Footprint
Cusco & the Inca Trail

Ben Box & Steve Frankham
2nd edition

 S0-BJL-716

In the variety of its charms, the power of its spell, I know of no place in the world which can compare with it.
Hiram Bingham describing Machu Picchu in *Lost city of the Incas*

Cusco & the Inca Trail Highlights

See colour maps at back of book

❶ Cusco, Plaza de Armas
The Incas' Place of Tears, now the heart of the gringo capital of South America

❷ Cusco, Qoricancha
Hidden inside a Catholic church is the Incas' Temple of the Sun

❸ Sacsayhuaman
Striking zigzag walls and massive masonry define this Inca ceremonial centre

❹ Pisac
If you only take in one market in the area, make it Pisac, with great Inca ruins above

❺ Moray
Huge depressions become crop laboratories beneath snow-capped mountains

❻ Salinas
White and brown salt pans tumble down a hillside, still productive after thousands of years

❼ Ollantaytambo
Another magnificent Inca fortress and temple, with a genuine Inca town below

❽ Machu Picchu
Where else? The focus of most people's visit to Peru and one of the world's finest archaeological ruins

❾ Inca Trail
The only way to Machu Picchu, four days of tough but unforgettable hiking

10 The White Rock
The most sacred site of the Incas, now in a remote, but beautiful area

11 Vilcabamba
An exhausting five-day trek away, the last city of the Incas

12 Choquequirao
Another lost city, another hard walk – but what a reward when you get there!

13 Raqchi
Here stands the Temple of Viracocha, the creator of all things, with a festival on 24 June

14 Andahuaylillas
The Sistine Chapel of the Andes: a simple 17th-century church covered in the most amazing frescoes

15 Pongo de Mainique
Where the Andes meet the Amazon, 'the most beautiful place on earth' to some; 'gateway to the underworld' to others

16 Manu Biosphere Reserve
No rainforest reserve can compare with Manu for the diversity of life forms

17 Tambopata National Reserve
Another marvellous place for wildlife, with macaw clay licks and hospitable lodges

18 Rafting on the Río Apurímac
The most exacting of several rafting options in the area; this is a highly dramatic river

Contents

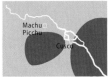

At Salinas, near Urubamba, thousands of terraced Inca salt pans cascading down the landscape are still in production today.

Southern Jungle

Lima

Background

Footnotes

7

1 *Perfect Inca stonework serves as the foundations for many colonial buildings in Cusco.* ▸▸ *See page 82.*

2 *Reminders of the Spaniards' religious legacy are everywhere to be seen in the city.* ▸▸ *See page 283.*

3 *Orchids such as the* Sobralia dichotom *grow in the humid forest along the Inca Trail.* ▸▸ *See page 164.*

4 *To the Incas, giants such as the glaciated peak of La Verónica were* apus, *beings to be worshipped.* ▸▸ *See page 134.*

5 *Brightly coloured macaws congregate to eat the clay at one of the collpas (macaw licks) in the Manu Biosphere Reserve.* ▸▸ *See page 221.*

6 *The Inca's agricultural terraces are still used to this day.* ▸▸ *See page 264.*

7 *The Jesuits' church of La Compañía de Jesús remains one of the most beautiful and ornate, despite the loss of many valuables following the Jesuits' expulsion from Peru.* ▸▸ *See page 76.*

8 *In the days of the Inca Empire, many thousands of kilometres of roads such as this crossed the difficult Andean terraìn.* ▸▸ *See page 164.*

9 *Look out for the natural dyes and materials in Cusco, the weaving centre of Peru.* ▸▸ *See page 109.*

10 *The busy market at Pisac has one section aimed at tourists and another where the people of the highlands sell or trade their produce.* ▸▸ *See page 137.*

11 *The ubiquitous (and cheap) mate burilado, or engraved gourd, is one of the most genuine expressions of folk art in Peru.* ▸▸ *See page 49.*

12 *As well as Inca ruins, the legendary Inca Trail combines unforgettable views, magnificent mountains, exotic vegetation and extraordinary ecological variety.* ▸▸ *See page 164.*

Sacred city
Towering Huayna Picchu provides the extraordinary backdrop for the sacred city.
There are steps right up to the top, but it's not a climb for the faint-hearted.

A foot in the door

Can you imagine a city laid out in the shape of a puma; a stone to tie the sun to; a city of fleas? Are you willing to meet the Earth Changer, Our Lord of the Earthquakes and Mother Earth? If so, prepare to follow the pilgrimage to Cusco, the place that every Inca endeavoured to visit once in a lifetime. Navel of the world, Spanish colonial showpiece, gringo capital of South America, Cusco is all these things and more.

Cusco will forever be associated with the Incas and there are Inca ruins within the city itself and conveniently close by in the surrounding hills and valleys. This makes it the ideal centre for visiting one of the Western Hemisphere's greatest empires. Its position, high up in the heart of the Andes, kept it largely isolated until the beginning of the 20th century when the railway arrived. As a result, although it has grown into a sprawling city of almost 300,000 inhabitants, its centre still has the feel of an unspoilt colonial town. But don't be lulled into thinking that a holiday here is going to be a mere trip back in time. Cusco is alive with the traditions of the descendants of the Incas and the legacy of 300 years of Spanish rule, as well as the latest trends of the 21st century. There is no need, either, to limit yourself to the city. The quintessential South American tourist site, Machu Picchu is only a train ride away, and a short bus trip will take you to Andean markets selling essentials for the locals and intricate handicrafts for the tourist. There are hot springs, charming places to stay and thrilling, exhausting hikes that traverse 4,000-m passes and dense jungle to lost cities – all reachable from Cusco. What's more, you have access to some of the main features that make Peru one of the eight 'mega-diverse' countries on earth. Below snow-covered peaks, a vast array of habitats drop into river canyons, or descend the eastern slopes of the Andes to the vast lowlands of the Amazon Basin.

Culture clash

For all their elegance, the Spanish churches and opulent mansions of Cusco have not fared as well as the matchless stonemasonry of the Inca foundations on which they were imposed. The best example of this uneasy marriage is the Qoricancha/Santo Domingo complex, the site of the Inca's Temple of the Sun. The colonial buildings also have their own elegance, in dominant churches and opulent mansions.

Mountains worship

From the tremendous zigzag walls of the ceremonial centre of Sacsayhuaman to the Inca suspension bridge of Qeswachaca, there are sites of historical interest in every direction. Just an hour from Cusco is the market town of Pisac and its superb fortress. Follow the Río Urubamba west, beneath sacred mountains, to Ollantaytambo, which has a well-preserved Inca town and an unfinished temple, whose pre-Columbian stonework is among the finest in the country. All along the valley, with its fields of cereals and steep agricultural terracing, stand the *apus*, the imposing snow-capped peaks worshipped by the Incas.

Lost city of the Incas

Machu Picchu, the only major Inca retreat to escape Spanish looting, is Peru's most-visited archaeological site. Getting there is a lot easier now than it was for Hiram Bingham, who discovered it in 1911. If the comfortable train ride sounds too easy, take the authentic approach along the Inca Trail. This four-day hike includes Inca tunnels, knee-shattering staircases and stretches of beautiful cloudforest. But don't overlook the shorter and longer variations to the main trail, which offer many new perspectives.

Wilderness beckons

Cusco is a city that you can walk out of. In little more than 10 minutes you leave the crowds and enter the solitude of the *cordillera*. If you just want to escape for a day, no problem. Alternatively, follow the footsteps of Incas, *conquistadores* and *campesinos* from one river valley to another over the highest of passes. Where there are trails, now there is mountain biking and you can climb as many hills as your muscles can take, or plummet 1,400 metres in two hours. Cusco is a paradise for rafting, too, with gentle half-day trips for beginners, heart-stopping whitewater runs for adrenaline-junkies and everything else in between.

Rainforest sanctuaries

In Peru's southern jungle are the Manu Biosphere Reserve and the Tambopata National Reserve, both brilliant places to see wildlife and both accessible from Cusco. Manu is one of the largest protected areas of rainforest in the world, starting high in the Andes and going down through elfin, cloud and montane forest to the vast lowland jungle of the Amazon.

Essentials

Planning your trip

To see Cusco and the surrounding area properly you'll need between 10 and 14 days. This would allow you to explore the city, enjoy its nightlife, visit the towns and villages of the Urubamba Valley – including Pisac, Ollantaytambo, Urubamba and Chinchero – and, of course, hike the Inca Trail to Machu Picchu (four days). Added to that, you'll need at least four or five days for a jungle trip to Manu or Tambopata, plus a few more for mountain biking and whitewater rafting. Three or four weeks, therefore, would allow you to enjoy the region to its full, but the one problem with Cusco is that it is all too easy to find a colonial café with a balcony, toss the guidebook aside, and sit back in the blazing sun to watch the world go by!

Where to go

Your first port of call will be Cusco's **Plaza de Armas**, heart of the city since Inca times, and it is here that you will get an immediate feel for the city. Two grand churches and a series of arcades surround this great colonial space, which is filled with eating places, tourist businesses and people on the move. Behind the façade, you will gaze amazed at the gold altars of churches such as **La Compañía**, then that will fade into insignificance on entering the complex of the **Temple of the Sun**. Here the Spanish *conquistadores* found so much gold it took them three months to melt it down. It takes only a little imagination to picture the solar garden as it once was: filled with life-sized replicas of men, women and children, insects, plants and flowers – all made from gold. The 700 gold and silver plates that once covered the temple walls here may have gone, but their disappearance has revealed the stunning craftsmanship of the Inca stonemasons whose blocks fit together so perfectly it is impossible to fit even a razorblade into the joints – and that after two major earthquakes.

Out of the city you have to travel only a few hours to discover the wonderful **Sacred Valley**. Take a one-day bus trip if you are on a tight schedule, otherwise see the spectacular Inca ruins, busy indigenous markets and beautiful scenery under your own steam and at your own pace. Some choose to take the bus, others to go off-road on a mountain bike. If you have the stomach for it, sign up for a condor's-eye view and paraglide it in tandem with a professional.

For many, Cusco means one thing: **Machu Picchu**, one of only three places in the Americas that has been declared a World Heritage Site for both its natural beauty *and* its history (the other two are Palenque in Mexico and Tikal in Guatemala). The ancient **Inca Trail** is one of the world's classic trekking routes. After four days of climbing through dizzying 4,000-m-plus mountain passes, the weary hiker emerges at the Sun Gate to look down at last on one of the most awe-inspiring sights in the world. And its wonder is not confined to the young and fit. The site is accessible by luxury train followed by a bus ride up a switchback road.

If you have plenty of time to spare, then make one of the major treks: to **Choquequirao** over the **Vilcabamba** mountain range; to the last Inca stronghold at **Espíritu Pampa**; or around – and up! – ice-capped **Ausangate**, the mountain that dominates Cusco's eastern skyline. The passes here are over 5,000 m. Thrill-seekers can combine a jungle experience with whitewater rafting the turbulent waters of the **Apurímac**, the true source of the Amazon. There cannot be many places in the world where you can cast off amid snow-capped mountain scenery or take a trip that later leaves you bumping through caiman-infested jungle. The rivers around Cusco are between a gentle Grade II to a heady Grade V.

And no trip of more than two weeks would be complete without discovering the beauty of the **Manu Biosphere Reserve**, one of the largest conservation areas on earth. Over one-tenth of all the species of birds in the world live here. Your trip will take you through cloudforest on the eastern slopes of the Andes past the upper tropical zone where blue-headed and military macaws can be found to the untouched forests of the western Amazon.

When to go

There is no time of year when you will have Cusco and Machu Picchu to yourself. Having said that, Peru's high season is from June to September and at that time, Cusco is bursting at the seams. This also happens to be the time of year which enjoys the most stable weather for hiking the Inca Trail or trekking and climbing elsewhere. The days are generally clear and sunny, though nights can be very cold at high altitude. The highlands can be visited at other times of the year, though during the wettest months from November to April some roads become impassable and hiking trails can be very muddy. April and May, at the tail end of the highland rainy season, is a beautiful time to see the Peruvian Andes, but the rain may linger, so be prepared.

On the coast, the summer months are from December to April. If you arrive in Lima between May and October you will find the area covered with what's known locally as *la garúa*, a thick blanket of cloud and mist. As your plane heads towards Cusco in the *garúa* season, you will soon be into clear skies and the mountains below can be seen rising like a new coastline out of the sea of fog.

The best time to visit the jungle is during the dry season, from April to October. During the wet season, November to April, it is oppressively hot (40°C and above) and while it only rains for a few hours at a time, which is not enough to spoil your trip, it is enough to make some roads virtually impassable.

Tours and tour operators

UK and Ireland

Audley Latin America, *6 Willows Gate, Stratton Audley, Oxfordshire, OX27 9AU, T01869-276210, www.audleytravel.com*
Austral Tours, *20 Upper Tachbrook St, London SW1V 1SH, T020-7233 5384, www.latinamerica.co.uk*
Condor Journeys & Adventures, *2 Ferry Bank, Colintraive, Argyll PA22 3AR, T01700-841318, www.condorjourneys-adventures.com* Eco and adventure tourism with specially designed tours to suit your requirements.
Dragoman, *Camp Green, Debenham, Stowmarket, Suffolk IP14 6LA, T01728-861133, www.dragoman.co.uk* Overland camping and/or hotel journeys throughout South and Central America.
Exodus Travels, *Grange Mills, 9 Weir Rd, London SW12 0NE, T020-8675 5550, www.exodus.co.uk* Experienced in adventure

travel, including cultural tours and trekking and biking holidays.
Explore Worldwide, *1 Frederick St, Aldershot, Hampshire GU11 1LQ, T01252-760000, www.exploreworldwide.com* Highly respected operator, with 2- to 5-week tours in more than 90 countries worldwide including Peru.
Guerba Adventure and Discovery Holidays, *Wessex House, 40 Station Rd, Westbury, Wiltshire BA13 3JN, T0845-1309770, info@guerba.co.uk* Specializes in adventure holidays, from trekking safaris to wilderness camping.
Journey Latin America, *12-13 Heathfield Terrace, Chiswick, London, W4 4JE, T020-8747 8315, and 12 St Ann's Sq, 2nd floor, Manchester, M2 7HW, T0161-8321441, www.journeylatinamerica.co.uk* The world's leading tailor-made specialist for Latin America, running escorted tours throughout the region, they also offer a wide range of flight options.

JOURNEY LATIN AMERICA

The UK's No.1 Latin American Specialist

- **Tailor-made Holidays** - An unrivalled range of options
- **Escorted Groups** - Tours ranging from 9 days to 6 weeks
- **Active Adventures** - Hiking, biking, rafting, kayaking and riding trips
- **Spanish & Portuguese Courses** - 1-4 week courses with homestay
- **Low Cost Flights** - International and domestic flights plus airpasses

JLA
Your answer to
LATIN AMERICA

London: **020 8747 8315**
Manchester: **0161 832 1441**

JourneyLatinAmerica.co.uk
Fully bonded ATOL Protected 2828   ABTA (V2522)   IATA   AITO

KE Adventure Travel, *32 Lake Rd, Keswick, Cumbria, CA12 5DQ, T017687-73966,* www.keadventuretravel.com Specialist in adventure tours, including 3-week cycling trips in and around Cusco.

Kumuka Expeditions, *40 Earls Court Rd, London W8 6EJ, T0800-068 8855* *www.kumuka.com* Overland tour operator for small groups, escorted or truck-based.

Last Frontiers, *Fleet Marston Farm, Aylesbury, Buckinghamshire HP18 0QT, T01296-653000, www.lastfrontiers.co.uk* South American specialist offering tailor-made itineraries as well as discounted air fares and air passes.

Naturetrek, *Cheriton Mill, Cheriton, Alresford, Hampshire, SO24 0NG, T01962-733051, www.naturetrek.co.uk* Birdwatching tours throughout the continent, also botany, natural history tours, treks and cruises.

South American Experience, *47 Causton Street, Pimlico, London, SW1P 4AT, T020-7976 5511, www.southamericanexperience.co.uk* Apart from booking flights and accommodation, also offers tailor-made trips.

Steppes Latin America, *51 Castle St, Cirencester, Gloucestershire, GL7 1QD, T01285-885333, www.steppeslatinamerica.co.uk*

Travelbag, *3-5 High St, Alton, Hampshire, GU34 1TL, T0870-9001352, www.travelbag.co.uk*

Trips Worldwide, *14 Frederick Place, Clifton, Bristol, BS8 1AS, T0117-3114400, www.tripsworldwide.co.uk*

Tucan Travel, *London, T020-8896 1600, london@tucantravel.com* Offers adventure tours and overland expeditions.

Veloso Tours, *34 Warple Way, London W3 0RG, T020-87620616, www.veloso.com*

South American Tours, *Hanauer Landstrasse 208-216, D-60314, Frankfurt/M, Germany, T+49-69-405 8970, www.southamerican tours.de* For holidays, business travel, or special packages. Has own office at Av Miguel Dasso 117, 14th floor, San Isidro, Lima, T422 7254, satperu@terra.com.pe

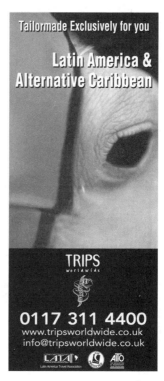

Tailormade Exclusively for you

Latin America & Alternative Caribbean

TRIPS
worldwide

0117 311 4400
www.tripsworldwide.co.uk
info@tripsworldwide.co.uk

LATA   ATO

Essentials Planning your trip

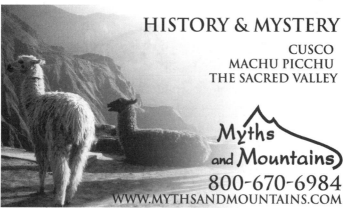

HISTORY & MYSTERY

CUSCO
MACHU PICCHU
THE SACRED VALLEY

Myths and Mountains

800-670-6984
WWW.MYTHSANDMOUNTAINS.COM

Essentials Planning your trip

Discover Peru Tours, *5775 Blue Lagoon Drive, suite 190, Miami, Florida 33126, T305-266 5827, www.discoverchile.com*
eXito, *108 Rutgers St, Fort Collins, CO 80525, T1-800-655 4053 T970-482 3019 (worldwide), www.exito-travel.com*
4starSouthAmerica, *3003 Van Ness NW Ste 5-823, Washington DC 20008, T1-800-7474540, www.4starSouthAmerica.com, UK T0871-711 5370, international T+49-700-4444 7824. Also has offices in Germany and Brazil.*
GAP Adventures, *19 Duncan St, Suite 401, Toronto, Ontario, M5H 3H1, T1-800-465 5600, www.gap.ca*
KE Adventure Travel, *1131 Grand Av, Glenwood Springs, CO 81601, T800-497 9675, www.keadventuretravel.com*
Ladatco Tours, *3006 Aviation Av, Suite 4C, Coconut Grove, FL 33133, T1-800-327 6162, www.ladatco.com* Based in Miami, run 'themed' explorer tours based around the Incas, mysticism, etc.
Lost World Adventures, *112 Church St, Decatur, GA 30030, T800-999 0558, T404-373 5820, www.lostworldadventures.com*
Myths and Mountains, *976 Tee Court, Incline Village, NV89451, T800-6706984, www.mythsandmountains.com*
Puchka Peru, *2280 Laurier Crescent, Prince George, BC, Canada V2M 2B1, T250-564 5884, www.puchkaperu.com* Specializes in textiles, folk art and market tours.
South American Journeys, *PO Box 12081, La Crescenta, CA 91214, T1-800-884 7474, www.southamericaexp.com* Small group tours off the beaten track with Peruvian guides, involvement in ecological projects.
Tambo Tours, *PO Box 60541, Houston, Texas 77205, and 23115 Calico Corners, Suite 1001, Spring, TX 77373, USA, T1-800-997 7378/1-888-246 7378, T001-281-528 9448, www.2GOPERU.com* Customized trips to the Amazon and archaeological sites of Peru for groups and individuals. Daily departures.

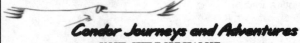

Condor Journeys and Adventures
YOUR CHILE SPECIALIST
* Archaeological excursions into the Atacama Desert and Easter Island.
* Adventure and ecological journeys on the Altiplano, into the prehistoric rain forests of the Lake District, the Austral Road and Torres del Paine, exploring outstanding national parks and scarcely visiteds areas.
* A wide range of outdoor activities such as hiking, horse riding, rafting, sea kayaking, fishing, climbing, biking and sailing.
* Andean Fjords, Magellan Strait and Antarctica cruises.
* Conventional, cultural, self drive and special interest tours.
  We tailor your dreamholidays to suit your most demanding wishes.
2 Ferry Bank, Colintraive, Argyll PA22 3AR, UK
Online brochure: http://www.condorjourneys-adventures.com
Tel: +44-1700 841-318   Fax: +44-1700 841-398   E-mail: info@condorjourneys-adventures.com

ANDINA TRAVEL
TREKS & ECO-ADVENTURES
LICENCED TOUR OPERATOR
ALTERNATIVE TREKS - TRADITIONAL TOURS - JUNGLE TRIPS -
MOUNTAIN BIKING-RIVER RAFTING -CUSTOMIZED ITINERARIES
Authorized Inca Trail Operators
Plazoleta Santa Catalina 219, Cusco, Perú   TelFax: 051 84 251892
www.andinatravel.com   Email: andinatravel@terra.com.pe

Wildland Adventures, *3516 NE 155 St, Seattle, WA 98155-7412, USA, T206-365 0868, www.wildland.com* Specialize in cultural and natural history tours to the Andes and the Amazon.

Australia

Adventure World, *73 Walker St, North Sydney, NSW 2060, T02-8913 0755, and 4th floor, 197 St Georges Terrace, Perth 6000, T08-9226 4524, www.adventureworld.com.au* Tour operator running a range of escorted group tours, locally escorted tours and packages to Peruand the rest of Latin America.
Kumuka Expeditions *Level 4, 46-48 York St, Sydney, NSW 2000, T1800-804277, 2-9279 0491, www.kumuka.com*
Tucan Travel *Sydney, T02-9326 4557, sydney@tucantravel.com*
Tempo Holidays, *1st floor, Beach St, Port Melbourne, Vic 3207, T03-9646 0277, www.yallatours.com.au* Tour operator specialising in group tours to Latin America, including Peru.

Special interest tours

Many tour operators handle more than one type of adventure tourism. Look under all types of sport for those with more than one activity on offer. See Cusco Tours and activities, p113 for more recommendations.

Climbing
Andes, *37a St Andrews St, Castle Douglas, Kirkcudbrightshire, Scotland, DG7 1EN, T01556-503929, www.andes.org.uk* Climbing and trekking trips in Peru (and many other destinations in Latin America).

Mountain biking
Andean Trails, *The Clockhouse, Bonnington Mill Business Centre, 72 Newhaven Rd, Edinburgh, EH6 5QG, T0131-467 7086, www.andeantrails.co.uk* Also for trekking and other adventure tours.
Peru Mountain Bike, *www.perumountainbike.com*, run from the USA, this agency organizes mountain bike trips in conjunction with Peruvian companies in Cusco and other parts of Peru.

TAMBO TOURS

ADVENTURE TRIPS TO THE
TAMBOPATA RESERCH CENTER & AMAZON

Daily departures for groups & individuals.

Offices in the US & CUZCO
Experience since 1988

toll free: US & Canada... **1-888-2GO-PERU** (246-7378)

www.2GOPERU.com e-mail - tambo@tambotours.com

TAMBO TOURS PO BOX 60541- HOUSTON, TEXAS 77205

International:
001-281-528-9448
fax: 281-528-7378

18

▼ ▼ ▼ ▼ ▼ ▼ ▼ ▼ ▼ ▼

Learn Spanish & Portuguese

Brazil • Ecuador • Guatemala • Puerto Rico • Perú • Chile
Bolivia • Argentina • México • Costa Rica • Panamá
Uruguay • Venezuela • Dominican Republic • Spain

▼ Learn the RIGHT way FAST
▼ For all ages and levels
▼ Most programs start weekly
▼ Private tutor or small groups
▼ 3-8 hours a day
▼ Exciting excursions
▼ Academic credit available
▼ Pre-departure assistance
▼ Travel insurance
▼ Easy to book online
▼ All major credit cards accepted

▼ ▼ **Now Featuring!** ▼ ▼

Additional Languages
Academic Study Abroad
Volunteer and Internship Placements

AmeriSpan programs can also be found at STA Travel offices around the world

USA & Canada: 1-800-879-6640
Worldwide: 215-751-1100
Fax: 215-751-1986
Web: **www.amerispan.com**
Email: info@amerispan.com
USA Office: P.O. Box 58129, Philadelphia, PA 19102
Guatemala Office: 6a Avenida Norte #40, Antigua, Tel/Fax 502-8-320-164

AmeriSpan
THE BRIDGE BETWEEN CULTURES

Essentials Planning your trip

Finding out more

Outside Peru, tourist information can be obtained from Peruvian embassies and consulates, see page 24. For Tourism organizations within Peru, see page 34. For newspapers, radio and TV websites, see Keeping in touch, page 64.

Websites

Cusco and Machu Picchu
There are many websites providing tourist information for Cusco and Machu Picchu. Good ones are:
www.aboutcusco.com, in English and Spanish.
www.cuscoonline.com, in Spanish, English, French, German, Italian and Portuguese.
www.cuscoperu.com, in English, Spanish, French and German.
www.enjoyperu.com/guiadedestinos/cusco/intro/index2.htm, in English and Spanish.
www.cusco.net an **www.cuscoperu.com** are also useful.
www.machupicchu.org More than just Machu Picchu, a library of all things related to the Inca region and Peru, very comprehensive.
www.machupicchu.com For Machu Picchu, the site of Machu Picchu Inc, of Key Biscayne, Florida.

Tourist and other information
www.magicperu.com (English and Spanish) **www.geocities.com/perutraveller/** (English) both have information for tourists, the latter aimed at independent travellers.
www.oanda.com Currency converter and for all your other financial needs.
www.peru.com/turismo Peru.com's travel page (Spanish and English).
www.perucultural.org.pe An excellent site for information on cultural activities, museums and Peruvian pre-Columbian textiles (Spanish).
www.perurail.com The website of Peru Rail (trains in the Cusco/Puno area).
www.rree.gob.pe Ministry of Foreign Relations' site, which contains addresses of all Peruvian embassies and consulates.
www.SAexplorers.org South American Explorers webpage, full of useful information and advice. Recommended.
www.terra.com.pe Go to *Turismo* for tourist information (in Spanish).
www.traficoperu.com On-line travel agent with lots of useful information (Spanish and English).
www.yachay.com.pe Red Científica Peruana, click on *Turismo* to get to the travel page.
www.adonde.com and **www.perulinks.com/** The latter is in Spanish and English and is easier to use.
http://gci275.com/peru/ Peruvian Graffiti, a site with politics, culture, economics and recent history.
http://gibbons.best.vwh.net Andean culture and Quechua (English).

It is better to seek advice on security before you leave from your own consulate rather than from travel agencies. Before you travel you can contact: **British Foreign and Commonwealth Office, Travel Advice Unit,** *T020-7238 4503,* *F020-7238 4545*. **Footprint is a partner in the Foreign and Commonwealth Office's Know before you go campaign** *www.fco.gov.uk/knowbeforeyougo* **US State Department's Bureau of Consular Affairs, Overseas Citizens Services,** *T202-647 4225,* *F202-647 3000,* *http://travel.state.gov/travel_warnings.html* **Australian Department of Foreign Affairs,** *T06-6261 3305,* *www.dfat.gov.au/consular/advice.html*

Essentials Planning your trip

Language

The official language is Spanish. Quechua, the language of the Inca empire, has been given some official status and there is much pride in its use, but despite the fact that it is spoken by millions of people in the Sierra who have little or no knowledge of Spanish, it is not used in schools. Another important indigenous language is Aymara, used in the area around Lake Titicaca. The jungle is home to a plethora of languages but Spanish is spoken in all but the remotest areas. English is not spoken widely, except by those employed in the tourism industry (eg hotel, tour agency and airline staff). Some basic Spanish for travellers will be found in the Footnotes section.

AmeriSpan, PO Box 58129, Philadelphia, PA 19102, T215-751 1100 (worldwide), T1-800-879 6640 (USA, Canada), F251-751 1986, www.amerispan.com offers language programmes in Cusco.

Disabled travellers

As with most underdeveloped countries, facilities for the disabled traveller are sadly lacking. Wheelchair ramps are a rare luxury and getting a wheelchair into a bathroom or toilet is well nigh impossible, except for in some of the more upmarket hotels. The entrance to many cheap hotels is up a narrow flight of stairs. Pavements are often in a poor state of disrepair (even fully able people need to look out for uncovered manholes and other unexpected traps). Visually and hearing-impaired travellers are similarly poorly catered for as a rule, but experienced guides can often provide tours with individual attention. Disabled Peruvians obviously have to cope with these problems and mainly rely on the help of others to get on and off public transport and generally move around.

The Ministerio de la Mujer y Desarrollo Social (Ministry for Women and Social Development) incorporates a Consejo Nacional de Integración de la Persona con Discapacidad, CONADIS (National Council for the Integration of Disabled People, www.conadisperu.gob.pe – in Spanish). CONADIS, together with PromPerú, private business, SATH (see next paragraph) and Kéroul of Québec, has been involved in a project called 'Peru: Towards an Accessible Tourism' and the 'First Report on Accessibility in Peru for Tourists with Disabilities' was published in 2001. The report identifies many challenges in a selected number of major tourist sites. For instance, archaeological sites such as Machu Picchu, being a World Heritage Site, may not be altered for accessibility. Specially trained personnel, however, can provide assistance to those with disabilities in these cases. The project can be accessed through the PromPerú website; click on Turismo accesible.

Some travel companies are beginning to specialize in exciting holidays, tailor-made for individuals depending on their level of disability. For those with access to the internet, a Global Access Disabled Travel Network Site is www.geocities.com/Paris/1502 It is dedicated to providing information for 'disabled adventurers' and includes a number of reviews and tips from members of the public. Another informative site, with lots of advice on how to travel with specific disabilities, plus listings and links belongs to the Society for Accessible Travel and Hospitality, www.sath.org You might want to read Nothing Ventured, edited by Alison Walsh (Harper Collins), which gives personal accounts of worldwide journeys by disabled travellers, plus advice and listings. One company in Cusco which offers tours for disabled people is **Apumayo**, see Cusco Tours and activities page 113.

Gay and lesbian travellers

Movimiento Homosexual de Lima (MHOL), Calle Mariscal Miller 828, Jesús María, T01-433 5519/433 6375 (English from 1630 on), mhol@terra.com.pe Great information about the gay community in Lima. On-line resources for gay travellers in Peru are http://gaylimape.tripod.com (a good site, in English, with lots of links and information) www.deambiente.com and www.gayperu.com (both in Spanish). In Cusco the scene is not very active (perhaps the best place to enquire is the **Café Macondo**). This does not imply, however, that there is hostility towards gay and lesbian travellers. As a major tourist centre which welcomes a huge variety of visitors, Cusco is probably more open than anywhere else in Peru.

Student travellers

Essentials Planning your trip

If you are in full-time education you will be entitled to an International Student Identity Card, which is distributed by student travel offices and travel agencies in 77 countries. The ISIC gives you special prices on all forms of transport (air, sea, rail etc), and access to a variety of other concessions and services. If you need to find the location of your nearest ISIC office contact the **ISIC Association**, Herengracht 479, 1017 BS Amsterdam, Holland, T+31-20-421 2800, F+31-20-421 2810, www.isic.org

Students can obtain very few reductions in Peru with an international student's card, except in and around Cusco. To be any use in Peru, it must bear the owner's photograph. An ISIC card can be obtained in Lima from **Intej**, Avenida San Martín 240, Barranco, T477 2864, www.intej.org They can also extend student cards. In Cusco student cards can be obtained from Portal Comercio 141, p 2, T621351.

Travelling with children → *Visit www.babygoes2.com For Health, see page 57.*

Travel with children can bring you into closer contact with local families and, generally, presents no special problems – in fact the path is often smoother for family groups. Officials tend to be more amenable where children are concerned and they are pleased if your child knows a little Spanish.

South American Explorers in Cusco and Lima (see pages 71 and 241) can provide lots of useful information on travelling with children in Peru.

Getting from A to B usually involves a lot of time waiting for buses, trains, and especially for aeroplanes. You should take reading material with you. When travelling by road in the Sacred Valley, you must be prepared for cramped colectivo travel.

Food can be a problem if the children are not adaptable. A small immersion heater and jug for making hot drinks is invaluable, but remember that electric current varies. In restaurants, you can normally buy children's helpings, or divide one full-size helping between two children.

On all long-distance buses you pay a **fare** for each seat, and there are no half-fares if the children occupy a seat each. For shorter trips it is cheaper, if less comfortable, to seat small children on your knee. On sightseeing tours you should *always* bargain for a family rate – often children can go free.

In all **hotels**, try to negotiate family rates. If charges are per person, always insist that two children will occupy one bed only, therefore counting as one tariff. You can almost always get a reduced rate at cheaper hotels.

▪ A child's survival guide to Peru

I went to Peru for three months and loved it. We lived in a place in Urubamba called K'uychi Rumi, which was brilliant because it shared a big garden with the other houses and we visited Cusco a lot.

The ruins are interesting to visit but you don't want to spend your whole time trudging up and down them. There is plenty else to do.

I really liked the horse riding. To start, try riding from Sacsayhuaman to the X-Zone (I love that name!) and around to Qenqo. This was my first horse-riding trip ever, so if you haven't been before, don't worry. It was quite flat and even my seven-year-old brother Owen managed on his own horse. My other brother Leo, who's four, rode with Dad.

The next ride wasn't flat at all. We went up a very steep hill in the Sacred Valley, from Lamay to a ruin called Huchuy Cusco. It was amazing. We went up a steep windy path between two hills and when I was on the path, I looked up and couldn't believe that I was going to do that – but we did.

After these trips you are fully prepared for camping in the High Andes. We went up to, wait for it, 4,200 m and it was cool in every sense, including temperature. The two nights in a tent were the coldest I have ever been in my life – but don't let me put you off because it was great fun and it warmed up during the day.

River-rafting on the Urubamba was fab. The first bit was gentle, but the second part near Ollantaytambo got rough, including a Grade III bit, which had a 2-m waterfall that we went over.

After all that exercise you might need some food. The place to go in Cusco is Jack's Café, which has toasted sandwiches, big breakfasts, chips and milkshakes. For a more fancy dessert, try the Due Monde ice cream place in Santa Catalina Ancha. My favourite flavour was naranja (orange)-split, and there are a lot of unusual flavours like *lúcuma* (egg-fruit) and *maracuya*, but don't try the spaghetti one.

In Urubamba, Los Geranios is recommended, as is anywhere which does fried chicken, which luckily is very popular around Cusco.

By Daisy Thomson (aged 9)

Women travellers

Generally women travellers should find visiting Peru an enjoyable experience. However, machismo is alive and well here and you should be prepared for this and try not to overreact. When you set out, err on the side of caution until your instincts have adjusted to the customs of a new culture. It is easier for men to take the friendliness of locals at face value; women may be subject to much unwanted attention. To help minimize this, do not wear suggestive clothing and do not flirt. By wearing a wedding ring, carrying a photograph of your 'husband' and 'children', and saying that your 'husband' is close at hand, you may dissuade an aspiring suitor. If politeness fails, do not feel bad about showing offence and departing. When accepting a social invitation, make sure that someone knows the address and the time you left. Ask if you can bring a friend (even if you do not intend to do so).

If, as a single woman, you can befriend a local woman, you will learn much more about the country you are visiting as well as finding out how best to deal with the barrage of suggestive comments, whistles and hisses that will invariably come your way. Travelling with another *gringa* may not exempt you from this attention, but at least should give you moral support.

Unless actively avoiding foreigners like yourself, don't go too far from the beaten track. There is a very definite 'gringo trail' which you can join, or follow, if seeking company. This can be helpful when looking for safe accommodation, especially if arriving after dark (which is best avoided). Remember that for a single woman a taxi at night can be as dangerous as wandering around on her own. A good rule is always to act with confidence, as though you know where you are going, even if you do not. Someone who looks lost is more likely to attract unwanted attention.

Working in Peru

There are many opportunities for volunteer work in Peru (**South American Explorers**, pages 71 and 241, have an extensive database). In Cusco, some ideas are given in The Good Samaritans, page 86. The **Amauta Spanish School** also offers volunteering opportunities; in Cusco, *T084-241422, www.amautaspanish.com/amauta/english/volunteer.html* For information outside Peru on voluntary work and working abroad, try: **www.workingabroad.com**, *2nd floor Office Suite, 59 Lansdowne Rd, Hove, East Sussex, BN3 1FL, T01273-711406*; **www.i-to-i.com**, *One Cottage Rd, Headingley, Leeds, LS6 4DD, T0870-333 2332*; **www.questoverseas.org**; **www.raleigh international.org**; **www.projecttrust.org.uk**; **www.gapyear.com** The website **www.amerispan.com**, which is principally concerned with language learning and teaching, also has a comprehensive list of volunteer opportunities.

Before you travel

Getting in

Visas and permits
No visa is necessary for countries of Western Europe, Asia, North or South America or citizens of Australia, New Zealand or South Africa. Travellers from Fiji and India do need visas. **Tourist cards** are obtained on flights arriving in Peru or at border crossings. The tourist card allows you up to a maximum of 90 days in Peru. The form is in duplicate and you give up the original on arrival and the copy on departure. **Note** This means you need to keep the copy as you will need to give it to the officials when you leave. A new tourist card is issued on re-entry to Peru but extensions are obtained with your current tourist card so you just take it and your passport to immigration when asking for extensions. If your tourist card is lost or stolen, apply to get a new one at **Inmigraciones**, Avenida España 700 y Avenida Huaraz, Breña, Lima, between 0900 to 1330, Monday to Friday. It shouldn't cost anything to replace your tourist card if you replace it in Lima.

Tourist visas for citizens of countries not listed above cost £9.60 (approximately US$14), for which you require a valid passport, a departure ticket from Peru, two colour passport photos, one application form and proof of economic solvency.

All foreigners should be able to produce on demand some recognizable means of identification, preferably a passport. You must present your passport when reserving tickets for internal, as well as international, travel. An alternative is to photocopy the important pages of your passport – including the immigration stamp, and have it legalized by a notario público, which costs US$1.50. This way you can avoid showing your passport.

Travellers arriving by air are not asked for an onward flight ticket at Lima airport, but it is quite possible that you will not be allowed to board a plane in your home country without showing an onward ticket.

Remember that it is your responsibility to ensure that your passport is stamped in and out when you arrive in the country or cross borders. The absence of entry and exit stamps can cause serious difficulties: seek out the proper migration offices if the stamping process is not carried out as you cross. You should always carry your passport in a safe place about your person, or if not leaving the city or town you're in, deposit it in the hotel safe. If staying in Peru for several weeks, it is worthwhile registering at your consulate. Then, if your passport is stolen, replacing it is simplified and faster.

Renewals and extensions The extension process in Lima immigration is as follows: go to the third floor and enter the long narrow hall with many 'teller' windows. Go to window number five and present your passport and tourist card. The official will give you a receipt for US$20 (the cost of a one-month extension) which you will pay at the **Banco de la Nación** on the same floor. Then go back to the teller room and buy form F007 for S/.22 (US$6.45) from window 12. Fill out the form and return to window five. Give the official the paid receipt, the filled-out form, your passport and tourist card. You have now finished your part of the process. Next, you will wait 10 or 15 minutes for your passport to be stamped and signed. You have just completed a not-so-painful Peruvian bureaucratic process. **Note** Three extensions like this are permitted, although it's unlikely that you will be allowed to buy more than one month at a time. Peruvian law states that a tourist can remain in the country for a maximum of six months, after which time you must leave. Crossing the border out of Peru and returning immediately is acceptable. You will then receive another 90 days and the process begins again.

To summarize: you are given 90 days upon entering the country. You can buy 90 more days for US$20 each (not at the same time) for a total of six months (180 days). Once your six months is completed, you must leave Peru (no exceptions). This simply means crossing into a bordering country for the day (depending on where, you can come back immediately) and returning with a fresh 90 days stamped in your passport.

If you let your tourist visa expire you can be subject to a fine of US$20 per day, but this is up to the discretion of the immigration official so it's a good idea to be very courteous. You can extend your visa in Lima, Cusco and Puerto Maldonado (also in Puno, on the shores of Lake Titicaca, and Iquitos on the Amazon), but in the provinces it can take more time than in Lima.

Business visas Visitors who are going to receive money from Peruvian sources must have a business visa: requirements are a valid passport, two colour passport photos, return ticket and a letter from an employer or Chamber of Commerce stating the nature of business, length of stay and guarantee that any Peruvian taxes will be paid. The visa costs US$31. On arrival business visitors must register with the **Dirección General de Contribuciones** for tax purposes.

Student visas To obtain a one-year student visa you must have: proof of adequate funds, affiliation to a Peruvian body, a letter of recommendation from your own and a Peruvian Consul, a letter of moral and economic guarantee from a Peruvian citizen and four photographs (frontal and profile). You must also have a health check certificate which takes four weeks to get and costs US$10. Also, to obtain a student visa, if applying within Peru, you have to leave the country and collect it in La Paz, Arica or Guayaquil from Peruvian immigration (it costs US$20).

Peruvian embassies and consulates abroad

Australia, *40 Brisbane Av Suite 8, Ground floor, Barton ACT 2600, Canberra,*

PO Box 106 Red Hill, T61-2-6273 8752, www.embaperu.org.au Consulate in Sydney. **Austria**, *Gottfried Keller-Gasse 2, 8th floor, T713 4377, embperu.austria@peru.jet2web.at* **Belgium**, *Av de Tervuren 179, 1150 Brussels,*

T32-2-733 3185, comunicaciones@embassy -of-per.be

Bolivia, *C Fernando Guachalla 300, Sopocachi, La Paz, T591-2-244 1250, embbol@caoba.entelnet.bo*

Canada, *130 Albert St, Suite 1901, Ottawa, Ontario, K1P 5G4, T1-613-238 1777, emperuca@bellnet.ca* Consulates in Montréal, Toronto and Vancouver.
Denmark, *Trianhlen 4, 4 TV, DK-2100, Copenhagen, T45-3-526 5848, www.peruembassy.dk*

France, *50 Av Kleber, 75116 Paris, T33-1-5370 4200, www.amb-perou.fr/*

Germany, *Mohrenstrasse 42, 10117 Berlin, T49-30-206 4103, www.embajada-peru.de* Consulates in Frankfurt and Hamburg.

Israel, *37 Ha-Marganit Shikun Vatikim, 52 584 Ramat Gan, Israel, T972-3-613 5591, emperu@021.net.il*

Italy, *Via Francesco Siacci N 4, 00197 Roma, T39-06-8069 1510, amb.peru@agora.stm.it* Consulates in Genoa and Milan.

Japan, *4-4-27 Higashi 1-Chome, Shibuya-ku, Tokyo 150-0011, T81-3-3406 4243, embperutokyo@embperujapan.org*

Netherlands, *Nassauplein 4, 2585 EA, The Hague, T31-70-365 3500, embperu@bart.nl*

New Zealand, *Level 8, 40 Mercer St, Cigna House, Wellington, T64-4-499 8087, embassy.peru@xtra.co.nz*

South Africa, *Infotech Building, Suite 201, Arcadia St, 1090 Hatfield, 0083 Pretoria, T27-12- 342 2390, emperu@iafrica.co*

Spain, *C Príncipe de Vergara 36, 5to Derecha 28001 Madrid, T34-91-431 4242, lepru@ embajadaperu.es* Consulate in Barcelona

Sweden, *Brunnsgatan 21 B, 111 38 Stockholm, T46-8-440 8740, F46-8-205592, www.webmakers/peru*

Switzerland, *Thunstrasse No 36, CH-3005 Berne, T41-31-351 8555, lepruberna02@ bluewin.ch* Consulates in Geneva and Zurich.

UK, *52 Sloane St, London SW1X 9SP, T020-7235 1917, F020-7235 4463, www.peruembassy-uk.com*

USA, *1700 Massachusetts Av NW, Washington DC 20036, T1-202-833 9860, lepruwash@aol.com* Consulates in Los Angeles, Miami, New York, Chicago, Houston, Boston, Denver and San Francisco.

Customs

Duty-free allowance When travelling into Peru you can bring 20 packs of cigarettes (400 cigarettes), 50 cigars or 500 g of tobacco, three litres of alcohol and new articles for personal use of gifts valued at up to US$300. There are certain items that are blacked out and therefore cannot be brought in duty-free: these include computers (but laptops are OK). The value-added tax for items that are not considered duty-free but are still intended for personal use is generally 20%. Personal items necessary for adventure sports such as climbing, kayaking and fishing are duty-free. Most of the customs rules aren't a worry for the average traveller, but anything that looks like it's being brought in for resale could give you trouble.

Export ban It is illegal to take items of archaeological interest out of Peru. This means that any pre-Columbian pottery or Inca artefacts cannot leave Peru. If you are buying extremely good replicas make sure the pieces have the artist's name on them or that they have a tag which shows that they are not originals. No matter how simple it seems, it is not worth your time to try and take anything illegal out of the country – this includes drugs. The security personnel and customs officials are experts at their job. Understand that this is a foolhardy idea and save yourself the horror of 10 years in jail.

Vaccinations For more information, see page 57. Before you travel, have a check up with your doctor and arrange your vaccinations well in advance. Contact a specialist travel clinic if your own doctor is unfamiliar with health in Latin America. You should be protected against typhoid, polio, tetanus and hepatitis A. A yellow fever vaccination certificate is only required if you are coming from infected areas of the world or, for your own protection, if you are going to the Peruvian jungle. Check malaria prophylaxis for all lowland rural areas to be visited and particularly if you will be on the borders of Bolivia and Brazil. Vaccination against cholera is not necessary, but occasionally immigration officials might ask to see a certificate. For a full and detailed description of necessary vaccinations and all matters relating to health, see Health page 57.

What to take

Everybody has their own preferences, but listed here are the most often mentioned. These include: an inflatable **travel pillow** for neck support; hiking boots; waterproof clothing; wax earplugs (vital for noisy hotels); rubber sandals (to wear in showers to avoid athlete's foot); a sheet sleeping-bag to avoid sleeping on filthy sheets in cheap hotels; a **clothes line**; a **water bottle**; a universal bath – and basin – **plug** of the flanged type that will fit any waste-pipe; **Swiss Army knife** (do not carry it in your hand luggage on aeroplanes); an **alarm clock** for those early morning departures; **candles** and/or a **torch/flashlight**; an **adaptor**; **padlocks** (for doors of the cheapest hotels, tent zips, and backpacks as a deterrent to thieves); a small **first aid kit**; and a **sun hat**.

A list of useful medicines and health-related items is given in the Health section on page 57. To these might be added some lip salve with sun protection, and pre-moistened wipes (such as 'Wet Ones'). Always carry toilet paper, which is especially important on long bus trips. Contact lens solution is readily available in pharmacies.

Insurance

Always take out travel insurance before you set off and read the small print carefully. Check that the policy covers the activities you intend or may end up doing. Also check exactly what your medical cover includes, ie ambulance, helicopter rescue or emergency flights back home. Also check the payment protocol. You may have to cough up first (literally) before the insurance company reimburses you. It is always best to dig out all the receipts for expensive personal effects like jewellery or cameras. Take photos of these items and note down all serial numbers. You are advised to shop around for an insurance company

Insurance companies

STA Travel and other reputable student travel organizations offer good value policies. Young travellers from North America can try the International Student Insurance Service (ISIS), which is available through **STA Travel**, *T1-800-836 4115*, *www.statravel.com*

Other recommended travel insurance companies in North America include: **Travel Guard**, *T1-800-8261300*, *www.noelgroup.com*

Access America, *T1-800-2848300*.
Travel Insurance Services, *T1-800-9371387*.
Travel Assistance International, *T1-800-8212828*.

Older travellers should note that some companies will not cover people over 65 years old, or may charge higher premiums. The best policies for older travellers (UK) are offered by **Age Concern**, *T01883-346964* and **Saga**, *T0800 0565464*, www.saga.co.uk

Money

Currency → *In October 2003, the exchange rate was US$1 = S/. 3.60.*

The *nuevo sol* (new sol, S/.) is the official currency of Peru. It is divided in 100 *céntimos* (cents) with coins valued at S/.5, S/.2, S/.1 and 50, 20, 10 and 5 *céntimo* pieces, although the latter is being phased out as it is virtually worthless. Notes in circulation are S/.200, S/.100, S/.50, S/.20 and S/.10. Try to break down notes whenever you can as there is a country-wide shortage of change (or so it seems). It is difficult to get change in shops and museums and sometimes impossible from street vendors or cab drivers. Prices of airline tickets, tour agency services, non-backpacker hotels and hostels, among others, are almost always quoted in dollars. You can pay in soles or dollars but it is generally easiest to pay dollars when the price is in dollars, and in soles when the price is in soles. This will save you from losing on exchange rates. In Cusco and Lima dollars are frequently accepted.

Note Almost no one, certainly not banks, will accept dollar bills that are ripped, taped, stapled or torn. Do not accept torn dollars from anyone; simply tell them you would like another bill. Also ask your bank at home to give you only nice, crisp, clean dollars and keep your dollars neat in your money belt or wallet so they don't accidentally tear. Forgeries of dollars and soles are not uncommon. Always check the sol notes you have received, even at the bank. Money changers, especially at borders, mix fake notes with genuine bills when giving wads of soles for other currencies. Hold the bills up to the light to check the watermark. The line down the side of the bill in which the amount of the money is written should appear green, blue and pink at different angles; fake bills are only pink and have no hologram properties. There should be tiny pieces of thread in the paper (not glued on). Check to see that the faces are clear. The paper should not feel smooth like a photocopy but rougher and fibrous. Try not to accept brand new notes, especially if changing on the street, slightly used notes are less likely to be forgeries. There are posters in many restaurants, stores and banks explaining exactly what to look for in forged sol notes. In parts of the country, forged one-sol coins are in circulation. Fakes are slightly off- colour, the surface copper can be scratched off and they tend to bear a recent date.

Credit cards

Visa (by far the most widely accepted card in Peru), **MasterCard, American Express** and **Diners Club** are all valid. There is often a commission of between 8% and 12% for all credit card charges. Often, it is cheaper to use your credit card to get money (dollars or soles) out of an ATM rather than to pay for your purchases with a card. Of course, this depends on your interest rate for cash advances on your credit cards – ask your bank or card provider about this. Another option is to put extra money on your credit cards and use them as a bank card. Most banks are affiliated with Visa/Plus system; those that you will find in Cusco and Lima, and most towns, are **BCP** (formerly **Banco de Crédito**), **BBVA Continental, Banco Weise Sudameris** and **Banco Santander Central Hispano** (BSCH). **Telebanco 24 Horas** ATMs (eg at **BCP**) accept Visa/Plus and American Express cards.

Interbank ATMs accept Visa, Plus, Mastercard, Maestro, Cirrus and American Express. There are also **Red Unicard** ATMs which accept Visa, Plus, MasterCard, Maestro and Cirrus. Note that not every branch of each bank offers the same ATM services (even branches within the same city). In comparison with widespread ATM use, businesses displaying credit card symbols may not accept foreign cards. Credit cards are not commonly accepted in smaller towns so go prepared with cash. Make sure you carry the phone numbers that you need in order to report your card lost or stolen. In addition, some travellers have reported problems with their credit cards being 'frozen' by their bank as soon as a charge from a foreign country occurs. To avoid this problem, notify your bank that you will be making charges in Peru.

Credit card assistance
American Express, *Jr Belén 1040, Lima (same building as Lima Tours), T01-330 4482/5,* Mon-Fri 0900-1700.
Diners Club, *Canaval y Moreyra 535, San Isidro, T01-221 2050.*

Mastercard, *Porta 111, 6th floor, Miraflores, T01-242 2700/311 6000, or T0800-307 7309.*
Visa Travel Assistance, *T108* and ask the operator for a collect call (*por cobrar*) to *T410-581 9994/3836 or, if local, call freephone T01-800-428 1888.*

Money exchange

US dollars are the only currency which should be brought from abroad (take some small bills). Other currencies carry high commission fees. Euros can only be exchanged at the money exchange booths at Lima airport. There are no restrictions on foreign exchange. Banks are the most discreet places to change travellers' cheques into soles. Some charge commission from between 1% and 3%, some don't, and practice seems to vary from branch to branch, month to month. The services of the **BCP** have been repeatedly recommended. Changing dollars at a bank always gives a lower rate than with *cambistas* (street changers) or *casas de cambio* (exchange houses). Always count your money in the presence of the cashier. For changing into or out of small amounts of dollars cash, the street changers give the best rates, avoiding paperwork and queuing, but you should take care: check your soles before handing over your dollars, check their calculators, etc, and don't change money in crowded areas. In Cusco many of the *cambistas* congregate around the top of Avenida Sol, so be careful. Think about taking a taxi after changing, to avoid being followed. Also, many street changers congregate near an office where the exchange 'wholesaler' operates; these

4starSouthAmerica

Great destinations...
...in great style!

Internet-Specials Now Available!

Argentina • Bolivia • Brazil • Chile • Ecuador • Paraguay • Peru • Uruguay

Have your vacation customized or join one of over 400 escorted scheduled Tours

Free Tour Brochure!
Flight Consolidator Fares!

Toll free 1-800-747-4540
Europe: +49(700)4444-7827
UK: 0871-711-5370

Tour-Info: www.4starSouthAmerica.com **Flights**: www.4starFlights.com

Cusco

... unlock the mysteries of the past, explore diverse natural beauty and experience colorful exotic cultures with a custom-designed vacation from LADATCO TOURS, The Destination Specialists to Central & South America and the Falkland Islands.

For information contact us at:
tailor@ladatco.com
www.ladatco.com

LADATCO TOURS
800-327-6162
Tel: 305-854-8422
Fax: 305-285-0504

will probably be offering better rates than elsewhere on the street. Soles can be
exchanged into dollars at the banks and exchange houses at Lima airport.

American Express will sell travellers' cheques to cardholders only, but will not exchange cheques into cash. Amex will hold mail for cardholders at the Lima branch only. They are also very efficient in replacing stolen cheques, though a police report is needed. Most of the main banks accept American Express travellers' cheques and **BCP** and **BSCH** accept Visa travellers' cheques. **Citibank** in Lima and some **BSCH** branches handle **Citicorp** cheques. Travellers have reported great difficulty in cashing travellers' cheques in the jungle and other remote areas. Always sign travellers' cheques in blue or black ink or ballpen.

Money transfer
To transfer money from one bank to another you must first find out which Peruvian bank works with your bank at home. You will then have to go to that bank and ask them what the process is to make a transfer. Depending on the bank, transfers can be completed immediately or will take up to five working days. Another option is to use **Western Union**, which has widespread representation.

Moneygram also has offices throughout the capital and the provinces. It exchanges most world currencies and travellers' cheques.

Cost of living
Living costs in the provinces are from 20 to 50% below those in Lima, although Cusco is a little more expensive than other, less touristy provincial cities. For a lot of low income Peruvians, many items are simply beyond their reach.

Cost of travelling
In 2003, the approximate budget for travelling, including transport, was US$25-35 per person a day for living comfortably, or US$12-15 a day for low budget travel. Your budget will be higher the longer you stay in Lima and depending on how many flights you take between destinations. Accommodation rates range from US$3-4 per person for the most basic *alojamiento* to over US$150 for luxurious hotels in Lima and Cusco. For meal prices, see Food and drink below.

Getting there

Air

From UK and Ireland
There are no direct flights to **Lima** from London. Cheap options are available with **Avianca** via Bogotá (also the simplest connection from Paris), **Iberia** via Madrid and **KLM** via Amsterdam. Alternatively, you can fly standby to Miami, then fly the airlines shown below. A little more expensive, but as convenient, are connections via Atlanta with **Delta**, or Houston with **Continental**. Other options are **British Airways** to Caracas then change to **Aeropostal**, or **Virgin Atlantic** to New York, then change to **LanChile**. From Dublin, either fly to Paris and then on to Bogotá for connections, or use the above options via other European capitals or US hubs.

From North America
Miami is the main gateway to Peru, together with Atlanta, Dallas, Houston, Los Angeles and New York. Direct flights are available from Miami with **Aero Continente**, **American Airlines**, **Lan Perú/Lan Chile** and **Copa** (via Panama City); through New

⁞ Discount flight agents

In the UK and Ireland
STA Travel, *86 Old Brompton Rd,
London, SW7 3LQ, T0870 160 0599,
www.statravel.co.uk* They have
other branches in London, as well as
in Brighton, Bristol, Cambridge,
Leeds, Manchester,
Newcastle-Upon-Tyne and Oxford
and on many University campuses.
Specialists in low-cost student/youth
flights and tours, also good for
student IDs and insurance.
Trailfinders, *194 Kensington High
St, London, W8 7RG, T020-7938 3939.*
They also have other branches in
London, as well as in Birmingham,
Bristol, Cambridge, Glasgow, Leeds,
Manchester, Newcastle, Oxford,
Dublin and Belfast.
In North America
Air Brokers International, *323
Geary St, Suite 411, San Francisco,
CA94102, T01-800-883 3273,
www.airbrokers.com* Consolidator
and specialist on RTW and Circle
Pacific tickets.
**Discount Airfares Worldwide
On-Line**, *www.etn.nl/discount.htm*
A hub of consolidator and discount
agent links.

**International Travel
Network/Airlines of the Web**,
www.itn.net/airlines Online air travel
information and reservations.
STA Travel, *T1-800-836 4115,
www.statravel.com* With branches
all over the US.
Travel CUTS, *187 College St, Toronto,
ON M5T 1P7, T1-866-246-9762,
www.travelcuts.com* Specialist in
student discount fares, IDs and other
travel services. Branches in other
Canadian cities as well as California.
Travelocity, *www.travelocity.com*
Online consolidator.
In Australia and New Zealand
Flight Centre, with offices
throughout Australia and other
countries. In Australia call *T133 133*
or log on to *www.flightcentre.com.au*
STA Travel, *T1300-360960,
www.statravel.com.au; 260 Hoddle St,
Abbotsford, Victoria 3067, T03-8417
6911.* In NZ: *Level 8, 229 Queen St,
Auckland, T09-309 9723.* Also in major
towns and university campuses.
Travel.com.au, *76 Clarence St,
Sydney, NSW, Australia, T02 9249
5232, outside Sydney: T1300 130 482,
www.travel.com.au*

York with **Continental**, which also flies from Houston and San Diego, and **Lan
Perú/Lan Chile**; from Atlanta with **Delta**; from Dallas with **American Airlines**, which
also flies from Orlando and Philadelphia; and from Los Angeles with **Lan Perú/Lan
Chile** and **Aero Mexico**. Daily connections can be made from almost all major North
American cities. From Toronto and Vancouver, there are connections in Los Angeles
and New York.

From Australia and New Zealand
There are no obvious connecting flights from either Australia or New Zealand to **Lima**.
One option would be to go to Buenos Aires from Sydney or Auckland (flights twice a
week with **Aerolíneas Argentinas**) and fly on from there with **Lan Chile**. Alternatively,
fly to Los Angeles and travel down from there. The round-the-world ticket offered by
Qantas/British Airways/American Airlines includes 12 free stops and goes via Miami.
Here you can pick up the American flight to **Lima**.

From Europe, Israel and South Africa
There are direct flights to **Lima** only from Amsterdam (**KLM** via Aruba) and Barcelona
and Madrid (**Iberia**). From Frankfurt, Rome or Milan, Lisbon or other European cities,
connections must be made in Madrid, Caracas, Brazilian or US gateways. The

⁝ Sites for flights

Aerolíneas Argentinas, www.aerolineas.com.ar	**Iberia**, www.iberia.com
AeroMexico, www.aeromexico.com	**KLM**, www.klm.com
Air France, www.airfrance.com	**LAB**, www.labairlines.com
American Airlines, www.aa.com	**Lacsa**, www.grupotaca.com
Avianca, www.avianca.com.co	**Lan Chile**, www.lanchile.com
British Airways, www.ba.com	**Lufthansa**, www.lufthansa.com
Continental, www.continental.com	**Qantas**, www.qantas.com
Copa, www.copaair.com	**Taca**, www.grupotaca.com
Delta, www.delta-air.com	**Tame**, www.tame.com.ec
El Al, www.elal.co.il	**Varig**, www.varig.com.brss

Essentials Getting there

alternatives from Tel Aviv to **Lima** are with **El Al** to New York, then **Lan Chile** on to **Lima**, or **El Al** to Madrid, then **Avianca** to **Lima** via Bogotá. From Johannesburg, make connections in Buenos Aires or São Paulo.

From Latin America

There are regular flights, in many cases daily, to Peru from most South American countries: Bogotá, **Avianca/Aces**, **Aero Continente** and **Aeropostal**; Buenos Aires, **Aerolíneas Argentinas**, **Taca** and **Lan Chile** (via Santiago de Chile); Caracas, **Aeropostal**, **Aero Continente** and **Taca**; Guayaquil and Quito, **Tame**, **Taca**, **Aero Continente** and **Aeropostal**; La Paz, **Lloyd Aéreo Boliviano** (LAB, also to Cochabamba and Santa Cruz), **Taca** (also to Santa Cruz) and **Aero Continente**; **Varig** to Rio de Janeiro and São Paulo (also **Taca**); Santiago de Chile, **Lan Perú/Lan Chile**, **Lacsa/Taca** and **Aero Continente**. From Central America: Mexico City, **Taca** and **AeroMexico**; Panama, **Copa**; San José, **Taca/Lacsa**.

From Asia

From Hong Kong, Seoul and Singapore, connections have to be made in Los Angeles. Make connections in Los Angeles or Miami if flying from Tokyo. You can also connect in New York in all cases except Singapore.

Baggage allowance

There is always a weight limit for your baggage, but there is no standard baggage allowance to Peru. If you fly via the USA you are allowed two pieces of luggage up to 32 kg per case. The American airlines are usually a bit more expensive but if you are travelling with a 40-kg bag of climbing gear, it may be worth looking into. On flights from Europe there is a weight allowance of 20 or 23 kg, although some carriers out of Europe use the two-piece system, but may not apply it in both directions. The two-piece system is gaining wider acceptance, but it is always best to check in advance. At busy times of the year it can be very difficult and expensive to bring items such as bikes and surf boards along. Many airlines will let you pay a penalty for overweight baggage – often this is US$5 per kilo – but this usually depends on how full the flight is. Check first before you assume you can bring extra luggage. The weight limit for internal flights is often 20 kg per person, or less, so remember this if you plan to take any internal flights.

Prices and discounts → *If you foresee returning home at a busy time (eg Christmas or Easter), a booking is advisable on any type of open-return ticket.*

Most airlines offer discounted fares on scheduled flights through agencies who specialize in this type of fare. The very busy seasons are from 7 December to

15 January and from 10 July to 10 September. If you intend travelling during those times, book as far ahead as possible. Between February and May and September and November special offers may be available. Examples of fares on scheduled airlines are: from the UK a return with flexible dates will cost about US$775, but travelling over the Christmas/New Year period can see prices rise to over US$4,000. The picture is the same from the USA: a low season return costs as little as US$250-330 from Miami, but high season is US$537. From Atlanta low season fares are US$490, but high season US$1,215; from Los Angeles low season US$410, high season US$1,470. From Sydney, Australia, a low season return is US$940-1,110, whereas a Christmas/New Year return will cost US$3,470.

Road

There are bus services from neighbouring countries to Peru. If coming from Bolivia, there are direct buses to Cusco and Puno from La Paz. On rare occasions, customs officials at international borders may ask for a forward ticket out of the country. This means you'll have to buy the cheapest bus ticket out of Peru before they let you in. Note that these tickets are not transferable or refundable.

Touching down

Airport information → For details on Cusco airport, see page 70.

Lima will be your point of entry into Peru. The city's Jorge Chávez Airport is located deep in the district of Callao, 16 km from the city centre. Passengers arriving from international flights will find the *aduana* (customs) process to be relatively painless and efficient (a push-button, red light/green light system for customs baggage checks). Once outside and past the gate separating arriving passengers from the public, you're subject to an inevitable mob of taxi drivers all offering you their services. Fares depend on where you pick up the taxi and how good you are at bargaining.

Transport into Lima
Taxis No taxis use meters, so make sure you fix the price before getting in and insist on being taken to the hotel of your choice, not the driver's. It's always best to have exact change in soles to avoid having to break a large bill along the way.

Remise taxis (Mitsui or CMV) have representatives at desks outside International Arrivals and National Arrivals, US$7.25 to San Miguel, US$11.75 to the city centre, US$14.50 to San Isidro and Miraflores, US$17.50 to Barranco. This is the safest option, but also the most expensive. There are many taxi drivers offering their services outside Arrivals with similar or higher prices (more at night). If you are feeling confident and not too jet-lagged, go to the car park exit and find a taxi outside the perimeter, by the roundabout. They charge US$3 to the city centre. The security guards may help you find a taxi. **Note** All vehicles can enter the airport for 10 minutes at no charge. After that, it's about US$1 every 30 minutes. Taxis that have been waiting for more than the allotted free time will try to make the passenger pay the toll upon leaving the airport. Always establish who will pay before getting in.

Buses There is a service called **Urbanito,** from the airport to the centre, Breña and San Miguel US$3, Pueblo Libre, San Isidro and Miraflores US$4.35 (a slow journey, as it calls at all hotels), T814 6932 (24 hours), urbanito@terra.com.pe Local buses

(US$0.35) and colectivos run between the airport perimeter and the city centre and suburbs. Their routes are given on the front window: 'Tacna' for the centre, 'Miraflores' for Miraflores. Outside the pedestrian exit are the bus, colectivo and taxi stops, but there is more choice for buses at the roundabout by the car entrance. At busy times (which is anytime other than very late at night or early morning) luggage may not be allowed on buses. **Note** Do not take the cheapest, stopping buses which go to the city centre along Avenida Faucett. They are frequently robbed. Pay a little more for a non-stopping bus.

Car hire All hire companies have offices at the airport. The larger international chains, **Budget, Dollar, Hertz,** are usually cheaper and have better-maintained vehicles than local firms. The airport in Lima is the best, most cost-effective place to arrange car hire. For transport in Lima, see page 259.

Airport facilities

The larger, more expensive hotels in Miraflores and San Isidro have their own buses at the airport, and charge for transfer. For details of hotels near the airport, see page 253. There are ATMs between the national and international foyers accepting American Express, Visa, Mastercard and the Plus, Cirrus and Maestro systems. There are *casas de cambio* (money changing desks) in the national foyer and in the international foyer. They are open 24 hours and change all types of travellers' cheque (they claim) and most major currencies, including Euros. There are also exchange facilities for cash in the international arrivals hall. **BCP** stands, in the national and international foyers, only collect the international or domestic airport tax that must be paid in order to get through the gate. **Note** The operators of the tax collection desks change frequently.

Although public telephones are everywhere in and around the airport, there is also a **Telefónica** office in the international foyer opposite desk 20, open 0700-2300 seven days a week. A fax service is available as well as internet facilities at US$3 per hour (must be one of the most expensive in the country). There are two post offices, one in the national foyer opposite desk 26, the other at the far end of the international foyer. Upstairs is **City Café** with fast computers for internet access at US$1.75 per hour (there is another one in departures, once through all the gates).

The left luggage lock-up is in the national flights concourse and offers safe 24-hour storage and retrieval for about US$3 per bag per day, or US$1 per hour.

Information desks can be found in the national foyer and in the international foyer (opposite desk 1) and beyond the check-in area, by the stairs. There is also a helpful desk in the international arrivals hall. It can make hotel and transport reservations. The Zeta bookstore upstairs has a good selection of English language guidebooks. **Zeta** has stalls in international and national departures, too.

On the second level there are other cafés besides **City Café**, some accepting major credit cards. Food tends to be pricey and not very good. Also upstairs are toilets.

Airport departure information

Airlines recommend that you arrive at the airport three hours before international flights and two hours before domestic flights. Check-in for international flights technically closes one hour before departure, 30 minutes for domestic flights, after which you may not be permitted to board. Cars entering the parking lot are subject to a document check of the driver, only.

Airport departure tax There is a US$28 departure tax for international flights which is never included in the price of your ticket. It may be paid in dollars or soles. For national flights (at all airports in Peru), the airport tax is US$5, payable only in soles. Tickets purchased in Peru will also have the 19% state tax, but this will be included in the price of the ticket. **Note** It is very important to reconfirm your flights when flying internally in Peru or leaving the country. This is generally done 48 to 72 hours in advance and can be done by phoning or visiting the airline office directly or, sometimes, by going to a travel agent for which you may have to pay a service charge. If you do not reconfirm your internal or international flight, you may not get on the plane. See also Customs, page 25.

Tourist information → *See also Websites, page 19.*

PromPerú, *Edificio Mitinci, located at the head of Av Carnaval y Moreyra in Corpac, 13th and 14th floor, San Isidro, T01-224 3279, www.peru.org.pe* Handles the promotion of tourism and information. They produce promotional material but offer no direct information service to individual tourists. The website does carry plenty of background and other information and they produce a monthly travel news magazine, *Kilca,* available by email: contact the press office, *perudirect@Promperu.gob.pe* PromPerú runs an information and assistance service, **i perú**, *T01-574 8000* (24 hours). Its main office in Lima is at *Jorge Basadre 610, San Isidro, T01-421 1227, iperulima@ promperu.gob.pe* Hours are Mon-Fri 0900-1830 and there is a 24-hr office at Jorge Chávez airport. There is also an office in Cusco, whose address is given in the text. **Indecopi** is the government-run consumer protection and tourist complaint bureau. They are friendly, professional and helpful. In Lima *T01-224 7888*, rest of Peru *T0800-42579 (not available from payphones), tour@indecopi.gob.pe*

Ministerio de Comercio Exterior y Turismo, *Calle Uno 050, Urb Córpac, San Isidro, Lima, T01-224 3347, www.mincetur.gob.pe* (for useful links go to *Turismo,* then *Otros Links*). In overall charge of tourism.

South American Explorers in Cusco (p71) and Lima (see p241), *www.SAExplorers.org,* is an excellent source of information.

Apavit (Asociación Peruana de Agencias de Viaje y Turismo), *Antonio Roca 121, Santa Beatriz, Lima, T01-433 7610, www.apavit.com*

Apotur (Asociación Peruana de Operadores de Turismo), *Bajada Balta 169, 2nd floor, Miraflores, Lima 18, T01-445 0382, apotur@amauta.rcp.net.pe*

Agotur (Asociación de Guías Oficiales de Turismo), *Baltazar La Torre 165, depto 101-D, San Isidro, Lima, T01-422 8937, agoturlima@yahoo.com*

Local customs and laws

Clothing

In general, clothing is less formal in the tropical lowlands, where men and women do wear shorts, than in the highlands, where people are more conservative, though wearing shorts is acceptable on hiking trails. Men should not be seen bare-chested in populated areas.

Courtesy

Politeness – even a little ceremoniousness – is much appreciated in Peruvian society. Men shake hands when introducing themselves to other men. Women or men meeting women usually greet each other with one kiss on the cheek. When introduced, Peruvians will probably expect to greet visitors in the same way. Always say *Buenos días* (until midday) or *Buenas tardes* and wait for a reply before proceeding further.

Always remember that the traveller from abroad has enjoyed greater advantages in life than most Latin American minor officials, and should be friendly and courteous at all times. Never be impatient and do not criticize situations in public (the officials may know more English than you think and they can certainly interpret gestures and facial expressions). In some situations, however, politeness can be a liability. Most Peruvians are disorderly queuers. In commercial transactions (buying a meal, goods

⁙ How big is your footprint?

• Where possible choose a destination, tour operator or hotel with a proven ethical and environmental commitment – if in doubt ask.

• Spend money on locally produced (rather than imported) goods and services and use common sense when bargaining – your few dollars saved may be a week's salary to others.

• Use water and electricity carefully – travellers may receive preferential supply while the needs of local communities are overlooked.

• Learn about local etiquette and culture – consider local norms and behaviour and dress appropriately for local cultures and situations.

• Protect wildlife and other natural resources – don't buy souvenirs or goods made from wildlife unless they are clearly sustainably produced and are not protected under CITES legislation (CITES controls trade in endangered species).

• Always ask before taking photographs or videos of people.

• Consider staying in local accommodation rather than foreign owned hotels – the economic benefits for host communities are far greater – and there are far greater opportunities to learn about local culture.

• The heart-breaking sight of children begging for money, shining shoes and selling sweets and postcards often at midnight in Cusco town centre leaves many visitors guilt-ridden if they refuse, or doubtful they have really helped if they do give money. The best advice is to give children food (fruit or a sandwich rather than sweets), or something to keep them warm such as a pair of gloves or a scarf.

• Otherwise make a donation to a local charitable organization such as **Los Niños** which is actively helping reverse the plight of hundreds of similar children.

in a shop, etc) politeness should be accompanied by firmness, and always ask the price first. Politeness should also be extended to street traders. Saying *No, gracias* with a smile is better than an arrogant dismissal.

In Peru it is common for locals to throw their rubbish, paper, wrappers and bottles into the street. Sometimes when asking a local where the rubbish bin is, they will indicate to you that it is the street. This does NOT give travellers the right to apply the 'when in Rome' theory. There are rubbish bins in public areas in many centres and tourists should use them. If there isn't one around, put the rubbish in your pocket. You will always find bins in bathrooms.

Time-keeping

Peruvians, as with most Latin Americans, have a fairly 'relaxed' attitude towards time. They will think nothing of arriving an hour or so late on social occasions. If you expect to meet someone more or less at an exact time, you can tell them that you want to meet *en punto*, or better still, meet in a bar or somewhere you don't mind waiting.

Tipping

In most of the better restaurants a 10% service charge is included in the bill, but you can give an extra 5% as a tip if the service is good. The most basic restaurants do not include a tip in the bill, and tips are not expected. Taxi drivers are not tipped – bargain the price down, then pay extra for good service if you get it. Tip cloakroom attendants and hairdressers (very high class only), US$0.50-$1; railway or airport porters,

US$0.50; car wash boys, US$0.30; car 'watch' boys, US$0.20. If going on a trek or tour it is customary to tip the guide, as well as the cook and porters.

Responsible tourism

Travel to the furthest corners of the globe is now commonplace and the mass movement of people for leisure and business is a major source of foreign exchange and economic development in many parts of South America. In some regions (eg Machu Picchu) it is probably the most significant economic activity.

The benefits of international travel are self-evident for both hosts and travellers – employment, increased understanding of different cultures, business and leisure opportunities. At the same time there is clearly a downside to the industry. Where visitor pressure is high and/or poorly regulated, adverse impacts to society and the natural environment may be apparent. Paradoxically, this is as true in undeveloped and pristine areas (where culture and the natural environment are less 'prepared' for even small numbers of visitors) as in major resort destinations.

The travel industry is growing rapidly and the impacts of this supposedly 'smokeless' industry are becoming apparent. These can seem remote and unrelated to an individual trip or holiday (eg air travel is implicated in global warming and damage to the ozone layer, resort location and construction can destroy natural habitats and restrict traditional rights and activities), but individual choice and awareness can make a difference in many instances (see box) and collectively, travellers are having a significant effect in shaping a more responsible and sustainable industry.

Of course, travel can have beneficial impacts and this is something to which every traveller can contribute – many national parks are part funded by receipts from visitors. Similarly, travellers can promote patronage and protection of important archaeological sites and heritage through their interest and contributions via entrance and performance fees. They can also support small-scale enterprises by staying in locally run hotels and hostels, eating in local restaurants and by purchasing local goods, supplies and arts and crafts.

There has been a phenomenal growth in tourism that promotes and supports the conservation of natural environments and is also fair and equitable to local communities. This 'ecotourism' segment is probably the fastest growing sector of the travel industry and provides a vast and growing range of destinations and activities. While the authenticity of some ecotourism operators' claims need to be interpreted with care, there is clearly both a huge demand for this type of activity and also significant opportunities to support worthwhile conservation and social development initiatives. If you are concerned about the application of the principles of ecotourism, in Peru as elsewhere, you need to make an informed choice by finding out in advance how establishments such as jungle lodges cope with waste and effluent disposal, whether they create the equivalent of 'monkey islands' by obtaining animals in the wild and putting them in the lodge's property, what their policy is towards employing and training local staff, and so on.

Organizations such as **Conservation International** (T001-202-912 1000 or T1-800-406 2306, www.ecotour.org), the **Eco-Tourism Society** (T001-802-651 9818, http://ecotourism.org), **Planeta** (www.planeta.com) and **Tourism Concern** (T+44-020-7753 3330, www.tourismconcern.org.uk) have begun to develop and/or promote ecotourism projects and destinations and their websites are an excellent source of information and details for sites and initiatives throughout South America. Additionally, organizations such as **Earthwatch** (T+44-1865-318838 or in US T978-461 0081, or T1-800-776 0188, www.earthwatch.org) and **Discovery Initiatives** (T+44-1285-643333, www.discoveryinitiatives.com) offer opportunities to participate directly in scientific research and development projects throughout the region.

Safety

More police patrol the streets, trains and stations in Cusco than in the past, which has led to an improvement in security, but you still need to be vigilant. Look after your belongings, leaving valuables in safe keeping with hotel management, not in hotel rooms. Places in which to take care are: when changing money on the streets; in the railway and bus stations; the bus from the airport; the Santa Ana market; the San Cristóbal area and at out-of-the-way ruins. Also take special care during Inti Raymi. Avoid walking around alone at night on narrow streets, between the stations and the centre, or in the market areas. Stolen cameras often turn up in the local market and can be bought back cheaply. If you can prove that the camera is yours, contact the police.

On no account walk back to your hotel after dark from a bar, nightclub or restaurant; strangle muggings and rape are on the increase. For your own safety pay the US$1 taxi fare, but not just any taxi. Ask the club's doorman to get a taxi for you.

The tourist police in Lima are excellent and you should report any incidents to them (see page 262). Dealings with the tourist police in Cusco have produced mixed reviews; you should double check that all reports written by the police in Cusco actually state your complaint. There have been some mix-ups, and insurance companies seldom honour claims for 'lost' baggage. In the event of a vehicle accident in which anyone is injured, all drivers involved are automatically detained until blame has been established, and this does not usually take less than two weeks.

Advice and suggestions → *You can check at South American Explorers (see pages 71 and 241) for latest travel updates.*

Be especially careful arriving at or leaving from bus and train stations. Stations are obvious places to catch people (tourists or not) with a lot of important belongings. Do not set your bag down without putting your foot on it, even just to double check your tickets or look at your watch; it will grow legs and walk away. Take taxis to stations, when carrying luggage, before 0800 and after dark (look on it as an insurance policy). Avoid staying in hotels too near to bus companies as drivers who stay overnight are sometimes in league with thieves. Also avoid restaurants near bus terminals if you have all your luggage with you it is hard to keep an eye on all your gear when eating. Try to find a travel companion if alone, as this will reduce the strain of watching your belongings all the time.

Keep all documents secure and hide your main cash supply in different places or under your clothes. Keep cameras in bags, take spare spectacles (eyeglasses) and don't wear wrist-watches (even cheap ones have been ripped off arms!) or jewellery. If you wear a shoulder-bag in a market, carry it in front of you. Backpacks are vulnerable to slashers: a good idea is to cover the pack with a plastic sack, which will also keep out rain and dust. It's best to use a pack which is lockable at its base. Make photocopies of important documents and give them to your family, embassy and travelling companion, this will speed up replacement if documents are lost or stolen and will still allow you to have some ID while getting replacements. Alternatively, before you leave home, send yourself an email containing all your important details and addresses which you can access in an emergency. If someone tries to extract a bribe from you, insist on a receipt.

Ignore mustard smearers and paint or shampoo sprayers, and don't bend over to pick up money or other items in the street. These are all ruses intended to distract your attention and make you easy for an accomplice to steal from. Ruses involving 'plainclothes policemen' are infrequent, but it is worth knowing that the real police only have the right to see your passport (not your money, tickets or hotel room). Before handing anything over, ask why they need to see it and make sure you understand the reason. Insist on seeing identification and know that you have the right to write it all down. Do not get in a cab with any police officer, real or not, tell them you will walk to the nearest police station. Do not hand over your identification freely and insist on going to the station first. A related scam is for a 'tourist' to gain your confidence, then accomplices create a reason to check your documents.

We have received reports of nightclubs denying entrance to people on the basis of skin colour and assumed economic status. This has happened in Lima and in Cusco. It is not possible to verify if this is the establishments' policy or merely that of certain doormen.

Drugs

Soft and hard drugs are part of the scene in Cusco and are easy to score, but be aware that anyone found carrying even the smallest amount is automatically assumed to be a drug trafficker. The use or purchase of drugs is punishable by up to 15 years' imprisonment and the number of foreigners in Peruvian prisons on drug charges is still increasing. If arrested on any charge the wait for trial in prison can take up to a year and is particularly unpleasant. Be wary of anyone approaching you in a club and asking where they can score – the chances are they'll be a plain-clothes cop. Also, we have received reports of drug-planting, or mere accusation of drug-trafficking by the PNP on foreigners in Lima, with US$1,000 demanded for release. If you are asked by the narcotics police to go to the toilets and have your bags searched, insist on taking a witness.

Getting around

Air

Low promotional tariffs are renewed monthly; often it is best to wait to purchase internal flights until your arrival. There are no deals for round trip tickets and prices can rise within four days of the flight.

It is not possible to take an international flight direct to Cusco, other than from Bolivia. You have to fly via Lima and while it may be possible to make a connection to get you to Cusco the same day you land in Peru, as often as not you will have to spend some time in the capital on the coast before flying up to the highlands. Many organized tours build a day or so in Lima as a matter of course. This allows you to get your bearings after your flight and see a bit of the city.

Lima to Cusco is the main tourist axis in Peru and there are plenty of flights between the two cities. The flight takes just one hour and all are in the morning, giving people in organized groups and independent travellers an early start. If you prefer to go by road, be aware that it's a full-day's journey. Getting around the country overland can be a difficult task and this is to be expected in a country whose geography is dominated by the Andes, one of the world's major mountain ranges. Great steps have been taken to improve major roads and enlarge the paved network linking the Pacific coast with the Highlands. It is worth taking some time to plan a journey in advance, checking which roads are finished, which have roadworks and which will be affected by the weather. The highland and jungle wet season, from mid-October to late March, can seriously hamper travel. It is important to allow extra time if planning to go overland at this time.

If you're on a tight schedule, then by far the best option is to fly **Lima-Cusco** (55 minutes, daily services), and **Cusco-Puerto Maldonado** if you're planning a trip to Tambopata (30 minutes, also daily services). Flights to Boca Manu for Manu are normally arranged through a tour operator (also 30 minutes). The main national

Domestic airlines

Aero Continente, *Av José Pardo 605, Miraflores, T01-241 4816, www.aerocontinente.com.pe* Flights to most major destinations in Peru.
Aviandina is a subsidiary of Aero Continente.
Lan Perú, *Av José Pardo 513, Miraflores, Lima, T01-213 8200/8300, www.lanperu.com* Flights from Lima to Arequipa, Chiclayo, Cusco, Juliaca, Puerto Maldonado and Trujillo.
Tans, *Jr Belén 1015, Lima Centre, Av Arequipa 5200, Miraflores, Lima, T01-213 6000, www.tans.com.pe* Flights to most major destinations in Peru.
Taca Perú, *Av Comandante Espinar 331, Miraflores, Lima, T01-213 7000, www.grupotaca.com* Flights between Lima and Cusco.
Star Up, *Av José Pardo 269, Miraflores, Lima, T01-445 6032.* Flights to Ayacucho, Cusco, Huánuco, Andahuaylas and Tingo María.

airlines serving the most travelled routes (of which Cusco is the prime example) are **AeroContinente** and its sister airline, **Aviandina**, and **Tans**. **Lan Perú**, a subsidiary of **Lan Chile**, and **Grupo Taca** (the Central American airline) also offer service on the Lima-Cusco route. These airlines generally cost the same, between US$63 and US$176 one-way anywhere in the country from Lima (there are very few seats at the cheapest price). The closer you get to departure date, the higher the fare. For shorter flights fares may cost a bit less. It is not unusual for the prices to go up at holiday times (Easter, May Day, Inti Raymi, 28-29 July, Christmas and New Year), and for elections. During these times, in school holidays (May, July, October and December to March) and the northern hemisphere summer seats can be hard to come by, so book early. **Lan Perú** and **Taca** are generally reckoned to have the better service. For details of flight prices email cheapairtickets@peru.com If you book tickets online and need to change your flight, you may be charged up to US$60 to do so.

If you wish to move on from Cusco to Bolivia, there are flights on Tuesday, Thursday and Saturday to/from **La Paz** (55 minutes) with **Lloyd Aéreo Boliviano** (**LAB**).

Advice and information

On the Cusco-Lima route there is a high possibility of cancelled flights during the wet season; tourists are sometimes stranded for several days. It is possible for planes to leave early if the weather is bad. Always give yourself an extra day between national and international flights to allow for any schedule changes. Flights are often overbooked so it is very important to reconfirm your tickets at least 24 hours in advance of your flight and in the high season make sure you arrive at the airport two hours before departure to avoid problems. By law, the clerk can start to sell reserved seats to stand-by travellers 30 minutes before the flight. To save time and hassle, travel with carry-on luggage only (48cm x 24cm x 37cm). This will guarantee that your luggage arrives at the airport when you do.

❖ Sit on right side of the aircraft for the best view of the mountains when flying Cusco-Lima; it is worth checking in early to get these seats

Internal flight prices are given in US dollars but can be paid in soles and the price should include the 19% sales tax. Tickets are not interchangeable between companies but sometimes exceptions will be made in the case of cancellations. Do check with companies for special offers.

Road

Peru is no different from other Latin American countries in that travelling by road at night or in bad weather should be treated with great care. It is also true that there are many more unpaved than paved roads, so overland travel is not really an option if you only have a few weeks' holiday. In the Cusco area a number of roads in the Sacred Valley are paved, but in the main, mountain roads are of dirt, some good, some very bad. Each year they are affected by heavy rain and mud slides, especially those on the eastern slopes of the mountains. Repairs can be delayed because of a shortage of funds. This makes for slow travel and frequent breakdowns. Note that some of these roads can be dangerous or impassable in the rainy season. Check beforehand with locals (not with bus companies, who only want to sell tickets) as accidents are common at these times.

Bus → *It is best to try to arrive at your destination during the day; it is safer and easier to find accommodation.*

Services south of Lima and inland to Cusco are improving as the road gets better. The main route is Lima-Nasca-Abancay-Cusco; the entire route is paved. There are direct (*ejecutivo*) service buses (different companies use different titles for their top class or executive services, eg **Imperial, Ideal, Royal**). As well as *ejecutivo* many bus companies have regular (local) service and the difference between the two is often great. There are several bus lines that run between Lima and the towns enroute to Cusco.

With the better companies or *ejecutivo* service you will get a receipt for your luggage, it will be locked under the bus and you shouldn't have to worry about it at stops because the storage is not usually opened. Tickets for *ejecutivo* service buses, however, can cost up to double those of the local service buses. For mountain routes, take a fleece and sleeping bag as the temperature at night can drop quite low. Night buses along the coast and into main highland areas are generally fine. Once you get off the beaten track, the quality of buses and roads deteriorates and you may want to stick to the day buses.

If your bus breaks down and you have to get on another bus, you will probably have to pay for the ticket, but keep your old ticket as some bus companies will give refunds. The back seats tend to be the most bumpy and the exhaust pipe is almost always on the left-hand side of the bus.

Note Prices of tickets are raised 60-100% during Semana Santa (Easter), Fiestas Patrias (Independence Day – 28 and 29 July), Navidad (Christmas) and special local events. Prices will usually go up a few days before the holiday and possibly remain higher a few days after. Tickets also sell out during these times so if travelling then, buy your ticket as soon as you know what day you want to travel.

Car hire

The minimum age for renting a car is 25. If renting a car, your home driving licence will be accepted for up to six months. Car hire companies are given in the text. They do tend to be very expensive, reflecting the high costs and accident rates. Hotels and tourist agencies will tell you where to find cheaper rates, but you will need to check that you have such basics as spare wheel, toolkit and functioning lights etc.

Check exactly what the hirer's insurance policy covers. In many cases it will only protect you against minor bumps and scrapes, not major accidents, nor 'natural' damage (eg flooding). Ask if extra cover is available. Also find out, if using a credit card, whether the card automatically includes insurance. Beware of being billed for scratches which were on the vehicle before you hired it.

The **Touring y Automóvil Club del Perú**: Avenida César Vallejo 699, Lince, T01-221 2432, postmaster@touringperu.com.pe, offers help to tourists and particularly to country; regional routes and the South American sections of the Pan-American Highway available (US$5).

Combis, colectivos and trucks

Combis operate between most small towns in the Andes on one- three-hour journeys. This makes it possible, in many cases, just to turn up and travel within an hour or two. On rougher roads, combis are minibuses, while on better roads there are also slightly more expensive and much faster car colectivos. Both operate in the Sacred Valley area. Colectivos are shared taxis which, usually charge twice the bus fare and leave only when full. Most firms have offices. If you book one day in advance, they will pick you up at your hotel or in the main plaza. Trucks are not always much cheaper than buses. They charge 75% of the bus fare, but are wholly unpredictable. They are not recommended for long trips, and comfort depends on the load.

Cycling

Unless you are planning a journey almost exclusively on paved roads, a mountain bike is strongly recommended. The good quality ones are incredibly tough and rugged, with low gear ratios for difficult terrain, wide tyres with plenty of tread for good road-holding, cantilever brakes, and a low centre of gravity for improved stability. A chrome-alloy frame is a desirable choice over aluminium as it can be welded if necessary. Once an aluminium frame breaks, it's broke. *Richard's New Bicycle Book* (Pan, £12.99) makes useful reading for even the most mechanically minded.

South American Explorers, *www.SAexplorers.org*, have valuable cycling information that is continuously updated. The Expedition Advisory Centre, administered by the **Royal Geographical Society**, *1 Kensington Gore, London SW7 2AR*, has published a useful monograph entitled *Bicycle Expeditions*, by Paul Vickers. Published in March 1990, it can be downloaded from the RGS's website (www.rgs.org). A useful website is **Bike South America**, *www.e-ddws.com/bsa/* Also recommended is **Cyclo Accueil Cyclo** (**CAC**), *3 rue Limouzin, 42160 Andrezieux, cacoadou@netcourier.com* An organization of long-haul tourers who open their homes for free to passing cyclists.

Hitchhiking

Hitchhiking is not easy, owing to the lack of private vehicles, and requires a lot of patience. It can also be a risky way of getting from A to B, but with common sense, it can be an acceptable way of travelling for free (or very little money) and a way to meet a range of interesting people. For obvious reasons, a lone female should not hitch by herself. Besides, you are more likely to get a lift if you are with a partner, be they male or female. The best combination is a male and female together. Three or more and you'll be in for a long wait. Your appearance is also important. Someone with matted hair and a large tattoo on their forehead will not have much success. Remember that you are asking considerable trust of someone.

Note Drivers usually ask for money but don't always expect to get it. In mountain and jungle areas you usually have to pay drivers of lorries, vans and even private cars; ask the driver first how much he is going to charge, and then recheck with the locals.

Motorcycling

The motorcycle should be off-road capable. A road bike can go most places an off-road bike can go at the cost of greater effort. Most hotels will allow you to bring the bike inside (see accommodation listings in the travelling text for details). Look for hotels that have a courtyard or more secure parking and never leave luggage on the bike overnight or whilst unattended.

Taxi prices are fixed and cost around US$0.60-1.55 in the urban areas. In Lima prices range from US$1.20-2.50, but fares are not fixed. Some drivers work for companies that do have standard fares. Ask locals what the price should be and always set the price beforehand. Taxis at airports are often a bit more expensive, but ask locals what the price should be as taxi drivers may try to charge you three times the correct price. Many taxi drivers work for commission from hotels and will try to convince you to go to that hotel. Feel free to choose your own hotel and go there. If you walk away from the Arrivals gate a bit, the fares should go down to a price that is reasonable.

Train

Peru's national rail service was privatized in 1999. The lines in the Cusco area are all run by **PerúRail SA**. Service has improved, but prices have also risen substantially.

PerúRail's services are **Cusco-Machu Picchu** and **Cusco-Juliaca-Puno**. For information, *T084-221992, www.perurail.com*

Sleeping

Cusco is full of excellent value hotels throughout the price ranges and finding a hotel room to suit your budget should not present any problems. The exception to this is during the Christmas and Easter holiday periods, Carnival, in June and Independence celebrations at the end of July, when all hotels seem to be crowded. It's advisable to book in advance at these times and during school holidays and local festivals (see Holidays and festivals, page 48).

Accommodation, as with everything else, is more expensive in Lima, where good budget hotels are fewer and, therefore, tend to be busy. Remote jungle towns such as Puerto Maldonado tend to be more expensive than the norm. And if you want a room with air conditioning expect to pay around 30% extra.

All hotels and restaurants in the upper price brackets charge 19% general sales tax (IGV) and 10% service on top of prices (neither is included in prices given in the accommodation listings, unless specified). The more expensive hotels also charge in dollars according to the parallel rate of exchange at midnight. Most lower grade hotels only charge the 19% sales tax but some may include a service charge.

By law all places that offer accommodation now have a plaque outside bearing the letters **H** (**Hotel**), **Hs** (**Hostal**), **HR** (**Hotel Residencial**) or **P** (**Pensión**) according to type. A hotel has 51 rooms or more, a *hostal* 50 or fewer, but the categories do not describe quality or facilities. Generally speaking, though, a *pensión* or *hospedaje* will be cheaper than a hotel or *hostal*. Most mid-range hotels have their own restaurants serving lunch and dinner, as well as breakfast. Few budget places have this facility, though many now serve breakfast. Many hotels have safe parking for motor cycles. Most places are friendly and helpful, irrespective of the price, particularly smaller *pensiones* and *hospedajes*, which are often family run and will treat you as another member of the family. Cheaper places don't always supply soap, towels and toilet paper. In colder (higher) regions they may not supply enough blankets, so take your own or a sleeping bag.

Youth hostels

The office of the Youth Hostel Association of Peru (Asociación Peruana de Albergues Turísticos Juveniles) in Lima is at Avenida Casimiro Ulloa 328, Miraflores, Lima, T446-5488, F444-8187. It has information about youth hostels all around the world. For information about International Student Identity Cards (ISIC) and lists of discounts available to cardholders contact **Intej**, see page 21.

⦂ A bed for the night

LL (over US$150) to **AL** (US$66-99) Hotels in these categories are usually only found in Cusco, Lima and the main tourist centres. They should offer pool, sauna, gym, jacuzzi, all business facilities (including email), several restaurants, bars and often a casino. Most will provide a safe box in each room.

A (US$46-65) and **B** (US$31-45) The better value hotels in these categories provide more than the standard facilities and a fair degree of comfort. Most will include breakfast and many offer 'extras' such as cable TV, minibar, and tea and coffee making facilities. They may also provide tourist information and their own transport. Service is generally better and most accept credit cards. At the top end of the range, some may have a swimming pool, sauna and jacuzzi.

C (US$21-30) and **D** (US$16-20) Hotels in these categories range from very comfortable to functional, but there are some real bargains to be had. At these prices you should expect your own bathroom, constant hot water, a towel, soap and toilet paper, TV, a restaurant, communal sitting area and a reasonably sized, comfortable room with air conditioning (in tropical regions).

E (US$11-15) and **F** (US$7-10) Usually in these ranges you can expect some degree of comfort and cleanliness, a private bathroom with hot water (certainly in **E**, less common in **F**) and perhaps continental breakfast thrown in.

Again, the best value hotels will be listed in the travelling text. Many of those catering for foreign tourists in the more popular regions offer excellent value for money and many have their own restaurant a nd offer services such as laundry, safe deposit box, money exchange and luggage store.

G (up to US$6) A room in this price range usually consists of little more than a bed and four walls, with barely enough room to swing the proverbial cat. If you're lucky you may have a window, a table and chair, and even your own bathroom, though this tends to be the exception rather than the rule. Prices given in the accommodation listings are for two people sharing a double room with bathroom (shower and toilet) in high season. Where possible, prices are also given per person, as some hotels charge almost as much for a single room.

Camping

This presents no problems in Peru. There can, however, be problems with robbery when camping close to a small village. Avoid such a location, or ask permission to camp in a backyard or *chacra* (farmland). Most Peruvians are used to campers. Be casual about it, do not unpack all your gear, leave it inside your tent (especially at night) and never leave a tent unattended.

Camping gas in little blue bottles is available. Those with stoves designed for lead-free gasoline should use *ron de quemar*, available from hardware shops (*ferreterías*). White gas is called *bencina*, also available from hardware stores. If you use a stove system that uses canisters make sure you dispose of the empty canisters properly. Keep in mind that you are responsible for the trash that your group, guide or muledriver may drop and it is up to you to say something and pick it up.

Advice and suggestions

If travelling alone, it's usually cheaper to share with others in a room with three or four beds. If breakfast is included in the price, it will almost invariably mean continental

⦂ Eating categories

Prices for individual restaurant meals given in the text refer to a two-course meal for one person, without tips or drinks, or, where stated, the price of a main course only.

Expensive over US$12
Mid-range US$5-12
Cheap under US$5

breakfast. During the low season, when many places may be half empty, it's often possible to bargain the room rate down. Reception areas in hotels may be misleading, so it is a good idea to see the room before booking. Many hoteliers try to offload their least desirable rooms first. If you're shown a dark box without any furniture, ask if there's another room with a window or a desk for writing letters. The difference is often surprising.

Note The electric showers used in many hotels (basic up to mid-range) are a health and safety nightmare. Avoid touching any part of the shower while it is producing hot water asnd always get out before you switch it off.

When booking a hotel from an airport, or station by phone, always talk to the hotel yourself; do not let anyone do it for you (except an accredited hotel booking service). You will be told the hotel of your choice is full and be directed to a more expensive one.

Toilets
Except in the most upmarket hotels and restaurants, most Peruvian toilets are barely adequate at best. The further you go from main population and tourist centres, the poorer the facilities, so you may require a strong stomach and the ability to hold your breath for a long time. Almost without exception used toilet paper or feminine hygiene products should not be flushed down the pan, but placed in the receptacle provided. This applies even in quite expensive hotels. Failing to observe this custom will block the pan or drain, which can be a considerable health risk.

Eating and drinking

Peruvian cuisine → *For a glossary of food and drink terms, see Footnotes.*
Not surprisingly for a country with such a diversity of geography and climates, Peru boasts the continent's most extensive and varied menu. In fact, Peru is rivalled in Latin America only by Mexico in the variety of its cuisine. One of the least expected pleasures of a trip to Peru is the wonderful food on offer, and those who are willing to forego the normal traveller's fare of pizza and fried chicken are in for a tasty treat.

Not surprisingly, the best coastal dishes are those with seafood bases, with the most popular being the jewel in the culinary crown, *ceviche*. This delicious dish of raw white fish marinated in lemon juice, onion and hot peppers can be found in neighbouring countries, but Peruvian is best. Traditionally, *ceviche* is served with corn-on-the-cob, *cancha* (toasted corn), yucca and sweet potatoes. Another mouth-watering fish dish is *escabeche* – fish with onions, hot green pepper, red peppers, prawns (*langostinos*), cumin, hard-boiled eggs, olives, and sprinkled with cheese. For fish on its own, don't miss the excellent *corvina*, or white sea bass. You should also try *chupe de camarones*, which is a shrimp stew made with varying and somewhat surprising ingredients. Other fish dishes include *parihuela*, a popular bouillabaisse with *yuyo de mar*, a tangy seaweed, and *aguadito*, a thick rice and fish soup said to have rejuvenating powers.

The staples of highland cooking, corn and potatoes, date back to Inca times and are found in a remarkable variety of shapes, sizes and colours. Two good potato dishes are *Causa* and *carapulca*. *Causa* is made with yellow potatoes, lemons, pepper, hard-boiled eggs, olives, lettuce, sweet cooked corn, sweet cooked potato, fresh cheese, and served with onion sauce. Another potato dish is *papa a la huancaina*, which is topped with a spicy sauce made with milk and cheese. The most commonly eaten corn dishes are *choclo con queso*, corn on the cob with cheese, and *tamales*, boiled corn dumplings filled with meat and wrapped in a banana leaf.

Meat dishes are many and varied. *Ollucos con charqui* is a kind of potato with dried meat, *sancochado* is meat and all kinds of vegetables stewed together and seasoned with ground garlic and *lomo a la huancaína* is beef with egg and cheese sauce. A dish almost guaranteed to appear on every restaurant menu is *lomo saltado*, a kind of stir-fried beef with onions, vinegar, ginger, chilli, tomatoes and fried potatoes, served with rice. *Rocoto relleno* is spicy bell pepper stuffed with beef and vegetables, *palta rellena* is avocado filled with chicken or Russian salad, *estofado de carne* is a stew which often contains wine and *carne en adobo* is a cut and seasoned steak. Others include *fritos*, fried pork, usually eaten in the morning, *chicharrones*, deep fried chunks of pork ribs and chicken, and *lechón*, suckling pig. And not forgetting that popular childhood pet, *cuy* (guinea pig), which is considered a real delicacy.

Very filling and good value are the many soups on offer, such as yacu-chupe, a green soup which has a basis of potato, with cheese, garlic, coriander leaves, parsley, peppers, eggs, onions, and mint, and *sopa a la criolla* containing thin noodles, beef heart, bits of egg and vegetables and pleasantly spiced. And not to be outdone in the fish department, *trucha* (trout) is delicious, particularly from Lake Titicaca.

The main ingredient in much **jungle cuisine** is fish, especially the succulent, dolphin-sized *paiche*, which comes with the delicious *palmito*, or palm-hearts, and the ever-present yucca and fried bananas. Other popular dishes include *sopa de motelo* (turtle soup), *sajino* (roast wild boar) and *lagarto* (caiman). *Juanes* are a jungle version of *tamales*, stuffed with chicken and rice.

The Peruvian sweet tooth is evident in the huge number of **desserts** and confections from which to choose. These include: *cocada al horno* – coconut, with yolk of egg, sesame seed, wine and butter; *picarones* – frittered cassava flour and eggs fried in fat and served with honey; *mazamorra morada* – purple maize, sweet potato starch, lemons, various dried fruits, sticks of ground cinnamon and cloves and perfumed pepper; *manjar blanco* – milk, sugar and eggs; *maná* – an almond paste with eggs, vanilla and milk; *alfajores* – shortbread biscuit with *manjar blanco*, pineapple, peanuts, etc; *pastelillos* – yuccas with sweet potato, sugar and anise fried in fat and powdered with sugar and served hot; and *zango de pasas*, made with maize, syrup, raisins and sugar. *Turrón*, the Lima nougat, is worth trying. *Tejas* are pieces of fruit or nut enveloped in *manjar blanco* and covered in chocolate or icing sugar – delicious.

The various Peruvian fruits are wonderful. They include bananas, the citrus fruits, pineapples, dates, avocados (*paltas*), eggfruit (*lúcuma*), the custard apple (*chirimoya*) which can be as big as your head, quince, paw paw, mango, guava, the passion-fruit (*maracuyá*) and the soursop (*guanábana*). These should be tried as juices or ice cream – an unforgettable experience.

Eating out → *For a full list of restaurants, see under Eating for each town.*

Lunch is the main meal, and apart from the most exclusive places, most restaurants have one or two set lunch menus, called *menú ejecutivo* or *menú económico*. The set menu has the advantage of being ready and is served almost immediately and it is usually cheap. The *menú ejecutivo* costs US$2 or more for a three-course meal with a soft drink and it offers greater choice and more interesting dishes than the *menú económico*, which costs US$1.50-2.50. Don't leave it too late, though, most Peruvians

⁞ A limp excuse

Did you know there is a potato that has the opposite effect of Viagra? It's a tuber named *año* and Cusqueño women have been known to use it to take revenge on cheating husbands. If a man is unfaithful, his wife will boil his trousers in a vat containing the potato – enough to stop him rising to any occasion!

Stories like these are part of the fun of discovering Cusco's markets. Wandering round one is a great experience, packed with new sights, smells and the bright colours of unknown fruit and veg. At San Jerónimo you'll find huacatay – a mint grown at high altitude and used in the preparation of guinea pig – bulls' testicles, which are boiled, sliced and used in salads, huge sacks of dirt-cheap garlic, massive 20-25 kg pumpkins, *pepiño* (which has a creamy-coloured skin and is very refreshing), as well as strawberries from the coast, basil, coriander, green chilli peppers and spinach.

There is caihua, from the cucumber family, which grows only in sub-tropical valleys and which can be stuffed or chopped for stir-fry or salad. Then there is a dried black potato which smells of bad feet when it is cooked, but is favoured by locals nevertheless; they grind it up and add it to food.

Then there are potatoes frozen overnight as hard as rocks to bring out their flavour; these are mixed with salt and eaten with cheese. These, together with olives, oranges and tomatoes piled high in large mounds, are weighed by indigenous women who proudly show off their region of origin by the different hats they wear.

Most westerners will shirk at ever sampling some of these foodstuffs – especially when a lamb´s head, complete with lipless, grinning teeth bobs to the surface of the favourite soup here (*caldo de cabeza*) for which locals pay a premiusm if it includes brain and tongue.

However, the sight of so much variety, of brown guinea pigs scurrying around cages, of bright yellow bananas balanced chest-high and of heady herbs sold by the sackful, is one worth seeking out. Just don't try the tuber named *año*! Aurelio Aguirre of Andes Nature Tours offers tailor-made tours around the markets of Cusco (see page 113).

eat lunch around 1230-1300. There are many Chinese restaurants (*chifas*) which serve good food at reasonable prices. For really economically minded people the *comedores populares* found in the markets of most cities offer a standard three-course meal for as little as US$1 (see Health, page 57).

For those who wish to eschew such good value, the menu is called la carta. An à *la carte* lunch or dinner costs US$5-8, but can go up to an expensive US$80 in a first-class Lima restaurant, with drinks and wine included. Middle- and high-class restaurants add 11% tax and 17% service to the bill (sometimes 19% and 13% respectively). This is not shown on the price list or menu, so check in advance. Less fancy retaurants charge only 5% tax, while cheap, local restaurants charge no taxes. Dinner in restaurants is normally about 1900 onwards, but choice may be more limited than lunchtime.

The situation for vegetarians is improving, but slowly. In Cusco you should have no problem finding a vegetarian restaurant (or a restaurant that has vegetarian options), and the same applies to Lima. Elsewhere, choice is limited and you may find that, as a non-meat eater, you are not understood. Vegetarians and people with allergies should be able to list (in Spanish) all the foods they cannot eat. By saying *No* como carne (I don't eat meat), people may assume that you eat chicken and eggs. If you do eat eggs, make sure they are cooked thoroughly. Restaurant staff will often bend over backwards to get you exactly what you want but you need to request it.

Drink

Peru's most famous drink is *pisco*, a grape brandy, used in the wonderful pisco sour, a deceptively potent cocktail which also includes egg whites and lime juice. The most renowned brands come from the Ica Valley. Other favourites are *chilcano*, a longer refreshing drink made with *guinda*, a local cherry brandy, and *algarrobina*, a sweet cocktail made with the syrup from the bark of the carob tree, egg whites, evaporated milk, *pisco* and cinnamon.

Some Peruvian wines are good, others are acidic and poor. The best are the Ica wines Tacama and Ocucaje, and both come in red, white and rosé, sweet and dry varieties. They cost around US$5 a bottle, or more. Tacama blancs de blancs and brut champagne have been recommended, also Gran Tinto Reserva Especial. Viña Santo Tomás, from Chincha, is cheap, but Casapalca is not for the discerning palate.

Peruvian beer is good, but is becoming pretty much the same the country over now that many individual brewers have been swallowed up by the multinational Backus and Johnson. This has happened to the *Cusqueña*, *Arequipeña*, *Callao* and *Trujillo* brands. Peruvians who had their favourites are lamenting this change. In Lima, the *Cristal* and *Pilsener* are both pretty good and served everywhere. Those who fancy a change from the ubiquitous pilsner type beers should look out for the sweetish 'maltina' brown ale. A good dark beer is Trujillo Malta.

Chicha de jora is a strong but refreshing maize beer, usually home-made and not easy to come by, and *chicha morada* is a soft drink made with purple maize. Coffee in Peru is usually execrable. It is brought to the table in a small jug accompanied by a mug of hot water to which you add the coffee essence. If you want coffee with milk, a mug of milk is brought. Those who crave a decent cup of coffee will find recommended places listed in the café section of each town. There are many different kinds of herb tea: the commonest are *manzanilla* (camomile), *mate de coca* (often served in the highlands to stave off the discomforts of altitude sickness) and *hierbaluisa* (lemon grass).

Entertainment

In Cusco → Look out for the vast range of flyers, which give you free entry plus a complimentary drink.
One of Cusco's main attractions – apart from Inca ruins, colonial architecture, great trekking, wonderful scenery and wild adventure sports – is its nightlife. There is a staggering selection bars to suit all tastes and dispositions, all crammed into a few streets on and around the main Plaza de Armas. You can large it up in the frenzied atmosphere of the **Cross Keys**, get blissed out in the laid-back **Los Perros**, or go all Oirish in **Paddy Flaherty's**. The choice, as they say, is yours. After the bars close the nightclubs kick into action. The old favourites such as **Mama Africa** and **Ukuku's** have been joined by a rash of new pretenders, some with decent sound systems and DJs spinning the latest happening tunes. But its not all techno and thumping drum 'n' bass. There are also places where you can wiggle your hips to the sensuous sounds of salsa and merengue. If all that brings you out in a cold sweat, there are *peñas* offering relatively sedate folklore shows.

Be warned that Cusco's nightlife is so prolific you may be so off your face every night that you won't even have the energy to do the Inca Trail. More seriously, though, take it easy on the booze when you first arrive. Having altitude sickness and a hangover is no joke. Also be aware of the potential dangers of trying to score drugs in nightclubs (see page 38).

The chances are you won't have much time in Lima and will want to move on to Cusco as soon as possible. But if you do have a free night before flying you should check out the nightlife in Barranco, a pleasant, bohemian, seaside suburb of the capital. It's only a short taxi ride from Miraflores and at weekends is positively throbbing with young *limeños* out for a good time. It's also a great place for a romantic early evening drink while you watch the sun slip into the Pacific Ocean. There are lots of trendy bars and nightclubs in Miraflores, too.

Festivals and events

Festivals → *A full list of local festivals is listed under each town.*

Every bit as important as knowing where to go and what the weather will be like, is Peru's festival calendar. At any given time of the year there'll be a festival somewhere in the country, at which time even the sleepiest little town or village is transformed into a raucous mixture of drinking, dancing and water throwing (or worse). Not all festivals end up as choreographed drunken riots, however. Some are solemn and ornate holy processions. All draw people from miles around; it helps a great deal to know about these festivals and when they take place.

Two of the major festival dates are **Carnaval,** which is held over the weekend before **Ash Wednesday,** and **Semana Santa** (Holy Week), which ends on **Easter Sunday**. Carnival is celebrated in most of the Andes and **Semana Santa** throughout most of Peru. Accommodation and transport is heavily booked at these times and prices rise accordingly.

Another important festival is **Fiesta de la Cruz,** held on the first of **May** in much of the central and southern highlands and on the coast. In Cusco, the entire month of **June** is one huge fiesta, culminating in **Inti Raymi,** on **24 June,** one of Peru's prime tourist attractions. Accommodation can be very hard to find at this time in Cusco.

The two main festivals in Lima are **Santa Rosa de Lima,** on **30 August,** and **Señor de los Milagros,** held on several dates throughout **October**. Another national festival is **Todos los Santos** (All Saints) on **1 November,** and on **8 December** is **Festividad de la Inmaculada Concepción.**

For a description of some of the main festivals and their historic roots, see Culture, page 288. For more dates, check the websites of **PromPerú** and **South American Explorers** (see page 71). Also check out **www.whatsonwhen.com**

National holidays

Aside from the festivals listed above, the main holidays are: **1 January,** New Year; **6 January,** Bajada de Reyes; **1 May,** Labour Day; **28-29 July,** Fiestas Patrias (Independence) ; **7 October,** Battle of Angamos; **24-25 December,** Christmas.

Shopping

Most businesses such as banks, airline offices and tourist agencies close for the official holidays while supermarkets and street markets may be open. This depends a lot on where you are so ask around before the holiday. Sometimes holidays that fall during mid-week will be moved to the following Monday. Find out what the local customs and events are. Often there are parades, processions, special types of food or certain traditions (like yellow underwear at New Year) that characterize the event. The high season for foreign tourism in Peru is June to September while national

Prices rise and accommodation and bus tickets are harder to come by. If you know when you will be travelling buy your ticket in advance.

Almost everyone who visits Cusco will end up buying a souvenir of some sort from the vast array of arts and crafts (artesanía) on offer. The best, and cheapest, place to shop for souvenirs, and pretty much anything else, is in the street markets which can be found absolutely everywhere.

Bargaining

Sooner or later almost everyone has to bargain in Peru. Only the rich and famous can afford to pay the prices quoted by taxi drivers, receptionists and self-proclaimed guides. The great majority of Peruvians are honest and extremely hard working, but their country is poor and often in turmoil, the future is uncertain and the overwhelming majority of people live below the poverty line. Foreigners are seen as rich, even if they are backpackers or students. In order to bring prices down, it is extremely helpful to speak at least some Spanish and/or to convince locals that you live, work or study in Peru and therefore know the real price.

You can negotiate the price of a tour booked through a travel agency, but not an aeroplane, bus or train ticket. In fact, you will probably get better price directly from the airline ticket office.

Bargaining is expected when you are shopping for artwork, handicrafts, souvenirs, or even food in the market. Remember, though, that most handicrafts, including alpaca and woollen goods, are made by hand. Ask yourself if it is worth taking advantage of the piteous state of the people you are buying from. Keep in mind, these people are making a living and the 50 centavos you save by bargaining may buy the seller two loaves of bread. You want the fair price not the lowest one, so bargain only when you feel you are being ripped off. Remember that some Peruvians are so desperate that they will have to sell you their goods at *any* price, in order to survive. Please, don't take advantage of it.

What to buy

Good buys are: silver and gold handicrafts; Indian hand-spun and hand-woven textiles; manufactured textiles in Indian designs; llama and alpaca wool products such as ponchos, rugs, hats, blankets, slippers, coats and sweaters; *arpilleras* (appliqué pictures of Peruvian life), which are made with great skill and originality by women in the shanty towns; and fine leather products which are mostly hand-made. Another good buy is clothing made from high quality Pima cotton, which is grown in Peru.

The *mate burilado*, or engraved gourd, found in every tourist shop, is cheap and one of the most genuine expressions of folk art in Peru. Alpaca clothing, such as sweaters, hats and gloves, is cheaper in the Sierra, the best value being found in Puno. Nevertheless, Cusco is one of the main weaving centres and a good place to shop for textiles, as well as excellent woodcarvings (see the Shopping section on page 109). **Note** Geniune alpaca is odourless wet or dry, wet llama 'stinks'. For a more detailed look at Peruvian arts and crafts, see under Arts and crafts on page 284.

Pre-paid Kodak slide film cannot be developed in Peru and is also very hard to find. Kodachrome is almost impossible to buy. Some travellers (but not all) have advised against mailing exposed films home. Either take them with you, or have them developed, but not printed, once you have checked the laboratory's quality. Note that postal authorities may use less sensitive equipment for X-ray screening than the airports do. Developing black and white film is a problem. Often it is shoddily machine-processed and the negatives are ruined. Ask the store if you can see an example of their laboratory's work and if they hand-develop. Exposed film can be protected in humid areas by putting it in a balloon and tying a knot. Similarly, keeping your camera in a plastic bag may reduce the effects of humidity.

Sports and activities

Birdwatching

Peru is the number one country in the world for birds. Its varied geography and topography, and its wildernesses of so many different life zones have endowed Peru with the greatest biodiversity and variety of birds on earth. 18.5% of all the bird species in the world and 45% of all neotropical birds occur in Peru. This is why Peru is the best destination for birds on the continent dubbed 'the bird continent' by professional birders.

A birding trip to Peru is possible during any month of the year, as birds breed all year round. There is, however, a definite peak in breeding activity – and consequently birdsong – just before the rains come in October, and this makes it rather easier to locate many birds between September and Christmas.

Rainwear is recommended for the mountains, especially during the rainy season between December and April. But in the tropical lowlands an umbrella is the way to go. Lightweight hiking boots are probably the best general footwear, but wellingtons (rubber boots) are preferred by many neotropical birders for the lowland rainforests.

Apart from the usual binoculars, a telescope is helpful in many areas, whilst a tape recorder and shotgun microphone can be very useful for calling out skulking forest birds, although experience in using this type of equipment is recommended, particularly to limit disturbance to the birds.

The birds

If your experience of neotropical birding is limited, the potential number of species which may be seen on a three- or four-week trip can be daunting. A four-week trip can produce over 750 species, and some of the identifications can be tricky! You may want to take an experienced bird guide with you who can introduce you to, for example, the mysteries of foliage-gleaner and woodcreeper identification, or you may want to 'do it yourself' and identify the birds on your own. See also Background, page 292.

Key sites

The **Tambopata National Reserve** (page 228) and the **Manu Biosphere Reserve** (page 221) are two of the premier birding sites in Peru. Full details will be found in the text. Also worth considering are Machu Picchu and Abra Málaga: Machu Picchu may be a nightmare for lovers of peace and solitude, but the surrounding bamboo stands provide excellent opportunities for seeing the Inca wren. A walk along the railway track near Puente Ruinas station can produce species which are difficult to see elsewhere. This is *the* place in Peru to see white-capped dipper and torrent duck. From Ollantaytambo (see page 143), it is only two hours' drive to one of the most accessible polylepsis woodlands in the Andes, whilst the humid temperate forest of Abra Málaga is only 45 minutes further on. In the polylepsis some very rare birds can be located without too much difficulty, including royal cinclodes and white-browed tit-spinetail (the latter being one of the 10 most endangered birds on earth). The humid temperate forest is laden with moss and bromeliads, and mixed species flocks of multi-coloured tanagers and other birds are common. A great three-week combination is about 16 days in Manu, then two or three days in the highlands at Abra Málaga. You can extend this by including one or more of the other highly recommended spots outside the scope of this guidebook. More information on the birds of Peru is given on page 292.

Climbing and trekking

While Peru has some of the best climbing in the world, Cusco is not developed for the sport. Near the city are the Cordilleras Vilcabamba and Vilcanota (see page 203) have the enticing peaks of Salkantay (6,271 m) and Ausangate (6,398 m).

Peru has some outstanding trekking circuits around the Nevados, its snow-capped mountains. Among the best known is the Ausangate circuit. The other type of trekking for which Peru is justifiably renowned is walking among ruins, and, above all, for the Inca Trail (see page 164). However, there are many other walks of this type in a country rich in archaeological heritage. Beyond Machu Picchu, for example, there are magnificent, if strenuous treks, to Vilcabamba (see page 181) and Choquequirao (see page 210).

Most walking is on clear trails well trodden by campesinos who populate most parts of the Peruvian Andes. If you camp on their land, ask permission first and, of course, do not leave any litter. Tents, sleeping bags, mats and stoves can easily be hired in Cusco but check carefully for quality.

Conditions for trekking and climbing

May to September is the dry season in the Cordillera. October, November and April can be fine, particularly for trekking. Most bad weather comes from the east and temperatures plummet around twilight. The optimum months for extreme ice climbing are from late May to mid July. In early May there is a risk of avalanche from sheered neve ice layers. It is best to climb early in the day as the snow becomes slushy later on. After July successive hot sunny days will have melted some of the main support (compacted ice) particularly on north facing slopes. On the other hand, high altitude rock climbs are less troubled by ice after July. On south facing slopes the ice and snow never consolidates quite as well.

Contact addresses and websites
Andean Travel Web, *www.andeantravel web.com/peru*, Andean adventure travel, with advice, links and more (Spanish and English).
APTAE (Asociación Peruana de Turismo de Aventura y Ecoturismo), *San Fernando 287, Miraflores, Lima 18, T241 4765, www.aptaeperu.com.pe*

Asociación de Deportes de Montaña, Aire Puro, *http://argos/pucp.edu.pe/ ~airepuro*, trekking, climbing, biking.
El Excursionismo en el Perú, *www.geocities.com/TheTropics/Shores/8717*, details of treks in Spanish.
Montañistas 4.0, *www.geocities.com/ Yosemite/7363*, a climbing association dedicated to going above 4,000 m.

Cultural tourism

This covers more esoteric pursuits such as archaeology and mystical tourism. Several of the tour operators listed on page 13 offer customized packages for special interest groups. Local operators offering these more specialized tours are listed in the travelling text under the relevant location. Cultural tourism is a rapidly growing niche market. Under the umbrella heading *Al-Tur*, **PromPerú** has 31 interesting community-based tourism projects in archaeology, agro-tourism, education, jungle trips, llama trekking, nature tourism and traditional medicine. A CD-ROM (*Turismo Vivencial – Experiential Tourism*) and information are available from **PromPerú**; see Tourist information, above.

For information on specialized shamanic healing and mystical tourism, see Cusco Tours and activities, page 113.

Kayaking

Peru offers outstanding whitewater kayaking for all standards of paddlers form novice to expert. Many first descents remain unattempted due to logistical difficulties, though they are slowly being ticked off by a dedicated crew of local and internationally renowned kayakers. For the holiday paddler, you are probably best joining up with a raft company who will gladly carry all your gear (plus any non-paddling companions) and provide you with superb food while you enjoy the river from an unladen kayak. There is a surprising selection of latest model kayaks available in Peru for hire from approximately US$10-20 a day.

For complete novices, some companies offer two- to three-day kayak courses on the Urubamba and Apurímac that can be booked locally. For expedition paddlers, bringing your own canoe is the best option though it is getting increasingly more expensive to fly with your boats around Peru. A knowledge of Spanish is indispensable.

Mountain biking

With its amazing diversity of trails, tracks and rough roads, Peru is surely one of the last great mountain bike destinations yet to be fully discovered. Whether you are interested in a two-day downhill blast from the Andes to the Amazon Jungle or an extended off-road journey, then Peru has some of the world's best biking opportunities. The problem is finding the routes as trail maps are virtually non-existent and the few main roads are often congested with traffic and far from fun to travel along. A few specialist agencies run by dedicated mountain bikers are now exploring the intricate web of paths, single tracks and dirt roads that criss-crosses the Andes, putting together exciting routes to suit everyone from the weekend warrior to the long-distance touring cyclist, the extreme downhiller to the casual day tripper.

If you are considering a dedicated cycling holiday, then it is best to bring your bike from home. It's pretty easy, just get a bike box from your local shop, deflate the tyres, take the pedals off and turn the handlebars. It is worth checking first that your airline is happy to take your bike: some are, some will want to charge. Make sure your bike is in good condition before you depart as spares and repairs are hard to come by, especially if your bike is very complicated (eg: XT V-brake blocks are virtually impossible to find and rear suspension/disc brakes parts are totally unavailable). A tip from a Peruvian mountain bike guide: take plenty of inner tubes, brake blocks, chain lube and a quick release seat. Leave all panniers at home and rely on the support vehicle whenever you get tired as there will be plenty more riding later.

If you are hiring a bike, be it for one-day or longer, the basic rule is you get what you pay for. For as little as US$5-10 a day you can get a cheap imitation of a mountain bike that will be fine on a paved road, but will almost certainly not stand up to the rigors of off-roading. For US$20-25 you should be able to find something half-decent with front shocks, V-brakes, helmet and gloves. Bear in mind that there are not many high-quality, well-maintained bikes available in Peru so you should check any hire bike thoroughly before riding it.

Choosing the right tour When signing up for a mountain bike trip, remember that you are in the Andes so if you are worried about your fitness and the altitude, make sure you get a predominantly downhill trip. Check there is a support vehicle available throughout the entire trip, not just dropping you off and meeting you at the end. Check the guide is carrying a first aid kit, at the very least a puncture repair kit (preferably a comprehensive tool kit) and is knowledgeable about bike mechanics. Bikes regularly go wrong, punctures are frequent and people do fall off, so it is essential that your guide/company provides this minimum cover.

On longer trips ask for detailed trip dossiers, describing the ups and downs and total distances of the routes, check how much is just dirt-road (suitable for just about anyone of reasonable fitness) and how much is single-track (often requiring considerable experience and fitness). Also it is good to know what support will be provided in the way of experienced bike guides, trained bike mechanics on hand, radio communications, spare bikes, cooking and dining facilities, toilet facilities, etc.

Where to ride in the Cusco area From a half-day downhill exploring the nearby ruins to the ultimate 550-km Andes to Amazon challenge, Cusco offers a multitude of rides to suit all abilities. Here is a selection of the rides available. All ideally require a guide as its very easy to get lost in the Andes.

Cusco Ruins tour Cheat by taking a taxi to Puka Pukara and enjoying a tarmac descent (if unguided) via Tambo Machay, Qenqo and Sacsayhuaman (don't forget your combined entrance ticket – see Box, page 71). Alternatively, with a guide, explore some of Cusco's less-visited ruins on the mass of old Inca tracks available only to those in the know.

Chinchero-Moray-Maras-Las Salinas-Urubamba One of the finest one-day trips in Peru, best done with a guide as it is easy to get lost. Largely downhill on a mixture of dirt road and single track, this trip takes you to the interesting circular ruins of Moray and into the spectacular salt pans of Maras on an awesome mule track (watch out for mules!).

Huchuy Qosqo For experts only, this unbelievable trip is best described as 'trekking with your bike'. Various routes, again hard to find, are followed by what must be one of the hairiest single tracks in the world, along the top of and down into the Sacred Valley of the Incas. Totally radical!

Lares Valley This offers some incredible down and uphill options on two- or three-day circuits including a relaxing soak in the beautiful Lares hotsprings.

Abra Málaga From 4,200 m, an 80-km descent to the jungle, or, alternatively a radical Inca Trail back to Ollantaytambo, both brilliant rides.

Tres Cruces to Manu From Pisac to Manu is a 250-km, beautiful dirt road ride offering big climbs and an even bigger (two-day) descent. A side trip to Tres Cruces to see the sunrise is a must if time permits. Be warned that the road to Manu only operates downhill every other day, so be sure to check you've got it right or else beware irate truck drivers not giving way on a very narrow road!

Cusco-Puerto Maldonado Possibly the greatest Trans-Andean Challenge on a bike: 550 km of hard work up to 4,700 m and down to 230 m on one of the roughest roads there is (with the odd full-on single track thrown in for good measure). Be prepared to get wet as there are a lot of river crossings, sometimes up to waist deep. Either a nine-day epic, or cheat on the hills and enjoy some of the biggest downhills out (three to four days).

Agencies in Cusco are given in the Tours and activities part of the Cusco chapter.

Parapenting and hang-gliding

'Vuelo Libre' is just taking off in Peru. The area with the greatest potential is the Sacred Valley of Cusco which has excellent launch sites, thermals and reasonable landing sites. Some 45 km from Cusco is Cerro Sacro (3,797 m) on the Pampa de Chincheros with 550 m clearance at take-off. It is the launch site for cross-country flights over the Sacred Valley, Sacsayhuaman and Cusco. Particularly good for parapenting is the Mirador de Urubamba, 38 km from Cusco, at 3,650 m, with 800 m clearance and views over Pisac.

The season in the sierra is May to October, with the best months being August and September. Some flights in Peru have exceeded 6,500 m.

Rafting

Peru is rapidly becoming one of the world's premier destinations for whitewater rafting. Several of its rivers are rated in the world's top ten and a rafting trip, be it for one or ten days, is now high on any adventurer's list of activities while travelling in Peru. It is not just the adrenaline rush of big rapids that attract, it is the whole experience of accessing areas beyond the reach of motor vehicles, whether tackling sheer-sided, mile-deep canyons, travelling silently through pristine rainforest, or canoeing across the stark Altiplano, high in the Andes.

Before you leap in the first raft that floats by, a word of warning and a bit of advice will help you ensure that your rafting 'trip of a lifetime' really is as safe, as environmentally friendly and as fun as you want it to be.

Basically, the very remoteness and amazing locations that make Peruvian whitewater rivers so attractive mean that dealing with an emergency (should it occur) can be difficult, if nigh on impossible. As the sport of rafting has increased in popularity over the last few years, so too have the number of accidents (including fatalities), yet the rafting industry remains virtually unchecked. How then, do you ensure your safety on what are undoubtedly some of the best whitewater runs anywhere in South America if not the whole world?

If you are keen on your rafting and are looking to join a rafting expedition of some length, then it is definitely worth signing up in advance before you set foot in Peru. Some long expeditions have fewer than two or three scheduled departures a year and the companies that offer them only accept bookings well in advance as they are logistically extremely difficult to organize. For the popular day trips and expeditions on the Apurímac there are regular departures (the latter in the dry season only – see below). If you can spare a couple of days to wait for a departure then it is fine to book in Cusco. It also gives you the chance to talk to the company who will be operating your tour and to meet the guides. There are day trip departures all year and frequent multi-day departures in the high season. Note that the difficulty of the sections changes between the dry and rainy season. Some become extremely difficult or un-runable in the rainy season. The dry season is April/May to September (but can be as late as November), the rainy season December to March.

How do you choose your **operator**? It is hoped that by the end of 2003 the Peruvian government will have put in place new regulations governing rafting operators and their river guides. The new legislation demands that Class 4+ guides hold the internationally recognized qualifications of Swift Water Rescue Technician and hold current first aid certificates. All rafting equipment will be checked regularly to ensure it meets basic safety standards, eg life jackets that actually float etc. At present there are a number of guides with the relevant qualifications, but you will only find them at companies who operate the longer, multi-day trips. Moreover, equipment standards in some of the companies are woefully low so how exactly the new legislation will work will be interesting. It may prove difficult to enforce the new rules, should they be put in place, but at least it will be a step in the right direction.

At present (and probably in the foreseeable future), as with many of Peru's adventure options, it simply boils down to 'You get what you pay for'. Rafting is an inherently dangerous sport and doing it in Peru with the wrong operator can quite seriously be endangering your life. If price is all that matters bear in mind the following comments: the cheaper the price, the less you get, be it with safety cover, experience of guides, quality of equipment, quantity of food, emergency back up and environmental awareness.

Often on trips you will be required to show proof that your **travel insurance** will cover you for whitewater rafting (occasionally you may be asked to sign an insurance disclaimer). If you are unsure about it, and are planning to go rafting, it is worth checking with your insurance company before you leave, as some policies have an additional charge. Very few policies cover Grade V rafting – read the small print. When signing up you should ask about the experience of the guides or even, if possible, meet them. At present there is no exam or qualification required to become a river guide, but certain things are essential of your guide. Firstly, find out his command of English (or whatever language – there are a few German speaking guides available), essential if you are going to understand his commands. Find out his experience. How many times has he done this particular stretch of river? Many Peruvian guides have worked overseas in the off-season, from Chile to Costa Rica, Europe and New Zealand. The more international experience your guide has, the more aware he will be of international safety practices. All guides should have some experience in rescue techniques. All guides must have knowledge of first aid. Ask when they last took a course and what level they are at.

Good **equipment** is essential for your safe enjoyment of your trip. If possible ask to see some of the gear provided. Basic essentials include self-bailing rafts for all but the calmest of rivers. Check how old your raft is and where it was made. Satellite phones are an essential piece of safety equipment on long trips in remote areas: does the company use them (they are not yet standard on the Apurímac)? Paddles should be of plastic and metal construction. Wooden paddles can snap, but a few companies use locally made ones which can be excellent, but expensive (in either case, losing a paddle should be of less importance to the company than the safety of the rafter). Helmets should always be provided and fit correctly (again, home-made fibreglass copies are an accident waiting to happen). Life jackets must be of a lifeguard-recognized quality and be replaced regularly as they have a tendency to loose their flotation. Locally made jackets look the business, but in fact are very poor floaters. Does your company provide wetsuits (some of the rivers are surprisingly cold), or, at the very least, quality Splash jackets, as the wind can cause you to chill rapidly? On the longer trips, dry bags are provided – what state are these in? How old are they? Do they leak? There is nothing worse than a soggy sleeping bag at the end of a day's rafting. Are tents provided? And most importantly (for the jungle) do the zips on the mosquito net work and is it rain proof? Does the company provide mosquito netting dining tents? Tables? Chairs? These apparent excesses are very nice when camping for some time at the bottom of a sandfly-infested canyon!

Back onto first aid: ask to see the first aid kit and find out what is in there and, most importantly, do they know how to use it? When was it last checked? Updated? Pretty basic stuff, but if someone used all the lomotil you could come unstuck.

After a tough day on the river, the last thing you want to do is get sick from the **food**. Good, wholesome food is relatively cheap in Peru and can make all the difference on a long trip. Once again, you pay for what you get. Ask if there's a vegetarian option. On the food preparation, simple precautions will help you stay healthy. Are all vegetables soaked in iodine before serving? Do the cooks wash their hands and is there soap available for the clients? Are the plates, pots and cutlery washed in iodine or simply swilled in the river? (Stop and think how many villages up stream use that river as their main sewage outlet.) All are simple ways to avoid getting sick.

On the Apurímac, the operator should provide a chemical **toilet** and remove all toilet paper and other rubbish. In the past, certain beaches have been subject to a completely uncaring attitude over toilet paper and human excrement. At the very least your company should provide a lighter for burning the paper and a trowel to dig a hole; always bury it deep and watch out when burning the paper so as not to start a fire.

It is normal practice for guides to check the campsite on arrival to ensure it is clean and then again before leaving. If your company does not, make it your responsibility to encourage other members of the group to keep the campsites clean of **rubbish**. When cooking, bottled gas is used; neither drift wood nor cut trees should be burnt.

Above all it is your **safety** on the river that is important. Some companies are now offering safety kayaks as standard as well as safety catarafts on certain rivers. This is definitely a step in the right direction but one that is open to misuse. Sometimes safety kayakers have little or no experience of what they are required to do and are merely along for the ride, sometimes they are asked to shoot video (rendering the safety cover useless). A safety cataraft is a powerful tool in the right hands, but weigh it down with equipment and it is of little use. All companies should carry at the very least a 'Wrap kit' consisting of static ropes, carabiners, slings and pulleys should a raft unfortunately get stuck. But more importantly, do the guides know how to use it?

So if all this doom and gloom has not put you off, you are now equipped to go out there and find the company that offers what you are looking for at a price you think is reasonable. Bear in mind a day's rafting in the USA can cost between US$75 -120 for a basic one-day. In Peru you might get the same for just US$25, but ask yourself what you are getting for so little. As it is, rafts and equipment cost the same, in fact more, in Peru.

Rivers

The Cusco region is probably the 'rafting capital' of Peru, with more whitewater runs on offer than anywhere else in Peru.

Urubamba Perhaps the most popular day run in the whole country, but sadly one heavily affected in parts by pollution both from Cusco (the Río Huatanay joins the Urubamba by Huambutio and is one of the main sewage outlets of Cusco) and from the towns of the Sacred Valley of the Incas who regularly dump their waste directly into the river. A recent clean-up campaign organized by various rafting companies removed 16 tons of rubbish, predominantly plastic bags and bottles, but it just touched the surface of the problem (see also box, page 138).

Huambutio – Pisac (all year availability, Grade II): a scenic half-day float with a few rapids to get the adrenaline flowing right through the heart of the Sacred Valley of the Incas. Fits in perfectly with a day trip to Pisac Market. A sedate introduction to rafting for all ages.

Ollantaytambo-Chilca (all year availability, Grade III to IV+ depending on season): a fun half-day introduction to the exciting sport of whitewater rafting with a few challenging rapids and beautiful scenery near the Inca 'fortress' of Ollantaytambo. This trip also fits in perfectly with the start of the Inca Trail. Try to go early in the morning as a strong wind picks up in the late morning.

Huaran Canyon (all year, GradeIII+ to V+ depending on season): a short section of fun whitewater that is occasionally rafted and used as site of the Peruvian National Whitewater Championships for kayaking and rafting. Definitely not for beginners in the rainy season.

Santa María to Quillabamba (dry season, Grade III to IV): a rarely rafted two-day, high jungle trip. A long way to go for some fairly good whitewater but mediocre jungle.

Chuquicahuana (rainy season, Grade IV to V+, dry season, Grade II to IV): in the rainy season, this is a technically demanding one-day trip for genuine adrenaline junkies. In the dry season this section makes a good alternative from the now terribly polluted sections further downstream (Huambutio – Pisac, Ollantay- tambo – Chilca) and provides several hours of fun, with 3 km of rapids (technical) with much cleaner water and all in a very pretty canyon. Strict safety procedures are needed all year round.

Cusipata (rainy season, Grade III to IV, dry season Grade II to III) Often used as a warm up section in high water before attempting Chuquicahuana. This section has fun rapids and a beautiful mini-canyon, which, in low water, is ideal for inflatable canoes (duckies). Again the water purity is much better than the lower sections.

Pinipampa (All year grade I to II): a fun and beautiful section, rarely paddled but relatively clean – no major rapids but a fun canoeing or ducky trip for beginners. Get out at the Huambutio start point, before the Huatanay disgorges Cusco's raw sewage into the Urubamba.

Kiteni-Pongo Mainique (the bit made famous by Michael Palin): an interesting jungle gorge, but logistically hard to reach and technically pretty average except in the rainy season.

Río Apurímac Technically the true source of the Amazon, the Apurímac cuts a 2,000-m deep gorge through incredible desert scenery and offers probably some of the finest whitewater rafting sections on the planet.

Puente Hualpachaca-Puente Cunyac (May-November, Grade IV to V): three (better in four) days of non-stop whitewater adventure through an awesome gorge just 5 hours drive from Cusco. Probably the most popular multi-day trip, this is one definitely to book with the experts as there have been fatalities on this stretch.

The Abyss Below Puente Cunyac is a section of rarely run whitewater. This extreme expedition involves days of carrying rafts around treacherous rapids; it seldom gets done.

Choquequirao Another rarely run section, this 10-day adventure involves a walk in with mules, a chance to visit the amazing ruins of Choquequirao and raft huge rapids in an imposing sheer-sided canyon all the way to the jungle basin. Definitely only for the experts.

Tambopata (June-October, Grade III-IV): wilderness, wildlife and whitewater, the Tambopata is probably the ultimate jungle adventure for those looking to get away from the standard organized jungle package. Starting with a drive from the shores of Lake Titicaca to virtually the end of the road, the Tambopata travels through the very heart of the Tambopata National Reserve, which boasts over 1,200 species of butterfly, 800 species of birdlife and many rare mammals including jaguar, giant otter, tapir, capybara and tayra. Four days of increasingly fun whitewater followed by two days of gently meandering through virgin tropical rainforest where silent rafts make perfect wildlife watching platforms. The final stage is a visit to the world's largest macaw clay lick and a short flight out from Puerto Maldonado. Definitely book in advance with the experts as this is a total expedition through one of the remote places in all South America.

Health

By Dr Charlie Easmon, MBBS MRCP MSc Public Health DTM&H DoccMed Director of Travel Screening Services.

Cusco stands at 3,310 m, so you'll need time to acclimatize to the high altitude. If flying from Lima, don't underestimate the shock to your system of going from sea-level to over 3,000 m in 60 minutes. Two or three hours' rest after arriving makes a great difference. Also avoid smoking, and drink plenty of clear, non-alcoholic liquid, and remember to walk slowly. If you're arriving in Cusco by air, it makes a lot of sense to get down to the Urubamba Valley, at 2,800 m, 510 m lower than Cusco itelf, and make the most of your first couple of days. At this relatively low altitude you will experience no headaches and you can eat and sleep comfortably.

There are English- (or other foreign language) speaking doctors in Cusco and Lima who have particular experience in dealing with locally occurring diseases, but don't expect good facilities away from the major centres.

Before you go

Before travelling take out medical insurance. Make sure it covers all eventualities especially evacuation to your home country by a medically equipped plane, if necessary. You should have a dental check up (especially if you are going to be away for

Essentials Health

more than a month), obtain a spare glasses prescription, a spare oral contraceptive prescription (or enough pills to last) and, if you suffer from a chronic illness (such as diabetes, high blood pressure, ear or sinus troubles, cardiopulmonary disease or nervous disorder) arrange for a check up with your doctor, who can at the same time provide you with a letter explaining the details of your disability. Check the current practice for malaria prophylaxis (prevention). If you are on regular medication, make sure you have enough to cover the period of your travel.

Vaccinations recommended

Polio if nil in last 10 years.
Tetanus Recommended if nil in last 10 years (but five doses is enough for life).
Typhoid Recommended if nil in last three years.
Yellow fever if you are travelling around South America it is best to get this vaccine since you will need it for the northern areas.
Rabies Recommended if going to jungle and/or remote areas.
Hepatitis A Recommended – the disease can be caught easily from food/water.

What to take

Mosquito repellents Remember that DEET (Di-ethyltoluamide) is the gold standard. Apply the repellent every four to six hours but more often if you are sweating heavily. If a non-DEET product is used check who tested it. Validated products (tested at the London School of Hygiene and Tropical Medicine) include Mosiguard, Non-DEET Jungle Formula and non-DEET Autan. If you want to use citronella remember that it must be applied very frequently (ie hourly to be effective).

Anti-malarials Specialist advice is required as to which type to take. General principles are that all except Malarone should be continued for four weeks after leaving the malarious area. Malarone needs to be continued for only seven days afterwards (if a tablet is missed or vomited seek specialist advice). The start times for the anti-malarials vary in that if you have never taken Lariam (Mefloquine) before it is advised to start it at least two to three weeks before the entry to a malarial zone (this is to help identify serious side-effects early). Chloroquine and Paludrine are often started a week before the trip to establish a pattern, but Doxycycline and Malarone can be started only one or two days before entry to the malarial area. It is risky to buy medicinal tablets abroad because doses may differ and there may be a trade in false drugs.

Insect bite relief If you are prone to insect bites or develop lumps quite soon after being bitten, carry an Aspivenin kit. This syringe suction device, available from major chemists/pharmacies, draws out some of the allergic materials and provides quick relief.

Painkillers Paracetomol or a suitable painkiller can have multiple uses for symptoms but remember that more than eight paracetmol a day can lead to liver failure.

Antibiotics Ciproxin (Ciprofloxacin) is a useful antibiotic for traveller's diarrhoea. It can be obtained by private prescription in the UK which is expensive or bought over the counter in South American pharmacies, but if you do this check that the pills are in date. You take one 500 mg tablet when the diarrhoea starts and if you do not feel better in 24 hours the diarrhoea is likely to have a non-bacterial cause and may be viral. Viral causes of diarrhoea will settle on their own. However, with all diarrhoeas try to keep hydrated by taking the right mixture of salt and water. This is available as Rehydration Salts in ready-made sachets or can be made up by adding a teaspoon of sugar and a half teaspoon of salt to a litre of clean water. Flat carbonated drinks can also be used.

Diarrhoea treatment Immodium and Pepto-Bismol are great standbys for those diarrhoeas that occur at awkward times (ie before a long coach/train journey or on a trek). They certainly relieve symptoms but are not a cure for underlying disease. Be

Sun block   The Australian's have a great campaign, which has reduced skin cancer. It is called Slip, Slap, Slop. Slip on a shirt, Slap on a hat, Slop on sun screen. SPF stands for Sunscreen Protection Factor.

MedicAlert   These simple bracelets, or an equivalent, should be carried or worn by anyone with a significant medical condition.

Soap   Biodegradable soap for jungle areas or ordinary soap for emergencies.

Other   For longer trips involving jungle treks take a clean needle pack, clean dental pack and water filtration device.

On the road

AIDS

AIDS (SIDA) is increasing and is not confined to the well-known high-risk sections of the population, ie homosexual men, intravenous drug abusers and children of infected mothers. Heterosexual transmission is now the dominant mode and so the main risk to travellers is from casual sex. The same precautions should be taken as with any sexually transmitted disease.The HIV virus that causes AIDS can be passed by unsterilized needles which have been previously used to inject an HIV positive patient, but the risk of this is negligible. It would, however, be sensible to check that needles have been properly sterilized or disposable needles have been used. If you wish to take your own disposable needles, be prepared to explain what they are for. The risk of receiving a blood transfusion with blood infected with HIV is greater than from dirty needles because of the amount of fluid exchanged. Supplies of blood for transfusion should now be screened for HIV in all reputable hospitals, so again the risk is very small indeed.

Altitude sickness

Symptoms   This can creep up on you as just a mild headache with nausea or lethargy. The more serious disease is caused by fluid collecting in the brain in the enclosed space of the skull and can lead to coma and death. A lung disease with breathlessness and fluid infiltration of the lungs is also recognized.

   Cures   The best cure is to descend as soon as possible.

   Prevention   Get acclimatized. Do not try to reach the highest levels on your first few days of arrival. The peaks are still there and so are the trails, whether it takes you personally a bit longer than someone else does not matter as long as you come back down alive.

Chagas disease

Symptoms   The disease occurs throughout South America, affects locals more than travellers, but travellers can be exposed by sleeping in mud-constructed huts where the bug that carries the parasite bites and defaecates on an exposed part of skin. You may notice nothing at all or experience a local swelling, with fever, tiredness and enlargement of lymph glands, spleen and liver. The seriousness of the parasite infection is caused by the long-term effects which include gross enlargement of the heart and/or guts.

   Cures   Early treatment is required with toxic drugs.

   Prevention   Sleep under a permethrin treated bed net and use insect repellents.

Dengue fever

Symptoms   This disease can be contracted throughout South America. In travellers it can cause a severe flu-like illness with fever, lethargy, enlarged lymph glands and muscle pains. It starts suddenly, lasts for two or three days, seems to get better for two or three days and then kicks in again for another two or three days. It is usually all over in an unpleasant week. The local children are prone to the much nastier haemorrhagic form of the disease, which causes them to bleed from internal organs, mucous membranes and often leads to their death.

Cures The disease is self limiting and forces rest and recuperation on the sufferer.

Prevention The mosquitoes that carry the Dengue virus bite during the day unlike the malaria mosquitoes. Sadly this means that repellent and covered limbs are a 24-hour issue. Check your accommodation for flower pots and shallow pools of water since these are where the Dengue-carrying mosquitoes breed.

Diarrhoea/intestinal upset → *Up to 70% of all travellers may suffer during their trip.*
Symptoms Diarrhoea can refer either to loose stools or an increased frequency; both of these can be a nuisance. It should be short lasting. Persistence beyond two weeks, with blood or pain, require specialist medical attention.

Cures Ciproxin will cure many of the bacterial causes but none of the viral ones. Immodium and Pepto-Bismol provide symptomatic relief. Dehydration can be a key problem especially in hot climates and is best avoided by the early start of Oral Rehydration Salts (at least one large cup of drink for each loose stool).

Prevention The standard advice is to be careful with water and ice for drinking. Ask yourself where the water came from. If you have any doubts then boil it or filter and treat it. There are many filter/treatment devices now available on the market. Food can also transmit disease. Be wary of salads (what were they washed in? who handled them?), re-heated foods or food that has been left out in the sun having been cooked earlier in the day. There is a simple adage that says 'wash it, peel it, boil it or forget it'. Also be wary of unpasteurised dairy products; these can transmit a range of diseases from brucellosis (fevers and constipation), to listeria (meningitis) and tuberculosis of the gut (obstruction, constipation, fevers and weight loss). Handwashing is the safest way of preventing unwanted muck to mouth transmission before you eat.

Hepatitis
Symptoms Hepatitis means inflammation of the liver. Viral causes of Hepatitis can be acquired anywhere in South America. The most obvious sign is if your skin or the whites of your eyes become yellow. However, prior to this all that you may notice is itching and tiredness.

Cures Early on, depending on the type of Hepatitis, a vaccine or immunoglobulin may reduce the duration of the illness.

Prevention Pre-travel Hepatitis A vaccine is the best bet. Hepatitis B is spread through blood and unprotected sexual intercourse, both of which can be avoided. Unfortunately there is no vaccine for Hepatitis C or the increasing alphabetical list of other Hepatitis viruses.

Leishmaniasis
Symptoms Peru is one of the main areas for a skin form of this disease. If infected, you may notice a raised lump, which leads to a purplish discoloration on white skin and a possible ulcer. The parasite is transmitted by the bite of a sandfly. Sandflies do not fly very far and the greatest risk is at ground level, so if you can avoid sleeping on the jungle floor do so. Seek advice for any persistent skin lesion or nasal symptom.

Cures Several weeks' treatment is required under specialist supervision. The drugs themselves are toxic but if not taken in sufficient quantity recurrence of the disease is more likely.

Prevention Sleep above ground, under a permethrin-treated net, use insect repellent and get a specialist opinion on any unusual skin lesions soon after return.

Leptospirosis

Various forms of leptospirosis occur throughout Latin America, transmitted by a bacterium that is excreted in rodent urine. Fresh water and moist soil harbour the organisms, which enter the body through cuts and scratches. If you suffer from any form of prolonged fever consult a doctor.

Malaria

Fortunately much of Peru is above 1,500 m and this reduces the malaria risk. There is no risk of malaria in the central urban area of Iquitos city, Lima or its vicinity, coastal areas south of Lima, or in the southern highland tourist areas of Ayacucho, Huancayo, Puno, Lake Titicaca, Cusco, Machu Picchu and any intermediate tourist points in the Urubamba Valley. However, there is a significant risk of malaria in the Amazon region. Malaria can cause death within 24 hours. It can start as something just resembling an attack of flu. You may feel tired, lethargic, headachy or worse, develop fits, coma and then death. You should have a low index of suspicion because it is very easy to write off vague symptoms, which may actually be malaria. Whilst abroad and on return get tested as soon as possible, the test could save your life.

Symptoms The symptoms of malaria are wide ranging from fever, lethargy, headache, muscle pains, flu-like illness, to diarrhoea and convulsions.

Cures Treatment is with drugs and may be oral or into a vein depending on the seriousness of the infection.

Prevention This is best summarized by the B and C of the ABCD, see below: Bite avoidance and Chemoprophylaxis. Some would prefer to take test kits for malaria with them and have standby treatment available. However, the field test of the blood kits has had poor results. When you have malaria you do not perform well enough to do the tests correctly to make the right diagnosis. Standby treatment (treatment that you carry and take yourself for malaria) should still ideally be supervised by a doctor since the drugs themselves can be toxic if taken incorrectly. The Royal Homeopathic Hospital in the UK does not advocate homeopathic options for malaria prevention or treatment. Travellers to Latin America should take the following malarial precautions:

A for Awareness

B for Bite Avoidance Wear clothes that cover arms and legs and use effective insect repellents in areas with known risks of insect-spread disease. Use a mosquito net dipped in permethrin as both a physical and chemical barrier at night.

C for Chemoprophylaxis Depending on the type of malaria and your previous medical condition/psychological profile take the right drug before, during and after your trip. Always check with your doctor or travel clinic for the most up to date advice.

D for Diagnosis Remember that up to a year after your return an illness could be caused by malaria. Be forceful about asking for a malaria test, even if the doctor says it is 'only flu.'

Rabies

Remember that rabies is endemic throughout Latin America, so avoid dogs that are behaving strangely and cover your toes at night from the vampire bats, which also carry the disease. If you are bitten by a domestic or wild animal, do not leave things to chance: scrub the wound with soap and water and/or disinfectant, try to have the animal captured (within limits) or at least determine its ownership, where possible, and seek medical assistance at once. The course of treatment depends on whether you have already been satisfactorily vaccinated against rabies. If you have (this is worthwhile if you are spending lengths of time in developing countries) then some further doses of vaccine are all that is required.

Unprotected sex can spread HIV, Hepatitis B and C, Gonorrhea (green discharge), Chlamydia (nothing to see but may cause painful urination and later female infertility), painful recurrent Herpes, Syphilis and Warts, just to name a few. You can cut down on the risks by using condoms, a femidom, or if you want to be completely safe, by avoiding sex altogether. See also AIDS, above.

Stings and bites

It is a very rare event indeed for travellers, but if you are unlucky (or careless) enough to be bitten by a venomous snake, spider, scorpion or sea creature, try to identify the creature, without putting yourself in further danger. Snake bites in particular are very frightening, but in fact rarely poisonous. Victims should be taken to a hospital or a doctor without delay. Most serum has to be given intravenously so it is not much good equipping yourself with it unless you are used to making injections into veins.

Treatment of snake bite Reassure and comfort the victim frequently. Immobilize the limb by a bandage or a splint and get the person to lie still. Do not slash the bite area and try to suck out the poison because this sort of heroism does more harm than good. If you know how to use a tourniquet in these circumstances, you will not need this advice. If you are not experienced, do not apply a tourniquet. What you might expect if bitten are: fright, swelling, pain and bruising around the bite and soreness of the regional lymph glands, perhaps nausea, vomiting and a fever. Symptoms of serious poisoning would be: numbness and tingling of the face, muscular spasms, convulsions, shortness of breath or a failure of the blood to clot, causing generalized bleeding.

Precautions Do not walk in snake territory in bare feet or sandals – wear proper shoes or boots. If you encounter a snake, stay put until it slithers away and do not investigate a wounded snake. Spiders and scorpions may be found in the more basic hotels. If stung, rest, take plenty of fluids and call a doctor. The best precaution is to keep beds away from the walls and look inside your shoes and under the toilet seat every morning.

Sunburn

The burning power of the tropical sun, especially at high altitude, is phenomenal. Always wear a wide-brimmed hat and use some form of suncream lotion on untanned skin. Normal temperate zone suntan lotions (protection factor up to seven) are not much good; you need to use the types designed specifically for the tropics or for mountaineers or skiers with protection factors up to 15 or above. These are often not available in Peru.

Ticks and maggots

Ticks usually attach themselves to the lower parts of the body often after walking in areas where cattle have grazed. The important thing is to remove them gently, so that they do not leave their head parts in your skin because this can cause a nasty allergic reaction some days later. Do not use petrol, vaseline, lighted cigarettes, etc to remove the tick, but, with a pair of tweezers remove the beast gently by gripping it at the attached (head) end and rock it out in very much the same way that a tooth is extracted. Certain tropical flies that lay their eggs under the skin of sheep and cattle also occasionally do the same thing to humans with the unpleasant result that a maggot grows under the skin and pops up as a boil or pimple. The best way to remove these is to cover the boil with oil, vaseline or nail varnish so as to stop the maggot breathing, then to squeeze it out gently the next day. See Typhus, below.

Tuberculosis (TB)

Symptoms TB can cause fever, night sweats and a chronic cough. Some people cough up blood. You may not know you have it but your friends will remark on your gradual weight loss and lack of energy. The lung type of TB is spread by coughs. Sometimes TB causes swelling of the lymph glands. TB can be spread by dairy products. Gut or pelvic TB can cause abdominal lumps, gut obstruction and even infertility. All parts of the body can be affected by TB.

Cures After diagnosis at least six months continuous treatment with several drugs is required.

Prevention Unfortunately BCG vaccine may not protect against lung TB. The best you can do is avoid unpasteurised dairy products and do not let anyone cough or splutter all over you.

Typhoid fever

Symptoms This a gut infection which can spread to the blood stream. You get it from someone else's muck getting into your mouth. A classic example would be the waiter who fails to wash his hands and then serves you a salad. The fever is an obvious feature, occasionally there is a mild red rash on the stomach and often you have a headache. Constipation or diarrhoea can occur. Gut pain and hearing problems may also feature. Deaths occur from a hole 'punched' straight through the gut.

Cures Antibiotics are required and you are probably best managed in hospital.

Prevention The vaccine is very effective and is best boosted every three years. Watch what you eat and the hygiene of the place or those serving your food.

Typhus

This can still occur and is carried by ticks. There is usually a reaction at the site of the bite and a fever. Seek medical advice. See Ticks, above.

Water

There are a number of ways of purifying water. Dirty water should first be strained through a filter bag and then boiled or treated. Bringing water to a rolling boil at sea level is sufficient to make the water safe for drinking, but at higher altitudes you have to boil the water for a few minutes longer to ensure all microbes are killed. There are sterilizing methods that can be used and there are proprietary preparations containing chlorine (eg Puritabs) or iodine (eg Pota Aqua) compounds. Chlorine compounds generally do not kill protozoa (eg Giardia).

Further information

Organizations and websites

Foreign and Commonwealth Office
(FCO),*www.fco.gov.uk* This is a key travel advice site, with useful information on the country, people, climate and lists the UK embassies/consulates. . It has links to the Department of Health travel advice site, listed below.

Department of Health Travel Advice,
www.doh.gov.uk/traveladvice This excellent site is also available as a free booklet, the T6, from post offices. It lists the vaccine advice requirements for each country.

Medic Alert, *www.medicalalert.co.uk* This is the website of the foundation that produces bracelets and necklaces for those with

existing medical problems. Once you have ordered your bracelet/necklace you write your key medical details on paper inside it, so that if you collapse, a medical person can identify you as someone with epilepsy or allergy to peanuts, etc.

Blood Care Foundation,
www.bloodcare.org.uk The Blood Care Foundation is a Kent-based charity 'dedicated to the provision of screened blood and resuscitation fluids in countries where these are not readily available.' It will dispatch certified non-infected blood of the right type to your hospital/clinic.

Public Health Laboratory Service
www.phls.org.uk This site has the malaria advice guidelines for travel around the

world. It also has useful information for those who are pregnant, suffering from epilepsy or planning to travel with children.

Centers for Disease Control and Prevention (USA) *www.cdc.gov* This site from the US Government gives excellent advice on travel health, has useful disease maps and has details of disease outbreaks.

World Health Organization *www.who.int* The WHO site has links to the WHO Blue Book on travel advice. This lists the diseases in different regions of the world. It describes vaccination schedules and which countries have Yellow Fever Vaccination certificate requirements.

Tropical Medicine Bureau *www.tmb.ie* Irish-based site with a good collection of general travel health information and disease risks.

Fit for Travel *www.fitfortravel.scot.nhs.uk* This site from Scotland provides a quick A-Z of vaccine requirements and travel health advice for each country.

British Travel Health Association *www.btha.org* This is the official website of an organization of travel health professionals.

NetDoctor *www.netdoctor.co.uk* This general health advice site has a useful section on travel and has an 'ask the expert', interactive chat forum.

Travel Screening Services *www.travelscreening.co.uk* This is the author's website. A private clinic dedicated to integrated travel health. The clinic gives vaccine and travel health advice.

Books and leaflets

The Travellers Good Health Guide by Dr Ted Lankester (ISBN 0-85969-827-0).

Expedition Medicine (The Royal Geographic Society) Editors David Warrell and Sarah Anderson (ISBN 1 86197 040-4).

International Travel and Health, World Health Organization, Geneva (ISBN 92 4 158026 7).

The World's Most Dangerous Places by Robert Young Pelton, Coskun Aral and Wink Dulles (ISBN 1-566952-140-9).

The Travellers Guide to Health (T6) can be obtained by calling the Health Literature Line on T0800-555 777.

Advice for travellers on avoiding the risks of HIV and AIDS (Travel Safe) **Department of Health**, *PO Box 777, London SE1 6XH*.The **Blood Care Foundation**, *PO Box 7, Sevenoaks, Kent TN13 2SZ, T01732-742 427*.

Keeping in touch

Communications

Internet → *For more Cusco details, see page 125.*

You can find internet access everywhere. Cusco and Lima have internet cafés on almost every corner; many of them have net2phone (see Telephone, below). Internet cafés in smaller places are listed in the travelling text. Internet cafés are incredibly cheap to use, often less than US$1 per hour. The downside of this popularity is that cafés frequently have no free terminals, so you have to pick your time carefully. When they first open in the morning is often a good time. In addition, the system is often overloaded, so getting access to your server can take a long time. Internet access is more expensive in hotel business centres and in and out of the way places. **Terra** and **Red Científica Peruana (rcp)** dominate the market.

Post → *The name of the postal system is Serpost.*

Parcels Sending parcels and mail can be done at any post office but Correo Central on the Plaza de Armas in Lima is the best place. The office is open Monday to Friday from 0800 to 1800. Stamps, envelopes and cloth sacks (to send bigger parcels in) can all be bought there. It costs US$1 to mail a letter up to 20 g anywhere in the Americas, US$1.50 to Europe and US$1.70 to Australia. You can also mail letters 'expreso' for about US$0.55 extra to the Americas, US$0.90 to the rest of the world, and they will arrive a little more quickly. Don't put tape on envelopes or packages, wait until you get to the post office and use the glue they have. It is very expensive to mail large packages out of Peru so it is best not to plan to send things home from here. For emergency or important documents, **DHL** and **Federal Express** are also options in Lima. For Cusco post office, see page 126.

Receiving mail To receive mail, letters can be sent to Poste Restante/General Delivery (*lista de correos*), your embassy, or, for cardholders, American Express offices. Members of the **South American Explorers** (see pages 71 and 241) can have post and packages sent to them at either of the Peruvian offices. Remember that there is no W in Spanish; look under V, or ask. For the smallest risk of misunderstanding, use title, initial and surname only. If having items sent to you by courier (eg DHL), do not use Poste Restante, but an address such as a hotel: a signature is required on receipt. Try not to have articles sent by post to Peru – taxes can be 200% of the value.

Telephone

The main service provider is **Telefónica** (or **Telser** in Cusco) which has offices in all large- and medium-sized towns. In some cases, the **Telefónica** office is administrative and phones are provided on the street outside. Local, national and international calls can be made from public phone boxes with coins or, more commonly, prepaid phone cards. To use phone cards, remove the card from its plastic covering (which should not be broken) and, on the back, scratch off the dark grey strip to reveal the card's number. You have to dial this number when told to do so by the operator. Cards for **Telefónica** services, of which there are several, can be bought at **Telefónica** offices or the many private phone offices (could be just a counter with a phone on the street). Also on sale in larger towns are cards for a number of carriers for long-distance calls: **AT&T**, **Americatel, Nortek** and **Perusat** (international only). Their rates are very competitive and there are usually seasonal offers to take advantage of. In some cases calls are routed through North America, so there may be a delay on the line. Each carrier has a prefix code which you must dial, as well as the card's secret code. Not every phone takes cards; **Telefónica**, for instance, has its own phones for its 147 service (national and international). The SuperPlus 147 card for one long-distance call is very good value at S/.20 (US$5.70) for 48 minutes. So shop around for the best deal for the type of call you want to make, select a card which will give you the number of minutes you require and get dialling. The average cost for a call to Western Europe is between S/.1.75 and S/.5 per minute (US$0.50-1.40) and to the US S/.1.55 and S/.4 (US$0.45-1.10). Calls without cards from public phones cost US$1 per minute to North America, US$1.40 to Europe and US$1.50 to Australia and New Zealand. Collect calls are possible to almost anywhere by ringing the international operator (108). You can also reach a variety of countries' operators direct if you wish to charge a call to your home calling card. By ringing 108 you can obtain all the 0-800 numbers for the international direct options and they speak English. Your home telephone company can give you the number to call as well. You can also receive calls at many **Telefónica** offices, the cost is usually around US$1 for 10 minutes. Net Phones are becoming increasingly popular, especially in Lima. Costs and service varies but can be as cheap as US$5 per hour to the USA. Calls to everywhere else are usually at least 50%s more. Faxes cost about US$1.50 per page to North America, US$2 to most of Western Europe and US$2.50 to Israel. The cost to receive is about US$1 per page. For **Telefónica** office in Cusco, see page 126.

Mobile phones There are three networks in Peru, **Telefónica, TIM** and **Bellsouth**. Telefónica has the most extensive network. Mobile phones brought into Peru which operate at 800 mhz may be activated at a **Telefónica** technical services office. **TIM** phones from Europe will operate in Peru, but calls cannot be diverted to another line if the phone number dialled is unanswered. **Bellsouth** uses TDMA technology and their technical staff would have to see a foreign phone to verify its compatibility. European mobiles are not compatible with **Bellsouth**. If it is essential that you have a mobile phone, your best bet is to buy one locally. All three companies sell phones, which take prepaid cards, from about US$70.

Media

Newspapers There are several national daily papers. The most informative are *El Comercio* and *La República*. *El Comercio* is good for international news and has a near monopoly on classified ads. It also has a good weekly tourism section. *La República* takes a more liberal-left approach and contains the *Crónica Judicial*. Its weekly tourism section, *Andares*, is recommended. Among the others are *Expreso* and *Ojo*. *Gestión* is a business daily. Very popular are the sensationalist papers, written in raunchy slang and featuring acres of bare female flesh on their pages.

There are a number of sites that provide regular news updates: *El Comercio* www.elcomercioperu.com.pe, *Expreso* www.expreso.com.pe, *Gestión* www.gestion.com.pe, *La República* www.larepublica.com.pe, *Perú al Día* news service www.perualdia.com, or through www.rcp.net.pe The following also have access to the daily news: www.terra.com.pe, www.peru.com

Magazines The most widely read magazine is the weekly news magazine *Caretas*, which gives a very considered angle on current affairs and is often critical of government policy, www.caretas.com.pe A bi-monthly magazine called *Rumbos* (English and Spanish together) is a good all-round what's happening in Peru magazine, www.rumbos.delperu.com Articles, in English and Spanish, feature cultural events, people and places of Peru and the region. Monthlies include *Business*, *Proceso Económico*, *Debate* and *Idede*. There is a weekly economic and political magazine in English, the *Andean Report,* with useful information and articles.

Radio Radio is far more important in imparting news to Peruvians than newspapers, partly due to the fact that limited plane routes make it difficult to get papers to much of the population on the same day. There are countless local and community radio stations which cover even the most far-flung places. The most popular stations are **Radioprogramas del Perú** (www.rpp.com.pe), which features round-the-clock news, and **Cadena Peruana de Noticias** (www.terra.com.pe/cpn/index.shtml).

A shortwave (world band) radio offers a practical means to brush up on the language, keep abreast of current events, sample popular culture and absorb some of the varied regional music. International broadcasters such as the **BBC World Service**, the **Voice of America**, Boston (Mass)-based **Monitor Radio International** (operated by *Christian Science Monitor*) and the Quito-based Evangelical station, **HCJB**, keep the traveller informed in both English and Spanish. Detailed advice on radio models (£150 for a decent one) and wavelengths can be found in the annual publication, *Passport to World Band Radio* (Box 300, Penn's Park, PA 18943, USA, £15.50). Details of local stations are listed in *World TV and Radio Handbook* (WTRH), (PO Box 9027, 1006 AA Amsterdam, The Netherlands, £15.80). Both of these, free wavelength guides and selected radio sets are available from the BBC World Service Bookshop, Bush House Arcade, Bush House, Strand, London WC2B 4PH, UK, T020-7557 2576.

TV Many hotels have televisions in the rooms, the more expensive the hotel, the more cable channels there will be on the set. There will almost certainly be US channels, often the BBC, Italian and occasionally German channels. You can find movies, sports, music, nature/discovery and news (**CNN** in both English and Spanish). Local channels include **América Televisión** (www.americatv.com.pe), **Cable Mágico** (www.cablemagico.com.pe), **Frecuencia Latina** (www.frecuencialatina. com.pe) and **Panamericana** (www.pantel.com.pe).

Machu □
Picchu

Cusco ■

Cusco City

Introduction

Cusco stands at the head of the Sacred Valley of the Incas and is the jumping-off point for the Inca Trail and famous Inca city of Machu Picchu. Not surprising, then, that this is the prime destination for the vast majority of Peru's visitors. In fact, the ancient Inca capital is now the 'gringo' capital of the entire continent. And it's easy to see why. There are Inca ruins aplenty, as well as fabulous colonial architecture, stunning scenery, great trekking, river rafting and mountain biking, beautiful textiles and other traditional handicrafts – all within easy reach of the nearest cappuccino or comfy hotel room.

The history books describe the Incas' mythical beginnings, their rapid rise to power, their achievements and their equally rapid defeat by the Spaniards, who converted the pulse of the Inca Empire into a jewel of their own. Yet Cusco today is not some dead monument. Its history breathes through the stones and the Quechua people bring the city to life with the combination of prehispanic and Christian beliefs.

Cusco City

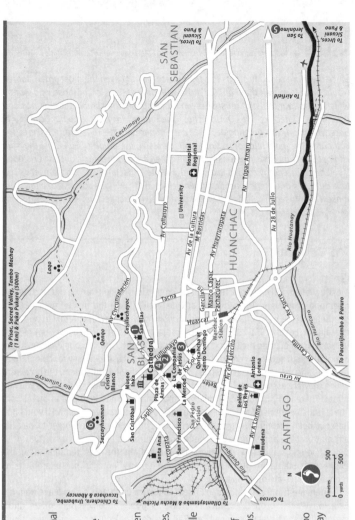

★ Don't miss...

1 **Church of San Blas** The carved pulpit is remarkable and you can get your fill of traditional crafts in the surrounding streets, see page 79.

2 **Santa Catalina** The museum of Cusqueño painting explains how European themes were adapted by local artists, see page 81.

3 **Colonial palaces** Visit one of the hotels that have been converted from colonial palaces, even if you are not staying there. The Novotel, Libertador and Monasterio are the best examples, see pages 92 and 95.

4 **Inca stonework** The Stone of 12 Angles on Calle Hatun Rumiyoc is the best example. See box, page 82.

5 **Shopping** The choice is endless, from piles of weavings to the most singular modern designs. Don't forget San Jerónimo market for weird and wonderful fruit and veg, see page 109.

6 **City tour** Take a car, horse, or go on foot, to Sacsayhuaman, Qenqo, Puka Pukara and Tambo Machay, the Inca sites outside the city on the way to Pisac, see page 113.

Cusco → Phone code 084. Colour map 5, A5. Population 275,000. Altitude 3,310 m.

Since there are so many sights to see in Cusco city, not even the most ardent tourist would be able to visit them all. For those with limited time, or for those who want a whistle-stop tour, a list of must-sees would comprise: the combination of Inca and colonial architecture at Qoricancha; the huge Inca ceremonial centre of Sacsayhuaman; the paintings of the Last Supper and the 1650 earthquake in the cathedral; the main altar of La Compañía de Jesús; the pulpit of San Blas; the high choir at San Francisco; the monstrance at La Merced; and the view from San Cristóbal. If you have the energy catch a taxi up to the White Christ and watch the sunset as you look out upon one of the most fascinating cities in the world. If you visit one museum make it the Museo Inka; it has the most comprehensive collection. ▸▸ For Sleeping, Eating and other listings, see pages 89-126.

Ins and outs

Getting there

Most travellers arriving from Lima will do so by **air**. No flights arrive in Cusco in the afternoon or at night. The airport is at Quispiquilla, near the bus terminal, 1.6 km southeast of the centre. ① *Airport information T084-222611/601.* A taxi to and from the airport costs US$1-2 (US$3.50 by radio taxi). Colectivos to the centre cost US$0.20 from outside the airport car park to the centre. You can book a hotel at the airport through a travel agency, but this is not really necessary. Many representatives of hotels and travel agencies operate at the airport, offering transport to the hotel with which they are associated. Take your time to choose your hotel, at the price you can afford. There is a post office, phone booths, restaurant and cafeteria at the airport. There is also a Tourist Protection Bureau desk, which can be very helpful if your flight has not been reconfirmed (not an uncommon problem). Do not forget to pay the airport tax at the appropriate desk before departure.

All long-distance **buses** arrive and leave from the bus terminal near the Pachacútec statue in Ttio district. Transport to your hotel is not a problem as representatives are often on hand.

There are two **train** stations in Cusco. To Juliaca and Puno, trains leave from the Estación Wanchac on *C Pachacútec, T084-221992.* The office here offers direct information and ticket sales for all **PerúRail** services. Look out for special promotional offers. When arriving in Cusco, a tourist bus meets the train to take visitors to hotels whose touts offer rooms on the train. Machu Picchu trains leave from Estación San Pedro, *T084-221313, opposite the Santa Ana market.* ▸▸ For further details, see Transport page 122. For trains to Juliaca and Puno, see page 124; to Machu Picchu, see page 160.

Getting around

The centre of Cusco is small and is easily explored on foot. Bear in mind, however, that at this altitude walking up some of the city's steep cobbled streets may leave you out of breath, so you'll need to take your time. It is even possible to walk up to Sacsayhuaman, but a better idea is to take a Combi to Tambo Machay and walk back downhill to town via Qenqo and Sacsayhuaman. Combis (minivans) are the main form of public transportation in the city: well-organized, cheap and safe. Taxis in Cusco are also cheap and recommended when arriving by air, train or bus. ▸▸ For further details, see Transport page 122.

If you wish to explore this area on your own, **Road Map** (*Hoja de ruta*) No 10 is an excellent guide. You can get it from the **Automóvil y Touring Club del Perú**, see

⁞ Visitors' tickets

A combined entry ticket to most of the sites of main historical and cultural interest in and around the city, called **Boleto Turístico Unificado** (BTU), costs US$12 (expected to rise to US$20) and is valid for five to 10 days. It permits entrance to the cathedral, San Blas, Santa Catalina Convent and Art Museum, Museo de Sitio Qoricancha (but not Santo Domingo/Qoricancha itself), Museo de Arte Religioso del Arzobispado, Museo Histórico Regional (Casa Inca Garcilaso de la Vega) and Museo Palacio Municipal de Arte Contemporáneo, plus the archaeological sites of Sacsayhuaman, Qenqo, Puka Pukara, Tambo Machay, Pisac, Ollantaytambo, Chinchero, Tipón and Piquillacta.

The BTU can be bought at the OFEC office (Casa Garcilaso), Plaza Regocijo, esquina Calle Garcilaso, Monday-Friday 0745-1800, Saturday 0830-1300, or at any of the sites included in the ticket. There is a 50% discount for students with a green ISIC card, which is only available at the OFEC office (Casa Garcilaso) upon presentation of the student card. Take your ISIC card when visiting the sites, as some may ask to see it.

Note that all sites are very crowded on Sunday, when many churches are closed to visitors, and the 'official' visiting times are unreliable. Photography is not allowed in the cathedral, churches and museums. On the back of the BTU is a map of the centre of Cusco with the main sites of interest clearly marked. It also includes a map of the tourist routes from Cusco to the Sacred Valley following the Río Urubamba towards Machu Picchu, as well as the southeastern area of Cusco on the road to Puno. The ticket includes days and hours of visiting.

Entrance tickets for Santo Domingo/Qoricancha, the Museo Inka (former Archaeological Museum), El Palacio del Almirante, and La Merced are sold separately. Machu Picchu ruins and Inca trail entrance tickets are sold at the Instituto Nacional de Cultura (INC), San Bernardo s/n entre Mantas y Almagro, Monday-Friday 0900-1300, 1600-1800, Saturday 0900-1100.

page 123. They have other maps. Motorists beware; many streets end in flights of steps not marked as such. There are very few good maps of Cusco available.

Tourist information

Tourist offices Official tourist information is at *Portal Mantas 117-A, next to La Merced church, T084-263176, 0800-2000*. There is also an **i perú** tourist information desk at the airport, *T084-237364, daily 0600-1300*, and another at *Portal de Carrizos 250, Plaza de Armas, T084-252974, daily 0830-1930*. **Ministry of Tourism**, *Av de la Cultura 734, 3rd floor, T084-223701, Mon-Fri 0800-1300*. See box above for OFEC offices and INC office for Machu Picchu.

South American Explorers, *Choquechaca 188, No 4, T084-245484, cuscoclub@saexploresrs.org, 0930-1700, Sun 0930-1300 from 1 Oct-30 Apr, Mon-Fri 0930-1700, Sat 0930-1300*; also in Lima (see page 241), an excellent resource and haven for the traveller. The Cusco club has recently moved to its swanky new location only a couple of minutes' walk from the Plaza de Armas. Great information on the Cusco area, along with an extensive English-language library, expedition reports, maps, and, of course, free coffee and hot chocolate for members.

Perú Verde, *Ricaldo Palma J-1, Santa Mónica, T084-243408, acss@telser.com.pe* For information and free video shows about Manu National Park and Tambopata National

Reserve. They are friendly and have information on programmes and research in the jungle area of Madre de Dios, as well as distributing of the beautiful but expensive book on the Manu National Park by Kim MacQuarrie and André Bartschi.

Tourist police, *C Saphi 511, T084-249654*. If you need a *denuncia* (a report for insurance purposes), which is available from the **Banco de la Nación,** they will type it out. Always go to the police when robbed, even though it will take a bit of time. The **Tourist Protection Bureau (Indecopi)**, protects the consumer rights of all tourists and help with any problems or complaints and can be helpful in dealing with tour agencies, hotels or restaurants. They are at the tourist office at *Portal Carrizos, Plaza de Armas* (see above). *Toll free T0800-42579 (24-hr hotline, not available from payphones). Head office is at Av de la Cultura 732-A, p 1, T084-252987, mmarroquin@indecopi.gob.pe*

Background

The ancient Inca capital is said to have been founded around AD 1100. According to the central Inca creation myth, the Sun sent his son, Manco Cápac and the Moon sent her daughter, Mama Ocllo, to spread culture and enlightenment throughout the dark, barbaric lands. The Sun pitied the people of this savage region because they could not cultivate the land, clothe themselves, make houses, nor had they any religion. Manco and Mama Ocllo emerged from the icy depths of Lake Titicaca and began their journey in search of the place where they would found their kingdom. They were ordered to head north from the lake until a golden staff they carried could be plunged into the ground for its entire length. The soil of the altiplano was so thin that they had to travel as far as the valley of Cusco where, on the mountain of Huanacauri, the staff fully disappeared and the soil was found to be suitably fertile. This was the sign they were looking for. They named this place Cusco, meaning 'navel of the earth'. The local inhabitants, on seeing Manco Cápac and Mama Ocllo with their fine clothes and jewellery (including the adornments in their long, pierced ears, which became a symbol of the Incas) immediately worshipped them and followed their instructions, the men being taught by Manco Cápac, the women by Mama Ocllo. (See also Children of the **Sun**, page 265, and The Inn of Origin, page 148.)

Thus the significance of Cusco and the sacred Urubamba Valley was established for many centuries to come. As Peter Frost states in his *Exploring Cusco*: "Cusco was more than just a capital city to the Incas and the millions of subjects in their realm. It was a Holy City, a place of pilgrimage with as much importance to the Quechuas as Mecca has to the Moslems. Every ranking citizen of the empire tried to visit Cusco once in his lifetime; to have done so increased his stature wherever he might travel."

Today, the city's beauty cannot be overstated. It is a fascinating mix of Inca and colonial Spanish architecture: colonial churches, monasteries and convents and pre-Columbian ruins are interspersed with hotels, bars and restaurants that have sprung up to cater for the tourists who flock here for the atmosphere. Almost every central street has remains of Inca walls, arches and doorways. Many streets are lined with perfect Inca stonework, now serving as the foundations for more modern dwellings. This stonework is tapered upwards (battered); every wall has a perfect line of inclination towards the centre, from bottom to top. The curved stonework of the Temple of the Sun, for example, is probably unequalled in the world.

Cusco has developed into a major commercial centre of 275,000 inhabitants, most of whom are Quechua. The city council has designated the Quechua, Qosqo, as the official spelling. Despite its growth, however, the city is still laid out much as it was in Inca times. The Incas conceived their capital in the shape of a puma and this can be seen from above, with the Río Tullumayo forming the spine, Sacsayhuaman the head and the main city centre the body. The best place for an overall view of the Cusco Valley is from the puma's head – the top of the hill of Sacsayhuaman.

Sights

Unless your Spanish is up to scratch a good guide can really improve your visit, as most of the sights do not have any information or signs in English. Either arrange this before you set out or grab one of those hanging around the sight entrances. The latter is much easier to do in the low season; good guides are often booked up with tour agencies at busy times of year. A tip is expected at the end of the tour; this gives you the chance to reward a good guide and get rid of a bad one!

Plaza de Armas

The heart of the city in Inca days was *Huacaypata* (the place of tears) and *Cusipata* (the place of happiness), divided by a channel of the Río Saphi. Today, Huacaypata is the Plaza de Armas and Cusipata is Plaza Regocijo. This was the great civic square of the Incas, flanked by their palaces, and was a place of solemn parades and great assemblies. Each territory conquered by the Incas had some of its soil taken to Cusco to be mingled symbolically with the soil of the Huacaypata, as a token of its incorporation into the empire.

As well as the many great ceremonies, the plaza has also seen its share of executions, among them the last Inca Túpac Amaru, the rebel *conquistador* Diego de Almagro the Younger, and the 18th-century indigenous leader Túpac Amaru II.

Around the present-day Plaza de Armas are colonial arcades and four churches. In the mid-1990s the mayor insisted that all the native trees be pulled down as they interrupted views of the surrounding buildings. The trees were replaced with the flowerbeds you see today. You may be forgiven for thinking the graceful, imposing church on the southeast side of the plaza is the cathedral. However, this is **La Compañía de Jesús**. When the Jesuits started building, the other Catholics asked the Pope to intervene complaining it was too ornate and overshadowed the presence of the cathedral. The Pope failed to act in time and La Compañía de Jesús was completed in all its splendour.

Cathedral

ⓘ *Open until 1000 for genuine worshippers – Quechua Mass is held 0500-0600. Those of a more secular inclination can visit Mon, Tue, Wed, Fri and Sat 1000-1130, or Mon-Sun 1400-1730. Entrance with the BTU tourist ticket.*

The early 17th-century baroque cathedral (on the northeast side of the square) forms part of a three-church complex: the cathedral itself, Iglesia Jesús y María (1733) on the left as you look at it and El Triunfo (1533) on the right. There are two entrances; the cathedral doors are used during Mass but the tourist entrance is on the left-hand side through Iglesia Jesús y María.

Two interesting legends surround the western tower of the cathedral. According to the first, a captured Inca prince is bricked up in the tower. His only means of escape is for the tower to fall, at which point he will reclaim his people and land. Believers' hopes were raised when the tower was severely damaged in the 1950 earthquake, but it failed to fall before restoration started, incarcerating the prince until this very day.

The same tower holds the largest bell in the city, weighing 5,980 kg. After two failed attempts at casting the bell, María Angola, an Afro-Peruvian woman, is said to have thrown a quantity of gold into the smelting pot on the third, successful attempt. The bell was then named after her. During the 1950 earthquake *María Angola* was damaged and her hoarse voice is now only heard on special occasions.

The cathedral itself was built on the site of the Palace of Inca Wiracocha (*Kiswarcancha*). Stones from Sacsayhuaman were used in its construction after the

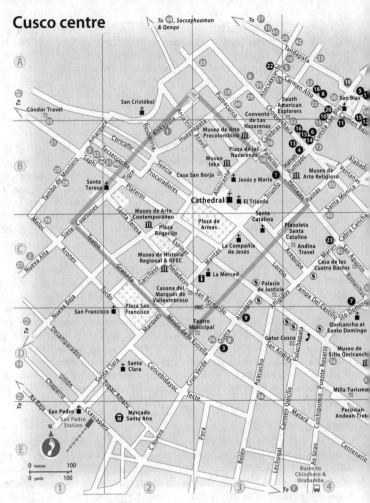

Cusco centre

architect, Juan Miguel de Veramendi, ordered the destruction of the Inca fortress.
Although Spanish designers and architects supervised its construction, it took nearly 100 years of Quechuan blood, sweat and tears to build. The ground plan is in the shape of a Latin cross with the transept leading into the two side-churches.

Built on the site of *Suntur Huasi* (The Roundhouse), **El Triunfo** was the first Christian church in Cusco. The name *El Triunfo* (The Triumph) came from the Spanish victory over an indigenous rebellion in 1536. It was here that the Spaniards congregated, hiding from Manco Inca who had besieged the city, almost taking it from the invaders. The Spaniards claim to have witnessed two miracles here in their hour of need. First, they were visited by the Virgin of the Descent, who helped put out the flames devouring the thatched roofs, then came the equestrian saint, James the Greater, who helped kill many indigenous people. The two divinities are said to have led to the Spanish victory; not only was it the triumph of the Spaniards over the Incas, but also of the Catholic faith over the indigenous religion.

The gleaming, newly renovated gilded main altar of the **Iglesia Jesús y María** draws the eyes to the end of the church. However, take the time to look up at the colourful murals which have been partially restored. The two gaudy, mirror-encrusted altars towards the front of the church are also hard to miss. Walking through into the cathedral's transept, the oldest surviving painting in Cusco can be seen. It depicts the 1650 earthquake. It also shows how within only one century the Spaniards had already divided the main plaza in two. *El Señor de los Temblores* (The Lord of the Earthquakes) can be seen being paraded around the Plaza de Armas while fire rages through the colonial buildings with their typical red-tiled roofs. Much of modern-day Cusco was built after this event. The choir stalls, by a 17th-century Spanish priest, are a magnificent example of colonial baroque art (80 saints and virgins are exquisitely represented), as is the elaborate pulpit. On the left is the solid-silver high altar; the original

Related maps
A Around Plaza de Armas, page 80

retablo behind it is a masterpiece of native wood carving by the famous Quechuan **Juan Tomás Tuyro Túpaq**. At the far right-hand end of the cathedral is an interesting local painting of the Last Supper. But this is the Last Supper with a difference, for Jesus is about to tuck into a plate of *cuy*, washed down with a glass of *chicha* (as opposed to the standard Cusco fare of pizza and chicken wings washed down with a bottle of *Cusqueño*). In the sacristy there is a good selection of artwork including portraits of all the bishops and archbishops of Cusco, including Vicente de Valverde, the Dominican friar who accompanied Pizarro and who was instrumental in the death of Atahualpa. He was bishop of Cusco until 1541, the year he died. The painting of the crucified Christ is strange because his body is rather effeminate. This is also noted in other paintings of Christ from the Cuzqueño school. This may be because the artists used female models, or could be simply how the Quechuan artists perceived him.

Many of the cathedral's treasures are hidden in a safe behind one of the carved doors. Much venerated is the crucifix of *El Señor de los Temblores* (**The Lord of Earthquakes**), the object of many pilgrimages and viewed all over Peru as a guardian against earthquakes. You may be forgiven for thinking he has a Quechuan complexion but this is actually due to many years' exposure to candle smoke! This is the most richly adorned Christ in the cathedral with his gold crown and his hands and feet pierced by solid gold, jewel-encrusted nails. The original wooden altar was destroyed by fire and dedicated locals are slowly covering the new plaster one with silver.

❖ Túpac Amaru was imprisoned next door, in San Ignacio chapel (now a craft market), before being executed in the plaza. His head was planted on a stick and placed on a hill by the main pass to the city.

The chapel of **St James the Greater** contains a statue of the saint on horseback. The painting depicts the saint killing the local indigenous people as he appeared in the miracle. Entering El Triunfo there is a stark contrast between the dark, heavy atmosphere of the cathedral and the light, simple structure of this serene church. The fine granite altar is a welcome relief from the usual gilding. Here the statue of the Virgin of the Descent resides and, above her, is a wooden cross known as the Cross of Conquest, said to be the first Christian cross on Inca land brought from Spain by Vicente de Valverde.

Going down into the catacomb (closed on Sundays), originally used to keep the bodies of important people, you will find a coffer containing half the ashes of the Cuzqueño chronicler Inca Garcilaso de la Vega, born of a Spanish father and Inca princess mother. The ashes were sent back from Spain only in 1978. The paintings of the parables which used to hang on the central columns have been moved to the Museo de Arte Religioso.

La Compañía de Jesús

On the southeast side of the plaza is the beautiful church of La Compañía de Jesús, built on the site of the Palace of the Serpents (*Amarucancha*, residence of the Inca Huayna Cápac) in the late 17th century. First it was given to Pizarro after the Spanish conquest, then it was bought by a family who eventually donated it to the Jesuits after their arrival in 1571. The church was destroyed in the earthquake of 1650. The present-day building took 17 years to construct and was inaugurated in 1668. When the Jesuits were expelled from Peru most of the valuables were taken to Spain. The altarpiece is a dazzling work of art. Resplendent in its gold leaf, it stands 21 m high and 12 m wide. It is carved in the baroque style, but the indigenous artists felt that this was too simple to please the gods and added their own intricacies in an attempt to reach perfection. Gold leaf abounds in the many *retablos* and on the carved pulpit. The painting on the left-hand side of the door as you enter is historically interesting. It depicts the marriage of Beatriz Qoya, niece of Túpac Amaru, to Martín García de Loyola, the nephew of one of Túpac's captors. Thus, de Loyola joins the line of succession for the Inca king's inheritance. The cloister is also noteworthy, though it has been closed since 1990 for restoration.

North and northeast of the Plaza de Armas

Museo Inka

ⓘ *Calle Ataud, To84-237380, Mon-Fri 0800-1700, Sat 0900-1600, US$1.40.*

The **Palacio del Almirante**, just north of the Plaza de Armas, is one of Cusco's most impressive colonial houses. Note the pillar on the balcony over the door, showing a bearded man from inside and a naked woman from the outside. During the high season local Quechuan weavers can be seen working in the courtyard. The weavings are for sale, expensive but of very good quality. It houses the interesting Museo Inka, run by the Universidad San Antonio Abad, which exhibits the development of culture in the region from pre-Inca, through Inca times to the present day. The museum has a good combination of textiles, ceramics, metalwork, jewellery, architecture, technology, photographs and 3-D displays. They have an excellent collection of miniature turquoise figures and other objects made as offerings to the gods. The display of deliberately deformed skulls with trepanning is fascinating, as is the full-size tomb complete with mummies stuck in urns! The section on coca leaves gives a good insight into the sacred Inca leaf. Old photographs of Machu Picchu are good to see after a visit for 'then and now' comparisons. The painting of the garrotting of Inca Atahualpa, watched over by Vicente de Valverde, is gory but informative. There are no explanations in English so a guide is a good investment.

Opposite, in a small square on Cuesta del Almirante, is the colonial house of **San Borja**, which was a Jesuit school for the children of upper-class mestizos.

Museo de Arte Religioso

ⓘ *Hatun Rumiyoc y Herrajes, 2 blocks northeast of Plaza de Armas, Mon-Sat, 0830-1130, 1500-1730. Entrance with BTU tourist ticket.*

The **Palacio Arzobispal** was built on the site of the palace occupied in 1400 by the Inca Roca and was formerly the home of the Marqueses de Buena Vista. It contains the Museo de Arte Religioso which has a fine collection of colonial paintings, furniture and mirrors. The Spanish tiles are said to be 100 years old and each carved wooden door has a different design. The collection includes the paintings by the indigenous master, **Diego Quispe Tito**, of a 17th-century Corpus Christi procession that used to hang in the church of Santa Ana. They now hang in the two rooms at the back of the second smaller courtyard.

The first picture on the right-hand side in the first room is an example of a travelling picture. The canvas can be rolled up inside the cylindrical wooden box which becomes part of the picture when it is hanging. The stained-glass windows in the chapel were made in Italy. The one on the left-hand side depicts the Lord of the Earthquakes. The priest's vestments belonged to Vicente de Valverde; the black was used for funerals, white for weddings and red for ceremonial masses. There are many paintings of the Virgin of the Milk, in which the Virgin Mary is breastfeeding Jesus, a sight not seen in Western religious paintings. The throne in the old dining room is 300 years old and was taken up to Sacsayhuaman for the Pope to sit on when he visited in 1986. Vistors can also see a bed that Simón Bolívar slept in.

Museo de Arte Precolombino

ⓘ *Plaza de las Nazarenas, daily 0900-2300, US$4.60, US$2.30 with student card.*

In the Casa Cabrera, on the northwest side of the plaza, this beautiful two-floor museum, set around a spacious courtyard, opened in June 2003. It is dedicated to the work of the great artists of pre-Colombian Peru. Within the expertly lit and well-organized galleries are many superb examples of pottery, metalwork (largely in gold and silver) and wood carvings. There are some vividly rendered animistic designs, giving an insight into the way Peru's ancient peoples viewed their world and

66 99 The masks on the walls represent the Spaniards when they arrived in Cusco – the eyes are red with greed and the skin yellow from all the gold they took ...

the creatures that inhabited it. At the time of writing some of the galleries were still under construction and most of the pieces on display originated from the Moche, Chimú, Paracas, Nasca and Inca empires. All the exhibits carry extensive explanations in English and Spanish, and there are some illuminating quotes regarding the influence of pre-Colombian art in Europe and beyond, for example, in the work of Pablo Picasso and his contemporaries. Highly recommended. The museum has a café (1000-1830) and restaurant (1830-2000) run by **Inka Grill** and stores such as **Alpaca 111** and **H Stern**.

There are many hostales and eating places on the steep, narrow streets which are good for a day-time wander, but take care after dark.

Convento de las Nazarenas

The Convento de las Nazarenas, on Plaza de las Nazarenas, is now an annex of **El Monasterio** hotel. You can see the Inca-colonial doorway with a mermaid motif, but ask permission to view the lovely 18th-century frescos inside. **El Monasterio** itself is well worth a visit – ask at reception if you can have a wander (see page 92). Built in 1595 on the site of an Inca palace, it was originally the **Seminary of San Antonio Abad** (a Peruvian National Historical Landmark). One of its most remarkable features is the baroque chapel, constructed after the 1650 earthquake. Look at the altar: to the right is a painting that slides to one side allowing access to a stairway, down which the statues of saints on high can be liberated for use in the Corpus Christi procession of June. Attempts have been made to restore the paintings outside in the cloister but, as can be seen in an alcove, the paint keeps peeling away and much is painted white. If you are not disturbing mealtimes, check out the dining room. This is where the monks used to sing. The masks on the walls represent the Spaniards when they arrived in Cusco – the eyes are red with greed and the skin yellow from all the gold they took. Moving back to the second cloister, turn left at the restored painting in the alcove to see a small courtyard which used to be a farm; guests claim to have seen ghosts here. One last curiosity is Samson's Martyrdom, an 18th-century painting in the Mestizo style, next to room 422. Look at the tray on the floor – those are Samson's eyes. Gruesome!

Only male visitors can see the place where monks were imprisoned for transgressions; today it's the men's toilets! In an inscription one monk tells how he was locked up for a day for ringing a bell 10 minutes late.

San Blas

The San Blas district, called Tococache in Inca times, has been put on the tourist map by the large number of shops and galleries which sell local carvings, ceramics and paintings. (See page 109). The small **church of San Blas** ① *Carmen Bajo, daily 1800-1130, 1400-1730, closed Thu mornings*, is a simple rectangular adobe building whose walls were reinforced with stone after the 1650 and 1950 earthquakes. It comes as some surprise to learn that it houses one of the most famous pieces of wood carving found in the Americas, a beautiful mestizo pulpit carved from a single cedar trunk. Eight heretics are carved at the basin of the pulpit. See if you can spot Henry VIII and Queen Elizabeth I of England among them. Above are carved the four Evangelists and, crowning the pulpit, supported by five archangels, is the statue of Saint Paul of Tarsus,

Museo de Arte Precolombino

Cusco's MAP (Museum of pre-Columbian Art) is a tribute to the talent of countless generations of anonymous Peruvian potters, weavers, gold and silversmiths, carvers, sculptors, painters and musicians. It is an extension of the prestigious Rafael Larco Herrera Museum, Lima, which itself contains one of the most complete collections of pre-Columbian Peruvian art. By establishing a museum in Cusco with exhibits from all Peru's cultures and historical periods, not just the local ones (ie Inca and perhaps Tiahuanaco), the founders of the MAP have broken the mould of regional museums. Now local residents and foreigners have the opportunity to see the full panoply of Peruvian cultural expression, with the artworks no longer displayed as the remains of long-dead civilizations, but in their Peruvian context and in relationship to other worldwide artistic expressions, right up to the present. And when the visitor steps out of the Casa Cabrera, it is not into the crowds of a 21st-century third world city like Lima, but into the timeless living museum which is Cusco.

The museum's most prized pieces are prominently displayed and well documented. But it's worth lingering over some of the 'minor' master-pieces. In the Formative showroom are two examples of small, finely carved stonework. One is a black granite mortar bowl belonging to the Cupisnique culture, finely polished and with large designs. Dated between 1000 BC and the beginning of the present era, it appears to possess a marked similarity to ancient Chinese Shang art of the same period. In a neighbouring showcase are a smaller mortar and pestle, the latter incised with a stylized puma, attributed to the Pacopampa culture (similar time period).

In the Mochica section you will be overwhelmed by the anthropo morphic deer, the perfect duck, the astounding cosmic potato, the triple portraits, the cormorants, etc. When you eventually make your way out, look for the 62 plates embedded in the wall framing the exit. Several of these deserve some attention: at the bottom right-hand side of the archway is a plate bearing a striking snake design. Four or five rows above, a larger plate represents that classic Mochica theme, warriors sporting elaborate body painting, headdresses and an array of personal weaponry, prancing in pursuit of one another in groves of opuntia cacti, with hum-mingbirds and insects above.

The seashell section contains spondylus-shell bead breast pieces and larger shell necklaces. The second display case to the right of the entrance features a bracelet composed of a strand of about 20-30 small pink snail shells, each serrated crosswise to its axis, making it look like a bouquet of miniature frosted candy roses (which never existed in pre-Columbian America). In the display case just before that hangs a necklace of larger creamy white snail shells, culminating in a pendant of a shell retaining its original barnacles.

Among the silver and gold works are a wide variety of nasal ornaments and a very dainty set of miniature Chimú royal crowns. It is, however, that room's main display, situated on the far wall, that sums up the tragic irony that characterized the demise of pre-Columbian era. Hundreds of gold and silver disks, which once decorated the tunics and shrouds of unknown lords, appear from a distance like so many gold and silver coins. And that is the only perspective from which the European *conquistadores* viewed this precious metalwork, and that is the end to which most of it came.

laza de Armas

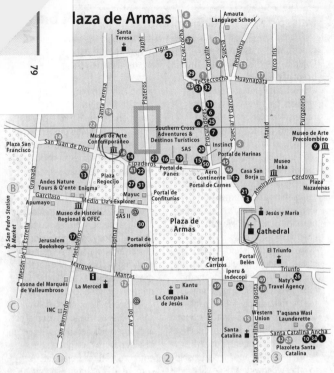

Plateros detail

0 metres 50
0 yards 50

Sleeping
El Procurador del
  Cusco **1** A2
Emperador Plaza **2** C3
Del Prado Inn **5** B3
Hostal Carlos V **4** A2
Hostal Corihuasi **6** A3
Hostal Imperial
  Palace **8** A2
Hostal Plaza de
  Armas **10** C2
Hostal Q'Awarina **11** A2
Hostal Qosqo **12** C2
Hostal Resbalosa **13** A3
Hostal Royal
  Frankenstein & Tangible
  Myth **14** B1
Hostal Santa María **15** C3
Hostal Turístico Plateros **7**
  Plateros detail
Munay Wasi **17** A3
Pensión Loreto **18** C2
Picoaga **19** A1
Posada del Viajero **20** C3
Royal Inka I **21** A1
Royal Inka II **22** A1
Tumi I **24** A1

Eating
Al Grano **1** C3
Ama Lur **2** Plateros detail
Ayllu **3** B3

Babieca **29** A2
Café Halliy **5** Plateros detail
Chez Maggy Clave
  de D **6** A2
Chez Maggy El
  Corsario **7** B2
Chez Maggy La Antigua
  8 A2
Deli, El Patio, Blueberry
  Lounge & Explorandes
  12 B3
Due Mondi **10** C3
El Cuate **11** A2
El Encuentro **34** C3
El Fogón **47** Plateros detail
El Mesón **22** B2
El Molino **48** Plateros detail
El Truco & Taberna
  del Truco **13** B1
Fallen Angel **9** B3
Inka Grill **16** B2
Keros **50** B2
Kintaro **17** B1
Kusikuy **18** Plateros detail
La Retama **19** B1
La Tertulia **20** B2
La Yunta **21** B3
Los Candiles & Café Amaru
  49 Plateros detail
Los Tomines **26** C3
Mesón de los Portales &
  Paccha **15** B2

Mía Pizza **4** A2
Pachacútec Grill &
  Bar **23** B2
Paititi **24** C3
Paloma Imbil **25** A2
Pizzería Marengo **27** B2
Pucará **28** Plateros detail
Trotamundos **30** B2
Tunupa & Cross
  Keys Pub **31** B2
Ukuku's **32** A2
Varayoc **14** B2
Víctor Victoria **33** A2
Yaku Mama **51** A2

Bars & clubs
El Garabato Video
  Music Club **41** B2
Excess **46** B3
Kamikaze **36** B2
Los Perros **37** A2
Magtas **45** B3
Mama **38** C3
Norton Rat's
  Tavern **39** C2
Paddy Flaherty's **40** C3
Rosie O'Grady's &
  Sky Travel **42** C3
Spoon **35** Plateros detail
Sunset Video Café **43** A2
Ukuku's **44** Plateros
  detail

although some believe it to be Jesus Christ. The skull is supposed to be that of the sculptor. There are many stories surrounding the artist. Some say he was an indigenous leper who dedicated his life to the carving after he was cleansed of the disease. The church was built and used by indigenous inhabitants and the Cusco baroque altarpiece was designed to compete with any in the city.

East and southeast of the Plaza de Armas

Santa Catalina
ⓘ *Arequipa at Santa Catalina Angosta, Sat-Thu 0900-1730, Fri 0900-1500. There are guided tours by English-speaking students; a tip is expected. Church open 0700-0800 daily.*

The church, convent and museum are magnificent. Santa Catalina was the founder of the female part of the Dominican Order, which also founded the beautiful convent of the same name in Arequipa. The Cusco convent is ironically built upon the foundations of the *Acllahuasi* (House of the Chosen Women), the most important Inca building overlooking the main plaza. The Quechuan women were chosen for their nobility, virtue and beauty to be prepared for ceremonial and domestic duties – some were chosen to bear the Inca king's children. No man was allowed to set eyes on the Chosen Women and if he had any relationship with one, he, his family and livestock would all be killed.

Today the convent is a closed order where the nuns have no contact with the outside world. There is a room at the back of the church where the nuns can participate in Sunday Mass. It is separated from the church by a heavy metal grill so although they cannot be seen their voices can still be heard. In this room there is the only signed painting in the museum. The artist was, of course, Spanish as local artists were either forbidden or unable to sign their work. The church has an ornate, gilded altarpiece and a beautifully carved pulpit. The altarpieces are all carved by different craftsmen and the paintings are anonymous.

The museum has a wonderful collection of Cuzqueño school paintings spanning the decades of Spanish rule – a good guide can point out how the style changes from the heavy European influence to the more indigenous style. One obvious difference can be seen in the paintings in the corridor of the Lord of the Earthquakes. Early paintings show Christ wearing a white loincloth typical of European paintings, but in others he is seen wearing a very light, almost transparent skirt. The beautifully coloured murals in the Scriptures Room show the difference between the devoted lives of the religious order in the upper section and the frivolity of the courtiers' life. The floral designs covering the lower section and the archways are the indigenous artists' way of paying tribute to *Pachamama*, Mother Earth. This can also be seen in the upstairs room, which has many paintings of the Virgin. The dresses are all triangular, the shape of mountains which were seen as gods by the indigenous people. Another addition can be seen in the painting of the Virgin of Bethlehem. The baby Jesus is held at an awkward angle because he has been swaddled tightly from neck to feet in the manner of indigenous babies. The gold patterns are applied to these paintings by the use of a stamp. This is carried out by a separate artist once the painting has dried. Many of the works of art, bureaux and ornaments were given to the Order by the families of the joining novices.

Also worth a visit is the palace called **Casa de los Cuatro Bustos**, whose colonial doorway is at San Agustín 400. This palace is now the Golden Tulip's **Hotel Libertador**. The general public can enter the hotel from Plazoleta Santo Domingo, opposite the Temple of the Sun/Qoricancha.

❖ The most fascinating article in this museum is the trunk which unfolds to reveal a religious tableau used by travelling preachers to take the word of the Lord to remote villages.

⁝ Getting stoned

Just wandering around the streets of Cusco gives you a sense of the incredible craftsmanship of the Inca stonemasons. Some of the best examples can be seen in the **Callejón Loreto**, running southeast past La Compañía de Jesús from the main plaza. The walls of the *Acllahuasi* (House of the Chosen Women) are on one side, and of the Amarucancha on the other. There are also Inca remains in **Calle San Agustín**, to the east of the plaza. The famous **Stone of 12 Angles** is in **Calle Hatun Rumiyoc** half-way along its second block, on the right-hand side going away from the plaza. The finest stonework is in the celebrated curved wall beneath the west end of **Santo Domingo**. This was rebuilt after the 1950 earthquake, at which time a niche that once contained a shrine was found at the inner top of the wall.

Excavations have revealed Inca baths below here, and more Inca retaining walls. Another superb stretch of late-Inca stonework is in **Calle Ahuacpinta**, outside Qoricancha, to the east or left as you enter. True Inca stonework is wider at the base than at the top and features ever-smaller stones as the walls rise. Doorways and niches are trapezoidal. The Incas clearly learnt that the combination of these four techniques helped their structures to withstand earthquakes. This explains why, in two huge earthquakes (1650 and 1950), Inca walls stayed standing while colonial buildings tumbled down. The walls of Hotel Libertador, near Santo Domingo, show an Inca stonemason following a Spanish architect – the walls are vertical and the doorways square. However, the stones are still beautifully cut and pieced together.

Qoricancha at Santo Domingo

ⓘ *Mon-Sat 0800-1700, Sun 1400-1600 (except holidays), US$1.15 (not on the BTU Visitor Ticket). There are guides outside who charge around US$2-3.*

This is one of the most fascinating sights in Cusco. Behind the walls of the Catholic church are remains of what was once the centre of the vast Inca society. The Golden Palace and Temple of the Sun was a complex filled with such fabulous treasures of gold and silver it took the Spanish three months to melt it all down. You will be able to see what was the Solar Garden – where life-sized gold sculptures of men, women, children, animals, insects and flowers were placed in homage to the Sun God – and marvel at near-complete temples with the best Inca stonework in Cusco. On the walls were more than 700 gold sheets weighing about 2 kg each. The *conquistadores* sent these back intact to prove to the King of Spain how rich their discovery was.

The first Inca, Manco Cápac, is said to have built the temple when he left Lake Titicaca and founded Cusco with Mama Ocllo. However, it was the ninth Inca, Pachacútec, who transformed it. When the Spaniards arrived, the complex was awarded to Juan Pizarro, the younger brother of Francisco. He in turn willed it to the Dominicans who ripped much of it down to build their church.

The temple complex Walk first into the courtyard then turn around to face the door you just passed through. Behind and to the left of the paintings (representing the life of Santo Domingo Guzmán) is Santo Domingo. This was where the Temple of the Sun stood, a massive structure 80 m wide, 20 m deep and 7 m in height. Only the curved wall of the western end still exists and will be seen (complete with a large crack from the 1950 earthquake), when you later walk left through to the lookout over the Solar

The festival of Inti Raymi

The sun was the principal object of Inca worship and at their winter solstice, in June, the Incas honoured the solar deity with a great celebration known as Inti Raymi, the sun festival. The Spanish suppressed the Inca religion, and the last royal Inti Raymi was celebrated in 1535.

However, in 1944 a group of Cusco intellectuals, inspired by the contemporary 'indigenist' movement, revived the old ceremony in the form of a pageant, putting it together from chronicles and historical documents. The event caught the public imagination, and it has been celebrated every year since then on 24 June, now a Cusco public holiday. Hundreds of local men and women play the parts of Inca priests, nobles, chosen women, soldiers (played by the local army garrison), runners, and the like. The coveted part of the Inca emperor, Pachacútec, is won by audition, and the event is organized by the municipal authorities.

It begins around 1000 at the Qoricancha – the former sun temple of Cusco – and winds its way up the main avenue into the Plaza de Armas, accompanied by songs, ringing declarations and the occasional drink of chicha. At the main plaza, Cusco's presiding mayor is whisked back to Inca times, to receive Pachacútec's blessing and a stern lecture on good government. Climbing through Plaza Nazarenas and up Pumacurcu, the procession reaches the ruins of Sacsayhuaman at about 1400, where scores of thousands of people are gathered on the ancient stones.

Before Pachacútec arrives the Sinchi (Pachacútec's chief general) ushers in contingents from the four Suyus (regions) of the Inca Empire. Much of the ceremony is based around alternating action between these four groups of players. A Chaski (messenger) enters to announce the imminent arrival of the Inca and his Coya (queen). Men sweep the ground before him, and women scatter flowers. The Inca takes the stage alone, and has a dialogue with the sun. Then he receives reports from the governors of the four Suyus. This is followed by a drink of the sacred chicha, the re-lighting of the sacred fire of the empire, the sacrifice (faked) of a llama, and the reading of auguries in its entrails. Finally the ritual eating of sankhu (corn paste mixed with the victim's blood) ends the ceremonies. The Inca gives a last message to his assembled children, and departs. The music and dancing continues until nightfall.

Garden. The Temple of the Sun was completely covered with gold plates and there would have been a large solar disc in the shape of a round face with rays and flames. One story, with no historic basis to it, is that conquistador Mancio Sierra de Leguizamo was given this in the division of spoils but he lost it one night playing dice. Whether a conquistador lost it, or the Incas spirited it away, the solar disc has not been found.

Still in the baroque cloister, close by and facing the way you came in, turn left and cross to the remains of the **Temple of the Moon**, identifiable by a series of niches. The Moon, or Mamakilla, was the Sun's wife. The walls were covered in silver plates and the dark horizontal stripe in the niches shows where they were attached. Have a look at the stonework. This is a fantastic example of polished joints so perfectly made it is impossible to slip even a playing card in between. In fact, all the walls of the temples around this courtyard are fine examples of Inca stonemasonry.

Further round the courtyard, heading anticlockwise, is a double door-jamb

⁞ Getting in a flap

Some love it, some hate it – but travel a couple of kilometres down the Avenida de la Cultura (the route to Paucartambo) and you won't miss it! Standing on a column in the middle of the road six storeys high is a massive condor, the Inca god called upon to protect the kingdom from the *conquistadores*. This modern-day marvel (or monstrosity, depending on your point of view) was built from the aluminium of a plane donated by the Army. The artist (who died young) also created the monument of Pachacútec, the greatest Inca ruler of all, which visitors see on arrival at Cusco airport.

The condor´s construction (which stands in sight of the poor barrios of San Sebastián) cost US$1.5 mn and three people's lives in two accidents. The day of its inauguration, the massive bird caused a flap among the dignatories below as an earth tremor started up and the wings began to move up and down! The beak is said to be gold, a sorry sight to the poor below who have no way of preying upon the treasure – the tower can be scaled only by locked stairs within.

doorway. Beyond this is the so-called **Temple of Venus and the Stars**. Stars were special deities used to predict weather, wealth and crops. There's a window around which, on the inside, holes can be seen where the Spaniards prised precious stones. The roofs of all these temples would have been thatched, but on the ceiling here was a beautiful representation of the Milky Way. The 25 niches would have held idols and offerings to the cult of the stars and the walls around them were plated in silver (notice again the dark stripes). In the **Temple of Lightning** on the other side of the courtyard is a stone. Stand on this and you will appreciate how good the Incas were as stonemasons: all three windows are in perfect alignment. The Lightning was the Sun's servant while the Rainbow, subject of the next and last temple, was also important because it came from the Sun. A rainbow was painted onto the gold plates which coated the walls.

The gold thread used in the vestments of Catholic priests (on display in the sacristy which you pass on your way to the Solar Garden) pales into insignificance when you consider the vast quantities of gold housed in this most special of Inca temple complexes. Yet, to the Incas, gold and silver had little monetary value, and were prized only for their religious significance. As you gaze over the grass lawn to the Avenida Sol, this may help you believe that there truly was once a garden here filled with flowers, insects, animals and people, all fashioned in gold and silver. What a sight that must have been!

Museo de Sitio Qoricancha

ⓘ *Mon-Fri 0800-1730, Sat 0900-1700. Entrance by the BTU Visitor Ticket, or US$2. The staff will give a guided tour in Spanish, but please give a tip.*

The former Museo Arqueológico is now housed in an underground site on Avenida Sol, in the gardens below Santo Domingo. It contains a limited collection of pre-Columbian artefacts, a few Spanish paintings of imitation Inca royalty dating from the 18th century, photos of the excavation of Qoricancha, and some miniature offerings to the gods. It's a good idea to visit Santo Domingo before the museum, in order to understand better the scant information given.

Other sights southeast of the centre

Between the centre and the airport on Alameda Pachacútec, the continuation of Avenida Sol, 20 minutes' walk from the Plaza de Armas, there is a statue of the **Inca**

Pachacútec placed on top of a lookout tower, from which there are excellent views of Cusco. Inside are small galleries and a coffee shop. ① *1000-2000, free.*

Avenida La Cultura, which runs southeast out of the city and eventually becomes the road to Sicuani and Lake Titicaca, passes through **Urbanización Magisterio**, one of the favoured areas to live in the city. Many foreigners, including overseas students, stay here. This is the other, modern side of Cusco, with all up-to-date services and it's just a US$0.60 taxi ride to the centre. Over the five blocks you'll find restaurants, including fast-food places with games for kids, every type of shop, internet cabins and long-distance phone services, laundries, safe long-term car parking, hairdressers, drugstores, dentists and video and DVD rental.

South and southwest of the Plaza de Armas

La Merced
① *On Márquez. The monastery and museum open 1430-1700. The church opens 0830-1200, 1530-1730, except Sun. US$0.85.*
La Merced was originally built in 1534 by the religious Order of Mercedarians (founded in 1223 by the French Saint Peter Nolasco), whose main aim was to redeem the natives. The church was razed in the 1650 earthquake and rebuilt by indigenous stonemasons in the late 17th century. The high altar is neoclassical with six gilded columns. There are a further 12 altars. Inside the church are buried Gonzalo Pizarro, half-brother of Francisco, and the two Almagros, father and son. Their tombs were discovered in 1946.

Attached is a very fine monastery. The first cloister is the most beautiful with its two floors, archways and pillars. The pictures on the first floor depict the Saints of the Order, but unfortunately those of the second floor have been removed for restoration. The small museum can also be found here. This houses the Order's valuables including the priceless monstrance (a vessel used to hold the consecrated host). It is 1.2 m high, weighs over 22 kg and is decorated with thousands of precious stones. Note the two huge pearls used for the body of a mermaid. There are many other precious religious objects including a small Christ carved in ivory, crowns and incense burners. The painting of the Holy Family is ascribed to Rubens. The superb choir stalls, reached from the upper floor of the cloister, can be seen by men only, but you must persuade a Mercedarian friar to let you see them.

The **Casona del Marqués de Valleumbroso**, on San Bernardo y Márquez, 3 blocks southwest of the Plaza de Armas, was gutted by fire in 1973 and is being restored.

Around Plaza Regocijo
Museo de Historia Regional, ① *Casa Garcilaso, C Garcilaso y Heladeros. 0730-1700. Entrance with BTU tourist ticket. A guide is recommended; they are usually available at the ticket office and many of them speak English*, tries to show the evolution of the Cuzqueño school of painting. It also contains Inca agricultural implements, a mummy from Nasca complete with 1 m-long hair, colonial furniture and paintings, a small photographic exhibition of the 1950 earthquake and mementos of more recent times. Upstairs there is an exhibition room which holds temporary exhibits from photography to recently excavated finds. The museum is disjointed and even the Spanish explanations are minimal.

If you are walking up Garcilaso, **Hostal Los Marqueses**, on the right, has one of the most unusual colonial courtyards. Attractive brick arches single this out from other patios in Cusco as do the sculpted faces of the previous noble owners which stare out from above them. This house is closed for renovation to a four-star hotel and it is not anticipated that it will reopen until at least mid-2004.

Good Samaritans

"Shoeshine? Shoeshine?" Everyone who visits Cusco will experience the sad sight of children as young as five struggling to shine shoes, or sell sweets or postcards.

Grubby, crouched in the gutter on a home-made box, knees poking through what´s left of their jeans, these urchins have been banned from the Plaza de Armas, but persevere to survive by pestering every tourist in sight in the streets nearby. Their plight is extraordinary. Often the offspring of alcoholic parents, many of them sleep huddled together in shacks you wouldn´t allow a pig to inhabit.

But equally amazing is the story of a pair of Dutch backpackers who have set out to change the children´s lives forever and the tale behind two other foreigners who are working to help Cusco's downtrodden and who need your help.

Titus Bovenberg and his girlfriend, Jolanda, came as tourists to Cusco in 1996. Seven years later they are still here – with a family of 12 adopted boys and a programme by the name of **Los Niños** that feeds and helps educate and clothe a further 250.

The 250 are the worst cases sent from three local schools. Many arrive with TB, bronchitis, pneumonia and numerous skin diseases. Some have been fainting through malnutrition; all are too small for their age. Doctors and dentists first attend to the children then Los Niños give the youngsters healthy food, ensure they clean their teeth and shower 10 or 15 of them every day at their centre.

This is all funded by an excellent hostel named Niños Hotel, its new offshoot, Niños 2, and a set of apartments (see page 97). Staying here is a way of directly helping the street children. No volunteers are taken.

Titus says: "We want to give these children not only food but hope that they can escape this; we must teach them they are human beings."

Meanwhile, in San Blas, another Dutch couple are battling for the underdogs through the **Hope Foundation**. In a dozen years Walter Meekes and his wife, Tineke, have built 20 schools in poor mountain villages and *barrios* around Cusco. They have a programme to teach teachers and, in town, there is a 30-bed burns unit at the hospital that would have been just a dream were it not for their efforts. Again, work is funded by an excellent hostel called **Marani**, see page 93, at which Walter will gladly tell you about his work. He does need volunteers.

A British woman, Suzy Butler, is spearheading Cusco's third amazing project, **Kiya Survivors**. At The Rainbow Centre in Urubamba, street children and children with special needs are being given basic education, therapy and access to theatre and sports. There is no other provision for these children or their families locally. Kiya Survivors has also opened a children's home called Mama Cocha.

Suzy says: "One of the kids is 16 and has Downs Syndrome. She had been out of her family house only once in all her life. Within two days of coming to us she was like a new person, smiling and wanting to write."

Suzy spends her time fundraising and organizing gap year students to help the project. Volunteers can work for 2, 3, 4 or 6 months and are asked to raise US$1,350-4,050, depending on the length of stay and type of volunteer programme. Spanish courses, an Inca Trail hike and other extras can be arranged.

To help Los Niños or the Hope Foundation, simply book a room at their hostels. For Kiya Survivors, visit *www.kiyasurvivors.org*, or write to *38 Hove Park Villas, Hove, East Sussex, UK, BN3 6HG, T01273-721092.*

with BTU tourist ticket, is only worth popping into if you are in the area and it is raining. The museum holds very few pieces and none of them has the artists' names, let alone any explanations.

Around Plaza San Francisco

San Francisco church, ⓘ *Plaza San Francisco, 3 blocks southwest of the Plaza de Armas. Church open 0600-0800, 1800-2000*, is an austere church reflecting many indigenous influences, but it has a wonderful monastery, cloister and choir. Although at the time of writing the monastery was not officially open to the public, it is possible to visit. Approach the door to the left of the church, shake it, look puzzled and the administrator will appear as if by magic. Agree on a price before you enter. If he starts asking for money to take photographs and then a further tip at the end because of his good service ask him for a *boleta de venta* for the money you paid up front.

The cloister is the oldest in the city, built in the Renaissance style, but with diverse influences. The ground floor has several crypts containing human bones. Some of the bones have been used to write out phrases to remind the visitor of his or her mortality! The fabulous high choir contains 92 detailed carvings of martyrs and saints. The rotating lectern inlaid with ivory skulls (the Franciscan monks' symbol) was used to hold large books. Over the years the wooden ledge has been worn away by the continuous turning of pages. On one of the stairways the largest painting (12 m high, 9 m wide) in South America can be seen. It records the 12 branches of the Franciscan Order – 683 people are present! Make sure you look up at the colourful, painted ceiling, restored after the 1950 earthquake.

Around Mercado Santa Ana

Heading towards Santa Ana market and San Pedro station from Plaza San Francisco, you pass Santa Clara arch and the nuns' church of **Santa Clara**. ⓘ *0600-0700*. It is singular in South America for its decoration, which covers the whole of the interior. Its altars are set with thousands of mirrors.

San Pedro, ⓘ *in front of the Santa Ana market, Mon-Sat 1000-1200, 1400-1700*, built in 1688, has two towers made from stones brought from an Inca ruin. The most interesting aspect of this church is the walk to it through the Santa Clara arch early in the morning. If you have only seen the Plaza de Armas and surrounding area a walk here will show you another side of Cusco life. The street stallholders will be setting up and the Santa Ana market is worth a visit.

Southern outskirts

The church of **Belén de los Reyes** was built by an indigenous architect in the 17th century. ⓘ *Mon, Tue, Wed, Thu and Sat 1000-1200, 1500-1700*. It has a striking main altar with silver embellishments at the centre and gold-washed *retablos* at the sides.

West and northwest of the Plaza de Armas

Above Cusco, on the road up to Sacsayhuaman, is **San Cristóbal**, built to his patron saint by Cristóbal Paullu Inca. The church's atrium has been restored and there is access to the Sacsayhuaman Archaeological Park. North of San Cristóbal, you can see the 11 doorway-sized niches of the great Inca wall of the **Palacio de Colcampata**, which was the residence of Manco Inca before he rebelled against the Spanish and fled to Vilcabamba. Above San Cristóbal church, to the left, is a private colonial mansion, **Quinta Colcampata**, once the home of the infamous explorer and murderer, Lope de Aguirre. It has also

Few tourists during restoration means this cloister can be visited in the peace and tranquillity for which it was meant.

been home to many other important personages including Simón Bolívar and Hiram Bingham during the years of his excavation of Machu Picchu in 1915-16. It has been restored but is not open to the public.

Cristo Blanco, arms outstretched and brilliantly illuminated at night, stands over the town and is clearly visible if you look north from the Plaza de Armas. He was given to the city as a mark of gratitude by Palestinian refugees in 1944. A quick glance in the local telephone directory reveals there is still a large Arab population in Cusco.

Sacsayhuaman

ⓘ *Daily 0700-1730. You can get in earlier if you wish and definitely try to get there before midday when the tour groups arrive. Free student guides are available, but you should give them a tip. There are lights to illuminate the site at night. The site is about a 30-min walk from the town centre. Walk up Pumacurco from Plaza de las Nazarenas.*
There are some magnificent Inca walls in the ruined ceremonial centre of Sacsayhuaman, on a hill in the northern outskirts. The Inca stonework is hugely impressive. The massive rocks weighing up to 130 tons are fitted together with absolute perfection. Three walls run parallel for over 360 m and there are 21 bastions.

Sacsayhuaman was thought for centuries to be a fortress, but the layout and architecture suggest a great sanctuary and temple to the Sun, rising opposite the place previously believed to be the Inca's throne – which was probably an altar, carved out of the solid rock. Broad steps lead to the altar from either side. Zigzags in the boulders round the 'throne' are apparently '*chicha* grooves', channels down which maize beer flowed during festivals. Up the hill is an ancient quarry, the Rodadero, now used by children as a rock slide. Near it are many seats cut perfectly into the smooth rock.

The hieratic, rather than the military, hypothesis was supported by the discovery in 1982 of the graves of priests, who would have been unlikely to be buried in a fortress. The precise functions of the site, however, will probably continue to be a matter of dispute as very few clues remain, due to its steady destruction. The site survived the first years of the conquest. Pizarro's troops had entered Cusco unopposed in 1533 and lived safely at Sacsayhuaman, until the rebellion of Manco Inca, in 1536, caught them off guard. The bitter struggle which ensued became the decisive military action of the conquest, for Manco's failure to hold Sacsayhuaman cost him the war, and the empire. The destruction of the hilltop site began after the defeat of Manco's rebellion. The outer walls still stand, but the complex of towers and buildings was razed to the ground. From then, until the 1930s, Sacsayhuaman served as a kind of unofficial quarry of pre-cut stone for the inhabitants of Cusco. For a detailed description, and map, of walks around Sacsayhuaman, see page 127.

Other sites near Cusco

Along the road from Sacsayhuaman to Pisac, past a radio station, at 3,600 m, is the temple and amphitheatre of **Qenqo**. These are not exactly ruins, but are of the finest examples of Inca stone carving *in situ*, especially inside the large hollowed-out stone that houses an altar. The rock is criss-crossed by zigzag channels that give the place its name and which served to course *chicha*, or perhaps sacrificial blood, for purposes of divination. The open space that many refer to as the 'plaza' or 'amphitheatre' was used for ceremonies. The 19 trapezoidal niches, which are partially destroyed, held idols and mummies.

The Inca fortress of **Puka Pukara** (Red Fort) was actually more likely to have been a *tambo*, a kind of post-house where travellers were lodged and goods and animals housed temporarily. It is worth seeing for the views alone.

A few hundred metres up the road is the spring shrine of **Tambo Machay**, still in excellent condition. There are many opinions as to what this place was used for. Some say it was a resting place for the Incas and others that it was used by Inca Yupanqui as a hunting place – the surrounding lands, even today, hide many wild animals including deer and foxes. As this Inca was a living god, Son of the Sun, his palace would also have been a sacred place. There are three ceremonial water fountains built on different levels. As water was considered a powerful deity it is possible that the site was a centre of a water cult. Water still flows by a hidden channel out of the masonry wall, straight into a little rock pool traditionally known as the Inca's bath.

It is safest to visit the ruins in a group, especially if you wish to see them under a full moon. Take as few belongings as possible and hide your camera in a bag.

Taking a guide to the sites mentioned above is a good idea and you should visit in the morning for the best photographs. Carry your multi-site ticket as there are roving ticket inspectors. You can visit the sites on foot. It's a pleasant walk through the countryside requiring half a day or more, though remember to take water and sun protection, and watch out for dogs. An alternative is to take the Pisac bus up to Tambo Machay (which costs US$0.35) and walk back. Another excellent way to see the ruins is on horseback, arranged at travel agencies. An organized tour (with guide) will go to all the sites for US$6 per person, not including entrance fees. A taxi will charge US$15-20 for three to four people. Some of these ruins are included in the many City Tours available. ▶▶ *For details, see page 113.*

🛏 Sleeping

Prices given are for double rooms with bathroom in the high season of Jun-Aug and include 28% tax and service, unless stated. When there are fewer tourists hotels may drop their prices by as much as half. Always ask for discounts; the prices shown at reception are usually negotiable. Also, hotel prices, especially in the mid to upper categories, are often lower when booked through tour agencies. You should book more expensive hotels well in advance through a good travel agency, particularly for the week or so around Inti Raymi, when prices are much higher.

Be wary of unlicensed hotel agents for mid-priced hotels, they are often misleading about details; their local nickname is *jalagringos* (gringo pullers), or *piratas* (pirates). Taxis and tourist minibuses meet arriving trains and take you to the hotel of your choice for US$0.50, but be insistent.

It is cold in Cusco and many hotels do not have heating. It is worth asking for an *estufa*, a heater, which some places will provide for an extra charge. When staying in the big, popular hotels, allow yourself plenty of time to check out if you have a plane or train to catch: front desks can be very busy. All the hotels listed below offer free luggage storage unless otherwise stated. Assume hotels have 24-hr hot water in pre-heated tanks unless otherwise stated. Cusco's low-power electric showers often do a poor job of heating the very cold water and their safety is sometimes questionable.

Plaza de Armas *p73, map p80*

L **Picoaga**, *Santa Teresa 344 (2 blocks from the Plaza de Armas),T084-227691, www.picoaga hotel.com* Price includes buffet breakfast. Originally the home of the Marqués de Picoaga, this beautiful colonial building has large original bedrooms set around a shady courtyard and a modern section, with a/c, at the back. All have cable TV, minibar and safe. There are conference facilities and the staff are very pleasant. Pricey but recommended.
L **Ruinas**, *Ruinas 472, T084-260644, www.hotelruinas.com* A comfortable hotel conveniently located close to the plaza (and **Rosie O' Grady's Irish Bar!**), **Ruinas** has good facilities (TV, minibar, etc) and comfortable beds, however it's possibly a little expensive given the competition in Cusco. Helpful staff, price includes buffet breakfast.
AL **Casa Andina B&B**, *Portal Espinar 142, T084-231733, www.casa-andina.com*

1½ blocks from the plaza, this brand new hotel has 40 rooms with cable TV, private bathroom and safe deposit box.

AL Royal Inka I, *Plaza Regocijo 299, T084-231067, royalin@ terra.com.pe* Price includes buffet breakfast. The 29 bedrooms, with cable TV and heating, are set in a colonial house around an enclosed shady central patio. Those to the front have balconies overlooking the plaza. The building is decorated with heavy colonial furnishings and has a tranquil atmosphere. There is a bar and the restaurant has a set menu, some days including roast leg of lamb! Recommended.

AL Royal Inka II, *close by, on Santa Teresa, same phone and website as above.* More modern and expensive but the price includes buffet breakfast, saunas and jacuzzi. Massages are an extra US$25. The old colonial façade hides a modern building, the rooms of which open out onto a huge atrium dominated by an incongruous, 3-storey high mural. All rooms have cable TV, heating and are identical, except for No 218 and 3 others which are much larger for the same price. These hotels run a free bus for guests to Pisac at 1000 daily, returning at 1800.

A Del Prado Inn, *Suecia 310, T084-224442, admin@delpradoinn.com* New and very smart hotel just off the plaza. 24-hr room service available, and closed-circuit TV in the public areas for additional security. Suites with jacuzzi cost US$90.

A Emperador Plaza, *Santa Catalina Ancha 377, T084-227412, emperador@terra.com.pe* Price includes buffet breakfast. A modern, light, airy hotel with friendly and helpful English-speaking staff. They will even order food for you from the Irish pub over the road! Rooms have cable TV, hairdryer, gas-heated showers and electric radiators. Winner of several hotel awards within its class.

A Hostal Plaza de Armas, *Plaza de Armas, corner of Mantas, T084-222351, hostal_plaza @terra.com.pe* Price includes breakfast, from 0500. This is a clean, modern hotel with 28 rooms, each with cable TV, mineral water and heaters. However, in spite of its excellent position, only the lacklustre restaurant has views over the plaza.

A-B Hostal Carlos V, *Tecseccocha 490, T084-223091, carlos_v_cus@starmedia.com* Price includes continental breakfast; heating is US$2.30 a night extra, TV costs more too. Take time to explore the 30 rooms and you should be able to find one with character and reasonable decor in the refurbished 1st-floor section. However, many bathrooms are shabby. With regards to prices, the owners are definitely open to negotiation. Worth a look.

B Hostal Corihuasi, *C Suecia 561, T084-232233, www.corihuasi.com* Price (can pay by Visa or AmEx) includes continental breakfast and airport pick-up. A tough climb up from the northernmost corner of the Plaza de Armas, this tranquil 18-bedroom guesthouse is popular with tour groups. It is friendly and has some good views (the best is from room No 1) as well as cable TV in each room. A solar heating system was being installed in 2003. Recommended.

B Hostal Qosqo, *Portal Mantas 115, near the Plaza de Armas, T084-252513.* Bargain hard for a discount. Price includes continental breakfast, a heater and cable TV. The state

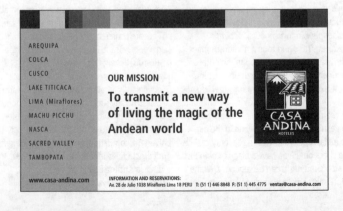

AREQUIPA
COLCA
CUSCO
LAKE TITICACA
LIMA (Miraflores)
MACHU PICCHU
NASCA
SACRED VALLEY
TAMBOPATA

www.casa-andina.com

OUR MISSION

To transmit a new way of living the magic of the Andean world

CASA ANDINA HOTELES

INFORMATION AND RESERVATIONS:
Av. 28 de Julio 1038 Miraflores Lima 18 PERU T: (51 1) 446 8848 F: (51 1) 445 4775 ventas@casa-andina.com

of decor and quality of mattress varies from room to room but most stay here for its proximity to the plaza. Clean, friendly and helpful.

B **Pensión Loreto**, *Pasaje Loreto 115, Plaza de Armas (it shares the same entrance as Norton's Rat pub), T084-226352, hloreto@terra.com.pe* Price includes continental breakfast and a heater which you will need as the original Inca walls make the rooms cold. Again, the best feature of this *hostal* is its location, although the rooms are spacious and they will serve you breakfast in bed if you are finding it too cold to get up. They have a laundry service and will help organize any travel services including guides and taxis. They also offer a free airport pick-up service. A bit pricey but where else can you fall out of a pub into your *hostal*?

C **Hostal Imperial Palace**, *Tecseccocha 490-B, T084-223324, celazo1@hotmail.com* (D without bathroom), price includes continental breakfast and some of the rooms have heaters. Hot water supply is patchy, with some rooms having a 24-hr supply, while others only have hot water in the early morning and evening. Rooms are large and have comfortable beds but are in need of redecoration. There is a café, bar and restaurant. Very friendly.

C **Hostal Q'Awarina**, *at the top of Suecia 575, T084-228130*. Price includes continental breakfast, heating is US$2 extra per night as is a TV in your room. No laundry service. Rooms are OK, ask for those with a view – they cost the same. There is a lovely living room with views across the city and the breakfast area upstairs is even better. Group rates available, good value.

D **Hostal Turístico Plateros**, *Plateros 348, T084-236878*. Price includes continental breakfast. Clean, good value *hostal* in a great location. There is a pleasant communal area with cable TV. The best rooms overlook the street.

D-E **Hostal Royal Frankenstein**, *San Juan de Dios 260, 2 blocks from the Plaza de Armas, T084-236999, ludwig_roth@hotmail.com* One thing is for sure, you will never forget this place. Greeted by a grinning skull whose eye sockets light up as you enter, things just become more peculiar. Passing through the fully equipped kitchen (just US$0.30 a day), you can sit next to a (caged) tarantula while watching cable TV in the living room or gaze at Franken Fish. Rooms, fortunately, follow this theme in name only, thus you can stay in Mary Shelley or the Laboratorio. Nearly all 10 have excellent mattresses but few have outside windows. Downstairs, with one exception, they also run straight off the living room, which has an open fire. However, Ludwig, the mildly eccentric German owner, has 2 excellent matrimonials/family rooms on the open-air top floor which are excellent and come with heaters. There is also a safe and laundry facilities. Next door is the rather funky jazz café, **Tangible Myth**. Recommended.

E **Munay Wasi**, *Huaynapata 253, not far from Plaza de Armas, T084-223661*. The price includes free hot drinks and laundry facilities. There are plans to put in cable TV. Bargain for a bed in this quiet, run-down colonial house. The 7 bedrooms are basic and very clean and most mattresses are sprung. The 2 front rooms have views of the Plaza de Armas. The owner is friendly and helpful.

E **Posada del Viajero**, *Santa Catalina Ancha 366, down lane next to Rosie O'Grady's, T084-261643*. Select your room carefully and you could find a real bargain at this centrally located *hostal*. Some are drab with dodgy mattresses piled 3 high but the owners are making real efforts and others have newly tiled bathrooms and comfy beds. Use of the kitchen costs US$0.60.

E **Hostal Resbalosa**, *Resbalosa 494, T084-224839*. Breakfast is US$1.45 extra; laundry costs US$0.75 per kg. For superb views of the Plaza de Armas from a sun-drenched terrace look no further. Owner Georgina is very hospitable but her best rooms are those with a view (US$1.45 extra). Others may be pokey and suffer from foam mattresses. The electric showers are reportedly cool, but most guests love this place. There is a safe in reception.

E **Hostal Santa María**, *Santa Catalina Angosta 156, near Plaza de Armas, down a passageway*. With its excellent location you can't expect any creature comforts with this price tag. Rooms are bare, dark but clean and the beds are fine.

F **El Procurador del Cusco**, *Coricalle 440, Prolongación Procuradores, at the end of Procuradores*. (G per person without bathroom), price includes use of the basic kitchen (no fridge) and laundry area. The rooms are basic too and the beds somewhat hard, but upstairs is better. There is a place to relax and gaze over the city and the staff are very friendly and helpful. This is good value for money. Recommended.

F Tumi 1, *Siete Cuartones 245, 2 blocks from Plaza de Armas, T084-244413*. Price includes use of the kitchen and laundry area. There is a free book exchange and laundry service costs US$0.85. This lovely colonial house has 16 bedrooms (none with bath) around a sunny, paved courtyard. All are clean, traditional and huge with bare wooden floors and walls in need of a lick of paint. The toilets all lack a toilet seat and it seems tight to charge poor backpackers US$1.40 if they have more than 1 shower (some are electric) a day. However, this is a very friendly, popular place and good value, especially if you bargain for longer stays.

North and northeast of the Plaza de Armas *p77, map p74*

LL El Monasterio, *Palacios 136, T084-241777, reservas@ peruorientexpress.com.pe* This 5-star, beautifully restored Seminary of San Antonio Abad is central and quite simply the best hotel in town for historical interest; it is worth a visit even if you cannot afford the price tag (see p78). Soft Gregorian chants follow you as you wander through the baroque chapel, tranquil courtyards and charming cloisters, admiring the excellent collection of religious paintings. There are 109 spacious rooms with all facilities, including cable TV, as well as 16 suites, including 2 royal suites at US$815 and 3 presidential suites at US$655. Some rooms even offer an oxygen-enriched atmosphere to help clients acclimatize, for an additional fee of US$25. Staff, who all speak English, are very helpful and attentive. The price includes a great buffet breakfast (US$17 to non- residents) which will fill you up for the rest of the day. The restaurant, where the monks used to sing, serves lunch and dinner à la carte. The chapel is used as a conference centre and there is email for guests (US$3 per hr), open 0930-1300, 1730-2130. Recommended.

LL Novotel, *San Agustín 239, T084-228282, reservations@novotelcusco.com.pe* 4-star, is US$50 cheaper (US$180 as opposed to US$230) in modern section; price includes buffet breakfast. This is probably the best hotel converted from a colonial house in Cusco. It was originally built as a home for *conquistador* Miguel Sánchez Ponce who accompanied Pizarro in the taking of Cajamarca. It was remodelled after the 1650 earthquake by General Pardo de Figueroa who built the lovely stone archways and commissioned paintings of the saints of his devotion on the grand stairway. Today the beautiful courtyard, roofed in glass, has sofas, coffee tables and pot plants around the central stone fountain. The modern 5-storey rear extension has 83 excellent, spacious, airy and bright rooms. All have sofas, cable TV, central heating and bathtubs. Those above the 2nd floor have views over Cusco's red-tiled rooftops. The 16 in the colonial section are not much different but have high, beamed ceilings and huge, 2-m-wide beds. There are 2 restaurants and a French chef.

A Hostal Cusco Plaza, *Plaza Nazarenas 181 (opposite El Monasterio), T084-246161*. Price includes continental breakfast. Situated on a lovely small plaza in the town centre, there are 33 clean rooms all with cable TV. Room 303 has the best view.

B Hostal El Arqueólogo, *Pumacurco 408, T084-232569, reservation@hotelarquelogo. com* Price includes buffet breakfast. Services include oxygen, a library and hot drinks. Heating costs US$5 extra per night. A colonial building on Inca foundations, this has rustic but stylish decor. There is a lovely sunny garden with comfy chairs and a small restaurant that serves interesting Peruvian food and fondue. French and English spoken. Recommended. Also has **Vida Tours**, *at this address, T084-227750, www.vidatours.com* Traditional and adventure tourism.

B Hostal Rumi Punku, *Choquechaca 339, T084-221102, www.rumipunku.com* A genuine Inca doorway leads to a sunny, tranquil courtyard. 20 large, clean, comfortable rooms, helpful staff and safe. Highly recommended. ·

C Hostal María Esther, *Pumacurco 516, T084-224382*. Price includes continental breakfast, and heating available for US$2 extra. This very friendly, helpful place has a lovely garden in which to relax and a variety of rooms. There is also a lounge with sofas and car parking. Recommended.

E **Casa Elena**, *Choquechaca 162, T084-241202, www.geocities.com/casa_elena* French/Peruvian hostel, very comfortable and friendly, breakfast included. Highly recommended.

E **El Balcón Colonial**, *Choquechaca 350, T084-238129, balconcolonial @hotmail.com* Price is per person. Continental breakfast is available at extra cost. Use of the kitchen costs US$1 per day and laundry costs US$0.70 per kg. There is accommodation for 16 people in 6 rooms of this family house. Rooms are basic with foam mattresses but the hospitality of the owner is exceptional. Free airport pick-up.

G **Hostal Pumacurco**, *Pumacurco 336, Interior 329, T084-243347 (3 mins from the Plaza de Armas)*. This is in the newly restored part of a very old colonial house. Everywhere is clean and secure and there are some large rooms as well as washing facilities. Owner Betty is very friendly and helpful.

San Blas *p78, map p74*

AL **Los Apus Hostal y Mirador**, *Atocsaycuchi 515 y Choquechaca, T084-264243, www.losapushostal.com* Price includes buffet breakfast and airport pick-up; laundry costs US$1 per kg. Character and mod-cons combine in this Swiss-owned *hostal*. It is all varnished wood, very clean and smart with beamed bedrooms fitted with cable TV and real radiators! Tall travellers will love the 2.3 m-long beds, but views are limited, even from the breakfast lookout on the top floor.

B **Hostal Casa de Campo**, *Tandapata 296-B (at the end of the street), T084-244404, info@hotelcasadecampo.com (or contact via La Tertulia , p 100)*. Price (10% discount for SAE members and Footprint Handbook owners) includes continental breakfast and free airport/rail/bus transfer with reservations. Guests get a work-out thrown in for free in the shape of many steep steps up to the multi-level hotel! Consequently the 26 bedrooms have fabulous views over Cusco. There is a safe deposit box, laundry service, meals on request and a sun terrace. Dutch and English are spoken; take a taxi there after dark. A new wing, with a further 24 rooms, was being opened in 2003.

B **Pensión Alemana**, *Tandapata 260, T084-226861, pensioalemana@terra.com.pe* Price includes American breakfast; laundry is US$1.10 per kg and heating extra. Car parking available. This Swiss-owned pension has clean, modern European decor with a comfy lounge area in which to watch cable TV or listen to music. There is a lovely garden with patio furniture. Recommended.

C **Hostal Amaru**, *Cuesta San Blas 541, T084-225933, www.cusco.net/amaru* (**D** without bathroom), Price includes breakfast and airport/train/bus pick-up. Services include oxygen, kitchen for use in the evenings only, laundry and free book exchange. Rooms are grouped around a pretty colonial courtyard, covered in geraniums in Jul. They have TVs with national channels only (cable in sitting area), good beds and carved wardrobes. This has pleasant places to relax and some Inca walls. Rooms in the first courtyard are best. Recommended.

C **Marani**, *Carmen Alto 194, T084-249462, marani@terra.com.pe* Breakfasts available. Services include beginnings of a book exchange and information on Andean life and culture. Walter Meekes and his wife, Tineke, opened this spotless *hostal* in 2000. The rooms are large with beamed ceilings and have heaps of character, set around a courtyard. There is a breakfast room to the same standards. Some of the rooms are decorated with gifts of gratitude from communities the couple have helped through their association, the **Hope Foundation** (*www.stichtinghope.org*). In 10 years the Dutch couple have built 20 schools in poor mountain villages and *barrios*, established a programme to teach teachers and set up a 30-bed burns unit in Cusco general hospital. Good value, a great cause and highly recommended.

C **Posada del Sol**, *Atocsaycuchi 296, T084-246394*. Includes American breakfast, heater and airport pick-up. Cheerfully decorated with rustic charm, the hotel also has a sun terrace with great views of Cusco and fantastic showers. Guests may use the kitchen and laundry costs only US$0. 50/kg. Food is available. The *hostal* is up some steps and cannot be reached by taxi. Recommended.

C **Hospedaje Turístico San Blas**, *Cuesta San Blas 526, T084-225781, sanblascusco@yahoo. com* The price includes continental breakfast and there is cable TV in the comfortable, covered courtyard. Heaters are extra. The bedrooms are very well decorated and the place has a lot of charm for a basic *hostal*.

D **El Arcano**, *Carmen Alto 288, T084-232703*. The old **Hostal Cristales** and **El Arcano** are now run by 1 person and share the same name. Breakfast and laundry are available in both, cheaper rooms with shared bath. On the one side there is a lovely little communal area with comfortable seating covered by a colourful glass roof and on the other there is a small breakfast area with cable TV and a book exchange. The owners are very friendly as is their large German shepherd dog. They will help arrange trips and own 2 lodges; one in the jungle and another in cloudforest. Highly recommended.

D **Hostal Kuntur Wasi**, *Tandapata 352-A, T084-227570*. (E without bathroom), services include a safe, use of the kitchen (for US$0.60 a day) and laundry (US$0.85 per kg). There are great views from the terrace where you can breakfast. Owned by a very welcoming, helpful family. The showers are electric. A very pleasant place to stay.

D **Hostal El Mirador de la Ñusta**, *Tandapata 682, T084-248039, elmiradordelnusta@hot mail.com* Snug and friendly family *hostal*, tucked in behind **The Muse** café, above the San Blas Plaza. The tasteful decor and location mean that this *hostal* is a real winner. Laundry service costs US$ 0.85 per kg, and there's a safe for valuables.

D **Hostal Pakcha Real**, *Tandapata 300, T084-237484, pakcharealhostal@ hotmail.com* Price includes breakfast, the use of the kitchen and free airport/train/bus pick-up; heaters are an extra US$1.50. This is a family-run *hostal* where you can expect all the comforts of home including a large lounge with a fireplace and cable TV. There is a laundry service and they own the shop next door. The rooms are spotless although sparsely decorated and the front 2 rooms have great views. Taxis can drop you at the door. A friendly, relaxed place.

D-E **Hospedaje Jhuno**, *Carmen Alto 281, T084-233579*. Breakfast is not included but guests can use the tiny kitchenette. A small

family-run *hospedaje* with 8 clean, decorated rooms and a family lounge with stereo.

D-E **Hospedaje Plaza de San Blas**, *Plazoleta San Blas 630, T084-235358, psanblas@ corihuasi.com* Colourful and welcoming *hospedaje* with a great location. Great value as the price includes continental breakfast. There's a snug little café in the same building. The 4-bed family room has a balcony and overlooks the plazoleta.

E **Hostal Familiar Mirador del Inka**, *Tandapata 160, off Plaza San Blas, T084-261384, miradordelinka@latinmail.com* This *hostal* was a bit of a building site at the time of writing, however many improve-ments were being made – a new bar had been set up in a luminous purple building overlooking the *hostal*, and a breakfast room was nearing completion. You can use the dilapidated kitchen and there is a laundry service. This *hostal* looks very stylish with its Inca foundations and white colonial walls but the interior courtyard is only good for a game of footie. The bedrooms, with private bathrooms, can be musty although they are spacious and some have great views. The owner's son Edwin runs trekking trips and has an agency on site.

E **Hostal Sambleño**, *Carmen Alto 114, T084-262979*. A lovely jumble of staircases overlooks a central courtyard in this San Blas cheapie which has some rooms of varying quality. Breakfast is available and there is a laundry service. Beds are comfortable but the showers are electric. Recommended.

E **Hostal Tikawasi**, *Tandapata 491, T084-231609, tikawasi@latinmail.com* Price includes breakfast; no private bathrooms. A family-run *hostal* with a nice garden overlooking the city, very quiet and pleasant.

F per person **Hospedaje Inka**, *Suytuccato 848, T084-231995*. Taxis leave you at Plaza San Blas, walk steeply uphill for 5-10 mins, or phone the *hostal*. Price includes bath and breakfast. There are wonderful views, the rooms are spacious and owner Américo is very helpful, with lots of information.

F **Hospedaje El Artesano de San Blas**, *Suytucato 790, T084-263968, manosandinas@yahoo.com* Newly refurbished, with many clean, bright and airy rooms. As with the **Hospedaje Inka**, you need to walk up from San Blas.

F Hostal Familiar Carmen Alto, *Carmen Alto 197, first on the right down steps (there is no sign), 3 blocks from central plaza, T084-224367.* If there's no answer when ringing the bell, go to the shop next door, it's run by the same family. Budget *hostal* owners could take a leaf out of owner Carmen's books: she has succeeded in giving basic rooms great character with traditional wall hangings and, in one case, by constructing a room around a huge live tree! This tranquil *hostal* is very much family run and guests can use the kitchen and washing machine. Carmen will make you a very good breakfast for US$2. All rooms have shared bath and the showers are electric. Recommended.

G Hospedaje Familiar Inti Quilla, *Atocsaycuchi 281, T084-252659.* Breakfast is not included and there are no facilities for either providing or making food. There are 6 colourfully decorated bedrooms around a pleasant little courtyard. It is situated on a quiet pedestrian street which means taxis cannot drop you off at the door. Good value.

LL Libertador, *in the Casa de los Cuatro Bustos at Plazoleta Santo Domingo 259 (see p82), T084-231961, www.libertador.com.pe* Buffet breakfast is US$15 extra. This splendid 5-star, award-winning hotel is built on Inca ruins (the walls can be seen in the restaurant and bar) and is set around courtyards. It has 254 well-appointed rooms; the attention to detail is so great there are even Nazca Lines drawn in the sand of the ashtrays! Enjoy Andean music and dance over dinner in the excellent **Inti Raymi** restaurant. Recommended.

AL Don Carlos, *Av Sol 602, T084-226207 (Lima T01-225 8633), www.hotelesdoncarlos.com* The price includes buffet breakfast. This 50-bedroom, modern hotel is clean and bright and has a friendly front desk but lacks character. All rooms have cable TV, a safe, fridge and heating as well as 24-hr room service. Some also have facilities for the disabled. Not the best value in this price range.

Cusco City Sleeping: East & southeast of the Plaza de Armas

The very best service in the best places of Perú

LIBERTADOR HOTELS
25 years
in the tourism industry

Perú has it all:
From a modern society that thrives next to centuries old cultural and historical landmarks, to wild nature and ancient cultures.

BECAUSE WE HAVE ONLY ONE BOSS: OUR GUEST

HOTELES LIBERTADOR
PERÚ

Afiliado a:
SUMMIT
HOTELS & RESORTS

[LIMA]   [CUSCO]   [PUNO]   [AREQUIPA]   [TRUJILLO]

Las Begonias 441 Of. 240 San Isidro | Lima 27 - PE | Telf.: (511) 442-1995 • 442-1996
Fax: (511) 442-2988 | E-mail: hotel@libertador.com.pe | http://www.libertador.com.pe

AL **San Agustín Internacional**, *San Agustín y Maruri 390, T084-221169, www.hotelsan agustin.com.pe* Price includes continental breakfast. There is a rustic Mexican feel to the lobby with its fireplace and water feature, while Andean music is piped to the communal areas. There are 76 heated bedrooms and the staff will organize tours.

AL **San Agustín Plaza**, *Av Sol 594, T084-238121, www.hotelsanagustin. com.pe* Price includes buffet breakfast. Decorated in a Spanish style with a central fireplace in the lobby, this hotel has 26 bedrooms which are well decorated, clean and airy. Street front rooms have views of Qoricancha.

AL **Savoy Internacional**, *Av Sol 954, T084-224322 (Lima T01-446 7965), www.hotelsavoyplaza.com* Price includes American breakfast. This is one of the earliest modern hotels in the city and some of the features such as TV sets (cable) and minibars are dated. However, bedrooms are spacious, with heating and some have good views, as does the Sky Room. There is also a bar, coffee shop, and the staff speak many languages. For a large hotel, this has a warm, friendly feel.

B **Los Portales**, *Matará 322, T084-223500, reservas@portalescusco.com* Price includes continental breakfast and airport pick-up; ask for a heater at no extra charge. Services include safe deposit box, laundry (US $3 per kg), oxygen and a money exchange. TV is local channels only and check-out time is an unfriendly 0900! A modern hotel with modern facilities, the whole place is painted in magnolia, relieved by wall paintings of local scenes. Very friendly and helpful, children welcome. Recommended.

E-F **Maison de la Jeunesse** *(affiliated to Hostelling International), Av Sol, Cuadra 5, Pasaje Grace, Edificio San Jorge (down a small side street opposite Qoricancha), T084-235617, elia25@msn.com* Very friendly French/Peruvian-run hostel with a selection of dormitories and private rooms. TV and video room, cooking facilities and very hot water add to its appeal. Price includes breakfast.

G **Estrellita**, *Av Tullumayo 445, parte Alta, T084-234134.* Price includes breakfast and tea and coffee all day. There is a TV, video and old stereo system in the tiny communal sitting area and a very basic kitchen. 11 rooms are multiples with shared bathrooms

and there are 2 with private bathrooms. It is basic but the wooden floors, good mattresses and clean decor make this excellent value. It is about a 15-min walk from the centre. When you arrive ring the bell several times and wait; you will be given your own keys when you register. Cars and bikes can be parked safely. Recommended.

South and southwest of the Plaza de Armas *p85, map p74*

C **El Inca**, *Quera 251, T084-246140, eschavez_pe@yahoo.com* Price (you can pay by Visa or MasterCard) includes breakfast; services include laundry (US$1.40 per kg). The unofficial prices are roughly half those displayed, and at these rates the hotel represents good value. Some of the rooms need redecorating and one smells damp, but if you choose carefully and avoid those on the 1st floor (there is a noisy disco in the basement) this can be a bargain find for a centrally located hotel.

D **Hostal Machu Picchu**, *Quera 282, T084-231111.* (E without bathroom). There is a public phone, a safe but no TVs; laundry costs US$0.85 per kg. This very clean colonial house is a central, pleasant place to stay if you can afford the better rooms. Those with a bathroom are of a high standard but those *sin baño* are dark inside. Floors are stylishly tiled and there are plenty of places to relax in the flower-filled garden and escape the busy road outside.

F **Hospedaje Magnolia's 2**, *Av Regional 898, T084-224898.* Price per person. Comfortable rooms with or without bath, quiet, safe, very clean and helpful, English spoken, laundry service, kitchen facilities, tourist information.

West and northwest of the Plaza de Armas *p87, map 74*

AL **Don Carlos Inca Tambo Hacienda Hotel**, *at Km 2, close to Sacsayhuaman, above the town, T084-221918 (Lima T01-224 0263), www.tci.net.pe/doncarlos* Price includes buffet breakfast and transport from the airport. Built on the site of Pizarro's original house, this 23-bedroom rustic-style hacienda is very peaceful, but this may not be enough to lure you out of town. The patio is a pleasant suntrap, but the garden is rough and, despite its height above the city, the views are not spectacular. Rooms have heaters and Peruvian-only TV. Perhaps a little expensive for the limited facilities on offer. Horse riding can be arranged in the 60 ha of hotel grounds or around the nearby ruins.

AL Cusco Plaza 2, *Saphi 486, T084-263000, F084-262001*. New hotel, with same management as the Cusco Plaza (see below). The 24, nicely decorated rooms are set around 3 charming covered patios. Price includes American breakfast, and all rooms have cable TV and heating.

A Hostal El Balcón, *Tambo de Montero 222, T084-236738, balcon1@terra.com.pe* Price includes breakfast and you can pay with Visa, AmEx, Diners and Visa electrón.This lovingly restored 1630 colonial house has 16 large rooms set around a beautiful, well-maintained garden. Ask for a TV if you want one – there is no extra charge. As well as a restaurant there is a kitchen for guests to use, and a laundry service. Homely atmosphere. Recommended.

B Hostal Cahuide, *Saphi 845, T084-222771, F084-248262*. Price (negotiate for a discount, especially for longer stays) includes American breakfast. Cable TV in all rooms, and ask for a heater at no extra charge. This is a modern 45-room hotel with 1970s furniture, plain white walls and comfortable beds. Helpful staff.

B Hostal San Isidro Labrador, *Saphi 440, T084-226241, labrador@qnet.com.pe* Very pleasant 3-star hotel with elegant but simple decor. Colonial arches lead to a breakfast area (continental breakfast included in the price) and 2 lovely patios. The location is good, there's plenty of hot water and heating and telephone in all rooms. Recommended.

B-C Hostal Andenes de Saphi, *Saphi 848, T084-227561, F084-235588*. Very friendly little hostel with an artistic and cosmopolitan atmosphere. Each room is decorated in a different style, so have a good look around before choosing. The 4-bed family room is very nice. Price includes continental breakfast and all rooms have heaters. Lovely entertainment/games room, and a small but pleasant garden.

C Niños Hotel, *C Meloc 442, T084-231424, www.ninoshotel.com* Price (US$30 with bathroom) does not include the excellent

breakfast (fruit salad, home-made wholemeal bread, locally produced jam, tea or coffee, fruit juice, etc) which costs US$1.70-2.50. Services include the cafeteria and laundry service (US$1.15 per kg). Dutch, English, German and French spoken. Spotless, beautiful rooms funding a fantastic charity established by Dutch couple, Titus and Jolande Bovenberg, who have converted this 17th-century colonial house into a stylish, comfortable place, typified by painted-wood floors and fresh lilies everywhere. All bedrooms lead onto a well-renovated courtyard. Those downstairs are named after the 12 streetchildren Titus and Jolande have adopted and care for at the back of the hotel, while upstairs rooms bear the names of various benefactors. Nearby are some equally well-appointed and spacious apartments, with a shared kitchen and bathroom, but are cold. Apartments (which can sleep several people) cost US$250 per month for the first person, US$100 per month for each additional resident. These help fund a restaurant in the same complex where the **Niños** foundation feeds, cares for and helps educate 250 more street children. Recently opened is the new **Niños 2**, on C Fierro, a little further from the centre. **Niños 2** follows the same model as the first hotel, with 20 nicely decorated, clean and airy rooms, surrounding the central courtyard. Use the contact details of the main hotel for reservations and information.

D Hostal Familiar, *Saphi 661, T084-239353*. (E without bathroom), luggage deposit costs US$2.85 a day for a big pack. For over 25 years the owners have run this popular 32-bedroom *hostal* in a pleasing colonial house with benches around a central courtyard, 3 blocks from the central plaza. Most beds are comfy and there is hot water all day from tanks. Recommended.

E Albergue Municipal, *Kiskapata 240, near San Cristóbal, T084-252506, albergue@municusco.gob* There are private rooms with double beds as well as dormitories in this very clean, helpful 56-bed youth hostel. Nice communal area with cable TV and video. No rooms have bath. It has the added bonus of great views as well as a cafeteria and place to wash clothes (laundry service US$0.75 per kg). Showers are electric and, unusually for a youth hostel, there is no kitchen.

E Hospedaje Killipata, *just off Tambo de Montero*, T084-236668. Very clean, family-run lodging with good showers and 24-hr hot water. Recommended.

E Hostal Qorichaska, *Nueva Alta 458*, T084-228974, F084-227094. Price includes a continental breakfast, use of the well-equipped kitchen and safe. Laundry is US$0.85 per kg. Rooms in this colonial house are clean, sunny although watch out for the odd sagging mattress in the new section. Ask for the older rooms which are bigger and have traditional balconies overlooking the paved courtyard. Friendly and recommended.

E Suecia II, *Tecseccocha 465 (no bell – knock!)*, T084-239757 (it is wise to book ahead). (**F** without bathroom), breakfast US$1.40. You'll find **Suecia II** opposite **Los Perros Bar** close to Gringo Alley. Rooms are set around a glass-covered colonial courtyard and consequently are warm. Beds have foam mattresses but they are thick and guests can sit at tables on verandas overlooking the patio. Drawbacks: no seats on the toilets, water not always hot or bathrooms clean, can be noisy and the luggage store is closed at night, otherwise OK.

E Hostal Rickch'airy, *Tambo de Montero 219*, T084-236606. (**F** without bathroom). This highly popular backpackers' haunt has views from the garden where travellers swap Machu Picchu tales while waiting for their tents to dry. Full breakfast is available (US$2) and owner Leo has tourist information and will collect guests from the station. Leo is in the process of building 15 new rooms each with private bathroom; at the time of writing 6 rooms were complete (**C**).

F Chaska Wasi, *Amargura 130 (there is no sign)*, T084-622831. For US$3 extra you'll be given cable TV in your room and American breakfast. Guests can also use the basic kitchen (there is no fridge) and there's a laundry service for US$1.40 per kg. This family house has character and 10

well-presented rooms. Sadly the beds are hard but showers are good and downstairs there is a clay oven in the living area but there are no double beds, otherwise this is excellent value for 1 block away from the central plaza.

F California, *Nueva Alta 444*, T/F084-242997. Services include free use of the somewhat grubby kitchen (which has no fridge), and there is a TV (no cable) in the living area downstairs. Some bedrooms are beamed, but the mattresses are ropey and the showers are electric. There's a good area to sit and eat or just chat and a second courtyard at the back where you can relax in the sun – but neither are too pretty. A step up from basic in a *hostal* of character. Very friendly and hospitable.

F Hospedaje Wiñay Wayna, *Vitoque 628 (at the top of Nueva Baja)*. T084-246794, miriamojeda@yahoo.com Price does not include breakfast, no rooms have bath. There is a safe and guests can use the kitchen. Laundry service costs US$0.70 per kg. This *hostal* is good value, perhaps reflecting its position away from plaza, near the market. All but 1 room is bright and airy, comfortable and pleasant, as is the cafeteria. Rugs on the floor typify this family's effort to make this colonial house a very pleasant place to stay.

G Hostal Luzerna, *Av Baja 205, near San Pedro train station (take a taxi at night)*, T084-232762. Price includes breakfast. A nice family runs this *hostal* which has hot water, good beds and is clean. It is safe to leave luggage. Recommended.

Family lodgings

There is a network of local families offering tourist accommodation in 3 categories:
Inti (room with private bath), *Quilla* (room with shared bathroom), and *Chaska* (rooms with use of family's bathroom). Guests are also invited to participate in family events. Contact: **Small Business Association of Family Lodgings**, C San Agustín 415, T084-244036, F084-233912.

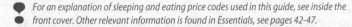

For an explanation of sleeping and eating price codes used in this guide, see inside the front cover. Other relevant information is found in Essentials, see pages 42-47.

🍴 Eating

Plaza de Armas *p73, map p80*

$$$ **Inka Grill**, *Portal de Panes 115, T084-262992*, 1000-2400 (Sun 1200-2400). According to many the best food in town is served here, specializing in Novo Andino cuisine (the use of native ingredients and 'rescued' recipes) and innovative dishes, also home-made pastas, wide vegetarian selection, live music, excellent coffee and home-made pastries 'to go'. A good place to spoil yourself, recommended.

$$$ **El Mesón**, *Espaderos y Plaza de Armas*, 2nd floor with balcony overlooking the plaza. Good *parrilladas* and other typical local dishes.

$$$ **Mesón de los Portales**, *Portal de Panes 163*. International and Peruvian cuisine.

$$$ **Pachacútec Grill and Bar**, *Portal de Panes 105*. International cuisine including seafood and Italian specialities, also features folk music shows nightly. Excellent value quality *menú* for just US$2.50.

$$$ **Paititi**, *Portal Carrizos 270*. Live music and good atmosphere in a setting with Inca masonry. Excellent pizzas but the service is variable depending on how busy they are.

$$$ **La Retama**, *Portal de Panes 123, 2nd floor*. Excellent Novo-Andino food and service. Recommend the mouth-watering trout sashimi as a starter followed by steak. There is also a balcony, an enthusiastic music and dance group and art exhibitions.

$$$ **El Truco**, *Plaza Regocijo 261*. Excellent local and international dishes, used a lot by tour groups, buffet lunch 1200-1500, nightly folk music at 2045, next door is **Taberna del Truco**, which is open 0900-0100.

$$$ **Tunupa**, *Portal Confiturías 233, 2nd floor (same entrance as Cross Keys)*. One of the finest restaurants on the plaza, its large restaurant (accommodates 120-140) is often used by tour groups. Also has the longest (glassed-in) balcony but this is narrow and best for couples only. Food is international, traditional and Novo Andino; try *piqueos del pescador* as a starter (US$11 for 2) and alpaca mignons or steak (US$10.30) to follow. Wine list, as everywhere in Cusco, is limited. Also an excellent buffet for US$15 including a *pisco sour* and a hot drink. In the evenings

there is an excellent gr[...]
17th-century-style Cusq[...]
their own composition a[...]
dancers. Recommended.

$$ **Al Grano**, *Santa Catalin[...] T084-228032, 1000-2100, clo[...]* Lunchtime menu US$2.15 is a good option if you are fed up with other menus. Evening serves 5 authentic Asian dishes for US$5.50, menu changes daily. Not a typical English curry but good and without doubt some of the best coffee in town, vegetarian choices. Also on the menu are breakfasts, including the 'Full English' variety, dubbed 'The Mother of all Breakfasts!', and jacket potatoes for those not smitten on all things hot and spicy! Recommended.

$$ **Keros**, *on the corner of Procuradores and Plaza de Armas, 2nd floor*. Lunchtime menu for US$4.30 includes *pisco sour*, 3 courses and a tea.

$$ **Kintaro**, *Heladeros 149*. 1200-2200, closed Sun. Excellent home-made food, set menu (1200-1500) particularly good value at US$3. Run by Japanese, the chicken teriyaki on rice is mouth-watering as is the sashimi of trout and avocado on sushi rice (watch out for the hot paste masquerading at the side of the plate as avocado!). Inca rolls and raw spinach in sesame is good, as is the tofu and saki. Low-fat food is said to be good for high altitude.

$$ **El Patio**, *Portal de Carnes 236, Plaza de Armas, left of the cathedral*. Closed 1530-1830. In a colonial courtyard, this has a short menu (great for the indecisive!) with great pasta, Mediterranean dishes and salads as well as a good-value lunch. Great for a quick meal; get there early as the sun disappears around 1300/1330. Recommended.

$$ **Pizzería Marengo**, *Plaza Regocijo 246, T084-252627*. Excellent pizzas for US$5-6 per person. Ask for a table in the back room next to the cosy clay oven and watch your food being prepared. Also does deliveries.

$$ **Los Tomines**, *Triunfo 384*. Excellent 4-course set meal for US$5-6. Recommended.

$$ **Varayoc**, *Espaderos 142, T084-232404*. Open daily 0800-2400. Swiss-owned restaurant including Peruvian ingredients (try bircher muesli for breakfast; cheese

...3 – the only place in Cusco ...it). Also has a variety of pastas, ...desserts, 'tea time' beverage and ...stry for US$2.80 accompanied by Andean harp music. It has a pleasant, literary atmosphere, established for 22 years and owner, Oscar, has a fine reputation.

$ **Babieca**, *Tecseccocha 418, T084-221122*. Walk to the top of Procuradores, turn left and this place is on the corner opposite the **Sunset Video Bar**. New in the summer of 2003, **Babieca** boasts some excellent pizzas with light, crispy bases and a varied selection of menus ranging from US$2-6. Warm decoration and efficient service add the finishing touch making this place a real winner.

$ **El Encuentro**, *Santa Catalina Ancha 384*. One of the best-value eateries in Cusco, 3 courses of good healthy food and a drink will set you back US$1.

$ **Paccha**, *Portal de Panes 167*. Good for breakfast, it also has a bookstore, posters for sale, English and French spoken.

$ **Víctor Victoria**, *Tigre 130*. Israeli and local dishes, highly recommended for breakfast, good value.

$ **La Yunta**, *Portal de Carnes, Plaza de Armas*. Good salads, pancakes and juices, also vegetarian, popular with tourists, same owners as **Instinct Travel Agency**.

Cafés, delis, panaderías and heladerías

Ayllu, *Portal de Carnes 208, to the left of the cathedral*, is probably one of the oldest cafés in Cusco and a great place to go. Fantastic breakfasts (have the special fruit salad, US$2.30), sandwiches, coffee and classical music as well as wonderful apple pastries. Try *leche asada*. Very much a local venue – menu refreshingly all-Spanish. Service superb, handled by blue-jacketed waiters permanently on the run.

The Deli, *Portal de Carnes 236, next to the Blueberry Lounge*. This is closest you'll get in Peru to a European delicatessen, and very nice it is too! Great salad bar, good takeaway including sandwiches, pricey, but worth it. They sell expensive imported products (including Marmite!).

Due Mondi, *Santa Catalina Ancha (near Rosie O'Grady's)*. 1000-2100. At just US$0.30 per delicious Italian scoop, this is an absolute

must. There's even *chicha* flavour!

Trotamundos, *Portal Comercio 177, 2nd floor*. This is one of the most pleasant cafés in the plaza if a bit pricey (hot chocolate US$1.40). Has a balcony overlooking the plaza and a warm atmosphere especially at night with its open fire. Good coffees and cakes, safe salads, *brochetas*, sandwiches and pancakes as well as 4 computers with internet access. Open Mon-Sat 0800-2400.

Procuradores (Gringo Alley) *map p80*

Procuradores, or Gringo Alley as the locals call it, is good for a value feed and takes the hungry backpacker from Mexico to Italy, to Spain and Turkey with its menus. None is dreadful, many are very good indeed, especially for the price; do not be too worried if a tout drags you into one (demand your free *pisco sour*) before you've reached the restaurant you have chosen from the list below:

$ **Chez Maggy**, have 3 branches: La Antigua (the original) at *Procuradores 365* and, on the same street, **El Corsario** *No 344* and **Clave de D** *No 374* (opens at 0700 for buffet breakfast).

$ **El Cuate**, *Procuradores 386*. Mexican food, great value, big portions and simple salads. Recommended.

$ **Mía Pizza**, *Procuradores 379*. Good range of cheap menus, including a good curry.

$ **Paloma Imbil**, *Procuradores 362*, has doner kebabs. The *rollo mixto* is US$3 and comes in delicious home-baked bread. For vegetarians and fans of Middle Eastern food the *rollo de falafel y queso* is a tasty option.

$ **Ukuku's Restaurant**, *at the very top of the alley*, has *menús* for US$2 which include a trip to the salad bar.

Cafés, delis, panaderías and heladerías

La Tertulia, *Procuradores 50, 2nd floor*. The breakfast buffet, served 0630-1300, includes muesli, bread, yoghurt, eggs, juice and coffee, eat as much as you like for US$3, superb value, vegetarian buffet daily 1800-2200, set dinner and salad bar for US$3.50, also fondue and gourmet meals, book exchange, newspapers, classical music, open till 2300.

Yaku Mama, *Procuradores 397*. Good for breakfast, unlimited fruit and coffee, good value.

Plateros *detail map p80*

Parallel with Gringo Alley but further south-west, Plateros also has good-value food.

$$ **Kusikuy**, *Plateros 348B, T084-262870*. 0800-2300 Mon-Sat. Some say this serves the best *cuy* (guinea pig, US$10.90) in town and the owners say if you give them an hour's warning they will produce their absolute best. Many other typical Cusco dishes on the menu. Set lunch is unbeatable value at only US$2. Good service, highly recommended.

$$ **Pucará**, *Plateros 309*. 1230-2200, closed Sun. Peruvian and international food. Japanese owner does very good US$2 set lunch and excellent *ají de gallina* (garlic chicken) and cream of potato soup, pleasant atmosphere. Recommended.

$ **Ama Lur**, *Plateros 325*. This is the restaurant below **Amalu** where you go for breakfast. Clean, cheap, very good set menu for US$2 as well as tasty evening meals.

$ **Auliya**, *C Garcilaso 265, 2nd floor*. Beautifully renovated colonial house, excellent vegetarian food, also stocks a wide range of dried food for trekking.

$ **Los Candiles**, *Plateros 323*. Good set lunch for US$2.50.

$ **El Fogón**, *Plateros 365*. Huge local *menú del día* for US$1.80 – no messing around, just good solid food at reasonable prices. Very popular with locals and increasingly so with travellers.

$ **El Molino**, *Plateros 339*. Snug little place that serves excellent pizza.

Cafés, delis, panaderías and heladerías

Amaru, *Plateros 325, 2nd floor*. Limitless coffee, tea, great bread and juices served, even on non-buffet breakfasts (US$1.15 for simple). Colonial balcony. Recommended.

Café Halliy, *Plateros 363*. Popular meeting place, especially for breakfast, good for comments on guides, has good snacks and *copa Halliy* (fruit, muesli, yoghurt, honey and chocolate cake, also good vegetarian menu and set lunch).

North and northeast of the Plaza de Armas *p77, map p74*

$$$ **Fallen Angel**, *Plazoleta Nazarenas 221, T084-258184, fallenangelincusco@hotmail. com* A potent new entry into the Cusco restaurant scene, this is the 2nd venture of Cusco native Andrés Zuñiga (the other being **Macondo** – see below). Extending his creative talents even further, you could almost say that Andrés has come up with an art gallery that just happens to serve great food. A 3-m tall silver angel dominates the central courtyard of this original *conquistador* residence, and the tables consist of glass-covered bath-tubes with goldfish swimming beneath. The menu features steaks of a quality to equal any in Peru, and there are some innovative pasta dishes, including the excellent Indonesian influenced *pastatai*. Cocktails are excellent. Andrés throws parties/fashion shows on a regular basis, and these are always events to remember.

$$$ **El Monasterio**, *Palacios 136, T084-241777*. Even if you are not staying here, it is worth visiting for its food as well as its architecture. The dining room is where the monks used to sing. Main courses will set you back around US$13/14. Breakfasts are huge (perhaps 'epic' would be a better word) and cost US$17.

$$$ **Novotel**, *San Agustín 239, T084-228282*, is in another historic building. The French chef creates dishes such as king prawns in puff pastry with leek in a mango sauce for US$10.

$$ **A Mi Manera**, *corner of Triunfo and Palacio*. Great-tasting food and good value if you ask for a set menu (not often advertised).

$ **Café Cultural Ritual**, *Choquechaca 140 and also San Blas (see below)*. Good value and tasty vegetarian *menú*, including some decent Indian dishes, for US$2.20.

Cafés, delis, panaderías and heladerías

Chocolate, *Calle Choquechaca 162, T974 9343 (mob)*. Good for coffee and cakes but the real highlights are the fresh gourmet chocolates – these come up to European standards. Great for an indulgence or as a gift to chocoholic friends.

Manzana Azul, *C Choquechaca 131a*. Great cakes, especially of the chocolate variety, but the coffee is terrible.

San Blas *map p74*

$$ **La Bodega**, *146 Carmen Alto*. Snug Dutch- and Peruvian-owned café/restaurant

of just 7 tables. You'll love it. Sip creamy hot chocolate by candlelight in the afternoons and read one of the English magazines. *House of the Rising Sun* sums up choice in music. *Pisco sour* US$1.70, *pollo al vino* US$3.70. The chicken curry (US$5.50) is very good. Dishes come with side trip to salad bar. They also serve a decent American breakfast for US$2.50, and the US$1.50 lunch menu is a bargain. Highly recommended.

$$ **Greens**, *Tandapata 700, behind the church on Plazoleta San Blas, T084-243820, greens_cusco@hotmail.com* Modern international, rich-tasting food in a trendy but warm and relaxed setting with sofas to kick back in while sipping wine and reading English magazines. Famous for huge Sun roasts (lunch and dinnertime, US$10, booking essential) as well as English breakfasts (0700-1500) and curries. Vegetarian options. Desserts and toasted sandwiches available 1500-1830, choose a video to watch; restaurant re-opens 1830, closes 2300. 2-for-1 cocktails 1830-1930. Games, book exchange and library. Good but perhaps overpriced.

$$ **Macondo**, *Cuesta San Blas 571, T084-229415, macondo@telser.com.pe* Bit pricier than others in this range but fantastic. Walking into **Macondo** is like walking into an artistic creation. Owner Andrés has dreamed up a casual, cosy, arty and comfortable restaurant with sofas of iron bedsteads covered in dozens of cushions mixed with chairs, tables and candles. Walls are decorated with local art, which changes every 15 days and his mum cooks in the kitchen of this colonial house that belonged to his grandmother. Popular, gay-friendly and a steep 3-block walk from the central plaza, **Macondo** has dishes of local ingredients with an artistic twist – eg vinaigrette of passion fruit with Amazonian salad. It is also renowned for its tasty alpaca mignon à la Parisienne (US$7). Sweets US$4.30 each – the Marquis au Chocolate is great. Daiquiris (US$3.70) are delicious. Happy hour 1500-1800. The tree house upstairs is great if you are 5 ft tall, otherwise take a seat fast! Visa attracts 10% surcharge. Recommended.

$$ **Jack's Café**, *on the corner of Choquechaca and San Blas. T084-806960.* Excellent and varied menu with very generous portions, all in a light and relaxed atmosphere. The American-style pancakes are the best in town and the freshly ground local coffee really gets you started in the morning. The kitchen can become overwhelmed in busy periods, eg lunchtime. Go when it's quieter for better service. **Jack's** opens at 0630, making this a good bet for pre-tour breakfast.

$$ **Pacha-Papa**, *Plazoleta San Blas 120, opposite church of San Blas, T084-241318.* A beautiful patio restaurant in a wonderful old colonial house. Very good typical Peruvian dishes with a European influence – owner Lucho has cooked abroad and has his own style. Excellent alpaca steaks, also try the trout in caper sauce. At night diners can sit in their own, private colonial dining room. Friendly, Andean harp music. Recommended.

$$ **Witches Garden**, *Carmen Bajo 169, just off Plazoleta San Blas, T084-9623866, witchesgardenrestaurant@hotmail.com* Good Novo Andino and international cuisine served in this warmly decorated little restaurant. The furry purple sofas are a highlight. Among the many tasty options the Aguaymanto beef medallions and spring rolls are recommended. There is a TV and video, with a selection of movies, available for patrons.

$ **Café Cultural Ritual**, *Plazoleta San Blas 614.* See northeast of Plaza de Armas, above.

$ **Granja Heidi**, *Cuesta San Blas 525, T084-238383.* US$2.50 gets you an excellent 3- or 4-course *menú del día* in a clean and relaxed environment. There are usually vegetarian options.

$ **Gypsy Pub**, *Carmen Alto 162-C.* Comfortable bar/restaurant a little further down the street from La Bodega. Good *menú del día* for US$2 and the chicken is some of the best in Cusco.

$ **Hatunrumiyoc**, *on the corner of Hatunrumiyoc and Choquechaca.* Good location on the 2nd floor with a nice balcony. Decent set menu at lunchtime, often including lasagna and sometimes trout. Served with a drink and soup this will set you back around US$2.50.

Cafés, delis, panaderías and heladerías

CentroPi, *Atocsaycuchi 599, San Blas, centropi@samerica.com* Yearning for a thick wedge of pecan or lemon meringue pie? Dreaming of apple crumble served with delicious home-made custard? If so, make your way to this wonderful and very chilled spot, a short walk from the Plazoleta de San Blas (at the end of Carmen Alto). The café exhibits local and international art, screens movies from its great selection of classics (not just Hollywood!) and even has a dark room for budding photographers.

Panadería El Buen Pastor, *Cuesta San Blas 579*. Very good bread and pastries, the proceeds from which go to a charity for orphans and street children. Serves up *empanadas* and endless hot drinks. Very popular with backpackers. Recommended.

Planet Cusco, *Carmen Alto 162, T084-223010*. Great buffet breakfast (fruit salad, eggs, bread, muesli, tea/coffee and juice) in a warm and stylish atmosphere for only US$1.40, plus 10 mins free internet, make this breakfast spot an absolute bargain.

The Muse, *Tandapata 682, Plazoleta San Blas*. Funky little café with a cosy feel and great views over the plaza. Fresh coffee, locally grown in Quillabamba, good food, including highly recommended vegetarian lasagne, chicken curry and carrot cake. There's often live music in the afternoons/evenings with no cover charge. English owner Clair is very helpful. **The Muse** will refill water bottles for a small charge in an attempt to minimize plastic waste in Cusco.

East and southeast of the Plaza de Armas *p81, map p74*

$$$**Parrilla Andina**, *Maruri*. Good-value meat-fest. Mixed grill will feed 2 people for around US$15. Features beef, chicken, alpaca and pork. Restaurant is part of the former palace of the Inca, Túpac Yupanqui.

$$**Inkanato**, *Plazoleta Santo Domingo 279, interior 2A, T084-222926*. Staff dressed in Inca and Amazonian outfits should not scare you off this interesting restaurant. Kitsch it may be but you can watch the staff preparing the food in the open-plan kitchen that stretches into the dining area.

$$**Los Toldos**, *Almagro 171 y San Andrés 219*. If you're feeling peckish, on a budget and fancy being served by waiters in a bow tie you could do worse than try their great chicken *brocheta*. Comes with fries, a trip to

the salad bar and is enough for 2 people at just US$2.30. Also *trattoria* with home-made pasta and pizza, delivery *T084-229829*.

$**Chifa Sipan**, *Quera 251* (better than their other branch for tourists in Plateros). Owner Carlos may not sound Chinese but he is and joins in the cooking at this excellent restaurant. There is no great ambience but it's busy at lunchtimes with locals which speaks volumes. Skip to the back of the menu for their better deals and try *chancho* (pork) *con tamarindo* (US$4) or wonton soup and *pollo tipakay* (US$4.20).

$**Mao's**, *Plaza Túpac Amaru 826, Wanchac, T084-252323 for delivery at no extra cost*. Cusco's answer to KFC/Burger King/ Macdonald's, the most popular place in town for wood-oven grilled or roast chicken, crisp French fries, kebabs, huge mixed meat barbecues and salads. It's large, has a games park for kids and electronic and video games. Good value, look out for promotions.

South and southwest of the Plaza de Armas *p85, map 74*

$**Túpac Amaru market** To eat really cheaply, and if your stomach is acclimatized to South American food, make your main meal lunch and escape the Plaza de Armas. Head for the market 5 blocks southwest at Túpac Amaru and eat at one of the many stalls. Food will cost no more than US$0.70 and 3-fruit juices are just US$0.45! Otherwise, look for the set *menús*, usually served between 1200-1500, although they are no good for vegetarians. Between 1200 and 1400 on Puente Rosario, just off Av Sol, pick up a piece of deep-fried potato or deep-fried, battered yucca from one of the street stalls for just US$0.15.

Cafés, delis, panaderías and heladerías

Café Manu, *Av Pardo 1046*. Good coffee and good food too in a jungle decor. It would be a sin to miss one of their liqueur coffees.

Moni, *San Agustín 311, T084-231029, www.moni-cusco.com* Peruvian/English-owned, good fresh food and breakfast, British music, magazines, bright, clean and comfy.

Picarones, *Ruinas y Tullumayo*, is good for doughnuts. It is very small, very local and very typical for classic Peruvian sweet stuff.

Happy hour trail

It is possible to spend half a day hopping from one happy hour to another in Cusco.

- Rosie O'Grady's
  1300-1400 (and 2030-2130)
- Macondo's
  1500-1800 (and 2130-2300)
- Green's 1830-1930
  Cross Keys
  1830-1930 (and 2130-2200)
  Blueberry Lounge
  1830-1930 (and 2200-2300)
- Paddy Flaherty's
  1900-2000 (and 2200-2230)
  Norton's Rat 1900-2100
- Amaru 2300-2200
- Excess 2100-2400

When it's time for a kebab, you can head straight up Gringo Alley to Paloma Imbil on the right. There are late-night sandwich and burger stalls on Plateros and Saphi, which are also good for a pre-club bite.

If you are still standing it is time to hit the clubs. Their happy hours change day to day but details are on all the flyers you will have picked up on your trail. As these usually provide you with a free drink you won't care too much when happy hour is. Enjoy, but don't forget to save US$1 for your taxi home!

Bars and clubs

Bars

Plaza de Armas *p73, map p80*
Blueberry Lounge, *Portal de Carnes 235, T084-742472*. Dark, moody and sophisticated, this is a slice of London's Soho on the Plaza de Armas. There's a good menu, featuring many Asian dishes.
Cross Keys Pub, *Portal Confiturías 233 (upstairs). 1100-0130*. Run by Barry Walker of **Manu Expeditions**, a Mancunian and ornithologist, darts, cable sports, pool, bar meals, happy hours 1800-1900 and 2130-2200, plus daily half price specials Sun-Wed, great *pisco sours*, very popular, loud and raucous, great atmosphere.
Norton Rat's Tavern, *Loreto 115, 2nd floor, on the plaza but has a side entrance off a road to the left of La Compañía (same entrance as Hostal Loreto), T084-246204, nortonrats@ yahoo.com* Pleasant pub with a pool table, dart board, cable TV and lots of pictures of motorbikes! Owner Jeffrey Powers loves the machines and can provide information for bikers. There's a balcony which offers great views of the Plaza de Armas. He has opened a juice bar inside the pub serving Amazonian specials – some even said to be aphrodisiacs. Happy hour 1900-2100 every night with other

daily specials such as Whisky Wednesday.
Paddy Flaherty's, *C Triunfo 124 on the corner of the plaza*, 1300-0100. It's an Irish theme pub serving cans of Guinness (beware! They cost US$3.40 a go). This is a great pub, deservedly popular and a good place to be for the Corpus Christi procession with its views over the Plaza de Armas. Now under new management with improved seating and great food – the jacket potatoes, shepherd's pie and baguettes are all highly recommended.

Elsewhere
Amaru Quechua Café Pub, *Plateros 325, 2nd floor, T084-246976*. Bar with pizzería, also serves breakfast for US$2.50, games, happy hour 1030-1130, 2000-2200.
Km 0 (Arte y Tapas), *Tandapata 100, San Blas*. Owners José Manuel Rabanal (Spanish) and Sara Pereira (Swiss-Italian) have really brought the warmth of Mediterranean Europe with them in this lovely themed bar tucked in behind San Blas. Good snacks and tapas (of course), affordable, and with live music every night (around 2200 – lots of acoustic guitar, etc), this place is a real gem.
Mandela's Bar, *Palacio 121, 3rd floor, T084-222424, www.mandelasbar.com*

Cutting-edge new bar/restaurant with an African theme and adobe-style walls. Good atmosphere and lots of space to spread out and relax. Serves breakfast, lunch and drinks in the evening, also Sun barbecues and special events through the year. Great 360º panorama from the rooftop.

Los Perros Bar, *Tecseccocha 436, above Gringo Alley (Procuradores)*. Completely different vibe and a great place to chill out on comfy couches listening to excellent music. Owner Tammy is very friendly and welcoming and occasionally locks the doors if there's a good party atmosphere going. She regularly returns to her native Australia to research new menus; the Thai-style wantons are famous in Cusco, but also give her sautéed chicken salad (US$3.40) with avocado a go. In addition, try the thick curried soups and good coffee. The chicken curry is the closest thing to Brick Lane that you'll find in Cusco, and you even get mango chutney! There's a book exchange, English and other magazines and board games. Opens 1100 for coffee and pastries; kitchen opens at 1300. Occasionally hosts live music and special events.

Rosie O'Grady's, *at Santa Catalina Ancha 360, T084-247935*. It's open 1100 till late (food served till midnight, happy hours 1300-1400, 1800-1900, 2300-2330). Has good music, tasty food. English and Russian (!) are both spoken.

Video bars

When you've seen enough ruins, colonial architecture or are simply in need of a rest, there are plenty of video bars in which to relax. Below are some of the best places, but new ones are opening all the time.

Centro Pi, *Atocsaycuchi 599, San Blas*. This very relaxed café has a private screening room, with DVD, projector and a wide selection of classic movies... Just turn up and pick your favourite.

Cursed Dragon, *Av La Cultura 2116-B, T9743708 (mob)*. Not a video bar, but the place to go for role-playing games, *Dungeons & Dragons, Vampire*, etc. The games room is on the 2nd floor and is open

1400-2000, US$0.30 all afternoon, phone to reserve; a great place to meet local students and gamers. Also has comics, posters, toys (authorized vendor of original products), bilingual staff.

Excess, *at the bottom of Suecia (see Clubs, below)*, usually has screenings mid-afternoon and at 1800.

Green's, *behind Plazoleta San Blas*, allows customers to this restaurant to choose a video between 1500 and 1800. It works on a first-come first-served basis, so get there early if you want to choose what you watch.

Mama Africa, *to the right of the cathedral (see Clubs, below)*, has 2 showings a day at 1545 and 1800. Films are free if you buy a drink.

Sunset Video Café, *inside Hostal Royal Qosqo, turn left at the top of Gringo Alley*, shows 3 films a day: 1600, 1900, 2130. It has good sound and you can order popcorn and other snacks while you watch. US$0.70.

Ukuku's, *on Plateros*, has 2 showings at 1600 and 1800. Films are free with any purchase.

Clubs

Before your evening meal don't turn down flyers being handed out around the Plaza de Armas. Then, over dinner, you should work out your free drink circuit – for each coupon not only gives you free entry, but it is worth a *cuba libre*. On the back of this tour you will be able to check out which club is the 'in' place to be that week – they are constantly changing. If you fancy learning a few Latin dance steps before hitting the local nightlife many of the clubs offer free lessons. Ask at the door for details or look out for flyers.

Excess, *on Suecia, next door to Magtas Bar (see below)*. An old Cusco staple. Movies are shown in the late afternoon and early evening, but after midnight this place really gets going with an extremely eclectic range of music, from 60's and 70's rock and pop to techno and trance. This place seems to give out more free drinks than most, so it's a good option for kicking off a big night on the town!

El Garabato Video Music Club, *Espaderos 132, 3rd floor. Daily 1600-0300*. Dance area, lounge for chilling, bar with saddles for stools, tastefully decorated in a colonial setting, with live shows 2300-0300 (all sorts of styles) and a large screen showing music videos. Their speciality is *té piteado*, hot tea or *mate de coca* with *pisco* and brown sugar. Recommended.

Kamikaze, *Plaza Regocijo 274, T084-233865. Peña at 2200*, good old traditional rock music, candle-lit cavern atmosphere, entry US$2.50 but usually you don't have to pay.

Magtas Bar, *Suecia 302 on the corner of the plaza*. This replaces the infamous **Uptown** at the same address, with a completely renovated chill-out section and dance floor. New in 2003, it seems to be aimed at the Peruvian market, with lots of salsa and Latin beats – even so, the odd pop-classic slips in.

Mama, *Portal Belén 115, 2nd floor*. The mother of all clubs in Cusco, **Mama Africa**, has experienced a rearrangement of management and become 2 separate entities. **Mama**, on the old **Mama Africa** site, is decorated in a jungle theme, with a dance floor to the far left and a large video screen, although people dance anywhere they can. The music is middle of the road, from local music through 70's classics to the latest releases. There is something for everyone. Free entry with a pass which you can get on the plaza. The club retaining the name of **Mama Africa** *now residing in the Portal de*

Harinas, 2nd floor, claims to have cooler music and be more of a serious clubber's spot, but Footprint will leave it to you to decide.

Spoon, *Plateros 334, 2nd floor, spoonclub@ peru.com 2000-0500*. In 2003, this was the hot club in town, replacing the equally hip **Eko** at the same venue. This joint tends to play more hard-core dance, trance and techno tunes than the other nightspots, but it still verges into hip-hop and funk on occasion. Free entry with a **Spoon** card, and happy hour from 2300-2400. Nights in **Spoon** rarely come to a close before the dawn light creeps through the windows.

Tangible Myth, *San Juan de Dios 260 (on the 2nd floor, next to Hostal Frankenstein), T084-260519*. Live jazz, sometimes edging into funk and Latin rhythms, Mon to Sat, usually warming up at around 2100. This is a great place to enjoy a relaxed night out. Just kick back and enjoy the mellow vibe!

Ukuku's, *Plateros 316*. US$1.35 entry or free with a pass. This is somewhat different to the other clubs as every night there is a live band that might play anything from rock to salsa. The DJ then plays a mixture of Peruvian and international music but the emphasis is on local. It has a good mix of Cusqueños and tourists. Happy hour 0730-0930.

♪ Entertainment

Centro Qosqo de Arte Nativo, *Av Sol 604, T084-227901*. There's a regular nightly folklore show here 1900-2030, entrance fee US$3.50.

Teatro Inti Raymi, *Saphi 605,* music nightly at 1845, US$4.50 entry and well worth it.

Teatro Municipal, *C Mesón de la Estrella 149*

(T084-227321 for information 0900-1300 and 1500-1900). This is a venue for plays, dancing and shows, mostly on Thu-Sun. Ask for their programmes. They also run classes in music and dancing from Jan-Mar which are great value.

● Festivals and events

On 20 Jan is a procession of saints in the **San Sebastián** district of Cusco.

Carnival in Cusco is a messy affair with flour, water, cacti, bad fruit and animal manure thrown about in the streets. Be prepared.

Easter Mon sees the procession of **El Señor de los Temblores** (Lord of the Earthquakes), starting at 1600 outside the

cathedral. A large crucifix is paraded through the streets, returning to the Plaza de Armas around 2000 to bless the tens of thousands of people who have assembled there.

On 2-3 May the **Vigil of the Cross**, which takes place at all mountaintops with crosses on them, is a boisterous affair.

In Jun is **Corpus Christi**, on the Thu after Trinity Sunday, when all the statues of the

⁞ It's no fun at the snow festival

Qoyllur Rit'i is not a festival for the unitiated or the faint-hearted. It can be very confusing for those who don't understand the significance of this ancient ritual. To get there involves a two hour walk up from the nearest road at Mawayani, beyond Ocongate, then it's a further exhausting climb up to the glacier. It's a good idea to take a tent, food and plenty of warm clothing. Many trucks leave Cusco, from Limacpampa, in the days prior to the full moon in mid-June; prices from US$2 upwards. This is a very rough and dusty overnight journey lasting 14 hrs, requiring warm clothing and coca leaves to fend off cold and exhaustion. Several agencies offer tours (see page 113). Peter Frost writes: "The pilgrimage clearly has its origins in Inca or pre-Inca times, although the historical record dates it only from a miraculous apparition of Christ on the mountain, around 1780. It is a complex and chaotic spectacle, attended by hundreds of dance groups, and dominated by the character of the *ukuku*, the bear dancer, whose night vigil on the surrounding glaciers is the festival's best-known feature. Under the best of circumstances the journey there is lengthy, gruelling and dusty, the altitude (4,600 m at the sanctuary) is extremely taxing, the place is brutally cold, very crowded, unbelievably noisy around the clock (sleep is impossible), and the sanitary conditions are indescribable."

Cusco City Festivals & events

Virgin and of Saints from Cusco's churches are paraded through the streets to the cathedral. This is a colourful event. The Plaza de Armas is surrounded by tables with women selling *cuy* (guinea pig) and a mixed grill called *chiriuchu* (*cuy*, chicken, tortillas, fish eggs, water-weeds, maize, cheese and sausage) and lots of Cusqueña beer.

In **early Jun**, 2 weeks before Inti Raymi (see below) is the highly recommended **Cusqueño Beer Festival**, held near the rail station, which boasts a great variety of Latin American music. The whole event is well-organized and great fun. Also in **Jun** is **Qoyllur Rit'i**, (Snow Star Festival), held at a 4,700-m glacier north of Ocongate (Ausangate), 150 km southeast of Cusco. It has its final day 58 days after Easter Sun.

On **24 Jun**, **Inti Raymi**, the Inca festival of the winter solstice (see p), where locals outnumber tourists, is enacted at the fortress of Sacsayhuaman. The spectacle starts at 1000 at the Qoricancha (crowds line the streets and jostle for space to watch), then proceeds to the Plaza de Armas. From there performers and spectators go to Sacsay huaman for the main event, which starts at 1300. It lasts 2½ hrs, and is in Quechua.

Locals make a great day of it, watching the ritual from the hillsides and cooking potatoes in pits in the ground. Tickets for the stands can be bought in advance from the **Emufec** office, *Santa Catalina Ancha 325 (opposite the Complejo Policial)*, and cost US$35. Standing places on the ruins are free but get there at about 1030 as even reserved seats fill up quickly, and defend your space. Travel agents can arrange the whole day for you, with meeting points, transport, reserved seats and packed lunch. Don't believe anyone who tries to persuade you to buy a ticket for the right to film or take photos. On the night before **Inti Raymi**, the Plaza de Armas is crowded with processions and food stalls. Try to arrive in Cusco 15 days before Inti Raymi. The atmosphere in the town during the build up is fantastic and something is always going on (festivals, parades, etc).

On the last Sun in **Aug** is the **Huarachicoy Festival** at Sacsayhuaman, a spectacular re-enactment of the Inca manhood rite, performed in dazzling costumes by boys of a local school.

On **8 Sep**, the **Day of the Virgin**, there is a colourful procession of masked dancers from the church of Almudena, at the

Corpus Christi in Cusco

Corpus Christi is an annual festival celebrated on the Thursday after Trinity Sunday (generally in early June) by Roman Catholics everywhere. In Cusco, Corpus is an exuberant and colourful pageant where profound faith and prayer share predominance with abundant eating and copious drinking.

All the Saints and Virgins are paraded through the city to the Plaza de Armas and, after being blessed, they are carried into the great cathedral to be placed in prearranged order, in two rows facing each other. The images are kept in the cathedral until the *octava* (the eighth day after their internment), when they are all escorted in procession back to their respective parishes and churches.

During these days and nights in each others' company, the Saints and Virgins, so the stories go, decide among themselves the future of the people for the forthcoming year. It is also said that they gamble at dice. Five hundred years ago, at the very same time of year and in this precise location, the mummified remains of the Incas were paraded in similar fashion and then laid in state. They consulted the Sun, the Moon, the Lightning and the Rains to learn what fate these elements were to bring in the course of the following year.

The Saints are the first in the parade. The traditional race between San Jerónimo and San Sebastián is a joyous event. San Cristóbal, carved from a single tree trunk, is an elaborately painted figure, who leans upon a great staff. His powerful muscles and thick sinews forever shoulder the body of the infant Jesus as they ford a river. It is the heaviest statue of all and popular legend tells that underneath it lies a *huaca*, or sacred rock.

Santiago, the warrior saint and patron of Cusco, enters astride his white horse, brandishing a sword. Trampled under the hooves of his steed lies a vanquished demon in the likeness of a Moorish soldier. Santiago's name was the battle cry of the Spanish soldiers, but he soon came to represent Illapa, the Andean deity of Thunder and Lightning.

Next come the Virgins, dressed in pomp, some accompanied by archangels and cherubs. They are seen as the equivalent of the Mother Earth, *Pachamama*. The Virgin of Belén is always first, escorted by San José, who stands by the entrance to the cathedral, waiting for all the Virgins to be carried inside. Santa Bárbara, the pregnant virgin, is the last.

Corpus is perhaps the city's greatest event. All the streets and the huge Plaza de Armas are thronged with enormous crowds. The revered images, each several hundred years old and from a distinct parish of the city, command a host of fervent followers, including a band of musicians and troupe of dancers. Most important and conspicuous are the bearers, whose strenuous efforts are relieved at resting points, known as *descansos*. The bier carrying the image is put on top of a scaffold and the bearers and followers are all given a round of *chicha*, and/or beer, while the band plays on and Ave Marias are prayed one after the other, like a mantra. The respite over, one final toast is made to the statue, also to *Pachamama* and to the surrounding mountain summits, *los apus*. In many cases this is accompanied by fresh coca leaves and lime. Then the parade resumes its journey. As the processions converge upon the centre, they merge together into a larger procession, which becomes engulfed by the multitudes in the Plaza de Armas. The images as they are carried along seem to become swaying vessels navigating a sea of humanity, riding its waves.

southwest edge of Cusco, near Belén, to the Plaza de San Francisco. There is also a fair at Almudena, and a bull fight on the following day.

On **8 Dec** is **Cusco Day**, when churches and museums close at 1200. And, on **24**

Dec, when all
tucked up
buying
of Ch
m

collection of Ande
designed by Japa
La Pérez, Urb N
Huanchac, T08
with a good
free pick-u
Primitiv
www.c
conte
the

◯ Shopping

Arts and crafts

Cusco has some of the best craft shopping in all Peru. In the Plaza San Blas and the surrounding area, authentic Cusco crafts still survive and woodworkers can be seen in almost any street. A market is held on Sat.

In its drive to 'clean up' Cusco, the authorites have moved the colourful artisans' stalls from the pavements of Plaza Regocijo to the main market at the bottom of **Av Sol**. There are, however, small markets of 10 or so permanent stalls dotted around the city which offer goods made from alpaca as well as modern materials. For example, at *Plateros 334*, the first stall in the doorway will tailor-make reversible fleeces in 2 colours for US$10.

Cusco is also the weaving centre of Peru and excellent textiles can be found at good value; but watch out for sharp practices when buying gold and silver objects and jewellery. Note that much of the wood used for picture frames, etc, is *cedro*, a rare timber not extracted by sustainable means.

Leading artisans who welcome visitors include the following:
Hilario Mendivil, *Plazoleta San Blas 634 and 619*, who makes biblical figures from plaster, wheatflour and potatoes.
Edilberta Mérida, *Carmen Alto 133*, who makes earthenware figures showing the physical and mental anguish of the indigenous peasant.
Antonio Olave Palomino, *Plazoleta San Blas 651*, makes reproductions of pre-Columbian ceramics and colonial sculptures.
Maximiliano Palomino de la Sierra, *Triunfo 393*, produces festive dolls and traditional wood-carvings.
Santiago Rojas, *Suytuccato 751, above San Blas*, makes statuettes.
Coordinadora Sur Andina de Artesanía, *C del Medio 130, off Plaza de Armas*, has a good assortment of crafts and is a non-profit

making organiz
Feria Artesanal Te
334. Daily 0900-2300. Ti.
corner of San Andrés and C.
good for local handicrafts.
Mercado Artesanal, *Av Sol, block 4, .*
for cheap crafts.
Museo Inca Art Gallery, *Huancaro M-B - L8,*
T084-231232 (PO Box 690), telephone between
0900 and 2100. Run by Amílcar Salomón Zorrilla, a good place for contemporary art.
Nemesio Villasante, *Av 24 de Junio 415,*
T084-222915. For Paucartambo masks.

Upmarket shops
Agua y Tierra, *Plazoleta Nazarenas 167, and also at Cuesta San Blas 595, T084-226951.* Excellent quality crafts from lowland rainforest communities, largely the Shipibo and Ashaninka tribes from the Selva Central whose work is considered to be among the finest in the Amazon Basin.
Andean Spirit, *Hatun Rumiyoc 487-B, T084-232962.* Potter Lucho Soler claims to use traditional Inca methods in his work. Whether this is true or not the ceramics on display are excellent, the quality beyond reproach.
Maky Artesanías, *Carmen Alto 101, T084-653643.* A great place to buy individually designed ceramics. Ask for discounts if buying several pieces.
La Mamita, *Portal de Carnes 244, Plaza de Armas*, sells the ceramics of Seminario-Behar, (see p141), plus cotton, basketry, jewellery, etc. A visit is highly recommended for those who cannot get to their studio in Urubamba.
Miori-Bernasconi Collection, *T084-271215, T965 2975 (mob).* The private collection of Andean art may be viewed by appointment. Pallay-Andean textile website www.geo cities.com/SoHo/Atrium/7785/ Quechua and Aymara pieces, 18th-19th century, antique coins, wooden *keros* and other objects.
Pedazo de Arte, *Plateros 334B.* A tasteful

n handicrafts, many
nese owner Miki Suzuki.
ateo Pumacahua 598,
4-232186. A big cooperative
selection. They will arrange a
p from your hotel.
, Hatun Rumiyoc 495, San Blas,
scio.com Excellent Peruvian
mporary art gallery, largely featuring
work of Federico Coscio.

lpaca and llama clothing and fabrics
Alpaca 111, *Plaza Regocijo 202, T084-243233*.
High-quality alpaca clothing, with shops also
in hotels **Monasterio**, **Libertador** and **Machu
Picchu Sanctuary Lodge** and at the airport.
Alpaca 3, *Ruinas 472*, and **Cuzmar II**, *Portal
Mantas 118T* (English spoken), also sell
quality alpaca items.
Away, *Procuradores 361, T084-229465*. Sells
blankets, leather goods and handmade shoes,
prices from US$15-40 for a pair, allow 2 days
delivery for your own design.
La Casa de la Llama, *Palacio 121,
www.llamactiva.com* The amount of fuss
and attention that gets given to alpaca
textiles these days and you'd be forgiven for
thinking that the poor old llama is only good
for hauling things around, being turned into
steaks in the city's various eateries or,
perhaps as a last resort, posing in photos
with tourists. Apparently this is not the case,
as this smart establishment proves rather
well, with a variety of excellent quality,
well-designed llama wool sweaters, scarves
and llama-leather bags.
**The Center for Traditional Textiles of
Cusco**, *Av Sol 603-A, T084-228117*. A non-profit
organization that seeks to promote, refine and
rediscover the weaving traditions of the area.
Tours of workshops in Chinchero and beyond
can de arranged, also weaving classes. In the
Cusco outlet you can watch weavers at work.
The textiles are of excellent quality and the
price reflects the fact that over 50% goes
direct to the weaver. Recommended.
Josefina Olivera, *Portal Comercio 173, Plaza
de Armas*. She sells old ponchos and antique
mantas (shawls), without the usual haggling.
Her prices are high, but it is worth it to save
pieces being cut up to make other items,
open daily 1100-2100.
Mon Repos, *Portal de Panes 139, Plaza de
Armas, T084-251600*. High-quality alpaca

clothing, expensive, but nicely presented
and with a wide selection.

Traditional musical instruments
Ima Sumac, *Triunfo 338, T084-244722*.
Taki Museo de Música de los Andes,
Hatunrumiyoq 487-5. Shop and workshop
selling and displaying musical instruments,
knowledgeable owner, who is an
ethnomusicologist. Recommended for
anyone interested in Andean music.

Jewellery
Carlos Chaquiras, *Triunfo 375 y Portal
Comercio 107, T084-227470,
www.carloschaquiras.com* 1000-1930. Very
upmarket, with lots of Inca figures, among
other designs, enhanced with semi-precious
stones and shells.
Joyería H Ormachea, *Plateros 372,
T084-237061*. Handmade gold and silver.
Spondylus, *Cuesta San Blas 505 y Plazoleta
San Blas 617, T084-226929,
spondyluscusco@mixmail.com* Interesting
jewellery in gold and silver, also using
semi-precious stones and shells. If you're
feeling creative and have your own jewellery
designs they'll make them up for you for a
reasonable fee. They sell some nice T-shirts
featuring Inca and pre-Inca designs.

Bookshops

**Centro de Estudios Regionales Andinos
Bartolomé de las Casas**, *Heladeros 129A*.
Good books on Peruvian history,
archaeology, etc, Mon-Sat 1100-1400,
1600-1900. The main branch, with the best
selection, is at *Limacpampa Grande 571,
Plaza Limacpampa*.
Jerusalem, *Heladeros 143, T084-235408*,
English books, guidebooks, music, postcards,
book exchange.
SBS (Special Book Services), *Av Sol 781-A,
opposite the post office, T084-248106*. Sells
Footprint's *South American Handbook*, *Peru
Handbook* and *Cusco and Inca Trail Handbook*.

Camping equipment

There are several places on Plateros which
rent out equipment but check it carefully as
it is common for parts to be missing. An
example of prices per day: tent US$3-5,

sleeping bag US$2 (down), US$1.50 (synthetic), stove US$1. A deposit of US$100 is asked, plus credit card, passport or plane ticket. Wherever you hire equipment, check the stoves carefully. White gas (*bencina*) costs US$1.50 per litre and can be bought at hardware stores, but check the purity. Stove spirit (*alcohol para quemar*) is available at pharmacies. Blue gas canisters, costing US$5, can be found at some hardware stores and at shops which rent gear. You can also rent equipment through travel agencies.
Soqllaq'asa Camping Service, *Plateros 365 No 2F, T084-252560*. Owned by English-speaking Sra Luzmila Bellota Miranda, recommended for equipment hire, from down sleeping bags (US$2 per day) to gas stoves (US$1 per day) and **ThermaRest** mats (US$1 per day); pots, pans, plates, cups and cutlery are all provided free by the friendly staff. They also buy and sell camping gear and make alpaca jackets, open Mon-Sat 0900-1300, 1600-2030, Sun 1800-2030.

Markets

To buy back your stolen camera, visit the Santiago area of Cusco on Sat morning There are a number of options.
San Jerónimo, *just out of town*, see p194, is the new location of the wholesale Sat morning fruit and vegetable market, but food just as good and not much more expensive (and washed) can be bought at the markets in town: **Huanchac**, *Av Garcilaso (not to be confused with C Garcilaso)*, or **Santa Ana**, *opposite Estación San Pedro*, which sells a variety of goods. The best value is at closing time or in the

rain. Take care after dark. Sacks to cover rucksacks are available in the market for US$0.75. Both Huanchac and Santa Ana open every day from 0700.

Just down from **Santiago Church** (an unsafe area at night because of drunks high on chemically produced alcohol) is a sprawling affair of stall upon stall laid out on the pavements. Everything from stolen car jacks to useless junk is for sale – well, would you have use for the arm of a doll or a broken-off piece of computer motherboard? It's a fascinating sight – just be sensible and leave the other camera at home.

The second less legitimate market – but equally well tolerated by Cusqueño authorities – is **El Molino**, *under the Puente Grau*, for contraband goods brought in from abroad without duty or tax being paid. Everything from computers to hi-fis, personal stereos to trekking boots, cheap camera film to wine can be bought here (take a taxi for US$0.60). It is clean and safe (but take the usual common sense precautions about valuables) and is open daily 0600-2030.

On Sat mornings you may see small plazas around the city for **furniture markets** where beds and wardrobes are sold at a fraction of the store price. **Plaza Túpac Amaru** doubles this up with a flower market, running from around 1000.

Supermarkets

La Canasta, *Av La Cultura 2000 block*. Very well stocked, takes credit cards, ATM outside. **D'Dinos Market**, *Av La Cultura 2003,*

SOUTH AMERICAN EXPLORERS
http://www.SAexplorers.org

Want to VOLUNTEER, STUDY, TRAVEL or EXPLORE?
JOIN the SOUTH AMERICAN EXPLORERS now!
Visit our clubhouses in Lima & Cusco (Peru) and Quito (Ecuador)

Call us at 800-274-0568 or 607-277-0488. You may also visit us at www.SAexplorers.org or email us at info@SAexplorers.org

⁝ Choosing a tour operator for the Inca Trail

To choose a tour group start first with the price. If the cost is under US$180, then you should be concerned. Bear in mind that the company has to pay for your train fare (US$59.50 for the full Backpackers' fare from Cusco, or US$47.20 from Ollantaytambo), US$50 to get you into Machu Picchu as well as supply food and equipment. If they're cutting costs this means that something has to give and usually this is the salary of the guides and porters (see The Inka Porter Project, page 168). However, you won't always get what you pay for. Agencies often pool their clients together to create commercially viable groups and trekkers sometimes find, en route, they paid hundreds of dollars more than others.

Ask the tour agencies some general questions and, if you're lucky, get them to put their answers in writing. Then, if you have a complaint, you can take it to Indecopi (see page 72) on your return and seek compensation. As well as the questions listed below, also ask if there's a toilet and dining tent (if this concerns you); if they carry a first aid kit which must (under the new regulations) include an oxygen bottle; do they carry radios; and, most of all, does the price include the return train ticket? Trekkers have been caught out unable to pay for their fare home – there is no bank in Aguas Calientes. Check also if the train takes you back all the way. The budget tour

companies buy the cheapest ticket back to Ollantaytambo and from there put you on a bus. This does, in fact, shave an hour off the 4½-hour return journey, but many are expected to stump up the US$2.85 bus fare. This should be part of the deal. Ask to see the equipment if possible (it has been known for tent pegs to be missing!), otherwise ask what tents they supply (some leak – this is the most frequent complaint we hear of). How good is the sleeping mat and sleeping bag (you need a down bag – pluma), if these are supplied?

Agencies vary in quality from week to week, season to season, but we can give the hassled reader some more concrete advice. The expensive agencies are all dependable. In the mid-range price bracket, **United Mice** consistently receives good reports for the Inca Trail. **SAS** is also excellent with only the odd bad report. At the budget end of the market, agencies band clients together to form groups so you don't always know who will be running the trip. This makes it difficult to recommend one above the other. However, **Wayki Trek** and **Exotic Adventures** have both received generally good reports.

Many of these agencies have their main offices away from the city centre, but have a local contact, mobile phone or hotel contact downtown.

T084-252656 for home delivery. Open 24-hrs, well supplied, takes credit cards.
Dimart, *Matará 271 y Av La Cultura 742*. Daily 0700-2200, credit cards accepted.
Gato's Market, *Portal Belén 115*.
El Pepito, *Plaza San Francisco,* Mon-Sat

0900-2000, closed lunchtime. Sells a wide variety of imported goods and also has a delicatessen, stocks multi-packs of food (eg chocolate bars) much cheaper than other shops, a good bargain for trekking supplies.
Shop Market, *Plateros 352.* Daily 1000-0300.

▲ Tours and activities

There are a million and one tour operators in Cusco, most of whom are packed into the Plaza de Armas. The sheer number and variety of tours on offer is bewildering and prices for the same tour can vary dramatically. Do not deal with guides who claim to be employed by the agencies listed below without verifying their credentials. You should only deal directly with the agencies and seek advice from visitors returning from trips for the latest information. Agencies listed below are included under the field in which they are best known and for which they receive consistent recommendations. Many of these, and the alternatives they offer, can be found in the trip reports in the **South America Explorers'** clubhouse at *Choquechaca 188* (you must join first – it's excellent value). Beware also of tours which stop for long lunches at expensive hotels.

Ask questions such as: What is the itinerary? How many meals a day are there? What will the food be? Does the guide speak English (some have no more than a memorized spiel and every ruin is a 'sacred special place')? In general also beware agencies quoting prices in dollars then converting to soles at an unfavourable rate when paying. Check if there are cancellation fees. Students will normally receive a discount on production of an ISIC card.

Inca Trail and general tours

It is now impossible to trek the Inca Trail independently following regulations brought in at the beginning of 2001 (see p164).

Andean Life, *Plateros 372, T084-221491, www.andeanlife.com* Offer a number of variations on the Inca Trail, as well as Salkantay and Ausangate, day trips in and around Cusco and jungle trips.

Andes Nature Tours, *Garcilaso 210, Casa del Abuelo, oficina 217, T084-245961, ant@terra.com.pe* Owner Aurelio speaks excellent English and has 25 years' experience in Cusco and will tailor treks 'anywhere'. Specializes in natural history, trekking, botany and birdwatching. Machu

Picchu 4-day/3-night US$321 (cheaper if part of a group).

Andina Travel, *Plazoleta Santa Catalina 219, T084-251892, www.andinatravel.com* Agency specializing in trekking and biking. Among treks offered are Salcantay to Ollantaytambo, 7 nights, US$500 for 4-5 people, and the Ausangate Circuit, 6 nights, again US$500 for 4-6 people. One of the company's specialities is the Lares Valley programme, which works together with some of the valley's traditional weaving communities and provides employment for village residents; 4 nights with 4-6 people US$300. Recommended.

Apu Expediciones, *T084-271215, T995 7483 (mob), www.geocities.com/apuexpeditions* Deals mostly through internet. Cultural, adventure, educational/academic programmes, nature tours and jungle packages to Manu and Tambopata, bilingual personnel, very knowledgeable. Andean textiles a speciality. Mariella Bernasconi Cillóniz has 19 years' experience and can plan individually customized trips, as well as traditional and alternative routes to Machu Picchu.

Big Foot, *Triunfo 392 (oficina 213), T084-238568, www.bigfootcusco.com* Specialists in tailor-made hiking trips, especially in the remote corners of the Vilcabamba and Vilcanota mountains. On the more conventional side their Inca Trail will cost US$250 for 4-6 people, Salcantay to Machu Picchu with 6-9 people US$350 and Ausangate US$350-400, depending on the route taken.

Carla's Travel, *Plateros 320, T084-228454, T993 0855 (mob), carlastravel@telser.com* Cheap and cheerful – this is about as economical as they come, but as long as you have realistic expectations you should be fine. Inca Trail 4-day/3-night US$190 – excludes sleeping bag and bus from Machu Picchu to Aguas Calientes. Group size 12-16 people. Will also arrange treks to Ausangate with a minimum of 4 people US$80 – excludes sleeping bag.

Cóndor Travel, *C Saphi 848-A, T084-225961, www.condortravel.com.pe (for flights diviajes@condortravel.com.pe)* A high-

quality, exclusive agency that will organize trips throughout Peru and the rest of the world. They have a specialized section for adventure travel and are representatives for **American Airlines**, **Servivensa**, **Avensa**, **Continental** and most other international airlines with ticket sales, connections, etc. They have many programmes to complement business trips and conferences.
Destinos Turísticos, *Portal de Panes 123, oficina 101-102, Plaza de Armas, T084-228168, www.destinosturisticosperu.com* The owner speaks Spanish, English, Dutch and Portuguese and specializes in package tours from economic to 5-star budgets. Individuals are welcome to come in for advice on booking jungle trips to renting mountain bikes. Sacred Valley tours cost US$10 excluding lunch and groups are a maximum of 20 people. Ask in advance if you require guides with specific languages. Very informative and helpful.
Ecotrek Peru, *Choquechaca 229, T084-253653, T974 8058 (mob), www.ecotrekperu.com* Scot and long-time Cusco resident Fiona Cameron runs this

environmentally friendly tour agency from her spacious flat a couple of minutes' walk from the plaza. Fiona supplies biodegradable soap on all her trips and is often involved in river clean-ups in the area. Tour specialities currently focus on adventurous mountain biking trips in remote highland areas and jungle expeditions to the Pongo de Mainique and beyond. Prices vary depending on the type of service required, however, Maras/Moray biking trips start at around US$35 a day and a 2-day biking trip from the Abra de Lares (minimum 4 people) would start at around US$120 per person. A biking descent from the cloudforests of the Abra de Málaga to Quillabamba (3 days) entails a loss of 3,300 m in altitude – this should get any biker's adrenaline flowing!
Enigma, *C Garcilaso 132, T084-222155, www.enigmaperu.com* A new adventure tour agency run by Spaniard Silvia Rico Coll. **Enigma** has rapidly gained an excellent reputation for well-organized and innovative trekking expeditions in the region. In addition to the regular Inca Trail (US$245), she offers some new and interesting routes

TAMBO TOURS

ADVENTURE
TRIPS TO THE
TAMBOPATA
RESERCH CENTER
&
AMAZON

Daily departures for
groups & individuals.

Offices in the
US & CUZCO
Experience since
1988

toll free:
US & Canada... **1-888-2GO-PERU** (246-7378)

www.2GOPERU.com e-mail - tambo@tambotours.com

International:
001-281-528-9448
fax: 281-528-7378

TAMBO TOURS PO BOX 60541- HOUSTON, TEXAS 77205

in the Ausangate area, 5 nights for US$295; Lares Valley, 3 nights US$220; also some longer routes, for example Vilcabamba to Machu Picchu for 6 nights US$455. Silvia also runs cultural tours such as visits to traditional weaving communities and Ayahuasca Therapy.

Exotic Adventures, *Plateros 325, 2nd floor, T084-243826, www.exotic-adventures.com* One of the better budget operators. 4- day/ 3-night Inca Trail US$240; 2 days/1 night US$165. Maximum 10 people in a group, minimum 4 (at these prices). They offer a 9-day Huancacalle to Cachora trek, via Choquequirao and the pass of Choqueta-carpo at 4,600 m – a magnificent trek. With 4 clients this costs US$350 per person.

Explorandes, *Av Garcilaso 316-A (not to be confused with C Garcilaso in the centre), T084-245700, www.explorandes.com* Experienced high-end adventure company. Their main office is in Lima, *San Fernando 320, Miraflores, T01-445 0532*, however trips can also be arranged from Cusco. A 5-day/4-night Inca Trail costs US$590. They arrange a wide variety of mountain treks including some in Cordillera Blanca and Huayhuash further north. Also offered are single and multi-day sea kayaking trips on Lake Titicaca using professional equipment; 3 days/2 nights US$190. Through the website you can book a 13-day/12-night trip down the Río Tambopata, from mountains to rainforest. Also arranges tours across Peru for lovers of orchids, ceramics or textiles. Award-winning environmental practices.

Gatur Cusco, *Puluchapata 140 (a small street off Av Sol 3rd block), T084-223496, gatur@terra.com.pe* Esoteric, ecotourism, and general tours. Owner Dr José (Pepe) Altamirano is knowledgeable in Andean folk traditions. Excellent conventional tours, bilingual guides and transportation. City tour US$10 (US$10 general entry ticket not included), Sacred Valley US$25 and includes lunch. 1-day 1st-class train ride private trip to Machu Picchu is US$360 with lunch in the **Machu Picchu Sanctuary Lodge Hotel**. Guides speak English, French, Spanish and German. They can also book internal flights.

Inca Explorers, *Suecia 339, T084-241070, www.incaexplorers.com* Specialist trekking agency with a good reputation for small group expeditions executed in socially and

environmentally responsible manner. 4-day 3-night Inca Trail US$379. More demanding, adventurous trips include a 2-week hike in the Cordillera Vilcanota (passing Nevado Ausangate) for US$780, based on a group of 10 clients, and Choquequirao to Espíritu Pampa, again for 2 weeks and for the same price.

Kantu Perú, *Portal Carrizos 258, T084-243673, T965 0202 (mob), kantukik@telser.com.pe* Changing offices in late 2003, so the mobile number or email may be the best point of reference – another possibility is to contact them through **Hostel Glorie**, *C San Cristóbal 190*. Run by the enthusiastic, amiable Polack brothers who speak French and English. They organize all aspects of travel in Peru but specialize in adventure travel by trail bike and 4WD vehicles. Trips can be as long as 16 days, or vehicles can be hired daily, with or without a guide. They have all the back-up and equipment you would expect from a company that won the best agency award in 2000, including satellite telephones. 4WD vehicles cost US$120-140 per day with driver and full tank of fuel, 150 km free, then US$0.25 per extra km (extra for a guide). Trail bikes can be rented for US$35 for 250cc, US$45 for 600cc (extra for a guide). If you want to do the trip to the 4 mountain lakes and the Inca grass bridge (see p204) they can provide a vehicle with a guide/driver. They also specialize in mystic/religious tours and trips into Chile, Bolivia, Ecuador and Brazil.

Kinjyo Travel Service, *Av Sol 761, T084-231121, travel_express@msn.com* An agency that also deals with group bookings from overseas but they will arrange personalized itineraries for groups. They will book all international/national flights.

Lima Tours, *Av Machu Picchu D-24, Urb Mañuel Prado, T084-228431, www.limatours. com.pe* Offers a 5-day/4-night Inca Trail package for US$240-380 (depending on the number of clients) leaving daily between Mar-Nov. Sleeping bags are not included. They also offer city tours for US$11 (excluding entrance fees) and Sacred Valley tours for US$30, including lunch.

Liz's Explorer, *Medio 114B, T084-246619, www.lizexplorer.com* Inca Trail 4-day/ 3-night US$225 (minimum group size 10, maximum 16), other lengths of trips available including 1 day for US$110. Liz

...ly laid out list of what is and ...cluded. Down sleeping bags ...er day extra, fibre bags US$2. If ...de who speaks a language ...an English let her know in advance. City tours US$5-8 (not including entry fees) and Sacred Valley US$8 (not including lunch). Majority of reports are good.

Machete Tours, *Tecseccocha 161, T084-224829, T969 2369 (mob), info@machete tours.com* Founded by born-and-bred jungle hand Ronaldo and his Danish partner Tina, **Machete** were originally a specialist Manu operator for budget clients (to the cultural zone), however, expansion in the last couple of years has seen them add many innovative trekking trips. Especially recommended is a complete 8-day traverse of the Cordillera Vilcabamba from the Apurímac Canyon and Choquequirao across the range to Machu Picchu itself. With a minimum of 5 people, this trek, with horse and mule support, costs around $400. They also offer expeditions to Espíritu Pampa, Ausangate and, of course, the Inca Trail. They have recently opened a new rainforest lodge on the remote Río Blanco, south of the Manu Biosphere Reserve. Not all of the guides speak English so check this before trip details are confirmed. Eric is a recommended guide for Choquequirao.

Naty's Travel Agency, *Triunfo 338-42, T084-239437, www.natystravel.com* Inca Trail 4-day/3-night US$195 – excludes sleeping bag. Groups of 8-16 people. Guides speak English. Will organize all other trips including Puerto Maldonaldo and special fiestas. They also sell air tickets.

Peruvian Andean Treks, *Av Pardo 705, T084-225701, www.andeantreks.com* Open Mon-Fri 0900-1300, 1500-1800, Sat 0900-1300. Manager Tom Hendrickson has 5-day/4-night Inca Trail for US$500 using high-quality equipment and satellite phones. His 7-day/6-night Vilcanota Llama Trek to Ausangate (the mountain visible from Cusco) costs US$639 and includes a collapsible pressure chamber for altitude sickness. Incas and Llamas tour attaches this to Inca Trail for a total of US$1,452.

Peru Treks and Adventures, *Garcilaso 265 oficina 13 (2nd floor), T084-805863, www.perutreks.com* New trekking agency set up by Englishman Mike Weston and his partner Koqui González. They pride themselves on good treatment of porters and support staff (and tourists!). Treks offered include Salkantay, the Lares Valley and Vilcabamba Vieja. Prices depend on group size. Mike also runs the **Andean Travel Web**, *www.andeantravel web.com*, a web-based information service focusing on socially and environmentally sustainable tourism in the region.

Q'ente, *Garcilaso 210, int 210b, T084-222535, www.qente.com* Inca Trail 4-day/3-night, US$298 – excludes sleeping bag (rent fibre bag for US$8). Their Inca Trail service is recommended. They will organize private treks to Salkantay, Ausangate, Choquequirao, Vilcabamba and Q'eros. Prices depend on group size. Sacred Valley Tours US$15, also day tours to Piquillacta and Tipón, and Moras and Moray, enquire for prices. Horse riding to local ruins costs US$25 for 4-5 hrs. Very good, especially with children.

Servicios Aéreos AQP SA, *T084-243229, 24 hrs T084-620585, aqpsa-cusco@mail.inter place.com.pe* Offers a wide variety of tours within the country, agents for **American**, **Continental**, **LAB** and other airlines; head office in Lima, *Los Castaños 347, San Isidro, T01-2223312*.

Sky Travel, *Santa Catalina Ancha 366, interior 3-C (down alleyway next to Rosie O'Grady's pub), T084-261818, F084-261414*. English spoken. General tours around city (US$8, not including entry tickets) and Sacred Valley (US$18 including buffet lunch). Prides itself on leaving 30 mins before other groups, thus reaching sights and the lunch spot (!) before anyone else. 4-day/3-night Inca Trail is US$215 in good-sized double tents and a dinner tent. Continuing with the theme of concern for food, the group is asked what it would like on the menu 2 days before departure. Other trips include Vilcabamba and Ausangate (trekking only).

SAS Travel, *Portal de Panes 143, T084-237292 (staff in a 2nd office at Medio 137, mainly deal with jungle information and only speak Spanish), www.sastravel.com* Discount for SAE members and students. Inca Trail 4-day/3-night US$295 excludes sleeping bags (can rent down bags for US$12, fibre bags for US$8), the bus down from Machu Picchu to Aguas Calientes and lunch on the last day. SAS have their own hostel in Aguas

Calientes – if clients wish to stay in Aguas after the trail and return the next morning this can be arranged at no extra cost. Group sizes are between 8 and 16 people. To go in a smaller group, costs rise considerably. A personal porter costs US$35 for up to 9 kg carried and US$70 for up to 18 kg. They carry a cooking, dining and toilet tent. Before setting off they ensure you are told everything that is included and give advice on what personal items should be taken. Manu 8-day/7-night US$690, combination of platform camping and lodges. Also mountain bike, horse riding and rafting trips can be organized. All guides speak English (some better than others). Booking is available by email at no extra charge. They can book internal flights at much cheaper rates than booking from overseas. Robyn is Australian and very helpful. Responsible, good equipment and food.

Tambo Tours, *PO Box 60541, Houston, Texas 77205, and 23115 Calico Corners, Suite 1001, Spring, TX 77373, USA, T1-800-997 7378/1-888-246 7378, T001-281-528 9448, www.2GOPERU.com* Customized trips to the Amazon and archaeological sites of Peru for groups and individuals. Daily departures.

Top Vacations, *T965 1414 (mob), www.hikingperu.com* This company has closed its central Cusco office and therefore largely arranges tours through the internet. It no longer operates classic Inca Trail treks, preferring instead to concentrate on more remote, less beaten paths. 8-day treks to Espíritu Pampa, with, for example, 6 clients costs US$350; 7 days/6 nights around Ausangate US$150 with a minimum of 4 clients; 4-day/3-night Lares Valley Trek, also with 4 clients US$175.

Trekperu, *Ricaldo Palma N-9, Santa Mónica, T084-252899, www.trekperu.com* Experienced trek operator as well as other adventure sports and mountain biking. Offers 'culturally sensitive' tours. US$385 (with 4 clients), 5-day/4-night Cusco Biking Adventure visits Tipón ruins, Huacarpa Lake, Ninamarca burial towers, Paucartambo, Tres Cruces (superb views over Manu) as well as Pisac and Cusco. Includes support vehicle and good camping gear. Need sleeping bag. Inca Trail (5 days/4 nights) US$640.

Tucan Travel, *T084-241123, cuzco@tucan travel.com* Offer adventure tours and overland expeditions.

United Mice, *Plateros 351y Triunfo 392, T084-221139, www.unitedmice.com* Inca Trail, 4 days/3 nights, US$250 – excludes sleeping bag (US$12), bus back from Machu Picchu. Private porter costs US$80. Good English-speaking guides; Salustio speaks Italian and Portuguese. Discount with student card, good food and equipment. City Tours US$6 in Spanish and English, US$7 only in English, Sacred Valley Tours US$12 in Spanish and English, US$15 only in English. Staff speak English. They offer treks to Choquequirao for 5 days/4 nights for US$220.

Wayki Trek, *Procuradores 44, T084-224092, waykitrek@hotmail.com* Budget travel agency, recommended for their Inca Trail service 4 days/3 nights US$220 or 2 days/1 night US$175. Owner Leo grew up in the countryside near Ollantaytambo and knows the area very well. They run treks to several almost unknown Inca sites including Quillarumiyoc, described as a structure for mapping the lunar year. Leo offers many interesting variations on the 'classic' Inca Trail. They also run treks to Ausangate, Salkantay and Choquequirao.

River rafting, mountain biking and trekking

For rafting, unless you are on a tight budget, **Amazonas Explorers** come highly recommended. Among the budget operators **Instinct**, **Mayuc**, **Swissraft** and **Southern Rivers** have received good reports for rafting services. When looking for an operator please consider more than just the price of your tour. Competition between companies in Cusco is intense and price wars can lead to compromises in safety as corners are cut or less experienced (and therefore cheaper) guides are hired. Consider the quality of safety equipment (lifejackets, etc) and the number and experience of rescue kayakers and support staff. On a large and potentially dangerous river like the Apurímac (where fatalities have occurred), this can make all the difference. Much of the advice given on pages 113 and 112 also applies here. See also Sport and activities p 52.

Amazonas Explorers, *PO Box 722, Cusco, T084-227137, www.amazonas-explorer.com*

Experts in rafting, hiking and biking; used by BBC. English owner Paul Cripps has great experience, but takes most bookings from overseas (*T01874-658125 in England, Jan-Mar or T01437-891743, year-round*). However, he may be able to arrange a trip for travellers in Cusco. Rafting includes Río Apurímac (4-day/3-night, US$635) and Río Tambopata including Lake Titicaca and Cusco, all transfers from Lima (16-day/15-night, US$2,400). Also 5-day/4-night Inca Trail, US$695. Paul offers a 14-day expedition to the Río Tuichi in Bolivia, including several days of grade III and IV rafting for US$2,040. This is a rugged wilderness decent from the mountains to the tropical forests of Madidi National Park. Rafting and trekking trips also combined.

Apumayo, *C Garcilaso 265 interior 3, T084-246018 (Lima: T01-444 2320), www.apumayo.com* Mon-Sat 0900-1300, 1600-2000. Urubamba rafting (from 0800-1530 every day) US$25; 3- to 4-day Apurímac trip US$230. Also mountain biking (on Treks) for US$25 half-day to ruins around Cusco and US$40 for full-day trip to Maras and Moray in Sacred Valley. For Machu Picchu 4-day/3-night is US$395 and US$295 for a 2-day/1-night tour with 1st-class train trip there. This company also offers tours for disabled people, including rafting.

Eric Adventures, *Plateros 324, T084-228475, www.ericadventures.com* Specialize in adventure activities. They clearly explain what equipment is included in their prices and what you will need to bring. Rafting 1-day Río Urubamba, Class III from Jun-Dec, Class IV-V rest of year, US$25; 3-day/2-night Apurímac Canyon Class IV-V in high season (not viable in the low season) US$200; kayak course 3-day/2-night US$120; canyoning, level 1 initiation course, 1-day, US$25, hydrospeed, 1-day in Río Urubamba Class II-III; mountain biking to Maras and Moray, 1-day, US$35; Inca Trail to Machu Picchu, 4-day/3-night, US$160. They also rent motorcross bikes for US$45 (guide is extra). Prices are more expensive if you book by email, you can get huge discounts if you book in the office. A popular company.

Instinct, *Procuradores 50, T084-233451, www.instinct-travel.com Also at Plaza de Armas, Ollantaytambo, T084-204045.* 1 day Río Ollanta , Class II, III & IV US$25 – includes food, wetsuit and transport; 4-day/3-night Río Apurímac, up to Class V, US$240. **Instinct** also run a 2-day/1-night trip on the Apurímac for US$150, using the lower half of the normal 3-4 day run. This is a project run in conjunction with the local Quechua community of Pivil. Rafts and equipment are transported into the canyon using local mules and mule drivers, thus bringing employment to the community. Mountain biking in the Sacred Valley, US$25; they also hire mountain bikes. Juan and Benjamín Muñiz speak good English.

Mayuc Expediciones, *Portal Confiturías 211, Plaza de Armas, T084-232666, www.mayuc.com* One of the major river rafting adventure companies in Cusco. Rafting 1-day Río Urubamba Class III US$20; 4-day/3-night Río Apurímac Class III-V US$150, 6-day/5-night Tambopata-Cadamo jungle expedition Class III-IV US$790 (6-7 people), US$690 (8 or more people). Fixed departures are on the 1st and 3rd Sun of every month May-Nov. **Mayuc** now have a permanent lodge, **Casa Cusi**, on the upper Urubamba, which forms the basis of 2-day, Class III-IV trips in the area. *Casa Cusi* certainly makes a night on the Urubamba fairly comfortable but the real highlight is the on-location sauna to warm you up after a hard day on the river! Qualified guides with Advanced Swiftwater Association level 3 diplomas and first-aid training. Safety oriented and family friendly. Other tours include Inca Trail 4-day/3-night Premium service US$337 (4-7 people), economic service US$180 (4-7 people), they also offer an alternative route into Machu Picchu via Salkantay 7-day/6-day US$499 (for 6-7 people). An all-inclusive trip, 8-day/9-night, which includes a city tour, Sacred Valley tour, Inca Trail and all hotel accommodation is good value at US$567. A combination of horse-trekking and walking can be organized in the highlands of Peru. The helpful, English-speaking staff will organize any itinerary in Peru for their clients.

Southern Rivers Expeditions, *Plateros 319, T084-232061, www.southernrivers.net* Peruvian owner Willie Villafuerte Solís has huge experience leading rafting trips around the world and possesses many safety and rescue qualifications. Unlike many of his contemporaries, he still prefers life on the river to that in the office, hence he leads many trips personally. On offer are 3- and 4-day Apurímac trips, 1- and 2-day runs on the Urubamba, and, given enough clients, 10-day trips to the Río Tambopata (US$700). During the rainy season (Dec-Mar) Willie heads to Chile to run trips on the Río Futaleufú.

Swissraft-Peru, *Plateros 361, T084-246414, www.swissraft-peru.com* Another new entry into the Cusco-based rafting scene, this company has quickly acquired a good reputation for professionally run tours on the Apurímac and Urubamba rivers, with the focus above all on safety. Equipment is new and of good quality. 4-day expeditions on the Apurímac will cost US$170.

Jungle tours

Manu *p221*

For Manu you're unlikely to go wrong. The pristine reserve area within the park (where hunting is prohibited) is worked by only 9 licensed operators. Those which have received favourable reports are listed below. If any other agency is offering Manu, they will be taking you only to the culture area within the park, which is less protected. If you see Manu promoted in the many agencies along Plateros for US$300-400 that will be a trip to the cultural zone – whatever they tell you. This doesn't mean you are in for a bad trip but the destination and the experience will not be the same.

Andes Amazon Trails Peru, *T974 1735 (mob), www.amazontrailsperu.com* Small agency operated by Abraham Huaman León who has many years' experience guiding in the region. Mainly offers interesting itineraries in the buffer zones surrounding Manu, including the Amarakaeri Reserved Zone and Blanquillo, but trips to the former Reserved Zone (now part of the National Park) and the Casa Machiguenga are also possible.

Expediciones Vilca, *Plateros 363, T084-251872, www.cbc.org.pe/manuvilca/* Manu jungle tours: 8-day/7-night, US$650, other lengths of stay are available. Will supply sleeping bags at no extra cost. Minimum 5 people, maximum 10 per guide. Arto Ovaska, author of *Manu, Nature's Paradise* (available in Cusco and

recommended as a good introduction to the park and its wildlife), works as a guide for **Vilca** so if you want a Finnish guide – ask! This is the only economical tour which camps at the Otorongo camp, which is supposedly quieter than Salvador where many agencies camp. Clients returning to Cusco by boat and bus stay at the new **Yanayaco Lodge**, situated close to a small parrot clay lick (*collpa*). There are discounts for students and members of **SAE**. In the low season they will organize all other tours.

InkaNatura Travel, *Plateros 361, 1st floor, T084-251173 (in Lima: Manuel Bañón 461, San Isidro, T01-440 2022), www.inkanatura. com* InkaNatura states that it is a non-profit organization where all proceeds are directed back into projects on sustainable tourism and conservation. 4-day/3-night trip to the Manu Reserved Zone, US$750 (2-4 people), a 2-night extension costs a further US$450; Manu Wildlife Centre 4-day/3-night, US$890 (2-4 people), The Biotrip, 6-day/5-night, US$1190 (for 2-4 people) which takes you through the Andes to lowland jungle; **Sandoval Lake Lodge** in Tambopata, 4-day/3-night, US$260 (2-4 people), and also a tour into Machiguenga Indian territory, including the Pongo de Mainique, 4-day/3-night, US$590 (promotional price; normal price US$1,290). They have also recently opened the remote **Heath River Wildlife Center**, 1 hr up the Río Heath (4-5 hrs from Puerto Maldonado) on the Peru/Bolivia border. This is a cooperative project with traditional Ese'eja community of Sonene. 5-day/4-night visits, with 2 nights at the **HRWC** and 2 nights in **Sandoval Lake Lodge** cost US$620. Trips can get booked up months in advance so contact them early. Having said that they guarantee departures even if they only have 1 passenger, so don't rule out booking with them once you are in Cusco. In the office they sell copies of a book called *Peru's Amazonian Eden-Manu* for US$80 where proceeds are invested in the projects. The same title can be found in other bookshops at a much inflated price. 10% discount on all trips for Footprint Handbook readers.

Manu Ecological Adventures, *Plateros 356, T084-261640, www.manuadventures. com* Manu jungle tours, 8-day/7-night, US$610, economical tour in and out overland, 7-day/6-night, US$700 in by land, out by plane, giving you longer in the jungle, both leave on Sun. Other lengths of stay are available leaving on Mon and Tue. This company operates one of the most physically active Manu programmes, with options for a mountain biking descent through the cloudforest and 3 hrs of white-water rafting on the way to **Erika Lodge** on the upper Río Madre de Dios. They operate with a minimum of 4 people and a maximum of 10 people per guide. With a minimum of 8 people they will operate specialized programmes.

Manu Expeditions, *Av Pardo 895, PO Box 606, T084-226671, www.ManuExpeditions. com* English spoken, Mon-Fri 0900-1300, 1500-1900; Sat 0900-1300. Run by ornithologist and British Consul Barry Walker of the **Cross Keys Pub**. 3 trips available: US$1,595, 9-day/8-night (leaves Sun), visits reserve and Manu Wildlife Centre; US$1,235, 6-day/5-night (leaves Sun), takes passengers to the reserve only and US$1,199, 4-day/3-night (leaves Fri), goes only to wildlife centre. The first 2 trips visit a lodge run by Machiguenga people on the first Sun of every month and cost an extra US$150. Also runs tailor-made bird trips in cloud and rainforest around Cusco and Peru, and has horse riding and a 9-day/8-night trip to Machu Picchu along a different route from the Inca Trail, rejoining at Sun Gate. Barry runs horse supported treks to Choque-quirao, starting from Huancacalle. Highly recommended.

Manu Nature Tours, *Av Pardo 1046, T084-252721, www.manuperu.com* Owned by Boris Gómez Luna. English spoken. This company aims more for the luxury end of the market and owns 2 comfortable lodges in the cloudforest and reserved zone. Tours are very much based around these sites, thus entailing less travel between different areas. The standard tours do not include a visit to the Blanquillo Macaw Lick, preferring instead to focus on the Macaw colonies close to the **Manu Lodge**. Manu Lodge has an extensive trail system and also offers canopy climbing for an additional US$45 per person. In the cloudforest zone a novel 'Llama Taxi' service is offered, in conjunction with local community of Jajahuana. An 8-day/7-night tour staying at both lodges costs US$1,990;

5-day/4-night to **Manu Lodge** US$1,650. **Manu Cloud Forest Lodge** and camping trips in the Reserved Zone US$710. Extensions to the Blanquillo Macaw Lick cost US$505.

Pantiacolla Tours, *Plateros 360, T084-238323, www.pantiacolla.com* Manu jungle tours: 5-day, US$725; 7-day, US$795; 9-day US$765. The 5- and 7-day trips include return flights, the 9-day trip is an overland return. Prices do not include US$45 park entrance fee. Guaranteed departure dates regardless of number, maximum 10 people with 1 guide. The trips involve a combination of camping, platform camping and lodges. All clients are given a booklet entitled, *Talking About Manu*, written by the Dutch owner, Marianne van Vlaardingen, who is a biologist who studied Tamarin monkeys at the Cocha Cashu Biological station within Manu. She is extremely friendly and helpful. Marianne and her Peruvian husband Gustavo have recently opened an ecotourism lodge in conjunction with the Yine native community of Diamante. The lodge is a base for cultural tours in the area and will eventually (the project runs for 10 years) be independently owned and managed by the village. Yine guides are used and community members are being trained in the various aspects of running the project. For more details of tours to Manu, see page 221.

Tambopata *p228*
For Tambopata the picture is not so clear because operators do not have to be licensed. However, the market does not appear to be unscrupulous in the manner of the Inca Trail firms. Use one of the firms listed below, ask the right questions and you should be fine. See also **Apu Expeditions**, **Explorandes**, **Mayuc** and **InkaNatura**, which are all listed above.

Peruvian Safaris, *Plateros 365, T084-235342, www.peruviansafaris.com* For reservations for the **Explorer's Inn**, 3-day/2-night US$180 – excluding park entrance fees and flights.

Rainforest Expeditions, *Portal de Carnes 236, Plaza de Armas, T084-246243, www.peru nature.com* This company has developed an excellent reputation for their Tambopata services in the last few years. They own 2 lodges on the Río Tambopata. **Posada Amazonas**, close to Puerto Maldonado, is run in conjunction with local community of Infierno. Several of the guides are community members. Further upriver, in an area of pristine primary forest, is the **Tambopata Research Center**, situated next to the area's famed Macaw Lick. Due to its remote location this is superb area for observing rainforest wildlife, including large mammals. They also have an office in Lima, *C Aramburu 166-4B, Lima 18, T01-421 8347.*For more details of tours to Tambopata, see page 228.

Cultural tours

K'uichy Light International, *Av Sol 814, of 219, T084-264107, T962 1722 (mob), kuichy@amauta.rcp.net.pe* Ruben E Palomino specializes in spiritual tours, good value.
Milla Tourism, *Av Pardo 689 y Portal Comercio 195 on the plaza, T084-231710, www.millaturismo.com* Mon-Fri 0800-1300, 1500-1900, Sat 0800-1300. Mystical tours to Cusco's Inca ceremonial sites such as Pumamarca and The Temple of the Moon. Guide speaks only basic English. City tour US$19 (includes entry tickets), Sacred Valley tour US$20 (includes lunch) and Inca Trail: 4-day/3-night US$250 (minimum 10 people, maximum 15); 1-day backpacker US$105 and 1-day 1st-class US$141. Also private tours arranged to Moray agricultural terracing and Maras salt mines in Sacred Valley, US$150 for car and guide, can be split. They also arrange cultural and environmental lectures and courses.
Mystic Inca Trail, *Unidad Vecinal de Santiago, bloque 9, dpto 301, T084-221358, ivanndp@terra.com.pe* Specialize in tours of sacred Inca sites and study of Andean spirituality. This takes 10 days but it is possible to have shorter 'experiences'.
Personal Travel Service, *Portal de Panes 123, oficina 109, T084-225518, ititoss@terra.com.pe* Mainly deals with group bookings and package holidays. They will organize a personalized itinerary for individuals and groups including international and national flights. They specialize in cultural tours in the Urubamba Valley.

Shamans and drug experiences
San Pedro and Ayahuasca have been used since before Inca times, mostly as a sacred healing experience. The plants are prepared with special treatments for curative purposes; they have never been considered a drug. If you choose to experience these incredible healing/teaching plants, only do so under the guidance of a reputable agency or shaman and always have a friend with you who is not partaking. If the medicine is not prepared correctly, it can be highly toxic and, in rare cases, severely dangerous. Never buy from someone who is not recommended, never buy off the streets and never try to prepare the plants yourself. We suggest the following, whom we know to be legitimate:
Another Planet, *Triunfo 120, T084-229379, www.anotherplanetperu.net* Run by Lesley Myburgh (who also runs **Casa de La Gringa**, *C Pensamiento E-3, Urb Miravalle*, 5 mins by taxi from plaza, sleeping in **D** range), who operates all kinds of adventure tours and conventional tours in and around Cusco, but specializes in jungle trips anywhere in Peru. Lesley is an expert in San Pedro cactus preparation and she arranges San Pedro journeys for healing at physical, emotional and spiritual levels in beautiful remote areas. The journeys are thoroughly organized and a safe, beautiful, unforgettable experience.
Casa de la serenidad, *T084-222851, www.shamanspirit.net* A shamanic therapy centre run by a Swiss-American healer and Reiki Master who uses medicinal 'power' plants. It also has bed and breakfast and has received very good reports.

Paragliding and ballooning
Richard Pethigal, *T993 7333 (mob), cloudwalker@another.com* Richard offers a condor's-eye view of the Sacred Valley. From May-Sep he runs half-day tandem paraglider flights from Cusco. He is a very experienced pilot and uses high-quality equipment. Be aware that the Sacred Valley offers exciting but challenging paragliding so if wind conditions are bad, flights may be delayed till the following day. Magnificent scenery, soaring close to snow-capped mountains makes this an awesome experience. He is licensed and charges US$60.
Globos de los Andes, *Arequipa 271, T084-232352, T969 3812 (mob), www.globosperu.com* Hot-air ballooning in the Sacred Valley and expeditions with balloons and 4WD lasting several days.

Cusco City Tours & activities

All of those listed are bilingual. Set prices: City tour US$15-20 per day; Urubamba/ Sacred Valley US$25-30, Machu Picchu and other ruins US$40-50 per day.

Classic standard tours
Mireya Bocángel, *mireyabocangel@ latinmail.com* Recommended.
Boris Cárdenas, *boriscar@telser.com.pe* Esoteric and cultural tours.
José Cuba and Alejandra Cuba, *Urb Santa Rosa R Gibaja 182, Urb Santa Rosa R Gibaja 182, T084-226179, T968 5187 (mob), alecuba@ Chaski.unsaac.edu.pe* Both speak English, Alejandra speaks German and French, very good tours.
Roberto Dargent, *Urb Zarumilla 5B-102, T084-247424, T962 2080 (mob), dargent travelperubolivia@hotmail.com* Very helpful.

Mariella Lazo, *T084-264210*. Speaks German, experienced, also offers river rafting.
Haydee Mogrovejo, *T084-221907,*

Aymoa@hotmail.com
Victoria Morales Condori, *San Juan de Dios 229, T084-235204.*
Juana Pancorbo, *Av Los Pinos D-2, T084-227482.*
Percy Salas Alfaro, *c/o Munditur, T084-2402887, T962 1152 (mob), smunditur@hotmail.com* Serious, friendly, English-speaking.
Satoshi Shinoda, *T084-227861* and **Michiko Nakazahua**, *T084-226185*, both Japanese-speaking guides.

Adventure trips
Roger Valencia Espinoza, *José Gabriel Cosio 307, T084-251278, vroger@qenqo.rcp.net.pe*

● Transport

Air

Airline offices
See also Lima, p259.
Aero Continente, *Portal de Carnes 254, Plaza de Armas, T084-243031, F084-235666, airport T084-235696 (toll free T0800-42420).*
American Airlines, *Saphi 848, T084-226605, F084-231161 (toll free T0800-40350)*, reconfirm 72 hrs in advance, represented by **Cóndor Travel**. **LAB**, *Santa Catalina Angosta 160, T084-222990, F084-222279, airport T084-229220*. **Lan Perú**, *Av Sol 627-B, T084-225552, F084-255555, airport T084-255550*. **Taca**, *Av Sol 226, T084-249921, airport T084-246858 (national and international reservations T0800-48222)*, good service. **Tans**, *San Agustín 315-317, T084-251000, airport T084-244906*, 0900-1930.

Bus

Local El Tranvía de Cusco is actually a motor coach which runs on the route of the original Cusco tramway system which operated from 1910-40. The route starts in the Plaza de Armas (except on Sun morning when the weekly flag ceremony takes place) and ends

at the Sacsayhuaman Archaeological Park. There is a 10-min stop at the mirador by the Cristo Blanco before descending to the Plaza de Armas. Departures 1000, 1150 and 1500, 1 hr 20 mins, with explanations of the city's history, architecture, customs, etc; US$2, US$1.40 for students with ID. For group reservations, *T084-740640*.

Long distance A new bus terminal, the Terminal Terrestre, has been opened on Prolongación Pachacútec.

All direct buses to **Lima** (20-24 hrs) now go via **Abancay** (Department of Apurímac), 195 km, 5 hrs (longer in the rainy season), and **Nasca** (Department of Ica), on the Panamerican Highway. This route is now almost entirely paved, however floods in the wet season often damage large sections of the highway. If prone to carsickness, be prepared on the road to Abancay, there are many, many curves, but the scenery is magnificent (it also happens to be a great route for cycling). At Abancay, the road forks, the other branch going to **Andahuaylas**, a further 138 km, 10-11 hrs from Cusco, and **Ayacucho** in the Central Highlands, another 261 km, 20 hrs from Cusco. On both routes at night, take a blanket or sleeping bag to ward off the cold. All buses leave daily from the Terminal Terrestre.

Molina, *Av Pachacútec, just past the railway station*, has buses on both routes. They run 3 services a day to Lima via **Abancay** and **Nasca**, and 1, at 1900, to **Abancay** and **Andahuaylas**; Expreso Wari leaves at 0800, 1400, 1600 and 2000 to **Abancay**, **Nasca** and **Lima**. With the improvement of the road, Cruz del Sur now also run this direct route to **Lima** via Abancay. Their cheaper *Ideal* service leaves at 0730 and 1400, while their more comfortable *Imperial* service departs at 1500 and 1600. San Jerónimo has buses to **Abancay**, **Andahuaylas** and **Ayacucho** at 1830. Turismo Ampay goes to Abancay at 0630, 1300 and 2000, **Turismo Abancay** at 0630, 1300 and 2000, and Expreso Huamanga at 1600. Fares to **Abancay** US$4.30, **Andahuaylas** US$6.50 (**Molina**), **Ayacucho** US$15, **Nasca** US$17-20, **Lima** US$20 (**Cruz del Sur**, *Ideal* class) to US$32 (**Cruz del Sur**, *Imperial* class). After 2½ hrs buses pass a checkpoint at the Cusco/ Apurímac departmental border. All foreigners must get out and show their passport. In Cusco you may be told that there are no buses in the day from Abancay to Andahuaylas; this is not so – **Señor de Huanca** does so. If you leave Cusco before 0800, with luck you'll make the onward connection at 1300, which is worth it for the scenery.

To **Lake Titicaca** and **Bolivia**: To **Juliaca**, 344 km, 5-6 hrs, US$10, **Imexco**, day and night buses, and **Tour Perú**, night buses, US$8. The road is fully paved, but after heavy rain buses may not run. To **Puno**, 44 km from Juliaca, there is a good service with **Ormeño** at 0900, US$10, 6 hrs. This service continues to **La Paz**, Bolivia. Other services are run by **Imexco** (daytime), **Pony Express**, **Tour Perú** and **Libertad** (at night), US$8, 6½-8 hrs. **Tour Perú** also offers a direct service to **La Paz**, US$15. For another service between Peru and Bolivia, call Litoral, *T084-248989*, which runs buses between the 2 countries, leaving Cusco at 2200, arriving La Paz 1200, US$30, including breakfast on the bus and a/c. Travel agencies also sell this ticket.

To **Arequipa**, 521 km, **Cruz del Sur** use the direct paved route via Juliaca and have 3 *Ideal* services leaving daily, 10½ hrs, US$7, and 1 *Imperial* service at 1930, 10 hrs, US$10. **Ormeño**'s fare is US$16. Other buses join the

new Juliaca-Arequipa road at Imata, 10-12 hrs, US$7.75 (eg **Carhuamayo**, 3 a day).

Car

Avis, *Av El Sol 808 and at the airport, T084-248800, avis-cusco@terra.com.pe* **Touring y Automóvil Club del Perú**, *Av Sol 349, T084-224561, cusco@touringperu.com.pe* A good source of information on motoring, car hire and mechanics (membership is US$45 per year).

Combi and taxi

Local Combis run from 0500 to 2200 or 2300, US$0.15. Combis run to all parts of the city, including the bus and train stations and the airport, but are not allowed within 2 blocks of the Plaza de Armas. Stops are signed and the driver's assistant calls out the names of stops. By law all passengers are insured. After 2200 combis may not run their full route; demand to be taken to your stop, or better still, use a taxi late at night.

Taxis have fixed prices: in the centre US$0.60 (a little more after dark); and to the suburbs US$0.85-1.55 (touts at the airport and train station will always ask much higher fares). In town it is safest to take taxis which are registered; these have a sign with the company's name on the roof, not just a sticker in the window. Taxis on call are reliable but more expensive, in the centre US$1.25 (**Ocarina** *T084-247080*, **Aló Cusco** *T084-222222*).

Long distance Taxi trips to **Sacsayhuaman** cost US$10; to the ruins of **Tambo Machay** US$15-20 (3-4 people); a whole-day trip costs US$40-70. For US$50 a taxi can be hired for a whole day (ideally Sun) to take you to **Chinchero**, **Maras**, **Urubamba**, **Ollantaytambo**, **Calca**, **Lamay**, **Coya**, **Pisac**, **Tambo Machay**, **Qenqo** and **Sacsayhuaman**.

Cycle repair

Atoq, *Saphi 704, T993 9725 (mob), atoqis@hotmail.com* Run by Juan Carlos Salazar Triveño, high-end bike hire, repairs, spare parts, information and guided tours, English spoken. See also Tours for mountainbiking, p117.

Train

All details of the train services out of Cusco can be found on *www.perurail.com*

The train to **Juliaca** and **Puno** leaves at 0800, on Mon, Wed and Sat, arriving in Juliaca at 1545 and Puno at 1645 (sit on the left for the best views). The train makes a stop to view the scenery at La Raya. Trains return from Puno on Mon, Wed and Sat at 0800, arriving in Cusco at 1645. Fares: tourist class, US$14.16, 1st class US$88.50.

Tickets can be bought up to 5 days in advance. The ticket office at Wanchac station is open Mon-Fri 0800-1700, Sat 0900-1200. Tickets sell out quickly and there are queues from 0400 before holidays in the dry season. In the low season tickets to Puno can be bought on the day of departure. You can buy tickets through a travel agent, but check the date and seat number. Meals are served on the train. Always check whether the train is running, especially in the rainy season, when services might be cancelled.

● Directory

Banks and money exchange

All the banks along Av Sol have ATMs from which you can withdraw dollars or soles at any hour. Whether you use the counter or an ATM, choose your time carefully as there can be long queues at both. Most banks are closed between 1300 and 1600.

Banco de Crédito, *Av Sol 189*. Gives cash advances on Visa and changes TCs to soles with no commission, 3% to dollars. It has an ATM for Visa. It also handles Amex. **Interbank**, *Av Sol y Puluchapata*. Charges no commission on TCs and has a Visa ATM which gives dollars as well as soles. Next door is **Banco Continental**, also has a Visa ATM and charges US$5 commission on TCs. **Banco Santander**, *Av Sol 459*. Changes Amex TCs at reasonable rates. Has Red Unicard ATM for Visa/Plus and MasterCard. **Banco Latino**, *Almagro 125 y Av Sol 395*. Has ATMs for MasterCard. **Banco Wiese**, *Maruri between Pampa del Castillo and Pomeritos*. Gives cash advances on MasterCard, in dollars. Emergency number for lost or stolen Visa cards, 0800-1330.

As well as the **ATMs** in banks (most of which have 24-hr police protection), there are ATMs on the *Plaza de Armas at the entrance to Inka Grill, Portal de Panes, Supermercado Gato's, Portal Belén*, and *the entrance to Cross Keys and Tunupa, Portal de Confiturías*. There are other ATMs on *Av la Cultura, beside Supermercado Dimart and beside Supermercado La Canasta*. **Western Union** at *Santa Catalina Ancha 165, T084-233727*. Money transfers in 10 mins; also at **DHL**, see below.

Many travel agencies and **casas de cambio** change dollars. Some of them change TCs as well, but charge 4-5% commission. There are many *cambios* on the west side of the Plaza de Armas (eg *Portal Comercio Nos 107 and 148*) and on the west side of Av Sol, most change TCs (best rates in the *cambios* at the top of Av Sol). The **street changers** hang around Av Sol, blocks 2-3, every day and are a pleasure to do business with. Some of them will also change TCs. In banks and on the street check the notes.

Embassies and consulates

Consulates Belgium, *Av Sol 954, T084-221098, F084-221100*. Mon-Fri 0900-1300, 1500-1700. **France**, *Jorge Escobar, C Micaela Bastidas 101, 4th floor, T084-233610*. **Germany**, *Sra Maria-Sophia Júrgens de Hermoza, San Agustín 307, T084-235459, Casilla Postal 1128, Correo Central*. Mon-Fri, 1000-1200, appointments may be made by phone, it also has a book exchange. **Holland**, *Marcela Alarco Zegaria, behind Hotel Savoy on Av Pardo, T084-264103, 965 0204 (mob)*. **Ireland**, *Charlie Donovan, Santa Catalina Ancha 360 (Rosie O'Grady's), T084-243514*. **Italy**, *Sr Fedos Rubatto, Av Garcilaso 700, T084-224398*. Mon-Fri 0900-1200, 1500-1700. **Netherlands**, *Sra Marcela Alarco Zegarra, Av Pardo 854, T084-264103*. **Spain**, *Sra Juana María Lambarri, T965 0106 (mob)*. **UK**, *Barry Walker, Av Pardo 895, T084-239974, bwalker@ amauta.rcp.net.pe* **US Agent**, *Dra Olga Villagarcía, Apdo 949, Cusco, T084-222183, F084-233541, or at the Binational Center (ICPNA), Av Tullumayo 125, Wanchac*.

Immigration

Av Sol, block 6, close to post office, T084-222740. Mon-Fri 0800-1300. Reported as not very helpful.

Internet

You can't walk for 5 mins in Cusco without running into an internet café, and new places are opening all the time. Most have similar rates, around US$0.60 per hr, although if you look hard enough you can find cheaper places. The main difference between cafés is the speed of internet connection and the facilities on offer. The better places have scanners, webcams and CD burners, among other gadgets, and staff in these establishments can be very knowledgeable. Listed below are some locations that stood out at the time of writing.

Internet Station, *Tecseccocha 422.* The owner here speaks excellent English and is very knowledgeable with computers. Excellent range of equipment with very helpful staff.

Inti Net, *Choquechaca 115c, T/F222037.* Good machines and fairly fast connection. Scanner and CD burner available, and this is a good place to make international phone calls which are charged at a reasonable rates.

Metro Sistemas, *Afligidos (first left down Av Sol), T/F084-263553.* All the facilities you could want, plus a fast connection and reasonable rates – excellent.

Mundo Net, *Santa Teresa 344, T/F084-260285.* Especially recommended, this café features very good machines with fast connection and large clear screens in a pleasant environment. Good coffee and snacks available.

World Net, *Santa Catalina Ancha 315.* Cheaper but still with a fast connection, has scanner and netphone; food and drinks also available.

If none of these places appeals, there are many more cafés around the Plaza de Armas and to the south of the centre.

Language classes

Academia Latinoamericana de Español, *Av Sol 580, T084-243364, latinocusco@goalsnet. com.pe* The same company also has schools in Ecuador (Quito) and in Bolivia (Sucre). They can arrange courses that include any combination of these locations using identical teaching methods and materials. Professionally run with experienced staff. Many activities per week, including dance lessons and excursions to sites of historical and cultural interest. Private classes US$170 for 20 hrs, groups, with a maximum of 4 students US$125, again for 20 hrs.

Acupari, *San Agustín 307, T084-242970.* The German-Peruvian Cultural Association, Spanish classes are run here.

Amauta, *Suecia 480, 2nd floor, T084-241422, PO Box 1164, www.amautaspanish.com* Spanish classes, individual or in small groups, also Quechua classes and workshops in Peruvian cuisine, dance and music, US$9.50 per hr individual, but cheaper and possibly better value for group tuition (2-6 people), US$88 for 20 hrs. They have pleasant accommodation on site, as well as a free internet café for students, and can arrange excursions and can help find voluntary work. They also have a school in Urubamba and can arrange courses in the Manu rainforest, in conjunction with Pantiacolla Tours.

Amigos Spanish School, *Zaguán del Cielo B-23, T084-242292, www.spanishcusco.com* Profits from this school support a foundation for disadvantaged children. Private lessons for US$8 per hr, US$100 for 20 hrs of classes in a group. Homestays available.

La Casona de la Esquina, *Purgatorio 395, corner with Huaynapata, T084-235830, www.spanishlessons.com.pe* US$5 per hr for one-to-one classes. Recommended.

Cusco Spanish School, *Garcilaso 265, oficina 6 (2nd floor), T084-226928, www.cuscospanish school.com* US$7.75 for private classes, cheaper in groups. School offers homestays, optional activities including dance and music classes, cookery courses, ceramics, Quechua, hiking and volunteer programmes. They also offer courses on an hacienda at Cusipata in the Vilcanota Valley, east of Cusco.

Excel, *Cruz Verde 336, T084-232272 , www. Excel-spanishlanguageprograms-peru.org* Very professional, US$7 per hr for private one-to-one lessons. US$200 for 20 hrs with 2 people, or US$80 per person in groups of 3 or more. The school can arrange accommodation with local families.

San Blas Spanish School, *Tandapata 688, T084-247898, www.spanishschoolperu.com* Private classes US$7 per hr, groups, with 4 clients maximum, US$80 for 20 hrs tuition.

Laundry

There are several cheap laundries on Procuradores, and also on Suecia and Tecseccocha. **Dana's Laundry**, *Nueva Baja y Unión*. US$2.10 per kg, takes about 6 hrs. **Lavandería Louis**, *Choquechaca 264, San Blas*. US$0.85 per kg, fresh, clean, good value. **Splendid Laundry Service**, *Carmen Alto 195*. Very good, US$0.75 per kg, laundry sometimes available after only 3-4 hrs. **Lavandería T'aqsana Wasi**, *Santa Catalina Ancha 345*. Same-day service, they also iron clothes, US$2 per kg, good service, speak English, German, Italian and French, Mon-Fri 0900-2030, Sat 0900-1900. **Lavandería**, *Saphi 578*. 0800-2000 Mon-Sat, 0800-1300 Sun. Good, fast service, US$1 per kg. String markers will be attached to clothes if they have no label.

Medical services

Clinics and doctors Clínica **Panamericana**, *Av Infancia 508, Wanchac, T084-222644, T9651552 (mob)*. 24-hr emergency and medical attention. **Clínica Pardo**, *Av de la Cultura 710, T084-240387, T9930063 (mob), www.clinica pardocusco.com* 24-hr emergency and hospitalization/medical attention, international department, trained bilingual personnel, handles complete medical assistance coverage with international insurance companies, free ambulance service, visit to hotel, discount in pharmacy, dental service, X-rays, laboratory, full medical specialization. The most highly recommended clinic in Cusco. Director is Dr Alcides Vargas. **Clínica Paredes**, *C Lechugal 405, T084-225265*. Newly expanded premises and medical attention. Director is Dr Milagros Paredes, whose speciality is gynaecology. Recommended. **Hospital Regional**, *Av de la Cultura, T084-227661, emergencies T084-223691*.

  Dr Ilya Gomon, *Av de la Cultura, Edif Santa Fe, oficina 207, T9651906 (mob)*. Canadian chiropractor, good, reasonable prices, available for hotel or home visits. **Dr Gilbert Espejo** and **Dr Boris Espejo Muñoz**, *both in the Centro Comercial Cusco, oficina 7, T084-228074 and T084-231918 respectively*.

If you need a yellow fever vaccination (for the jungle lowlands, or for travel to Bolivia or Brazil where it is required), it is available at the paediatric department of the **Hospital Antonio Lorena** from 0830 on Mon, Wed and Fri; they are free and include the international vaccination certificate. **Dentists** Dr Eduardo Franco, *Av de la Cultura, Edif Santa Fe, oficina 310, T084-242207, T965 0179 (mob)*. 24-hr.

Post offices

Central office, *Av Sol at the bottom end of block 5, T084-225232*. Mon-Sat 0730-2000, 0800-1400 Sun and holidays. Poste restante is free and helpful. Sending packages from Cusco is not cheap. **DHL**, *Av Sol 627, T084-244167*. For sending packages or money overseas.

Public conveniences

Conveniences can be found at the top of Plateros, at its junction with Saphi. US$0.50.

Telephone

Telefónica, *Av del Sol 386, T084-241111*. For telephone and fax, Mon-Sat 0700-2300, 0700-1200 Sun and holidays. International calls can be made by payphone or go through the operator – a long wait is possible and a deposit is required. To send a fax costs (per page): US$4.75 to Europe and Israel; US$2.80 to North America. To receive a fax costs US$0.70 per page.

Radio messages Radio Alex, *Quinta Jardín 288, Villa Militar, T084-238219*. For radio use to and from the jungle and other regions, with the potential to connect with phone lines. Alex Galindo charges 1 sol per min (plus phone charges if required); very reliable. You can also try **Radio América**, *Túpac Amaru E-6, San Sebastián, T084-271428* and **Radio Tawantinsuyo**, *Av Sol 806, T084-228411*. Mon-Fri 0730-1900, Sat 0700-1300, messages are sent out between 0500 and 2100 (you can choose the time), in Spanish or Quechua, price per message is US$1. This is sometimes helpful if things are stolen and you want them back.

▲ Walks around Sacsayhuaman

Sacsayhuaman to Tambo Machay

From Sacsayhuaman, the route leads east by northeast, part of the way along the modern paved highway, until reaching the turn-off for Qenqo, about 2 km away. First pass **Qenqo Chico**, then **Qenqo Grande** (see also page 88) and then following the exit road out of Qenqo – just before it joins the main paved highway running to the northeast, another smaller road feeds into it from the right. Follow this road which will soon curve left before reaching a large group of houses (Villa San Blas), about 200 m away, on the other side of a gully.

In the immediate vicinity of **Villa San Blas**, the paved road circles around a small rock outcropping with finely cut and polished niches and small platforms, a *huaca* (shrine). From that point, an older dirt track heads off in a northerly direction. Continue along this track for about 50 m, enough to steer comfortably clear of the houses, the children and the dogs, and then leave this secondary road altogether, striking off at right angles to the right of it and begin hiking east, skirting around fields and depressions (the remains of reservoirs), following any of several footpaths, but always maintaining a fairly straight course.

About 400 m away, there is a gentle descent into a shallow creek bed. After crossing it and walking on for almost 100 m, you will find some Inca stone walls. This marks the beginning of a semi-subterranean archaeological site similar to Qenqo. Because it does not protrude significantly above the level of the surrounding terrain, it is not easy to distinguish from many other rocky outcrops scattered throughout the area. It is, however, a conglomeration of large boulders with walkways and interconnecting galleries between them. The rocks are extensively sculpted with the usual array of niches and platforms and a great profusion of carvings, many of which represent monkeys and snakes, as well as what is thought to have been a large

Walks around Sacsayhuaman

	Sacsayhuaman to Tambo Machay
	Tambo Machay to Sacsayhuaman return
	Alternative route Laqo to Cusco
	Sacsayhuaman to Chacán

sculpted stone representing a toad. There are also remains of a liturgical fountain and a very battered, partially defaced but still clearly perceptible stone sculpture of a large feline, possibly a puma, perhaps a jaguar (a plausible explanation given the presence of other examples of jungle fauna, the monkeys and snakes). This was once a *huaca* of great importance. The name given to this site is **Cusilluchayoc** ('place of the monkeys', from *kusillo*, monkey in Quechua). In Spanish it is sometimes called Templo de los Monos. The original Inca name is unknown.

Also unknown is the reason why so many of these *huacas* are partially or almost totally buried. Archaeological research has revealed as much as 3 m of niches, pedestals, carvings and masonry below present ground level. Throughout the Sacsayhuaman Archaeological Park all the lower sections of the various *huacas* uncovered over the last 25 years are much lighter in colour, in many cases almost white, in marked contrast with the weathered grey patina of the parts exposed for hundreds of years. The lower levels retain the original luminosity of the polished limestone, traces of what must have been a dazzling landscape. Did the Incas themselves attempt to conceal their religious shrines from the *conquistadores*? Or was it the fanatic persecution of heathen idolatry undertaken by the Christians during and after the conquest that entombed the native places of worship? Alternatively, the consistency of the landfill and uniformity of the depth throughout the area could suggest a natural or geological cause. Landslides brought about by earthquake or flooding are possibilities. Although records from the last 500 years detail devastating earthquakes in the Cusco region, as well as floods and similar natural disasters, there are no specific references to great displacements of earth having obliterated this area.

After walking through Cusilluchayoc, you reach a well-defined, straight dirt track, flanked by sections of adobe walls with cacti and agave growing on them. This is a section of the ancient **Inca road** from Cusco to Pisac, still used by highland folk descending from the hills to Cusco. Turn left on this road and head northeast (away from Cusco) for about 300 m, towards a very prominent rock outcrop rising some 40 m above the surrounding fields. This is yet another important Inca *huaca*, currently known as **Laqo** (although the original Inca name is unknown). *Laqo* has more than one meaning in Quechua: it can be interpreted as 'confusing, misleading, enigmatic', but it is also the name of an algae found along Andean streams and marshes. And such a stream runs just below the site and so the place name would seem to derive from that. Still, it is also an enigmatic place. The name more commonly used by the local inhabitants is **Salonniyuc**, a hybrid Spanish-Quechua word roughly meaning '(place)...of the salón (hall, room in Spanish)'. Another name is 'Salapunku' or 'Salonpunku', with the same Spanish noun plus the Quechua *punku* (door, doorway). It is always Laqo on maps.

Laqo is a formation of grey, porous limestone, some 50 m high. A split, large enough to walk through, cuts into the rock. There are two large caves with remains of zoomorphic sculptures similar to those in Cusilluchayoc. Carved in the rock are niches and an altar upon which sunlight and moonlight fall at certain times of the year, filtered through the fissure above (hence another name for the place, **Templo de la Luna** – Temple of the Moon). The external surfaces also have carvings, sculptures, niches, stairways and the remains of a sundial, similar to the *intihuatanas* at Machu Picchu and Pisac.

Laqo has always been an observatory. Standing at the summit it is easy to appreciate why. It is the best single vantage point from which to view not only the Cusco countryside, but also to see through the fabric of Andean time. To the southeast, about 100 km away as the crow flies, rises the great snowy peak of **Ausangate**, 'the one that pulls – or herds – the others', 6,350 m above sea level, revered *apu* of the eastern Andes and grandfather of mountains. Some 70 km closer, in the same direction, loom the dark, jagged crags of **Pachatusan**, 'pillar – or fulcrum – of the earth', 4,950 m, one of the children of Ausangate. And only 10 km away,

⋮ Ceques – the cosmic dials

To understand the basis on which many Inca roads were laid out, one needs to know a little about the *ceque* system. This involves a complex series of lines and associated *huacas* (shrines) that radiated out from Cusco and had astronomical, calendric and sacred connotations. The centre point of this giant dial is generally taken to be the Qoricancha, although some say a pillar and the tower of the Suntur Huasi on the Huacaypata (the Plaza de Armas) were the sighting points. Forty-one lines emanated from the hub, some hundreds of kilometres long. The lines were not necessarily marked on the ground, but ran dead straight towards the horizon. Four were the intercardinal roads to the four quarters of Tahuantinsuyo, others aimed at the equinox and solstice points, others to the points where different stars and constellations rise. On or near these rays, about 328 *huacas* pillars, and survey points were distributed. The lines served various purposes. They were used for tracking the movements of sun and stars; they helped predict the best time for planting crops and were instumental in irrigation (about a third pointed to springs and other water sources). Certain *ceques* and their *huacas* were under the jurisdiction of particular *panacas* (clans). As well as delineating panaca property, the lines helped to define the organization of land, water and work and the rituals and ceremonies which began and closed work cycles.

aligned with father and grandfather, the young and green **Pikol**, one of the local *apus*, 4,200 m high. Every mountain, every hill, is an *apu*. Every *apu* possesses its individual identity and name. The *apus* are masculine and they all belong to a hierarchical order. At the same time, each *apu* is both offspring and consort of Mother Earth, *Pachamama*, source of all life, the indivisible and fundamental feminine element in nature.

Almost all the limestone outcroppings scattered throughout the countryside are in effect *huacas*, all intricately carved and sculpted. There are also groves of eucalyptus trees, imported to Peru from Australia (via California) in the mid-19th century; adobe walls belonging to kilns and brickworks from colonial times; ancient irrigation canals contouring many kilometres of mountain slopes; fields of native amaranth, maize, beans and potatoes interspersed with other fields sown with cereals of European origin, such as wheat, barley and oats.

At the northern end of Laqo, there is a dirt road, about 10 m wide, running east to west. Beyond it, lies a flat open field about 50 m long, which culminates on the side of a steep ravine with a shallow stream descending from the north. This runs through the many carved limestone outcrops, turns slightly to the southeast and flows on in the direction of Cusco. The same Inca road followed from Cusilluchayoc to Laqo descends into this ravine, crosses the stream and continues its northeasterly course, gradually climbing and skirting around the southeastern flanks of the mountains, crossing into a small valley and then into a larger one, eventually reaching the village of **Chilcapuquio**, about 2 km from Laqo. The cliffs and rocky canyon walls along this section display many overhangs and cave-like openings, some at ground level and others many metres higher. These are the remains of burials dating back to Inca times. It is not uncommon to find remains of ceremonial offerings, such as bouquets of flowers, candles, coca leaves and tobacco, tributes by the people of today to the eternal spirits of the mountains.

Cusco City Walks around Sacsayhuaman

Beyond Chilcapuquio, the main trail swerves to the right and gradually begins
heading eastward, climbing about 100 m towards **Yuncaypata**, another, larger,
community. Before the main trail comes to and crosses another

🔊 *Most of these hiking routes can also be done on horseback and perhaps as many can be ridden on a mountain bike. Horse and mountain bike rentals are readily available.*

stream, called the Ccorimayo on maps, it is best to strike away
from it, following any of several smaller trails which will be
found on the left heading north. These paths follow the course
of the Ccorimayu, always on the left side of its ravine, gradually
pulling away from it and climbing above it. About 2 km to the
north of the point where one has struck off the main trail, and
200 m higher, poised atop a prominent rock buttress, lies the

site of **Puka Pukara** and, a further kilometre beyond it, crossing the modern paved
road from Cusco to Pisac, are the ruins of **Tambo Machay** and the finishing point of
this hike (see page 89).

The return from Tambo Machay

You can return from Tambo Machay to Cusco by simply following the main paved
road. There is also (time permitting) an interesting off-road alternative. Begin by
following the main paved road going back to Cusco, retracing your steps past Puka
Pukara. The road soon reaches the vicinity of the modern community of
Huayllacocha. On the left side of the road, a small ravine can be seen, descending
southward. This is the **Qenqomayu**, the zigzagging river, the same which eventually
flows 50 m past the northern end of Laqo and which the trail from there to
Chilcapuquio and Puka Pukara earlier crosses. Several footpaths, along either the left
or right slopes of the gully, descend for about 3 km to reach the vicinity of Laqo.

About 500 m after starting the descent there is a notable feature on the right bank
of the canyon: the western canyon walls become vertical cliffs, extensively
pockmarked with open holes, most of them many metres above ground level. They
are all graves (all looted) dating back to Inca times and representing one of the largest
cemeteries in the department of Cusco. A similar one can be seen opposite the
northern side of the ruins of Pisac. Facing the vertical necropolis in the Qencomayu
gully is an Inca wall, of fine masonry, running for about 100 m. Its function is not
known but it may indicate a shrine buried in the hill behind it, or some kind of
canalization of the Qencomayu, channeling its course toward Cusco.

You approach Laqo, but to avoid visiting the site again, gradually climb above
and away from the Qencomayu, at a southwesterly angle, eventually to descend
and meet the dirt road which runs in front of the northern end of Laqo from east to
west. Once on this road, head left (west) for about 1 km, until rejoining the main
paved highway from Pisac to Cusco, now heading south toward Cusco. Cross the
highway, turn left, and less than 50 m south there is turnoff to the right (west).
Directly above, lies another limestone promontory containing another enigmatic
huaca. The outer surface displays many carvings, though none as fine as the ones in
Laqo or Cusilluchayoc. But the inner part of the *huaca* is a labyrinth of passageways
and narrow caves. The official name of this site is **Lanlacuyoc**, which roughly
translates as 'that which has an evil (or mischievous) spirit'. Its more popular name
is Zona X, no doubt bestowed upon it 25 years ago during Cusco's Hippy period (the
Katmandu of the west, as it was called), when this particular archaeological site
acquired a keen degree of interest.

Leaving the recent and ancient past behind, follow the paved road for about 3
km, past the ruins of a colonial kiln, an Inca quarry, countless clumps of intricately
carved limestone and occasional parked cars with romantic couples in pursuit of the
timeless ritual. Soon after the first few turns, Sacsayhuaman comes into view. Any
options for getting off the road, as long as they are on the left and head down towards
Sacsayhuaman, are good.

Both of these hiking routes can be undertaken in reverse. It is also possible to hike from Laqo, after coming there from Cusilluchayoc, northward, following the course of the Qenkomayu upward for about 3 km eventually reaching Huayllacocha on the main paved Cusco-Pisac highway, a few hundred metres before Puka Pukara. This avoids the longer roundabout way from Laqo to Chilcapuquio. The routes can be modified and combined according to time limitations and weather conditions. Likewise, it is possible to take motor transport to the furthest point, in this case Tambo Machay, and from there begin walking back in the direction of Sacsayhuaman and Cusco.

An alternative route Laqo-Cusco

After walking 1 km beyond Laqo, head northeast along the Inca road from Cusilluchayoc (which goes to Pisac) and follow it uphill to the right of the hill. The trail crosses from a narrow valley to a wider valley. After a grove of eucalyptus you will see well-preserved Inca terraces, to the right of which is **Inkiltambo**. Here is a vast area of carved niches, which housed the mummies of the ancestors of the Inca community that looked after the *huaca*.

From Inkiltambo you go down the *quebrada* (ravine) of **Choquequirau**, taking the trail on the right side of the stream. You pass colonial kilns and then take a trail that goes up the right side of the valley, leading to a superb view of the **Huatanay Valley** and **San Jerónimo** (see page 194). The outskirts of Cusco are reached through a gap in the ridge. A dirt track crosses the hillside towards Cusco to meet the paved road, which you follow to the right for about 100 m until you find the path again on the opposite side. This leads to **Titicaca** (or Tetekaka) *huaca*, which now has a cross and chapel. The shrine stands on the *ceque* (see page 129) of the winter solstice and Peter Frost (in his *Exploring Cusco*) associates this fact with the alignment of the *huaca* with the legendary birthplace of the sun in Lake Titicaca. Above the shrine, the path splits; take the upper fork and continue to the *huaca* called **Mesa Redonda**, so called for its flat, table-like rock. Beyond, you go downhill into the city.

Hike to Chacán from Sacsayhuaman

You can reach the paved perimeter road around the north side of Sacsayhuaman from the centre of Cusco on foot. From the Plaza de Armas walk up Calle Suecia (straight up from the Portal de Carnes), or up Cuesta del Almirante to Plaza Nazarenas (turn left onto Calle Pumacurco), or via Calle Saphi and any of the pedestrian streets to the right of this street (eg Resbalosa or Amargura staircase). All of these will lead you to a small ticket booth just a few metres above San Cristóbal church. Leave the paved road at the booth to climb a wide path heading north to the Sacsayhuaman archaeological site. If you cross the esplanade of Sacsayhuaman and the paved road you will find traces of an Inca road on the left of the modern trail. This will bring you to an irrigation channel made of concrete. Do not miss this channel, as it leads directly to **Chacán**. Follow the channel upstream for 2 km, where it meets the Tica Tica Valley. Here a natural bridge (Chacán means 'bridge place') carries the channel across the gorge while the stream runs 25 to 30 m below. Above this exceptional barrier stands a large carved rock built between stone walls. This is another of Cusco's sacred *huacas*. If you cross the bridge and go down to your right towards the edge of the cliff, you will reach a lookout point at the front of a cave, which has Inca carvings. Below you can see the Río Tica Tica emerging from another cave, which runs beneath Chacán.

One kilometre upstream from Chacán are the ruins of **Ñustapacana**. The surroundings of this site are full of fine terraces, stone walls and another *huaca*.

Back at Chacán, walk west on the high trail above the river. Look for a eucalyptus plantation (or the remains of it if it has been cut down), on the opposite side of the river. Walk down to the river at this point and cross over. Along this path you will see rocks carved in the shape of pyramids and other Andean religious motifs. Most prominent is a rock, some 2½ m in height, whose central symbol has been defaced. This is **Quispe Wara** (Crystal Loincloth). Associated with this shrine are high quality Inca walls and aqueducts, which can be seen on the return to Cucso. Stay on the left bank of the river at Quispe Wara and climb straight uphill until you reach a narrow road. A leisurely 2-km descent passes, as a point of reference, the **Inkatambo Hotel** on your left. After this, turn left for 100 m to get back to the paved road at the bend just below Sacsayhuaman.

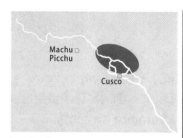

Machu
Picchu

Cusco

The Sacred Valley

Introduction

The Río Urubamba cuts its way through fields and rocky gorges beneath the high peaks of the Cordillera. The presence of giants such as **Pitusiray** and **La Verónica** is a constant reminder that to the Incas such mountains were apus (beings to be worshipped). The landscape is forever changing as shafts of sunlight fall upon plantations of corn, precipitous Inca terraces, tiled roofs, or the waters of the river itself. Brown hills, covered in wheat fields, separate Cusco from this beautiful high valley. Major Inca ruins command the heights – **Pisac**, **Huchuy Cusco** and **Ollantaytambo** are the best examples – and traditional villages guard the bridges or stand on the highlands.

The road from Cusco climbs up to a pass, then continues over the pampa before descending into the densely populated Urubamba Valley, which stretches from Sicuani (on the railway to Puno) to the gorge of Torontoi, 600 m lower, to the northwest of Cusco. Upstream from Pisac, the river is usually called the **Vilcanota**, downstream it is the **Urubamba**. Beyond Ollantaytambo, the river begins its descent to the Amazonian lowlands, becoming wilder as it leaves the valley behind. That the river was of great significance to the Incas can be seen in the number of strategic sites they built above it. They enhanced the valley's fertility by building vast stretches of terraces on the mountain flanks and the Inca rulers had their royal estates here. It is from the Incas' own name for the river that the section from Pisac to Ollantaytambo is called Sacred today.

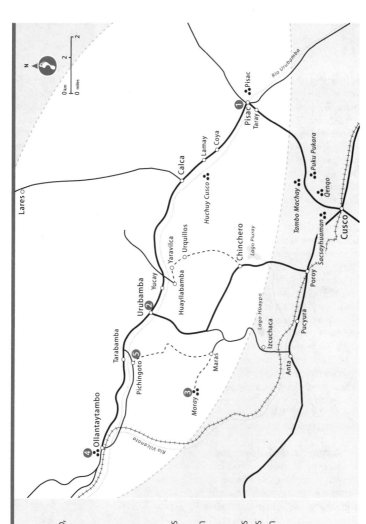

The Sacred Valley

★ **Don't miss...**

❶ **Pisac** After a good breakfast at the Hostal Pisaq on the plaza, or at the Presidencial Beho, walk up to the ruins at Pisac. As you climb, the views of the Urubamba Valley just get better and better, see page 136.

❷ **Urubamba** Visit the pottery workshop of Seminario-Behar, where pre-Columbian techniques and designs are used to make very desirable ceramics, see page 141.

❸ **Moray** In the hills above Urubamba, Moray's three large depressions, converted into terraced crop laboratories, show to perfection the Incas' thorough understanding of their environment, see page 143.

❹ **Ollantaytambo** Don't only see the Inca ruins here, but also the town, half of which retains its Inca layout (the llaqta). The town's museum is well worth a visit too, see page 143.

❺ **Pichingoto** The extraordinary, ancient salineras (salt pans) are quite spectacular, see page 143.

The Sacred Valley

For the visitor, paved roads, plentiful transport and a good selection of hotels and eating places make this a straighforward place to explore. You can choose either a quick visit from the city or, better still, linger for a few days, savouring the sights and atmosphere. The valley itself is great for cycling and there are plenty of walking trails for one- to two-day excursions. Horse riding and rafting are also popular in this most visitor-friendly of tourist destinations. Furthermore, if the altitude of Cusco itself is too much, you can hop on a minibus down to the valley – the 500-m difference can do wonders for your health. The best time to visit this area is April to May or October to November. The high season is from June to September, but the rainy season, from December to March, is cheaper and pleasant enough.

Ins and outs

Getting there From Cusco you can get to the Sacred Valley by bus, car, taxi or as part of an organized tour. The road from Cusco which runs past Sacsayhuaman and on to Tambo Machay (see page 88), climbs up to a pass, then continues over the pampa before descending into the densely populated Urubamba Valley. As the road drops from the heights above Cusco, there are two viewpoints, Mirador C'orao and Mirador Taray, over the plain around Pisac, and, beyond, the Pitusiray and Sawasiray mountains. This road then crosses the Río Urubamba by a bridge at Pisac and follows the north bank to the end of the paved road at Ollantaytambo. It passes through Calca, Yucay and Urubamba, which can also be reached from Cusco by the beautiful, direct road through Chinchero (see page 142). A taxi costs US$20-25 for the round trip up the valley and back to Cusco. An organized tour to Pisac can be fixed up anytime with a travel agent for US$5 per person. Tours can also be arranged to Chinchero, Urubamba and Ollantaytambo with a Cusco travel agency. To Chinchero, US$6 per person. Usually only day tours are organized for visits to the valley. ▸▸ *See under Cusco Tour operators, page 113.*

Getting around Don't hurry; most organized tours are too fast. Explore it on foot, by bike or on horseback. Using public transport and staying overnight in Urubamba, Ollantaytambo or Pisac allows much more time to see the ruins and markets. ▸▸ *See also Transport, page 154.*

Pisac → *Phone code: 084.*

Only 30 km north of Cusco is the little village of Pisac, which is well worth a visit for its superb Inca ruins, perched precariously on the mountain, above the town. They are considered to be amongst the very finest Inca ruins in the valley. Strangely, however, most visitors don't come to Pisac for the ruins. Instead, they come in droves for its Sunday morning market.

Pisac

Sleeping
Hospedaje Familiar
Kinsa Ccocha **1**
Hostal Pisaq **3**
Parador **2**
Residencial Beho **4**
Royal Inca Pisac **5**

Eating
Bakery **1**
Doña Clorinda **2**
Valle Sagrado **3**

⁞ A market for beads

A major feature of Pisac's popular market is the huge and varied collection of multicoloured beads on sale. Commonly called 'Inca beads', this is in fact something of a misnomer; for, although the Incas were highly talented potters and decorated their ware with detailed geometric motifs, they are not known to have made ceramic beads.

These attractive items have become popular relatively recently.

They used to be rolled individually by hand and were very time-consuming to produce. Now, in a major concession to consumerism, they are machine-made and produced in quantity, then hand-painted and glazed.

Today, the clay beads are produced in countless, often family-run, workshops in Cusco and Pisac. Some are made into earrings, necklaces and bracelets, but many thousands are sold loose.

Pisac is usually visited as part of a tour from Cusco but this often allows only 1½ hours here, not enough time to take in the ruins and splendid scenery. ▸▸ *For Sleeping, Eating and other listings, see pages 150-155.*

Pisac market

The market is described variously as colourful and interesting, or touristy and expensive, which is in part explained by the fact that it contains both sections for the tourist and for the local community. Traditionally, Sunday is the day when the people of the highlands come down to sell their produce (potatoes, corn, beans, vegetables, weavings, pottery, etc). These are traded for essentials such as salt, sugar, rice, noodles, fruit, medicines, plastic goods and tools. The market comes to life after the arrival of tourist buses around 1000, and is usually over by 1500. However, there is also an important ceremony every Sunday, in which the *Varayocs* (village mayors) from the surrounding and highland villages participate in a Quechua Catholic mass in **Pisac church**. It is a good example of the merging of, and respect for, different religious cultures. This aspect of the traditional Pisac Sunday market is still celebrated at 1100 sharp. Pisac has other, somewhat less crowded, less expensive markets on Tuesday and Thursday morning; it's best to get there before 0900.

On the plaza, which has several large *pisonay* trees, are the church and a small interesting **Museo Folklórico**. The town, with its narrow streets, is worth strolling around, and while you're doing so, look for the fine façade at Grau 485. There are many souvenir shops on Bolognesi.

Inca ruins

ⓘ *0700-1730. If you go early (before 1000) you'll have the ruins to yourself. Entry is by multi-site ticket. Guides charge US$5, but the wardens on site are very helpful and don't charge anything to give out information.*

The ruins of Inca Pisac stand on a spur between the Río Urubamba to the south and the smaller Chongo to the east. It is not difficult to imagine why this stunning location was chosen, as it provides an ideal vantage point over the flat plain of the Urubamba, the terraces below and the terraced hillsides across the eastern valley. In *The Conquest of the Incas*, John Hemming describes Pisac as one of the Incas' 'pleasure houses' in the Yucay Valley (another name for this stretch of the Urubamba). If it were merely that, it would have been some country estate. There were, however, many other facets to the site – defensive, religious and agricultural – all contributing to one of the largest Inca ruins in the vicinity of Cusco. The main buildings that can be seen

Rubbish

Every year on 16 September hundreds of students, campesinos, gringos, local companies and other volunteers board a bus in Cusco with rubber gloves and rubbish bags in their hands. What are they doing? Saving the Río Urubamba.

The Urubamba, sacred river of the Incas, is a Peruvian national treasure. This historical waterway, however, is being polluted. El Río Willkamayu (as it is known in Quechua) is a danger to the health of the local people as it is seriously contaminated by plastic, oil, petrol and any number of other non-biodegradeable products. In the 2002 Clean-up, nappies, clothing and labels that have been out of production for more than 10 years were found.

To start the ball rolling the *Día del Río* (Day of the River) will be used as a celebration of ecology and education. The idea is to enlighten the young people of Peru through teaching and by example. To preserve this great site South American Explorers is leading a clean up effort in partnership with many other companies. Meetings are held roughly once a month at the South American Explorers clubhouse (*Choquechaca 188, Cusco, T084-245484*) and lots of ideas have resulted concerning cleaning the river and recycling in general.

Cusco is becoming more progressive on all ecological subjects. A new recycling plant has been opened to deal with the inorganic rubbish. It will take time but in a few years it is hoped that all households in Cusco will be separating their refuse.

What you can do:
- Bring a water bottle and fill it in designated areas.
- Always leave plastic bottles in recycling bins.
- Bring or buy biodegradable soap.
- Say no to plastic bags in shops. Carry a backpack.
- Join the next *Día del Río*.

There are many ways to help. For more information, check out www.perurivers.org or

today have been dated to the reign of Pachacútec (see page 264), to whom, it is said, the estate belonged. To appreciate the site fully, allow five or six hours if going on foot. Even if going by car, do not rush as there is a lot to see and a lot of walking to do.

The walk up to the ruins begins from the plaza, passing the Centro de Salud and a new control post. The path goes through working terraces, giving the ruins a context. The first group of buildings is **Pisaqa**, with a fine curving wall. Climb up to the central part of the ruins, the **Intihuatana** group of temples and rock outcrops in the most magnificent Inca masonry. Here are the **Reloj Solar** (Hitching Post of the Sun – now closed because thieves stole a piece from it – palaces of the moon and stars, solstice markers, baths and water channels. From Intihuatana, a path leads around the hillside through a tunnel to **Q'Allaqasa** (military area). Across the valley at this point, a large area of Inca tombs in holes in the hillside can be seen. The end of the site is **Kanchiracay**, where the agricultural workers were housed. At dusk you will hear, if not see, the *pisaca* (partridges), after which the place is named, and you may see deer too.

Road transport approaches from the Kanchiracay end. The drive up from town takes about 20 minutes. Walking up, although tiring, is recommended for the views and location. It's at least one hour uphill all the way. The descent takes 30 minutes. Horses are available for US$3 per person. Combis charge US$0.60 per person and taxis US$3 one way up to the ruins from near the bridge. Then you can walk back down (if you want the taxi to take you back down negotiate a fare). Overnight parking is allowed in the car park.

Pisac to Urubamba

The first village on the road from Pisac towards Urubamba is **Coya** (see Festivals, page 154). Next is **Lamay** (see Festivals, page 154) and the nearby warm springs, which are highly regarded locally for their medicinal properties.

Calca, 18 km beyond Pisac at 2,900 m, was the headquarters of Manco Inca at the beginning of his uprising against the Spaniards in 1536. Today it is a busy hub in the valley, with a plaza which is divided into two parts. Urubamba buses stop on one side, and Cusco and Pisac buses on the other side of the dividing strip. Look out for the *api* sellers with their bicycles loaded with a steaming kettle and assortment of bottles, glasses and tubs.

It is a two-day hike from Cusco to Calca, via Sacsayhuaman, Qenqo, Puka Pukara, Tambo Machay and Huchuy Cusco with excellent views of the Eastern Cordilleras, past small villages and along beautifully built Inca paths. There are many places to camp, but take water.

There are mineral baths at **Machacancha**, 8 km east of Calca. These springs are indoors, pleasantly warm and will open at night for groups. They are half an hour by taxi from town. About 3 km beyond Machacancha are the Inca ruins of **Arquasmarca**.

Huchuy Cusco

The ruins of a small Inca town, Huchuy Cusco, are reached across the Río Urubamba and after a stiff three- to four-hour climb. Huchuy Cusco (also spelt Qosqo), which in Quechua means 'Little Cusco', was the name given to this impressive Inca site some time in the 20th century. Its original name was Kakya Qawani, which translates as 'from where the lightning can be seen'. According to the Spanish chronicler Pedro de Cieza de León, the palaces and temples at Huchuy Cusco were built by the eighth Inca, Viracocha, who conquered the area by defeating the ethnic groups settled there.

Huchuy Cusco is dramatically located on a flat esplanade almost 600 m above the villages of Lamay and Calca in the Sacred Valley. The views from the site are magnificent, with the Río Urubamba far below meandering through fertile fields, and the sombre Pitusiray massif opposite, surrounded by other snowy peaks.

The ruins themselves consist of extensive agricultural terraces with high retaining walls and several buildings made from both the finely wrought stonework the Incas reserved for their most important constructions, and adobe mud bricks. The Peruvian National Culture Institute (INC) began restoration work at the site in July 2001.

There are several ways to reach Huchuy Cusco. The ruins can be accessed most easily by following the steep trail behind the village of Lamay, which is reached by crossing the bridge over the river. There is also a clearly marked trail from the village of Calca. Another longer route leads to Huchuy Cusco from Tambo Machay near Cusco, a magnificent one- or two-day trek along the route once taken by the Inca from his capital to his country estate at Huchuy Cusco; some sections of the original Inca highway remain intact.

Valle de Lares

In this hike you walk through the beautiful landscape of the Lares Valley, with its magnificent mountains, lakes and llamas and meet local people and stay in small villages. Several agencies in Cusco offer trekking and biking tours to the region and some offer this trek as an alternative Inca Trail. The 1:100,000 **Instituto Geográfico Nacional** map should be useful here. Treks usually include transport by bus, guide, cook, porters or horses to carry food and equipment, food from lunch on the first day to lunch on the fourth day and camping equipment. Dineke Veerman writes:

Day 1 By bus it's 1½ hours to the start of the hike near an old hacienda in **Huarán** (2,830 m) in the Sacred Valley. You walk along the river for about five hours, slowly getting higher, having lunch and arriving at the pampa of **Cancha-Cancha** at 3,800 m. Camp there.

Day 2 After breakfast start the climb to the first pass, **Pachacútec** (4,420 m), which is about 3½ hours up. The views of the glaciers of Pachacútec, Pitusiray and the lake Pachacútec are fantastic. It takes 1½ hours down before lunch near the lake **Chihuapampa**. Then two hours to the campsite in **Kishuarani** (3,700 m), passing the **Canchispaqcha** waterfalls.

Day 3 From Kishuarani start to climb for about three hours, first passing the lake of **Queñacocha**, then to the second pass, **Kkochuyckaza** (4,240 m), where there are views of snow-covered mountains and the **Huillke** lakes. It is one hour until lunch near Huillke lakes (3,960 m) and one hour more down to the campsite in **Concani** (3,800 m).

Day 4 An easy walk, all downhill, leads in about 2½ hours to the hot springs near **Lares**. You then continue for about an hour to the village of Lares, from where buses run to Calca, and then back to Cusco.

A variation on the hike adds an extra day, with camping at the village of **Patacancha** on the fourth night, then a final hike or transport to Ollantaytambo.

Yucay

A few kilometres east of Urubamba, Yucay has two large, grassy plazas divided by the restored colonial church of **Santiago Apóstol**, with its oil paintings and fine altars. On the opposite side from Plaza Manco II is the **adobe palace** built for Sayri Túpac (Manco's son) when he emerged from Vilcabamba in 1558.

Urubamba

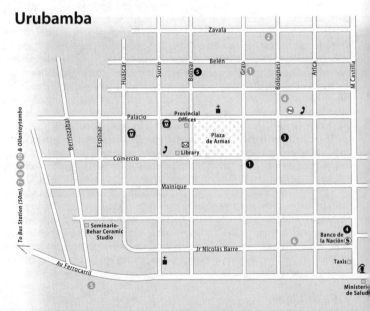

Sleeping
Capulí **1**
Hospedaje Perla de
  Vilcanota **3**
Hostal Urubamba **4**
Incaland **5**
K'uychi Rumi **8**
Las Chullpas **10**
Las Tres Marías **2**
Macha Wasi **6**
Perol Chico **9**
San Agustín Urubamba
  11
Sol y Luna **7**

Back along the road towards Yucay a bridge crosses the river to the village of
Huayllabamba (see page 142). If you are not dashing along the road at the speed of a local minibus, it is pleasant to cross the river and amble along the quieter bank, through farmland and small communities.

Urubamba → *Phone code: 084. Colour map 2, B2. Altitude: 2,863 m.*

Like many places along the valley, Urubamba has a fine setting, with views of the Chicón snow-capped peaks and glaciers, and enjoys a mild climate. The main plaza, with a fountain capped by a maize cob, is surrounded by buildings painted blue. Calle Berriózabal, on the west edge of town, is lined with pisonay trees. The large market square is one block west of the main plaza. The main road skirts the town and the bridge for the road to Chinchero is just to the east of town.

▸▸ *For Sleeping, Eating and other listings, see pages 150-155.*

Sights

Seminario-Behar Ceramic Studio, ⓘ *Calle Berriózabal 111, a right turning off the main road to Ollantaytambo. To84-201002, kupa@terra.com.pe Open every day, just ring the bell,* founded in 1980, is located in the beautiful grounds of the former **Hostal Urpihuasi**. The Seminario has investigated the techniques and designs of pre-Columbian Peruvian cultures and has created a style with strong links to the past. Each piece is handmade and painted, using ancient glazes and minerals, and is then fired in reproduction pre-Columbian kilns. The resulting pieces are very attractive. Reservations to visit the studio and a personal appointment with the artists (Pablo and Marilú) are welcomed. Recommended.

Around Urubamba

Five kilometres west of Urubamba is the village of **Tarabamba**, where a bridge crosses the Río Urubamba. If you turn right after the bridge you'll come to **Pichingoto**, a tumbled-down village built under an overhanging cliff. Also, just over the bridge and before the town to the left of a small, walled cemetery is a salt stream. Follow the footpath beside the stream and you'll come to **Salinas**, a small village below which are a mass of terraced Inca *salineras* (salt pans), which are still in production after thousands of years. It's a particularly spectacular sight as there are over 5,000. The cascade of centuries-old rectangular basins is like a giant artwork by a Cubist painter obsessed with the colour white. These are now a fixture on the tourist circuit and can become congested with buses. The walk to the salt pans takes about 30 minutes. Take water as it can be very hot and dry here.

9 de Noviembre
❸

To Cusco via Calca; Yucay & Cusco via Calca

❷ ⓐ

Coliseo Municipal
❻

To Cusco via Chinchero

66 99 The cascade of centuries-old rectangular basins is like a giant artwork by a Cubist painter obsessed with the colour white.

Chinchero → *Phone code: 084. Colour map 2, B3. Altitude: 3,762 m.*

ⓘ *The site is open daily, 0700-1730, and can be visited on the combined entrance ticket (see page 71). Chinchero is northwest from Cusco, high on the pampa just off a direct road to Urubamba. The streets of the village wind up from the lower sections, where transport stops, to the plaza which is reached through an archway.*

The great square appears to be stepped, with a magnificent Inca wall separating the two levels. Let into the wall is a row of trapezoidal niches, each much taller than a man. From the lower section, which is paved, another arch leads to an upper terrace, upon which the Spaniards built an attractive church, recently painted white. The interior of the church has been restored to reveal the paintings in all their glory. The ceiling, beams and walls are covered in beautiful floral and religious designs. The altar, too, is fine. The church is open on Sunday for mass and at festivals. Ask in the tourist office in Cusco if it is open at other times as it is worth spending a quiet moment or two inside. From the upper earth- and grass-covered plaza, there are superb views over the mountain ranges. Opposite the church is a small local museum. Excavations have revealed many Inca walls, terraces and various other features.

The local produce **market** on Sunday morning is fascinating and very colourful, and best before the tour groups arrive. It's on your left as you come into town. There's also a small handicraft market, also on Sunday, up by the church. Chinchero attracts few tourists, except on Sunday. ▶▶ *For Festivals, see page 154.*

Chinchero to Huayllabamba hike

There is a scenic path from Chinchero to Huayllabamba, the village on the left bank of the Río Urubamba between Yucay and Calca (see page 141). The hike is quite beautiful, with fine views of the peaks of the Urubamba Range, and takes about three to four hours. Follow the old Chinchero-Urubamba dirt road, to the left of the new paved road. Ask the locals when you are not sure. It runs over the pampa, with a good view of Chinchero, then drops down to the Urubamba Valley. The end of the hike is about 10 km before the town of Urubamba. You can either proceed to Urubamba or back to Cusco.

An alternative hike from Chinchero follows the spectacular Maras-Moray-Pichingoto salt mines route (see below). This brings you to the main Urubamba valley road, about 10-12 km beyond the town of Urubamba. You could also take the more direct main road from Chinchero to Urubamba, with occasional shortcuts, but this route is a lot less interesting.

Moray

ⓘ *US$1.45.* This remote but beautiful site lies 9 km to the west of the little town of **Maras** and is well worth a visit. There are three 'colosseums', used by the Incas, according to some theories, as a sort of open-air crop nursery, known locally as the laboratory of the Incas. The great depressions do not contain ruined buildings, but are lined with fine terracing. Each level is said to have its own microclimate. The scenery around here is absolutely stunning. As you leave Maras, look back to the village with its church, tiled roofs and adobe walls framed by snowy mountains. All around are fields of wheat and other crops, such as *kiwicha*, whose tall, thin, violet-coloured flowers produce a protein-rich grain. At harvest-time the whole area turns from rich green to every shade of gold and brown imaginable. To the northwest stands the majestic white peak of La Verónica. The light is wonderful in the late afternoon, but for photography it's best to arrive in the morning. The road eventually arrives at the guardian's hut, but there is little indication of the scale of the colosseums until you reach the rim.

About 1½ km below Maras are the *salineras* (salt pans) at **Pichingoto**, which are well worth a visit (see page 141). At **Tiobamba**, near Maras, an indigenous market-festival is held on 15 August (see Festivals, page 154). The most interesting way to get to Moray is from Urubamba via the Pichingoto Bridge over the Río Urubamba. The climb up from the bridge is fairly steep but easy, with great views of Nevado Chicón. The path passes by the spectacular salt pans. Moray is about 1½ hours further on. If you cannot get transport to Maras, so take any combi going between Urubamba and Chinchero, get out at the junction for Maras and walk from there.

❧ Moray is a very atmospheric place, which, many people claim, has mystical powers.

It's 30 minutes to Maras; once through the village, bear left a little, and ask directions to Moray. It's 1½ hours' walk in total. Hitching back to Urubamba is quite easy, but there are no hotels at all in the area, so take care not to be stranded. The **Hotel Incaland** in Urubamba can arrange horses and guide and a pick-up truck for the return, all for US$30-40 per person (see page 151). Another option is to hire a taxi with driver to take you to Moray.

Ollantaytambo → *Phone code: 084. Colour map 2, A2. Altitude: 2,800 m.*

A trip to Ollantaytambo is a journey into the past, to a world governed by a concept of time very different to the one which holds sway nowadays. Today, the descendants of the people who founded Ollantaytambo continue to live there, watched over still by the sacred mountains of Verónica and Alankoma. They work the land as they have always done, with the same patience and skill that their ancestors employed to shape and then move the huge blocks of stone with which they built both their homes and the temples in which they worshipped. The attractive little town now sits at the foot of some spectacular Inca ruins and terraces, and is built directly on top of the original Inca town. ▸▸ *For Sleeping, Eating and other listings, see pages 150-155.*

Ins and outs

Getting there Ollantaytambo can be reached by bus from Cusco, Urubamba and Chinchera. The best way of getting to Machu Picchu is by train. You won't be allowed on the station unless you have previously bought a ticket for the train. The gates are locked and only those with tickets can enter. ▸▸ *See also Transport, page 155.*

History

The Tambo Valley, as the Spanish chroniclers called it, is a fertile stretch of land sown with fields of maize which hug the banks of the Río Urubamba (Vilcanota) from Ollantaytambo to Machu Picchu. Long before the arrival of the Incas, the valley was inhabited by the Ayarmaca, who had migrated from Lake Titicaca, far to the southeast. On their long journey, this race of farmers followed the course of the Vilcanota, abandoning the harsh altiplano in their search for a better climate for their agricultural activities. The Ayarmacas, known in the Spanish chronicles as Tampus, came from the same ethnic stock as the Incas of Cusco, and maintained with them many cultural, linguistic and family ties which would ensure them, at least for a while, a degree of regional autonomy during the period of Inca imperial expansion. When Inca Pachacútec did begin to take control of neighbouring areas (see History section, page 264), one of his first conquests was the Tambo Valley. The chronicles tell of two *curacas* (local chieftains), Paucar Ancho and Tokori Tupa, who led the resistance against the Inca, only to be defeated in the mid-15th century. Pachacútec sacked their town, subjugated its people and made their lands his royal estate.

Upon the death of Pachacútec in 1471, his properties were passed to the members of his *panaca* (royal household), the Hatun Ayllu (Great Clan). This was the Inca's extended family and formed the social, political and religious elite from whose ranks the new Inca would emerge. The Hatun Ayllu set about converting Ollantaytambo into a great agricultural complex by extending its terraces beyond the town. To reclaim still more land for cultivation, they straightened a 3-km stretch of the river, as well as building canals and irrigation channels to bring fresh water from the area's snow- capped peaks and highland lakes. They ordered the construction of *qolqas* (barns) to store the harvest, as well as establishing checkpoints to control access to the centre known today as Ollantaytambo. To link Ollantaytambo to the rest of their empire via the Royal Inca Highway (*Capac Ñan*), the Incas built a tremendous suspension bridge across the river. Undiminished after more than five centuries, the single supporting central buttress of that ancient bridge now supports a modern metal structure.

When Manco Inca decided to rebel against the Spaniards in 1536, he fell back to Ollantaytambo from Calca to stage one of the greatest acts of resistance to the *conquistadores*. Hernando Pizarro led his troops to the foot of the Inca's stronghold which, later, Hernando's brother Pedro described as "so well fortified that it was a thing of horror". Under fierce fire, Pizarro's men failed to capture Manco and retreated to Cusco, but Manco could not press home any advantage. The Inca siege of the Spaniards in Cusco turned into stalemate and Manco was unable to capitalize on the arrival of Diego de Almagro's army from Chile to threaten the Pizarro brothers' hold on Cusco. In 1537, feeling vulnerable to further attacks, Manco left Ollantaytambo for Vilcabamba.

Ollantaytambo

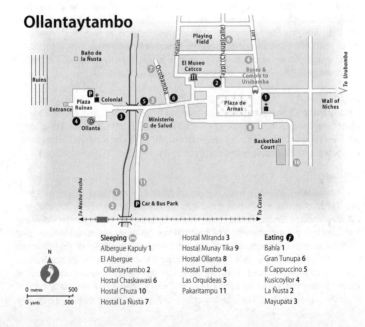

Sleeping		Eating
Albergue Kapuly **1**	Hostal Miranda **3**	Bahía **1**
El Albergue	Hostal Munay Tika **9**	Gran Tunupa **6**
Ollantaytambo **2**	Hostal Ollanta **8**	Il Cappuccino **5**
Hostal Chaskawasi **6**	Hostal Tambo **4**	Kusicoyllor **4**
Hostal Chuza **10**	Las Orquídeas **5**	La Ñusta **2**
Hostal La Ñusta **7**	Pakaritampu **11**	Mayupata **3**

0 metres 500
0 yards 500

It is easy to see, even today, how daunting an assault on the Inca's defences must have seemed to Pizarro. Great walled terraces of fine masonry climb the hillside, at the top of which is an unassailable sanctuary. The entire construction is superb, including the curving terraces following the contours of the rocks overlooking the Urubamba. It was these terraces which were successfully defended by Manco Inca's warriors. Manco built the defensive wall above the site and another wall closing the Yucay Valley against attack from Cusco. These are still visible on either side of the valley. Walking up the terraces is taxing enough, but imagine how impossible it must have been for armed *conquistadores* trying to scale the hill under a hail of missiles.

Entering Ollantaytambo

Entering Ollantaytambo from Urubamba, the road is built along the long wall of 100 niches. Note the inclination of the wall towards the road. Since it was the Incas' practice to build with the walls leaning towards the interiors of the buildings, it has been deduced that the road, much narrower then, was built inside a succession of buildings. The road leads into the main plaza, in the middle of which is a fountain on whose top rim stand the statues of two white geese. Public transport congregates in the centre of the square and there is a small church in the southeast corner. The original Inca town is behind the north side of the plaza and you can enter it by taking any of the streets of the plaza, or the street that runs beside the Río Patacancha. The road from the northwest corner of the plaza looks up to the Inca temple, but to get there you have to cross the bridge over the river and go down to the colonial church with its *recinto* (enclosure). Beyond is a grand plaza (and car park) with entrances to the archaeological site.

The fortress

ⓘ *0700-1730. Admission is by combined entrance ticket (see page 71), which can be bought at the site. Otherwise it's US$6.50. If possible arrive very early, 0700, before the tourists. Guides at the entrance charge US$2. Avoid Sun afternoons, when tour groups from Pisac descend in their hundreds.*

The ruins, known as 'the fortress', were, in fact, a religious complex, with temples dedicated to the many divinities which comprised the Inca pantheon. The gods the Incas worshipped represented the forces of nature, and were seen, therefore, to control the agricultural life of the community. At the fortress, we find the Temple of Viracocha, the creator god, as well as those devoted to the sun, water, earth and lightning. The magnificent terraces which lead up to the temple site were almost certainly used by astronomer-priests for the cultivation of corn for ceremonial purposes; the maize they grew there would mark the seasons for planting and harvesting for the rest of the community.

When you visit Ollantaytambo you will be confronted by a series of 16 massive, stepped terraces of the very finest stonework after crossing the great high-walled trapezoidal esplanade known as *Mañariki*. Beyond these imposing terraces lies the so-called Temple of Ten Niches, a funeral chamber once dedicated to the worship of the Pachacútec *panaca* (royal household). Immediately above this is the site popularly known as The Temple of the Sun, although it is not known for certain whether it was ever intended for that purpose. The remains of this temple consist of six monolithic upright blocks of rose-coloured rhyolite, forming a wall which, in common with other Inca temples, runs from east to west. A narrow, vertical course, like stone beading, separates the giant monoliths, on which traces of relief carving can be seen. Typical Andean motifs like the *chakana* (Andean cross), as well as other zoomorphic figures are just legible. These designs were defaced by the Spanish shortly after the conquest, as part of a systematic campaign by the victors physically to erase the indigenous religion. They have also suffered, though, from erosion; sketches by the American traveller Ephrain George Squier, who visited Ollantaytambo in the 1870s, show that the figures were much more complete then. Below the

'Temple of the Sun', the dark grey stone is embellished today with bright orange lichen. Note how most of the stones have one or two protrusions at the bottom edge, a feature you will not see in Cusco or Pisac.

You can either descend by the route you came up, or follow the terracing round to the left (as you face the town) and work your way down to the Valley of the Patacancha. On this route there are more Inca ruins in the small area between the town and the temple fortress, behind the church. Most impressive is the **Baño de la Ñusta** (Bath of the Princess), a grey granite rock, about waist high, beneath which is the bath itself. It is delicately finished with a three-dimensional *chakana* motif. The water falls over the relief arch into the pool, which was probably used for the worship of water in the form of ritual bathing. Some 200 m behind the Baño de la Ñusta along the face of the mountain are some small ruins known as **Inca Misanca**, believed to have been a small temple or observatory. A series of steps, seats and niches have been carved out of the cliff. There is a complete irrigation system, including a canal at shoulder level, some 15 cm deep, cut out of the sheer rock face.

The town

Tucked away below its more famous ruins and rarely visited, the town of Ollantaytambo gives those few travellers who do wander its narrow streets, unchanged for 500 years, a much clearer idea of what life must have been like under Inca rule. Unlike modern cities, *llaqtas* (Inca towns) were not designed to house large populations. Inca society was essentially agrarian and, among the common people, almost everyone worked and lived on the land. The towns and cities that the Incas did build were meant to serve as residential areas for the state's administrative and religious elite.

Throughout the Inca Empire of Tawantinsuyo, the *llaqtas* were divided into two zones, along blood lines, between the two principal *ayllus* (clans), of Hanan and Urin. In Ollantaytambo, the Urin occupied the area which today corresponds to the present-day village. Called *Qosqo Ayllu*, it was both an administrative centre and the home of the Pachacútec *panaca*. The streets were laid out in a simple grid pattern, with the whole forming the Inca trapezoid (see page 269). These streets, whose corners are marked with huge stone blocks, surround *canchas* (communal enclosures which house many families). Each *cancha* occupies half a block, with just one entrance on those streets which run parallel to the Río Patacancha. It is clear, from the elaborate double-jamb porticos which form their entrances, that these *canchas* were built for members of the Incas' social and religious elite. The Inca nobility did not work on the land, their *yanaconas* (servants) did it for them, and the remains of the homes of this servant class, built from much simpler materials, have been found in the northern part of the town.

El Museo Catcco (Centro Andino de Tecnología Tradicional y Cultural de las Comunidades de Ollantaytambo) ① *Casa Horno, Patacalle, 1 block from the plaza. T084-204024, catcco@mail.com Daily 0900-1800. US$1.45 (donations welcome). Tourist information is available in the museum. Information on the museum and other aspects of Ollantaytambo can be found in Spanish on www.cbc.org.pe/rao, the site developed from the Ollantaytambo Pilot Project, which was undertaken by Prom Perú and the European Union. The project, aimed at developing the town, its tourism and community participation, has produced much useful material and we recognize here our debt to it in researching this section. The museum is run by Sr Joaquín Randall.* If you are visiting Ollantaytambo, begin your tour here. Started with help from the British Embassy, Catcco houses a fine ethnographical collection. The Information Center gives tips on day-hikes, things to see and places to dine and stay. Local guides, trained at museum workshops, are available for tours of the town and surrounding areas. Outside the museum, Catcco runs non-profit cultural programmes including the Ollantaytambo Andean Library and Research Center, temporary exhibitions, concerts and lectures. Also on site is a ceramics workshop, a textile revitalization programme and an educational theatre project. Ceramics and textiles are sold in the museum shop; proceeds help fund the museum and other Catcco programmes. The museum has internet access. Note the canal down the middle of the street outside the museum.

Recently a two-dimensional '**pyramid**' has been identified on the west side of the main ruins of Ollantaytambo. Its discoverers, Fernando and Edgar Elorietta, claim it is the real Pacaritambo, from where the four original Inca brothers emerged to found their empire (see page 148). Whether this is the case or not, it is still a first-class piece of engineering with great terraced fields and a fine 750-m wall creating the optical illusion of a pyramid. The wall is aligned with the rays of the winter solstice, on 21 June. People gather at mid-winter dawn to watch this event.

The mysterious 'pyramid', which covers 50-60 ha, can be seen properly from the other side of the river. This is a pleasant, easy one-hour walk, west from the Puente Inca, just outside the town. You'll also be rewarded with great views of the Sacred Valley and the river, with the snowy peaks of the Verónica massif as a backdrop.

Around Ollantaytambo

Inca quarries at Cachiccata

It takes about a day to walk to the Inca quarries on the opposite side of the river and return to Ollantaytambo. The stone quarries of Cachiccata are located on the lands of the hacienda of the same name, some 9 km from Ollantaytambo. There are three quarries at the site: **Molle Puqro,** which the Incas were gradually abandoning at the time of the conquest; **Sirkusirkuyoc** and the smaller **Cachiccata**, which both seem to have been fully operational. The stone at Cachiccata, rose-coloured rhyolite, is just one of many types of stone used in the construction of Ollantaytambo, and it is still not known where the others came from. It would seem that all the quarries were abandoned when Manco Inca retreated from Ollantaytambo after confronting Hernando Pizarro's cavalry there in 1537.

Standing to the left of the six monolithic blocks which form the so-called Temple of the Sun at Ollantaytambo, you can see, looking west-southwest across the valley, the quarries of Cachiccata, below a mountain called Yana Urco. From here, you can appreciate the Herculean nature of the task that the builders of Ollantaytambo's magnificent temples set themselves. Several generations of stonemasons and labourers must have worked in their thousands to quarry the huge blocks that the Incas used in the construction of the Temple of the Sun and the Royal House of the Sun. Once extracted, the stones would have been roughly shaped before being transported to the building site. Possibly using rollers, or more probably using the simple brute force of the thousands of men that the Incas' highly organized society would have been able to dedicate to the task, the blocks were then dragged for more that 6 km across open country.

The Incas would have only been able to cross the Río Urubamba in winter, when its waters are at their lowest ebb, and even then they could probably have only done so by diverting the river's course. It is thought that they dug two channels; the stones would then have been dragged across the dry left-hand channel while the river was being diverted through the right-hand one. This right-hand channel would then be drained in its turn to allow the stones to continue their painstaking progress.

The next task was to raise the rhyolite blocks from the valley floor up to the site known as the fortress and to accomplish this, the Incas' engineers built a great ramp. Looking down from the Temple of the Sun, to the left of the six monoliths, the remains of this ramp can still be seen, and they are even more clearly visible when you look up at the ruins from the valley floor. It is difficult to appreciate from today's highly mechanized perspective just how hard the Incas laboured to build Ollantaytambo,

The Inn of Origin

One of the Incas' three creation stories is the *Inn of Origin*. This legend tells of Pacaritambo, the Inn, or House of Origin, which is also associated with another name, Tambotocco, the Place of the Hole. Like the *Children of the Sun* story, (see page 265), there are variations on the basic theme, which relates that four brothers and four sisters (three of each in some versions) emerged from the central cave of three in a cliff. The names of the brothers and sisters vary, but usually the men were called Ayar Cachi, Ayar Manco, Ayar Uchu and Ayar Sauca, and the women Mama Huaco, Mama Ocllo, Mama Coya and Mama Rahua. The brothers and sisters set out in search of good land on which to settle and on the way fell out with Ayar Cachi, who was much stronger, more violent and more arrogant than the others. They lured him back to the cave and walled him up inside before recommencing their journey. Soon, though, Ayar Cachi miraculously reappeared, telling them to move on to the valley of Cusco and found the city. He then went to the mountain of Huanacauri where his spirit remained, becoming a place of veneration for the Incas. In return for them worshipping him on the mountain, Ayar Cachi would intercede, on their behalf, to the gods to ensure prosperity and success in war. Ayar Manco then proceeded with his sisters to Cusco, where, according to some versions, he built Qoricancha as his first house

and quickly earned the respect of the local Indians. A bloody twist to this story recounts how one of the four sisters, on the lookout for the ideal land, came to Cusco and petrified the inhabitants by killing an Indian, ripping out his lungs and blowing them up as she entered the village.

This myth has several elements in common with the *Children of the Sun*: siblings teaching the unenlightened people and founding Cusco and the Inca dynasty; the discovery of fertile land on which to base the kingdom; the role of Huanacauri Mountain. Whereas the *Children of the Sun* borrows from the Lake Titicaca creation myth, the *Inn of Origin* borrows from another major American tradition; ancestors, especially brothers, coming out of rocks or the ground.

For the sake of completeness, the third main creation story concerns a Shining Mantle, the brightness of which as it reflected the sun's rays so dazzled the people that the wearer deceived them into believing that he descended from the Sun. Some versions say that Ayar Manco was the instigator of this trickery after he and his brothers emerged from Pacaritambo. He used sheets of silver strapped to his body to flash in the sun as he strode along a hilltop. An alternative version says that it was Sinchi Roca, Manco's successor, who was dressed in this magnificent robe by his mother. She thus led the people to believe that the boy was a ruler sent by the Sun.

employing as they did a patience and skill born of a concept of time very different to our own. The stones were found near the summit of a mountain on the other side of the river valley after a prolonged search. They then had to be quarried, hewn into a rough shape, and hauled across the valley floor and up to the temple. Once there, they were sculpted by the master masons to fit together perfectly, to the design of an architect, or architects, of consummate skill.

Between the ruins and the quarries of Cachiccata, more that 50 enormous stones that never reached their destination lie abandoned. The inhabitants of the area call them *las piedras cansadas*, or (the tired stones). It is still not known whether work on the temples ceased when the Spanish arrived, or did it stop during the civil war between Atahualpa and Huascar? The thousands of workers who were involved in the construction of Ollantaytambo, over a period of generations, almost certainly worked under the *mit'a* system (see page 266). For several months of each year they would have to leave their work to tend their crops, and in times of war, construction would have been abandoned and the workers integrated into the enormous conscripted armies upon which the Inca state depended. Another suggestion is that Colla workers from Lake Titicaca were employed in the construction of the site. This conclusion has been drawn from the similarities of the monoliths facing the central platform with the Tiahuanaco remains. According to this theory, the Colla are believed to have deserted halfway through the work, leaving behind all the unfinished blocks visible today. While most experts agree that the work on Ollantaytambo was begun under Pachacútec, it will probably never be known for certain exactly when Cachiccata's great stones first began to tire.

Pinkuylluna

Pinkuylluna Hill, on the western edge of Ollantaytambo, is home to the Sacred Valley's most impressive collection of *qolqas* (storehouses) structures which have often (and erroneously) been called prisons by local guides. The reason why these granaries were built so high up on the hillside is given by the 17th-century Spanish chronicler Bernabé Cobo, [the Incas] "built their storehouses outside their towns, in the high places that were fresh and well-ventilated...". It is impossible to know with any certainty what kinds of produce were stored at Pinkuylluna, but the main harvest was certainly maize, which was probably stored alongside other crops. Many observers take the gigantic image, known locally as the Tunupa, which appears on the hillside when viewed from the bridge in front of the ruins, to be a carved likeness of the Inca creator god, Viracocha.

Pincuylluna can be climbed with no mountaineering experience, although there are some difficult stretches – allow two or three hours going up. The path is difficult to make out, so it's best not to go on your own. Walk up the valley to the left of the mountain, which is very beautiful and impressive, with Inca terraces after 4 km.

Pumamarca

Hidden away in the hills beyond the historic town, Pumamarca lies about two hours on foot from Ollantaytambo through fertile countryside sculpted long ago into a magnificent series of agricultural terraces which to this day are sown with corn and *kiwicha*. Pumamarca is a small, well-preserved Inca citadel some 7 km north of, and 800 m above, Ollantaytambo. It lies at the confluence of the Río Patacancha and its tributary, the Yuracmayo (or White River). From there it dominates a strategic point, commanding a privileged view of both valleys, which would have once controlled access to Ollantaytambo from that direction, as well as guarding the canal which bears its name.

The ruins' high surrounding wall with its numerous zigzags suggests that the site was a fortress, although (as at Ollantaytambo) all the *qolqas* (storehouses), were built outside the main complex. Nobody knows for sure exactly when this citadel was built. Some researchers believe that it may have been another checkpoint, designed to limit access to Ollantaytambo from Antisuyo, the eastern *suyo* (quarter) of the Inca Empire. But the impressive nature of Pumamarca, built in classic Inca style, leads many scholars to conclude that it may have been one of the first Inca settlements in the area, and not just a simple outpost of Ollantaytambo.

The path to Pumamarca passes through the village of Munaypata and follows the Río Patacancha. At Pallata, 6 km from Ollantaytambo and 30 minutes before Pumamarca, the Miranda family will look after bicycles and other gear. They live in the first house in the village; the path from the road to the footbridge over the river passes their front door. Up the same valley are the indigenous villages of Marcacocha, Huilloc and Patacancha.

Cusichaca Valley

A major excavation project has been carried out since 1977 under the direction of Ann Kendall in the Cusichaca Valley, 26 km from Ollantaytambo, at the intersection of the Inca routes. Only 9 km of this road are passable by ordinary car. The Inca fort, **Huillca Raccay**, was excavated in 1978-80, and work is now concentrated on **Llactapata**, a site of domestic buildings. Ann Kendall is now working in the Patacancha Valley northeast of Ollantaytambo. Excavations are being carried out in parallel with the restoration of Inca canals to bring fresh clean water to the settlements in the valley.

● Sleeping

Pisac *p136, map p136*

AL **Royal Inca Pisac**, *Carretera Ruinas Km 1.5, T084-203064, royalin@terra.com.pe* In the same chain as the **Royal Incas I** and **II** in Cusco, this hotel can be reached by the hotels' own bus service. It is a short distance out of town, on the road that goes up to the ruins, a taxi ride after dark. Price includes taxes and breakfast. Camping is available for US$5 per person. A guide for the ruins can be provided. The rooms are comfortable, in a number of blocks in the grounds of a converted hacienda; they are pleasantly furnished, with all conveniences. There is a pool, sauna and jacuzzi (US$7), tennis court, horse riding and bicycle rental. The restaurant is good and there is a bar. The hotel is popular with day-trippers from Cusco. In the public area a rescued owl sits on a perch, casting an eye over the guests. A small deer wanders around the property, but there is also a puma in a cage. Staff are very helpful and accommodating.

E **Hostal Pisaq**, *at the corner of Pardo, on the plaza in front of the church and marketplace, Casilla Postal 1179, Cusco, T084-203062, hotelpisaq@terra.com.pe* Price per person. There is 1 room with bath in our **D** range. All others share bathrooms, which are spotless. Breakfast is US$2.50 extra (a bit more if you have eggs). Excellent brownies are on sale and pizza is served on Sun. There is hot water 24 hrs, pleasant decor, and a sauna. Friendly and knowledgeable staff who speak English, German and French. Recommended.

F **Residencial Beho**, *Intivatana 642, 50 m up the hill from the plaza, T/F084-203001*. Ask for a room in the main building. They serve a good breakfast for US$1. The *hostal* has a shop selling local handicrafts including

masks. The owner's son will act as a guide to the ruins at the weekend.

G **Hospedaje Familiar Kinsa Ccocha**, *on the plaza*. The rooms are basic and none has bath. Price per person; you pay less if you don't use hot water.

G **Parador**, *on the plaza, T084-203061*. Price per person. All rooms share bathrooms, which have hot water. Breakfast is not included, but the restaurant serves other meals.

Pisac to Urubamba *p139*

L-AL **Sonesta Posadas del Inca**, *Plaza Manco II de Yucay 123, Yucay, T084-201107, posada@sonestaperu.com* The price includes taxes and buffet breakfast. A converted 300-year-old monastery is now a hotel which is like a little village with plazas, lovely gardens, a chapel, and many different types of room (one even has its own ghost – ask for room 111 if you want to be spooked). As well as rooms in the old part, there are recent additions, which are comfortable and well appointed. The restaurant serves an excellent buffet lunch. There is a conference centre. Highly recommended.

AL **Sonesta Posada del Inca Yucay II**, *Plaza Manco II 104, Yucay, T084-201107*. In the same chain, and just a short way from **Posadas del Inca**. Also called **Posada del Inca Libertador**, or **Casona**, this colonial house was where Simón Bolívar stayed during his liberation campaign in 1824. The price includes taxes and breakfast. The 39 rooms have heating and, outside, there are 2 patios and gardens. There is a restaurant and pizzería. Various activities can be arranged: canoeing, horse riding, mountain biking and guided treks and tours.

B-C **Hostal Y'Llary**, *also on the plaza, Yucay, T084-201112*. The price includes bathroom and breakfast.

E **Hostal Pitusiray**, *Calca, on the edge of town.* Basic.

F **Hostal Jerseyhuasi**, *Lamay, beside the springs.* A nice little place, price includes breakfast, with generous portions of good food at other meals, clean and comfortable rooms. They also have camping possibilities.

G **Hostal Martín**, *Calca, opposite the market place, 1 block from the plaza.* Dirty, cold water only.

Urubamba *p141, map p140*
Out of town
LL-AL **Sol y Luna**, *west of town, T084-201620, www.hotelsolyluna.com* Attractive bungalows set off the main road in lovely gardens, pool, excellent buffet in restaurant, French-Swiss owned. Has **Viento Sur** adventure travel agency, for horse riding, mountain biking, trekking and paragliding, *www.aventurasvientosur.com*

L-AL **K'uychi Rumi**, *Km 73.5 on the road to Ollantaytambo, 3 km from town, T084-201169, www.urubamba.com* 6 cottages for rent with 2 bedrooms, fully equipped, fireplace, terrace and balcony, surrounded by gardens. Price is for 1-2 people, each house can accommodate 6.

AL **Incaland Hotel and Conference Center**, *Av Ferrocarril s/n, 5 mins' walk from the centre, T084-201126, www.incalandperu.com* Special rates are also available. 65 comfortable, spacious bungalows set in extensive gardens, English-owned, good restaurant serving buffet meals, bar, disco, 2 pools, also horse riding (eg to Moray), mountain biking, kayaking and rafting. The staff are helpful and service is good.

AL-A **San Agustín Urubamba**, *Km 71, T084-201443/44* (or book at *San Agustín Internacional* in Cusco, p96), 20 mins' walk from town, towards Yucay. Comfortable, small pool, restaurant serving a buffet on Tue, Thu and Sun for US$3.50.

B **Perol Chico**, *Km 77 on the road to Ollantaytambo, office Grau 203, Casilla postal 59, Correo Central, Urubamba, T084-201694, stables T084-624475, www.perolchico.com* Dutch/Peruvian-owned, private bungalows with fireplace and kitchen on a ranch, specializes in horse riding (see below). Recommended.

D per person **Las Chullpas**, *3 km west of town in the Pumahuanca Valley, T084-685713,*

www.laschullpas.com Very peaceful, includes excellent breakfast, vegetarian meals, English and German spoken, Spanish classes, natural medicine, treks, horse riding, mountain biking, camping US$3 with hot shower. *Mototaxi* from town US$0.85, taxi (ask for Querocancha) US$2.

In town
C **Las Tres Marías**, *Zavala 307, T084-201004 (Cusco T084-225252).* New, with beautiful gardens, hot water, welcoming. Recommended.

D **Macha Wasi**, *Jr Nicolás Barre, T084-201612, www.unsaac.edu.pe/machawasi* Canadian-owned guesthouse with comfortable rooms and a dormitory, delicious breakfast extra, safe, lovely garden, laundry. Spanish courses and treks can be arranged. Recommended.

F **Capulí**, *Grau 222.* With bath, hot water and TV. Price per person, or **G** per bed with shared bath.

F **Hostal Urubamba**, *Bolognesi 605.* Basic but pleasant, rooms with bath and cold water, or **G** without bath.

G **Hospedaje Perla de Vilcanota**, *9 de Noviembre, T084-201135.* Price is per bed, without bath, but shared bathrooms have hot water; some rooms are even cheaper.

Chinchero *p142*
F **Hotel Restaurant Antabaraj**, *just beyond ticket control, T084-306002 (Patricia Cagigao), antabaraj@hotmail.com* Basic rooms, take sleeping bag, kitchen facilities, good views, food at reasonable prices.

Ollantaytambo *p143, map p144*
AL **Ñustayoc Mountain Lodge and Resort**, *about 5 km west of Ollantaytambo, just before Chillca and the start of the Inca Trail, T084-204098 or Lima T01-275 0706, www.nustayoclodge.com* Large and somewhat rambling lodge in a wonderful location with great views of the snowy Verónica massif and other peaks. Lovely flower-filled garden and grounds. Nicely decorated, spacious rooms, all with private bath. Price includes continental breakfast served in the large restaurant area.

AL **Pakaritampu**, *C Ferrocarril s/n, T084-204020, www.pakaritampu.com* The price includes breakfast and taxes. This modern, 3-star hotel has 20 rooms with bath and views. There is a TV room, restaurant and bar, internet service for guests, laundry, safe and room service. Adventure sports such as rafting, climbing, trekking, mountain biking and horse riding can be arranged. Meals are extra: buffet US$13, dinner US$12-15. Excellent quality and service.

C **Hostal Munay Tika**, *on the road to the station, T084-204111, munaytika@latin mail.com* Price includes breakfast and bath. Dinner is served by arrangement. To use the sauna costs US$5 with prior notice. Also has a nice garden. New and good.

C-D **Albergue Kapuly**, *at the end of the station road, T084-204017.* Prices are lower in the off season. A quiet place with spacious rooms, some with and some without bath. The garden is nice and the price includes a good continental breakfast. Recommended.

D **El Albergue Ollantaytambo**, *within the railway station gates, T084-204014, www.rumbosperu.com/elalbergue/* Owned by North American Wendy Weeks, the *albergue* has 8 rooms with shared bathrooms. Price (per person) includes breakfast; box lunch costs US$4, full dinner US$7 on request. The rooms are full of character and are set in buildings around a courtyard and lovely gardens. Great showers (24 hrs a day) and a eucalyptus steam sauna (US$5). The whole place is charming, very relaxing and homely. See the office-cum-shop-cum-exhibition where interesting handicrafts can be bought. Also for sale is Wendy's digestif, *Compuesto Matacuy* (also sold at **Centro Pi** in Cusco). It's very convenient for the Machu Picchu train and good place for information. Private transport can be arranged to the salt mines, Moray, Abra Málaga for birdwatching and taxi transfers to the airport. Highly recommended.

E **Hostal Chaskawasi**, *Chaupicalle (also called C Taypi) north of the plaza, T084-208085, anna_machupicchu@ hotmail.com* New *hostal* snuggled away in the small alleys behind the plaza. Owner Anna is very friendly.

E **Hostal La Ñusta**, *C Ocobamba, T084-204035.* Ask about accommodation in the shop/restaurant of the same name on the plaza or in the **Pizzería Gran Tunupa**. This is a decent although uninspiring budget option. Proprietor Rubén Ponce

loves to share his knowledge of the ruins with guests. You get a good view of the ruins from the balcony. See below for the restaurant.

E **Hostal Ollanta**, *on the south side of the plaza, T084-204116.* Basic and clean, but with a great location. All rooms with shared bath.

E **Las Orquídeas**, *near the start of the road to the station, T084-204032.* Good accommodation at this *hostal*, price includes breakfast and meals are available.

F **Hostal Chuza**, *just below the main plaza I n town, T084-204113.* Very clean and friendly with safe motorcycle parking. They have a TV in the front room for guests and one of the rooms features a wonderful view of the ruins with the Nevado de Verónica framed perfectly behind – a wonderful sight to wake up to in the morning. Recommended.

F **Hostal Miranda**, *between the main plaza and the ruins, T084-204091.* A basic *hostal* with shower included. It's very friendly, clean and the flower-filled garden is pleasant.

G **Hostal Tambo**, *just walk up the street called Lari that heads north from the plaza.* After 20 m or so you'll see an unmarked blue door on the left-hand side... bang on the door! If this doesn't work keep walking, turn left down the first small alley and bang on that blue door instead! Once past this unassuming exterior you emerge into a mini Garden of Eden, full of fruit trees, flowers, dogs, cats and domesticated parrots in the trees. There's no hot water and only 3 basic rooms (price per person), but the family is very friendly and the Señora is a real character.

ⓐ Eating

Pisac *p136, map p136*
Good, cheap trout is available in many restaurants.

$$ **Valle Sagrado**, *just out of town along from the bridge going towards Urubamba.* Meals are not cheap, but the helpings are huge and good value. Recommended, especially for the fish.

$ **Bakery**, *Av Mcal Castilla 372,* sells excellent cheese and onion *empanadas* for US$0.25, suitable for vegetarians, and good wholemeal bread. The oven is tremendous – take a look even if you aren't hungry.

$ Doña Clorinda, *on the plaza opposite the church*, doesn't look very inviting but cooks tasty food, including vegetarian options. A very friendly place.

Pisac to Urubamba *p139*
There are some basic restaurants around the plaza in Calca.

Urubamba *p141, map p140*
$$ La Casa de la Abuela, *Bolívar 272, 2 blocks up from the Plaza de Armas, T084-622975*. Excellent restaurant with rooms grouped around a small courtyard. The trout is fantastic and food is served with baskets of roasted potatoes and salad. Recommended.

$$ Chez Mary, *Comercio y Grau, corner of main plaza, T084-201003*. Mary Cuba, the owner, is a local Urubambina, very pleasant and helpful, who speaks good English. She serves excellent food, good pasta and pizzas, and the atmosphere is very cosy and comfortable, with smart decor and good music. At night the bar has live music.

$$ El Fogón, *Parque Pintacha, T084-201534*. Traditional Peruvian food, large servings, nice atmosphere. Recommended.

$$ Pizzonay, *Av Mcal Castilla, 2nd block*. Pizzas, excellent lasagne. Mulled wine served in a small restaurant with nice decor. Clean, good value. Recommended.

$$ Quinta los Geranios, *on the main road before the bridge, T084-201043*. Regional dishes, excellent lunch with more than enough food, average price US$13.

$$ El Maizal, *on the road before the bridge, T084-201454*. Country-style restaurant with a good reputation, buffet service with a variety of typical Novo Andino dishes, plus international choices, beautiful gardens with native flowers and fruit trees. Recommended (they also have a hotel of the same name).

$ Pintacha, *Bolognesi 523*. Pub/café serving sandwiches, burgers, coffees, teas and drinks. Has games and book exchange, cosy, open till late.

Around Urubamba *p141*
$$$ Tunupa, *on left side of the road on the riverbank, in a new, colonial-style hacienda (same ownership as Tunupa in Cusco), zappa@ terra.com.pe* Excellent food served indoors or outdoors, bar, lounge, library, chapel, gardens, stables and an alpaca-jewellery shop. Outstanding exhibition of pre-Columbian objects and colonial paintings, and **Seminario**'s ceramics feature in the decor. People on valley tours (Tue, Thu, Sun) are served a varied buffet including Novo Andino cuisine; buffet lunch US$15, 1200-1500. Lunch and dinner (1800-2030) is available daily.

Ollantaytambo *p143, map p144*
$$ Fortaleza, *2 branches, one on Plaza Ruinas, the other on the north side of the main plaza*. Basic but good food, breakfasts, pizza and pasta – all the gringo restaurant favourites are on offer, as well as some more local dishes.

$$ Gran Tunupa, *corner of C ocobamba and Bentinerio, right-hand side between the plaza and the bridge*. Nice view and reasonable food but the pizzas suffer from the usual Peruvian lack of tomato sauce.

$$ Il Cappuccino, *just before the bridge on the right-hand side*. Offers the best cappuccino in town, great coffee generally, also café latte and expresso. Good continental and American breakfasts. Slightly more sophisticated ambience and service in comparison with many other establishments in town.

$$ Kusicoyllor, *on the Plaza Ruinas*. The same owners as **Il Cappuccino**, serving pizza, pasta and, once again, good coffee.

$$ Mayupata, *Jr Convención s/n, across the bridge on the way to the ruins, on the left, T084-204083 (Cusco)*. Serving international choices and a selection of Peruvian dishes, desserts, sandwiches and coffee. It opens at 0600 for breakfast, and serves lunch and dinner. The bar has a fireplace; river view, relaxing atmosphere.

$ Bahía, *on the east side of the plaza*. Very friendly, vegetarian dishes served on request.

$ La Ñusta, *on the plaza*, with the same owner as the hostel – see above, popular, serves good food; snacks available.

🌑 Bars and clubs

Urubamba *p141, map p140*
Tequila, Av Mcal Castilla 3rd block. The door is always closed so you must ring the bell. Disco, drinks, good coffee, open till late.

⊛ Festivals and events

Pisac *p136, map p136*
A local fiesta is held on **15 Jul**.

Pisac to Urubamba *p139*
The **Fiesta de la Virgen Asunta** is held in **Coya** on **15-16 Aug**. **Lamay** hosts a festival on **15 Aug**.

Urubamba *p141, map p140*
May and **Jun** are the harvest months, with many festivals following mysterious ancient schedules. Urubamba's main festival, **El Señor de Torrechayoc**, takes place during the first week of Jun.

Chinchero *p142*
The town celebrates the **Day of the Virgin**, on **8 Sep**.

Moray *p142*
At **Tiobamba**, near Maras, a fascinating indigenous market-festival is held on **15 Aug** where Sacred Valley yellow maize is exchanged for pottery from Lake Titicaca.

Ollantaytambo *p143, map p144*
On **6 Jan** there is the **Bajada de Reyes Magos** (the Magi), when people from the highland communities bring down to Ollantaytambo the Niño Jesús, dressed in a poncho, etc. There is some traditional dancing, a bull fight, local food and a fair. The **Fiesta de Compadres**, a moveable feast 10 days before Carnavales and 13 days before Ash Wednesday, is celebrated in the small, indigenous village of **Marcacocha**, close to Ollantaytambo by local transport or on foot. There is a delightful chapel on an Inca site, the dance of the *huayllata* (Andean goose), a mass and a bullfight inthe smallest bullring imaginable, all in beautiful surroundings. As elsewhere, **Semana Santa**, the week before **Easter**, is a lovely time of year. **End May-early Jun**: Pentecostes, 50 days after

Easter, is the **Fiesta del Señor de Choquekillca**, patron saint of Ollantaytambo. There are several days of dancing, weddings, processions, masses, feasting and drinking (the last opportunity to see traditional Cusqueño dancing). On **29 Jun**, following *Inti Raymi* in Cusco, there is a colourful festival, the **Ollanta-Raymi**, at which the Quechua drama, *Ollantay*, is re-enacted. **29 Oct** is the **Aniversario de Ollantaytambo**, a festival with dancing in traditional costume and many local delicacies for sale.

⊕ Sport and activities

Urubamba *p141, map p140*
Horse riding Perol Chico, *T084-695188*, see Sleeping p151. Owned and operated by Eddy van Brunschot (Dutch/Peruvian), 1- to 12-day trips out of Urubamba, good horses, riding is Peruvian Paso style; 1-day trip to Moray and the salt pans costs US$60 (6 hrs). Recommended. Also contact through **SAS Travel** in Cusco, p116.

⊙ Transport

To organize your own Sacred Valley transport, try one of these taxi drivers, recommended by **South America Explorers**: **Manuel Calanche**, *T084-227368, T969 5402 (mob)*; **Carlos Hinojosa**, *T084-251160*; **Ferdinand Pinares**, *Yuracpunco 155*; **Tahuantinsuyo**, *T084-225914, T968 1519 (mob)*, speaks English, French and Spanish); **Eduardo**, *T084-231809*, speaks English. Also recommended are: **Angel Marcavillaca Palomino**, *Av Regional 877, T084-251822, amarcavillaca@yahoo.com*, helpful, patient, reasonable prices; **Movilidad Inmediata**, *T962 3821 (mob)*, runs local tours with an English-speaking guide. **Angel Salazar**, *Marcavalle I-4 Huanchac, T084-224679 (to leave messages)*, is English-speaking and arranges good tours, very knowledgeable and enthusiastic; **Milton Velásquez**, *T084- 222638, T968 0730 (mob)*, is also an anthro- pologist and tour guide and speaks English.

   For public transport to the Sacred Valley, see below:

Pisac *p136, map p136*
Bus From C Puputi on the outskirts of Cusco, near the Clorindo Matto de Turner

school and Av de la Cultura. 32 km, 1 hr, US$0.85. Colectivos, minibuses and buses leave when full, between 0600 and 1600; also trucks and pick-ups. Buses returning from Pisac are often full. The last one back leaves around 2000. Taxis charge about US$20 for the round trip. To Pisac, **Calca** (18 km beyond Pisac) and **Urubamba**, buses leave from Av Tullumayo 800 block, Wanchac, US$1.

Urubamba *p141, map p140*

Road There is a paved road from the main road between **Chinchero** and Urubamba to **Maras** and from there an unpaved road in good condition leads to **Moray**. There is public transport from Chinchero to Maras and regular pick-up trucks which carry people and produce in and out. Maras and Moray are visited most easily via Chinchero nowadays. Transport stops running between 1700 and 1800; it costs between US$0.60-1.

The bus and combi terminal is just west of town on the main road.

Buses run from Urubamba to **Calca**, **Pisac** (US$0.80, 1 hr) and **Cusco** (2 hrs, US$1), from 0530 onwards. Also buses to Cusco via **Chinchero**, same fare.

Colectivos to **Cusco** can be caught outside the terminal and on the main road, US$1.15. Combis run to **Ollantaytambo**, 45 mins, US$0.30. Hotels such as the **Incaland** and **Posadas del Inca**, **Yucay**, run a twice-daily shuttle between Cusco airport and Urubamba for US$10. There ar ealso buses from here to Quillabamba.

Train See page 174 for the Sacred Valley Railway from Urubamba to **Aguas Calientes**.

Chinchero *p142*

Road Combis and colectivos for Chinchero leave from 300 block of Av Grau, **Cusco**, 1 block before crossing the bridge. 23 km, 45 mins, US$0.45; and for **Urubamba** a further 25 km, 45 mins, US$0.45 (or US$1 Cusco-Urubamba direct, US$1.15 for a seat in a colectivo). To **Ollantaytambo**, 0745 and 1945 direct, or catch a bus to Urubamba from Av Grau.

Ollantaytambo *p143, map p144*

Road For those travelling by car and intending to go to Machu Picchu, it is recommended to leave the car at Ollantaytambo railway station, which costs US$1 a day, or at suitable hotels (see Sleeping, above).

Bus: There is a direct bus service from Ollantaytambo to **Cusco** at 0715 and 1945; the fare is US$2.85. The station is 10-15 mins walk from the plaza (turn left at the sign that says 'Centro de Salud' between the Plaza de Armas and the ruins). There are colectivos at the plaza for the station when trains are due. Also, a bus leaves the station at 0900 for **Urubamba** (US$0.30) and **Chinchero** (US$1).

Train See page 174.

❶ Directory

Pisac *p136, map p136*

Banks If you need to change money, there is a shop on M Castilla, heading away from the plaza, near where the road bends; it will change Tcs. **Internet and telephone** On the same side of the plaza as the museum are the municipal building with a computer centre (internet for US$0.75 per hr, closed Sun morning) and a public phone booth.

Pisac to Urubamba *p139*

Internet In **Calca**, the municipal library has internet connection.

Urubamba *p141, map p140*

Banks Banco de la Nación, *M Castilla at the start of the 2nd block.*
Post Serpost, post office, is on the Plaza de Armas.
Telephone There are several phone booths around the centre. The one outside **Hostal Urubamba** can make international calls.

Ollantaytambo *p143*

Internet Internet Ollanta, just before the Plaza Ruinas on the left-hand side, opposite the Santiago Apóstol church. 3 machines, US$2 per hr, US$0.90 for 15 mins.

Machu Picchu & the Inca Trail

Introduction

There is a tremendous feeling of awe on first witnessing this incredible sight. The ancient citadel, 42 km from Ollantaytambo by rail, straddles the saddle of a high mountain with steep terraced slopes falling away to the fast-flowing Río Urubamba snaking its hairpin course far below in the valley floor. Towering overhead is Huayna Picchu, and green jungle peaks provide the backdrop for the whole majestic scene. In comparison with many archaeological ruins, there are so many standing buildings that it requires no stretch of the imagination to work out what the city looked like. What function some of those buildings had and the meaning of their enigmatic symbols is harder to guess at, but this adds to the allure of the site.

To almost anyone looking for a picture that sums up South America, Machu Picchu is usually what first springs to mind. On the television, in brochures, on packets of coffee, you name it, Machu Picchu has become a kind of shorthand for lost civilizations, the thrill of discovery, exotic travel and, above all, the mystery that can still be found in an increasingly technological world. At the same time it is accessible; hundreds of thousands of tourists visit it each year. And yet it transcends the many roles that it has acquired, photogenic image, tourist magnet, centre of controversy, through the strength of its stones, the way it is intimately tied to its surroundings, its enigmas and its beauty.

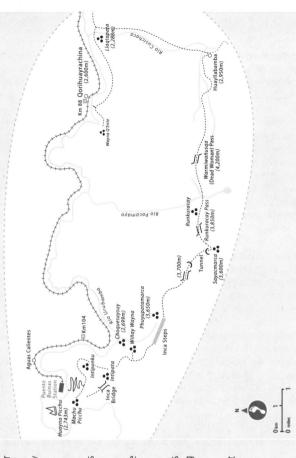

★ Getting the most out of Machu Picchu

1. Not everyone has the time or the stamina to trek up to Machu Picchu. There is still a thriving business in one- or two-day trips, but a quick visit hardly gives you time to recover from the initial sense of awe. It takes at least a day to appreciate the ruins and their surroundings fully.

2. Do find time to peer into corners, investigate the angles of stones, the weight of lintels, the outlook of windows. See how rocks and openings align themselves with peaks across the valley.

3. Try to be there for dawn or dusk to enjoy the changing of the light. A good time to visit is before 0830, when the views are at their best. The Watchman's Hut is an ideal place to spend the last few minutes of daylight.

4. Monday and Friday are bad days to visit because there is usually a crowd of people on guided tours who are going or have been to Pisac Market on Sunday, and too many people all want lunch at the same time.

5. The ruins are at their busiest in the morning. Although it is quieter in the afternoon, a lot of people do stay on to see the sun setting behind the mountains.

Ins and outs

Getting there There are two ways to get to Machu Picchu. The easy way is by train from Cusco, Ollantaytambo or Urubamba, with a bus ride for the final climb from the rail terminus at Aguas Calientes to the ruins. ▸▸ *See Transport, page 174, for the timetables.* The strenuous way is to hike the Inca Trail, which is described in its own section (see page 164). This is the only true way to get to Machu Picchu: sling your rucksack on your back and follow in the footsteps of the Incas. By trekking you are making a true pilgrimage and the sweat and struggle is all worth it when you set your eyes on this mystical site at sunrise from the Inca sun gate above the ruins. That way you see Machu Picchu in its proper context. Afterwards you recover in Aguas Calientes and soothe those aching limbs in the hot springs. The introduction of new regulations for walking the Inca Trail in 2001 opened up additional options for trekking to Machu Picchu, some shorter, some longer than the old route. So if you fancy widening the perspective of how the Incas walked to their sacred city, ask your chosen tour operator to show you the alternatives.

▸▸ *For Sleeping, Eating and other listings, see pages 172-176.*

Advice and information The Machu Pichu Sanctuary Lodge (see Sleeping, page 172) is located next to the entrance, with a restaurant serving buffet lunch. Beside the entrance and luggage store is a snack bar. Neither place is cheap so it's best to take your own food and drink, and take plenty of drinking water. Note that food is not officially allowed into the site.

Permission to enter the ruins before 0630 to watch the sunrise over the Andes, which is a spectacular experience, can be obtained from the **Instituto Nacional de Cultura** (INC) in Cusco, but it is often possible if you talk to the guards at the gate. The ruins are also quieter after 1530, but don't forget that the last bus down from the ruins leaves at 1730. The walk up takes 1½-two hours, following the Inca path. Walking down to Aguas Calientes, if staying the night there, takes between 30 minutes and one hour.

You are not allowed to walk back along the Inca Trail though you can pay US$4.50 at Intipunku to be allowed to walk back as far as Wiñay-Wayna. In the dry season sandflies can be a problem, so take insect repellent and wear long clothing.

The agency officially responsible for the site is **Unidad Gestión de Machu Picchu,** *C Garcilaso 223, Cusco, T084-242103.* It is an excellent source of information on Machu Picchu and this is the place to which any complaints or observations should be directed.

History

For centuries Machu Picchu was buried in jungle, until Hiram Bingham stumbled upon it in July 1911. It was then explored by an archaeological expedition sent by Yale University. Machu Picchu was a stunning find. The only major Inca site to escape 400 years of looting and destruction, it was remarkably well preserved. And it was no ordinary Inca settlement. It sat in an inaccessible location above the Urubamba Gorge, and contained so many fine buildings that people have puzzled over its meaning ever since.

Bingham claimed he had discovered the lost city of Vilcabamba, and for 50 years everyone believed him. But he was proved wrong, and the mystery deepened. Later discoveries revealed that Machu Picchu was the centre of an extensive Inca province. Many finely preserved satellite sites and highways also survive. This is craggy terrain and the value of a province with no mines and little agricultural land – it was not even self-sufficient – is hard to determine. Bingham postulated it was a defensive citadel on the fringes of the Amazon. But the architecture fails to convince us, and in any case, defense against whom?

The Incas were the first to build permanent structures in this region, which was unusual because they arrived at the tail end of 4,000 years of Andean civilization. 16th-century land titles discovered in the 1980s revealed that Machu Picchu was built by the Inca Pachacútec, founding father of the Inca Empire. But they do not tell us why he built it. One reasonable speculation is that this area provided access to coca plantations in the lower Urubamba Valley. However, the fine architecture of Machu Picchu cannot be explained away simply as a coca-collecting station.

Machu Picchu

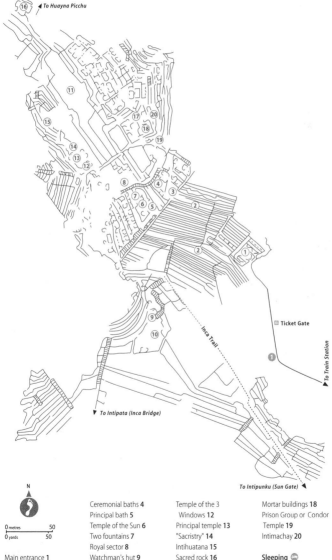

Main entrance **1**
Agricultural sector **2**
Dry moat **3**
Ceremonial baths **4**
Principal bath **5**
Temple of the Sun **6**
Two fountains **7**
Royal sector **8**
Watchman's hut **9**
Funerary rock **10**
Main plaza **11**
Temple of the 3
  Windows **12**
Principal temple **13**
"Sacristry" **14**
Intihuatana **15**
Sacred rock **16**
Living quarters &
  workshops **17**
Mortar buildings **18**
Prison Group or Condor
  Temple **19**
Intimachay **20**

Sleeping
Machu Picchu
  Sanctuary Lodge **1**

Recent studies have shown that the Temple of the Sun, or Torreón, was an observatory for the solstice sunrise, and that the Intihuatana stela is the centre-point between cardinal alignments of nearby sacred peaks. The Incas worshipped nature: the celestial bodies, mountains, lightning, rainbows, rocks – anything, in fact, that was imbued with spiritual power.

This spiritual component is the key to understanding Machu Picchu. The Bingham expedition identified 75% of the human remains as female, and a common belief is that Machu Picchu was a refuge of the Inca 'Virgins of the Sun'. However, the skeletons were re-examined in the 1980s using modern technology, and the latest conclusion is that the gender split was roughly 50/50.

Machu Picchu was deliberately abandoned by its inhabitants – when, we do not know. This may have happened even before the Spanish invasion, perhaps as a result of the Inca civil wars, or the epidemics of European diseases which ran like brushfires ahead of the Spanish in the New World. One theory proposes that the city ran dry in a period of drought; another suggests a devastating fire. Or the city may have been evacuated during the period of Inca resistance to the Spanish, which lasted nearly 40 years and was concentrated not far west of Machu Picchu.

Machu Picchu ruins → *Colour map 2, A2. Altitude: 2,380 m.*

ⓘ *The site is open from 0700 to 1730. Entrance fee is US$20. It is possible to pay in dollars, but only clean, undamaged notes will be accepted. You cannot take backpacks into Machu Picchu; leave them at the entrance for US$0.50. Guides are available at the site, they are often very knowledgeable and worthwhile, and charge US$15 for 2½ hrs. See also Advice and information, above.*

Once you have passed through the ticket gate you follow a path to a small complex of buildings which now acts as the main entrance to the ruins. It is set at the eastern end of the extensive terracing which must have supplied the crops for the city. Above this point, turning back on yourself, is the final stretch of the Inca Trail leading down from **Intipunku** (Sun Gate), see page 169. From a promontory here, on which stands the building called the **Watchman's Hut**, you get *the* perfect view of the city (the one you've seen on all the postcards), laid out before you with Huayna Picchu rising above the furthest extremity. Go round the promontory and head south for the **Intipata** (Inca bridge), see page 164. The main path into the ruins comes to a dry moat that cuts right across the site. At the moat you can either climb the long staircase which goes to the upper reaches of the city, or you can enter the city by the baths and Temple of the Sun.

The more strenuous way into the city is by the former route, which takes you past quarries, on your left as you look down to the Urubamba on the west flank of the mountain. To your right are roofless buildings where you can see in close up the general construction methods used in the city. Proceeding along this level, above the main plazas, you reach the **Temple of the Three Windows** and the **Principal Temple**, which has a smaller building called the **Sacristy**. The two main buildings are three-sided and were clearly of great importance, given the fine stonework involved. The wall with the three windows is built onto a single rock, one of the many instances in the city where the architects did not merely put their construction on a convenient piece of land. They used and fashioned its features to suit their concept of how the city should be tied to the mountain, its forces and the alignment of its stones to the surrounding peaks. In the Principal Temple, a diamond- shaped stone in the floor is said to depict the constellation of the Southern Cross.

Continue on the path behind the Sacristy to reach the **Intihuatana**, the 'hitching-post of the sun'. The name comes from the theory that such carved rocks (*gnomons*), found at all major Inca sites, were the point to which the sun was

66 99 The feeling of relief on reaching the top is immense and there's the added, sadistic pleasure of watching your fellow sufferers struggling in your wake...

symbolically 'tied' at the winter solstice, before being freed to rise again on its annual ascent towards the summer solstice. The steps, angles and planes of this sculpted block appear to indicate a purpose beyond simple decoration and researchers, such as Johan Reinhard in *The Sacred Center*, have sought the trajectory of each alignment. Whatever the motivation behind this magnificent carving, it is undoubtedly one of the highlights of Machu Picchu.

Climb down from the Intihuatana's mound to the **Main Plaza**. Beyond its northern end is a small plaza with open-sided buildings on two sides and on the third, the **Sacred Rock**. The outline of this gigantic, flat stone echoes that of the mountains behind it. From here you can proceed to the entrance to the trail to Huayna Picchu (see below). Returning to the Main Plaza and heading southeast you pass, on your left, several groups of closely packed buildings which have been taken to be **Living Quarters and Workshops, Mortar Buildings** (look for the house with two discs let into the floor) and the **Prison Group**, one of whose constructions is known as the **Condor Temple**. Also in this area is a cave called **Intimachay**.

A short distance from the Condor Temple is the lower end of a series of **Ceremonial Baths** or fountains. They were probably used for ritual bathing and the water still flows down them today. The uppermost, **Principal Bath**, is the most elaborate. Next to it is the **Temple of the Sun**, or Torreón. This singular building has one straight wall from which another wall curves around and back to meet the straight one, but for the doorway. From above it looks like an incomplete letter P. It is another example of the architecture being at one with its environment as the interior is taken up by the partly worked summit of the outcrop onto which the building is placed. All indications are that this temple was used for astronomical purposes. Underneath the Torreón a cave-like opening has been formed by an oblique gash in the rock. Fine masonry has been added to the opposing wall, making a second side of a triangle, which contrasts with the rough edge of the split rock. But the blocks of masonry appear to have been slotted behind another sculpted piece of natural stone, which has been cut into a four-stepped buttress. Immediately behind this is a two-stepped buttress. This strange combination of the natural and the man-made has been called the Tomb or Palace of the Princess. Across the stairway from the complex which includes the Torreón is the group of buildings known as the **Royal Sector**.

Huayna Picchu

Synonymous with the ruins themselves is Huayna Picchu, the verdant mountain overlooking the site. There are also ruins on the mountain itself, and steps to the top for a superlative view of the whole magnificent scene, but this is not for those with vertigo. The climb takes up to 90 minutes but the steps are dangerous after bad weather and you shouldn't leave the path, ① *0700-1300, with the latest return time being 1500*. You must register at a hut at the beginning of the trail. The other trail to Huayna Picchu, down near the Urubamba, is via the Temple of the Moon, in two caves, one above the other, with superb Inca niches inside, sadly blemished by graffiti. To reach the **Temple of the Moon** from the path to Huayna Picchu, take the marked trail to the left; it is in good shape. It descends further than you think it should. After the Temple you may proceed to Huayna Picchu, but this path is overgrown, slippery when wet and has a crooked ladder on an exposed part about 10 minutes before the top (not for the faint-hearted). It is safer to return to the main trail to Huayna Picchu, but this adds about 30 minutes to the climb. The round trip takes about four hours.

Intipata

The famous Inca bridge – Intipata – is about 45 minutes along a well-marked trail south of the Royal Sector. The bridge – which is actually a couple of logs – is spectacularly sited, carved into a vertiginous cliff-face. The walk is well worth it for the fine views, but the bridge itself is closed to visitors. Not only is it in a poor state of repair, but the path beyond has collapsed. There have been several accidents.

The Inca Trail

The wonder of Machu Picchu has been well documented over the years. Equally impressive is the centuries-old Inca Trail that winds its way from the Sacred Valley near Ollantaytambo, taking three to four days. What makes this hike so special is the stunning combination of Inca ruins, unforgettable views, magnificent mountains, exotic vegetation and extraordinary ecological variety. The government acknowledged all this in 1981 by including the trail in a 325 sq-km national park, the Machu Picchu Historical Sanctuary. Machu Picchu itself cannot be understood without the Inca Trail. Its principal sites are ceremonial in character, apparently in ascending hierarchical order. This Inca province was a unique area of elite access. The trail is essentially a work of spiritual art, like a Gothic cathedral, and walking it was formerly an act of devotion. ▸▸ *For Sleeping, Eating and other listings, see pages 172-176.*

Ins and outs

Entrance tickets and tours ▸▸ *For further details of tours, see page 112.*
An entrance ticket for the trail or its variations must be bought at the **Instituto Nacional de Cultura** (**INC**) office in Cusco; no tickets are sold at the entrance gates. Furthermore, tickets are only sold on presentation of a letter from a licensed tour operator on behalf of the visitor. There is a 50% discount for students, but note that officials are very strict, only an ISIC card will be accepted as proof of status. Tickets are checked at Km 82, Huayllabamba and Wiñay-Wayna.

On all hiking trails (Km 82 or Km 88 to Machu Picchu, Salkantay to Machu Picchu, and Km 82 or Km 88 to Machu Picchu via Km 104) adults must pay US$50, students and children under 15 US$25. On the Camino Real de los Inkas from Km 104 to Wiñay-Wayna and Machu Picchu the fee is US$25 per adult, US$15 for students and children (or US$20 and US$10 respectively if you don't camp at Wiñay- Wayna).

Tour operators in Cusco, including Tambo Tours, will arrange transport to the start, equipment, food, etc, for an all-in price, averaging around US$180-200 per person.

Advice and information
Although security has improved in recent years, it's still best to leave all your valuables in Cusco and keep everything inside your tent, even your shoes. Avoid the July-August high season and the rainy season from November to April (note that this can change, so check in advance). In the wet it is cloudy and the paths are very muddy and difficult. Also watch out for coral snakes in this area (black, red, yellow bands). Please remove all your rubbish, including toilet paper, or use the pits provided. Do not light open fires as they can get out of control. The **Annual Inca Trail Clean-up** takes place usually in September. Many agencies and organizations are

⦂ Inca Trail regulations

The year 2001 signalled the beginning of strict new rules on the Inca Trail; tourists should be aware of the following regulations:

- All agencies must have a licence to work in the area.

- Groups of up to seven independent travellers who do not wish to use a tour operator are allowed to hike the trails if they contact an independent, licensed guide to accompany them, as long as they do not contract any other persons like porters or cooks.

- A maximum of 500 visitors per is day allowed on the trail.

- Operators pay US$10 for each porter and other trail staff; porters are not permitted to carry more than 25 kg (although less scrupulous agencies often find ways to circumvent this requirement).

- Littering is banned, as is carrying plastic water bottles (canteens only may be carried).

- Pets and pack animals are prohibited, but llamas are allowed as far as the first pass.

- Groups have to use approved campsites; on the routes from Km 82, Km 88 and Salkantay, the campsites may be changed with prior authorization (Llulluchayoc, Llulluchapampa, Pacaymayo Valley, Runkurakay, or Phuyupatamarca).

As of August 2003 these regulations were being enforced with increasing efficiency. Particularly important for prospective trekkers to consider is the 500-person daily limit on the trail. In the high season (roughly June-September) this numerical limit means that there can be waiting lists of several days, sometimes up to a week. If you have limited time in the Cusco area, it is essential that you book your space on the Inca Trail well in advance of your intended departure date. Other aspects, such as limits on groups size, carrying medical kits with oxygen, responsible disposal of waste, were only being applied haphazardly. The best advice is to check in advance with a reputable tour company in Cusco (see the list given on page 113), with **South American Explorers** (www.saexplorers.org) or with a government agency such as **PromPerú** (www.peru.org.pe, www.peruonline.net) or the **Ministry of Tourism**.

(Machu Picchu The Inca Trail)

involved and volunteers should contact **South American Explorers** in Cusco (see page 71) for full details of ways to help.

Equipment

While hiking the Inca Trail note that it is cold at night, and weather conditions change rapidly, so it is important to take strong footwear, rain gear and warm clothing (this includes long johns if you want to sleep rather than freeze at night): dress in layers. Also take food, water, water purification tablets, insect repellent, sunscreen, a hat and sunglasses, a supply of plastic bags, coverings, a good sleeping bag, a torch and a stove for preparing hot food and drink to ward off the cold at night. It is worth paying extra to hire a down sleeping bag if you haven't brought your own. A paraffin (kerosene) stove is preferable, as fuel can be bought in small quantities in markets.

A tent is essential, but if you're hiring one in Cusco, check carefully for leaks. Walkers who have not taken adequate equipment have died of exposure. Caves marked on some maps are little better than overhangs and are not sufficient shelter to sleep in. You could also take a first-aid kit; if you don't need it the porters probably will given their rather basic footwear.

It is now forbidden to use trekking poles because the metal tips are damaging the trail. Instead, buy a carved wooden stick on sale in the main plaza in Ollantaytambo or at the trail head. Many will need this for the steep descents on the path. If you need knee/ankle/thigh supports go to **Ayala**, a shop down a small arcade in Cusco, to the right of **Taca Peru,** opposite the Palacio de Justicia near the top of Avenida Sol.

All the necessary equipment can be rented in Cusco (see page 113). Good maps of the trail and area can be bought from **South American Explorers** in Lima or Cusco (see pages 71 and 241). If you have any doubts about carrying your own pack, porters/guides are available through Cusco agencies. Carry a day-pack, water and snacks in case you walk faster or slower than the porters and you have to wait for them to catch you up or you have to catch them up.

Take around US$30 extra per person for tips and a drink at the end of the trail. If you're carrying your own gear it's wise to take another US$60 for when you realize the climb and altitude really is too much; freelance porters are everywhere on the trail and will carry your bags for US$8-15 per day.

The trek

Day 1

The trek to the sacred site begins either at Km 82, **Piscacucho**, or at Km 88, **Qorihuayrachina**, at 2,600 m. In order to reach Km 82 hikers are transported by their tour operator (see above) in a minibus on the road that goes to Quillabamba. From Piri onward the road follows the riverbank and ends at Km 82. Where there used to be an *oroya* (cable crossing), there is now a bridge. You can depart as early as you like and arrive at Km 82 faster than going by train. The Inca Trail equipment, food, fuel and

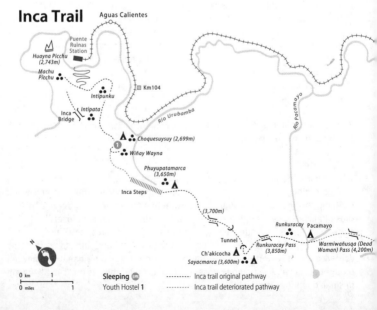

Inca Trail

Aguas Calientes
Puente Ruinas Station
Huayna Picchu (2,743m)
Machu Picchu
Intipunku
Km104
Inca Bridge
Intipata
Río Urubamba
Río pacamayo
Choquesuysuy (2,699m)
Wiñay Wayna
Phuyupatamarca (3,650m)
Inca Steps
(3,700m)
Tunnel
Runkuracay Pass (3,850m)
Runkuracay
Pacamayo
Warmiwañusqa (Dead Woman) Pass (4,200m)
Ch'akicocha
Sayacmarca (3,600m)

0 km 1
0 miles 1

Sleeping
Youth Hostel 1
.... Inca trail original pathway
.... Inca trail deteriorated pathway

field personnel reach Km 82 (depending on the tour operator's logistics) for the Inrena staff to weigh each bundle before the group arrives. When several groups are leaving on the same day, it is more convenient to arrive early. Km 88 can only be reached by train, subject to schedule and baggage limitations. The train goes slower than a bus, but you start your walk nearer to Llaqtapata and Huayllabamba. (See below for details of variations in starting points for the Inca Trail.)

The first ruin is **Llaqtapata**, near Km 88, the utilitarian centre of a large settlement of farming terraces which probably supplied the other Inca Trail sites. From here, it is a relatively easy three-hour walk to the village of **Huayllabamba**. Note that the route from Km 82 goes via **Cusichaca**, the valley in which Ann Kendall worked (see page 150), rather than Llaqtapata.

A series of gentle climbs and descents leads along the Río Cusichaca, the ideal introduction to the trail. The village is a popular camping spot for tour groups, so it's a better idea to continue for about an hour up to the next site, **Llulluchayoc** – 'three white stones' – which is a patch of green beside a fast-flowing stream. It's a steep climb but you're pretty much guaranteed a decent pitch for the night. If you're feeling really energetic, you can go on to the next camping spot, a perfectly flat meadow, called **Llulluchapampa**. This means a punishing 1½-hour ascent through cloudforest, but it does leave you with a much easier second day. There's also the advantage of relative isolation and a magnificent view back down the valley.

Day 2

For most people the second day is by far the toughest. It's a steep climb to the meadow, followed by an exhausting 2½-hour haul up to the first pass – aptly named **Warmiwañusqa** (Dead Woman) – at 4,200 m. The feeling of relief on reaching the top is immense and there's the added, sadistic pleasure of watching your fellow sufferers struggling in your wake. After a well-earned break it's a sharp descent on a treacherous path down to the Pacamayo Valley, where there are a few flat camping spots near a stream if you're too weary to continue.

Day2/3

If you're feeling energetic, you can proceed to the second pass. Halfway up comes the ruin of **Runkuracay**, which was probably an Inca *tambo* (post-house). Camping is no longer permitted here. A steep climb up an Inca staircase leads to the next pass, at 3,850 m, with spectacular views of Pumasillo (6,246 m) and the Vilcabamba Range. The rail descends to **Sayacmarca** (Inaccessible town), a spectacular site over the Aobamba Valley, where it's possible to camp. Just below Sayacmarca lies **Conchamarca** (Shell town), a small group of buildings standing on rounded terraces.

Day 3

A blissfully gentle two-hour climb on a stone highway, leads through an Inca tunnel and along the enchanted fringes of the cloudforest, to the third pass. This is the most rewarding part of the trail, with spectacular views of the entire Vilcabamba Range, and it's worth taking

The Inka Porter Project

When you're slogging up Dead Woman's Pass, sweating away and feeling sorry for yourself, spare a thought for the guy who just ran past you with your pack and half a kitchen on his back. Being a porter on the Inca Trail, or anywhere else in the Andes for that matter, is a tough business. Four days of literally backbreaking work and you'd be a lucky porter indeed to come away with US$30. Add to that unscrupulous tour operators who insist porters carry far in excess of the official 25-kg limit and fail to provide accommodation (a waterproof tent) other than a plastic sheet, and you have a line of work that no sane westerner would contemplate. Competition between tour agents in Cusco is fierce and, in the battle to maximize profits and minimize costs (and prices), it's often the porters who lose out.

For years porters on the Inca and other trails have had very little protection from these harsh conditions and have lacked an organization through which they could speak with a unified voice. This is where The Inka Porter Project, or *Porteadores Inka Ñan* (in Quechua, the first language of the majority of porters) comes in.

Facilitated by Alison Crowther, the project and its aims are directed by the porters themselves, who identify the issues and areas of concern. Working with tour agents, government bodies and international organizations the aim is to improve, in a practical way, working and environmental conditions on the Inca Trail and elsewhere in the Andes. Among projects currently underway

are the building of porter discussion groups, an equipment loan programme, tourist and agency awareness and the development and testing of a special porter backpack. To find out more, or if you're interested in the many volunteer opportunities, just swing round to the Porter Project office (details below) or South American Explorers in Cusco (see page 71).

Some practical ways to help:

Hire a porter! Providing employment is the most direct form of aid. Day 2 on 'The Trail' can be hard, so you'll save yourself some pain as well!

Ask your agent how much porters are paid. 100-150 soles for four days is a good wage, but most are paid less. Cheap trips often entail badly paid porters.

Let your agent know that porters' welfare is of concern to you.

Spend time with your porters – these guys are amazing people, and many have fascinating tales to tell!

Tip your porter. Get together with your group on the last night and arrange a tip. Thirty soles (US$8.50) per porter is fair. Give your tips directly to the porters themselves.

Make sure your guide takes care of sick porters on the trail.

Report all instances of neglect or abuse to the Porter Project office in Cusco or South American Explorers.

Contact details: **Porteadores Inka Ñan**, Dept 4, Choquechaca 188, Cusco, T084-246829, www.peruweb.org/porters The Porter Project is entirely funded through the generous contributions of volunteers and the public.

the time to dwell on the wonders of nature. Then it's down to the extensive ruins of **Phuyupatamarca** (Cloud-level town), at 3,650 m, where Inca observation platforms offer awesome views of nearby Salkantay (6,270 m) and surrounding peaks. There is a 'tourist bathroom' here, where water can be collected, but purify it before drinking.

From here an Inca stairway of white granite plunges more than 1,000 m to the spectacularly sited and impressive ruins of **Wiñay-Wayna** (Forever Young), offering views of newly uncovered agricultural terraces at **Intipata** (Sun place). A trail, not easily visible, goes from Wiñay-Wayna to the newly discovered terracing. There is a youth hostel at Wiñay-Wayna (see Sleeping, below) and there are spaces for a few tents, but they get snapped up quickly. After Wiñay-Wayna there is no water, and no place to camp, until Machu Picchu. A gate by Wiñay-Wayna is locked between 1530 and 0500, preventing access to the path to Machu Picchu at night.

Day 4
From Wiñay-Wayna it is a gentle hour's walk through another type of forest, with larger trees and giant ferns, to a steep Inca staircase which leads up to **Intipunku** (Sun gate), where you look down, at last, upon Machu Picchu, basking in all her reflective glory. Your aching muscles will be quickly forgotten and even the presence of the functional hotel building cannot detract from one of the most magical sights in all the Americas.

Alternative Inca routes

The Inca Trail from Km 104
A short Inca Trail, the **Camino Real de los Inkas**, is used by those who don't want to endure the full hike. It starts at Km 104, where a footbridge gives access to the ruins of Chachabamba and the trail which ascends through the ruins of Choquesuysuy, lately cleaned up, to connect with the main trail at Wiñay-Wayna. This first part is a steady, continuous three-hour ascent (take water) and the trail is narrow and exposed in parts. About 15 minutes before Wiñay-Wayna is a waterfall where fresh water can be obtained (best to purify it before drinking).

Salkantay to Machu Picchu
This route takes three nights. A trek from **Salkantay** joins the Inca Trail at Huayllabamba, then proceeds as before on the main trail through Wiñay- Wayna to Machu Picchu. There is no checkpoint at Salkantay for verifying that the relevant fees have been paid, but you will get checked at Huayllabamba. To get to Salkantay, you have to start the trek in **Mollepata**, northwest of Cusco in the Apurímac Valley. Buses of the **Ampay** company run from Arcopata on the Chinchero road, or you can take private transport to Mollepata (three hours from Cusco). It is down an unpaved road which turns off the main road after Limatambo. From Mollepata it's an all-day trek to **Salkantay Pampa**, also called Soraypampa. Camp below Salkantay (6,271 m). From Salkantay Pampa a very demanding ascent leads to the **Incachiriaska Pass** (4,900 m). Descend to camp at Sisaypampa. From there, trek to **Pampacahuana**, an outstanding and seldom-visited Inca ruin. The remains of an Inca road then go down to the singular Inca ruins of **Paucarcancha**. This entire section is done with mules and/or horses. There is an obligatory change from animals to porters before you reach Huayllabamba.

An alternative from Salkantay is to go to Huayllabamba, then down to Km 88, from where you can take the train to Aguas Calientes, or back to Cusco. ⓘ *There is an entrance fee of US$15 for this hike, but it does not include the entrance to Machu Picchu. If you combine this route with the short Inca Trail from Km 104, you have to pay the US$ 25 trail fee (see above for full details on prices).*

Paucarcancha to Machu Picchu
A four-night trek from Paucarcancha to Huayllabamba, then on the traditional Trail to Machu Picchu. Paucarcancha is an abandoned set of ruins on the descent from Pampacahuana, before the village of Huayllabamba on the main Inca Trail.

Paucarcancha is also shown as Incarakay on some maps. Nearby there are some hot springs. Paucarcancha is an important camping site on the trek from Salkantay, or from Ancascocha Lake pass on the route from the Sillque Valley. As an alternative to the Inca Trail, there is a trek from Paucarcancha to the Palcaycasa Pass between the Salkantay and Palcay snow peaks. From the pass you can walk on a wide, well-preserved Inca trail to Aobamba or the hydroelectric station.

Other routes

There are other routes which approach the Inca Trails to Machu Picchu, such as Km 77, Chillca, up the Sillque ravine in the Qente Valley, which is commonly called the Lago Ancascocha route. There is another access through the Millpo Valley in the Salkantay area. From the Vilcabamba mountain range, you can reach Machu Picchu by hiking down from Huancacalle to Chaulla by road, getting to Santa Teresa and walking to the hydroelectric (Aobamba) train station. Then it's an hour's train ride on the local train to Aguas Calientes (tourists are allowed to ride the local train for this short section).

A three-night trek goes from Km 82 to Km 88, then along the Río Urubamba to Pacaymayo Bajo and Km 104, from where you take the trail described above to Wiñay-Wayna and Machu Picchu.

Also, good hiking trails from Aguas Calientes have been opened along the left bank of the Urubamba river, for day hikes crossing the bridge of the hydroelectric plant to Choquesuysuy.

Aguas Calientes → *Phone code: 084. Colour map 2, A2.*

Only 1½ km back along the railway from Puente Ruinas, this is a popular resting place for those recovering from the rigours of the Inca Trail. It is called Aguas Calientes (or just Aguas) after the hot springs above the town. It is also called the town of Machu Picchu.

TAMBO TOURS

ADVENTURE
TRIPS TO THE
TAMBOPATA
RESERCH CENTER
&
AMAZON

Daily departures for
groups & individuals.

Offices in the
US & CUZCO
Experience since
1988

toll free:
US & Canada... **1-888-2GO-PERU** (246-7378)

www.2GOPERU.com e mail - tambo@tambotours.com

TAMBO TOURS PO BOX 60541- HOUSTON, TEXAS 77205

International:
001-281-528-9448
fax: 281-528-7378

Most activity is centred around the old railway station, on the plaza, or on Avenida Pachacútec, which leads from the plaza to the thermal baths.

The **baths** ⓘ *0500-2030. US$1.50*, consist of a rather smelly communal pool, 10 minutes' walk from the town. You can rent towels and bathing costumes for US$0.65 at several places on the road to the baths. There are basic toilets and changing facilities and showers. Take soap and shampoo and keep an eye on your valuables.

Aguas Calientes

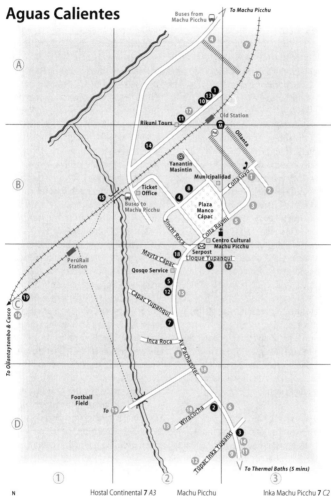

N

Not to scale

Sleeping 🛏
Gringo Bill's
  (Hostal Q'oñi Unu) **3** *B3*
Hatuchay Tower **4** *A2*
Hospedaje Inca Tambo **1** *B3*
Hospedaje Las
  Bromelias **5** *B3*
Hospedaje Quilla **6** *D3*

Hostal Continental **7** *A3*
Hostal Don Guiller &
  Pizzería El Candamo **8** *C2*
Hostal Ima Sumac **9** *D3*
Hostal Los
  Caminantes **10** *A3*
Hostal Pachakúteq **11** *D3*
Hostal Samana Wasi **12** *D2*
Hostal Wiracocha
  Inn **13** *D2*
Jardín Real **18** *D2*
La Cabaña **14** *D3*
Las Orquídeas **19** *D2*
Machu Picchu Inn **15** *C2*

Machu Picchu
  Pueblo **16** *C1*
Presidente & Hostal
  Machu Picchu **17** *A2*
Rupa Wasi **2** *B3*

Eating 🍴
Aiko **1** *A2*
Café Inkaterra **19** *C1*
Clave de Sol **2** *D2*
Govinda **3** *D3*
Illary **4** *B2*
Inca Wasi **5** *C2*
Indio Feliz **6** *C2*

Inka Machu Picchu **7** *C2*
Inka's Pizza Pub **8** *B2*
La Chosa Pizzería **10** *A2*
Las Qenas **11** *A2*
Machu Picchu **12** *C2*
Pizzería Samana
  Wasi **1 13** *A2*
Pizzería Samana
  Wasi **2 14** *B2*
Pueblo Viejo **18** *C2*
Toto's House **15** *B1*

Bars & clubs 🍸
Waisicha Pub **17** *C3*

An interesting day hike out of Aguas Calientes ascends Putucusi Mountain. Local people consider Putucusi to be a protector mountain for the area and it gives stupendous views of Machu Picchu and its surroundings. Follow the railway line out of town towards Machu Picchu and look for some stone stairs and a trail on your right (there is a blue sign). The climb to the top takes 1½-two hours, is very steep and involves several ladder sections – not for the faint-hearted.

● Sleeping

Machu Picchu ruins *p162, map p161*
LL **Machu Picchu Sanctuary Lodge**, *under the same management as the Hotel Monasterio in Cusco (Peru Orient Express Hotels), T084-241777, www.monasterio.orient- express.com* This hotel, at the entrance to the ruins, was completely refurbished in 2001 and has included some environmentally friendly features. They will accept American Express TCs at the official rate. The rooms are comfortable, the service is good and the staff helpful. Electricity and water are available 24 hrs a day. Food in the restaurant is well cooked and presented; the restaurant is for residents only in the evening, but the buffet lunch is open to all. The hotel is usually fully booked well in advance; if struggling for a booking try Sun night as other tourists find Pisac Market a greater attraction.
Camping is not allowed at Intipunku, nor anywhere else at the site; guards may confiscate your tent. There is a free campsite down beside the rail tracks at Puente Ruinas station.

Wiñay-Wayna *p169*
G **Youth Hostel**, price per person, with bunk beds, showers and a small restaurant. It is often fully booked. You can sleep on the floor of the restaurant more cheaply, but it is open for diners until 2300. There are also spaces for a few tents, but they get snapped up quickly too. The hostel's door is closed at 1730.

Aguas Calientes *p170, map p171*
Many hotels in Aguas Calientes seem to have increased their prices sharply in recent years, perhaps in response to the rising costs of train services and excursions on the Inca Trail. Whether based on fact or not, many establishments seem to presume that Aguas is attracting wealthier clients; bargain hard for good value accommodation.
LL **Hatuchay Tower**, *Carretera Puente Ruinas block 4, T084-211201 (reservations in Lima T01-447 8170), www.hatuchaytower.com.pe* Smart on the inside but in need of exterior renovation. Buffet breakfast and all taxes are included in the price, but the hot water system seems to be unreliable. There are standard rooms and luxury suites. It is below the old station.
LL **Machu Picchu Pueblo Hotel**, *Km 110. Reservations: Jr Andalucia 174, San Isidro, Lima, T01-6100404; in Cusco at Plaza las Nazarenas 211, T084-245314, www.inkaterra.com* Beautiful colonial-style bungalows have been built in a village compound surrounded by cloudforest 5 mins' walk along the railway from the town. The hotel has lovely gardens in which there are many species of birds, butterflies and orchids. There is a pool, an expensive restaurant, but also a **campsite** with hot showers at good rates. It offers tours to Machu Picchu, several guided walks on the property and to local beauty spots. The buffet breakfasts for US$12 are great. It also has the **Café Amazónico** by the railway line. The hotel is involved in a project to rehabilitate spectacled bears, and re-release them back into the wild. Recommended, but there are a lot of steps between the public areas and rooms.
AL **Machu Picchu Inn**, *Av Pachacútec 101, T084-211057, mapiinn@peruhotel.com.pe* The price includes bathroom and breakfast. A modern hotel, with a functional atmosphere.
A **Presidente**, *at the old station, T084-211034 (Cusco T084-244598), presidente@terra.com.pe* Next to **Hostal Machu Picchu**, see below, this is the more upmarket half of the establishment. Rooms without river view are cheaper, but the price includes breakfast and

taxes. There seems to be only minimal difference between this and **Machu Picchu**, which represents much better value for money.

B **Gringo Bill's (Hostal Q'oñi Unu)**, *Colla Raymi 104, T084-211046, gringobills@yahoo. com* Price includes bathroom and continental breakfast. **Gringo Bill's** is an Aguas Calientes institution, it's friendly and relaxed, with hot water, good beds, luggage store, laundry and money exchange. Good but expensive meals are served in **Villa Margarita** restaurant; breakfast starts at 0530 and they offer a US$4 packed lunch to take up to the ruins. They have opened a place for long-stay clients in Cusco (*Larapa H-11-2, San Jerónimo* – quite a distance from the centre).

B **La Cabaña**, *Av Pachacútec M20-3, T084-211048*. Price includes bathroom and continental breakfast. Rooms have hot water. There is a café, laundry service and a DVD player and TV (with a good selection of movies) for clients in the lounge. The staff are helpful and can provide information on interesting local walks. The hotel is popular with groups.

C **Hostal Ima Sumac**, *Av Pachacútec 173, T084-211021*. 5 mins before the baths, so quite a climb up from the station. Some of the rooms smell a little damp, but are generally of a reasonable standard; they exchange money.

C **Hostal Machu Picchu**, *at the old station, T084-211212*. Price includes breakfast and taxes. A clean, functional establishment, which is quiet and friendly (especially Wilber, the owner's son). There is hot water, a nice balcony over the Urubamba, a grocery store and travel information is available. Recommended.

C **Rupa Wasi**, *C Huanacaure 180, T084-211101, www.rupawasi.org* Rustic and charming 'eco-lodge', located up a small alley off Collasuyo. The lodge and its owners have a very laid-back, comfortable style, and there are great views from the balconies of the first floor rooms. This lodge is slowly adding to its environmentally friendly credentials with purified water available (so you don't have to buy more plastic) and an organic garden and rainwater collector in the pipeline. Great breakfasts for US$3.

C-D **Jardín Real**, *C Wiracocha 7, T084-211234, jardinrealhotel@hotmail.com* A clean, modern hotel with good hot water. At the unofficial price this hotel represents great value, so bargain hard. Same owner as **Pizzería Los Jardines** on Pachacútec.

D **Hostal Continental**, *near the old train station, T084-211065*. Very clean rooms with good beds, hot showers. This *hostal* was closed for renovation at the time of writing.

D **Hostal Don Guiller**, *Av Pachacútec 136, T084-211145*. Price includes breakfast. Rooms have bath and hot water. In the same building is the **Pizzería El Candamo**.

D **Las Orquídeas**, *Urb Las Orquideas A-8, T084-211171*. From Av Pachacútec, cross the bridge over the river to the football pitch and follow the small dirt path on the right. Rooms have bath and hot water and are clean. This is a quiet, pleasant place away from the main part of town.

D **Hostal Pachakúteq**, *up the hill beyond Hostal La Cabaña, T084-211061*. Rooms with bathroom and 24-hr hot water. Good breakfast is included, quiet, family-run. Recommended.

D **Hospedaje Quilla**, *Av Pachacútec, T084-211009, between Wiracocha and Túpac Inka Yupanki*. Price includes breakfast, bath and hot water. They rent bathing gear for the hot springs if you arrive without your costume and towel.

D **Hostal Wiracocha Inn**, *C Wiracocha, T084-211088*. Rooms with bath and hot water. Breakfast included. There is a small garden at this very friendly and helpful *hostal*. It's popular particularly with European groups.

D-E **Hospedaje Inca Tambo**, *C Huana- caure s/n, T084-211135, hostalinkatambo@ latinmail.com* Basic but clean, situated just below **Rupa Wasi** (see above); negotiate for a good price.

D-E **Hospedaje Las Bromelias**, *Colla Raymi, T084-211145*. Just off the plaza before **Gringo Bill's**, this is a small place which has rooms with bath and hot water. Accommodation is cheaper without bath.

E **Hostal Los Caminantes**, *Av Imperio de los Incas 140, by the railway just beyond the old station, T084-211007*. Price is per person for a room with bathroom. Hot water available but breakfast costs extra. It's basic but friendly and clean.

F Hostal Samana Wasi, *C Túpac Inka Yupanki, T084-211170, quillavane@ hotmail.com* Price includes bath and 24-hr hot water. There are cheaper rooms without bath at this friendly, pleasant place.

Camping

The only official campsite is in a field by the river, just below Puente Ruinas station. Do not leave your tent and belongings unattended.

🍴 Eating

Machu Picchu ruins *p162, map p161*
See under Sleeping, above.

Aguas Calientes *p170, map p171*
Pizza seems to be the most common dish in town, but many of the pizzerías serve other types of food as well. The old station and Av Pachútec are lined with eating places. At the station (where staff will try to entice you into their restaurant), are, among others: **Aiko**, which is recommended; **La Chosa Pizzería**, with pleasant atmosphere, good value; **Las Quenas**, which is a café and a baggage store (US$0.30 per locker); and 2 branches of **Pizzería Samana Wasi**. See also under Sleeping, above.

$$$ **Café Inkaterra**, *on the railway, just below the Machu Picchu Pueblo Hotel.* US $15 for a great lunch buffet with scenic views of the river.

$$ **Indio Feliz**, *C Lloque Yupanqui, T084-211090.* Great French cuisine, excellent value and service, set 3-course meal for US$10, good *pisco sours*. Highly recommended.

$$ **Inka's Pizza Pub**, *on the plaza.* Good pizzas, changes money and accepts TCs. Next door is **Illary**, which is popular.

$$ **Pueblo Viejo**, *Av Pachacútec, near the plaza.* Good food in a spacious but warm environment. Price includes salad bar.

$$ **Toto's House**, *Av Imperio de los Incas,*

on the railway line. Same owners as **Pueblo Viejo**. Good value and quality *menú*.

$ **Clave de Sol**, *Av Pachacútec 156.* Same owner as **Chez Maggy** in Cusco, serving Italian food for about US$4, changes money, also has a vegetarian menu, open 1200-1500, 1800-whenever.

$ **Govinda**, *Av Pachacútec y Túpac Inka Yupanki.* Vegetarian restaurant with a cheap set lunch. Recommended.

$ **Inca Wasi**, *Av Pachacútec.* A very good place to eat.

$ **Inka Machu Picchu**, *Av Pachacútec 122.* Another good place on the avenue. The menu includes vegetarian options.

$ **Inti Killa**, *Av Imperio de los Incas 47.* Good-value *menú* with excellent food and plenty of it. Credit cards accepted.

$ **Machu Picchu**, *Av Pachacútec.* Good food in a friendly atmosphere.

🎵 Bars and clubs

Aguas Calientes *p170, map 171*
Waisicha Pub, *C Lloque Yupanqui.* For good music and atmosphere.

⊖ Transport

Machu Picchu ruins *p162, map p161*
Bus
Buses leave **Aguas Calientes** for Machu Picchu every 30 mins from 0630 to 1300 and cost US$9 return, valid for 48 hrs. Buses run down from the ruins from 1200 to 1730. It is also possible to take a bus down between 0700 and 0900. The ticket office is opposite the bus stop. Tickets can also be bought in advance at **Consetur**, *Santa Catalina Ancha, Cusco,* which saves queuing when you arrive in Aguas Calientes.

Train
The **PerúRail** trains to Machu Picchu run from San Pedro station in **Cusco**. They pass through Poroy and Ollantaytambo to Aguas Calientes (the official name of this station is Machu Picchu). The station for the tourist trains at Aguas Calientes is on

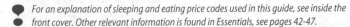

For an explanation of sleeping and eating price codes used in this guide, see inside the front cover. Other relevant information is found in Essentials, see pages 42-47.

the outskirts of town, 200 m from the **Pueblo Hotel** and 50 m from where buses leave for Machu Picchu ruins. The ticket office is open 0630-1730; there is a guard on the gate. A paved road in poor condition runs from Aguas Calientes to the start of the road up to the ruins.

There are 2 classes of tourist train: **Vistadome** and **Backpacker**. From **Cusco** the **Vistadome** costs US$88.50 return and the **Backpacker** costs US$59.50 return (a 1-way ticket is available for US$29.75, but only 48 hrs before departure). The **Vistadome** leaves Cusco daily at 0600, stopping at Ollantaytambo at 0805 and Machu Picchu at 0940. It returns from Machu Picchu at 1530, passing Ollantaytambo at 1700, reaching Cusco at 1920. The **Backpacker** leaves Cusco at 0615, passing Ollantaytambo at 0840 and Machu Picchu at 1010. It returns at 1555, passing Ollantaytambo at 1740, getting to Cusco at 2020.

The **Sacred Valley Railway Vistadome** service runs from **Urubamba** to Machu Picchu and costs US$69 return. It leaves Urubamba at 0600, reaching Machu Picchu at 0820, returning at 1645, reaching Urubamba at 1910.

There are further **Vistadomes** and **Backpackers** from **Ollantaytambo** to Machu Picchu, at US$69 and US$47.20 return, respectively. The Ollantaytambo **Vistadome** leaves at 1030 and 1455, arriving at 1145 and 1615, returning from Machu Picchu at 0845 and 1320, reaching Ollantaytambo at 1005 and 1440. The Ollantaytambo **Backpacker** leaves at 0925, arriving at 1100, returning from Machu Picchu at 1700, reaching Ollantaytambo at 1840. Seats can be reserved even if you're not returning the same day. The **Vistadome** tickets include food in the price. These trains have toilets, video, snacks and drinks for sale. Tickets for all trains should be bought at Wanchac station in Cusco, *Av Pachacútec*. The **Sacred Valley Railway** office, *Av El Sol 803, Cusco, T084-249076*, or *Casa Estación, Av Ferrocarril s/n, Urubamba, T084-201126/27, www.sacredvalleyrailway.com*

Several Urubamba and Yucay hotels offer free transport to and from the Urubamba station. Tickets can be bought through

PerúRail's website, *www.perurail.com* Services other than those listed above are entirely at the discretion of **PerúRail**. Note that the timetable and prices are subject to frequent change.

In August 2003, **PerúRail** introduced the **Hiram Bingham** service from Cusco to Machu Picchu, a super-luxury train with dining car and bar. It leaves Cusco 0900 with brunch on board, arriving Machu Picchu 1230. It leaves Machu Picchu 1830, cocktails, dinner and live entertainment on board, arriving Poroy at 2200 with bus service back to Cusco hotels. The cost, including all meals, buses and entry to the ruins, US$350.

At the other extreme, there is a cheap way to travel by train to Machu Picchu, but you have to check on this train's existence at the time of travel. **Backpacker** coaches are added to the local train which leaves Ollantaytambo at 1945, arriving Aguas Calientes 2120. It returns from Aguas at 0545, arriving Ollantaytambo at 0740. Tickets cost US$11.90 one way (possibly rising to US$12.50 in 2004), they can only be bought 1-2 days before departure and they sell out fast. Tourists are not allowed to travel in the carriages for local people. If you use this service you have to stay 2 nights in Aguas Calientes if you want to see Machu Picchu. Timetables are not published for this train and the inclusion of **Backpacker** coaches is not guaranteed.

◐ Directory

Aguas Calientes *p170, map p171*
Banks and money exchange There are no banks in Aguas Calientes. Those businesses that change money will not do so at rates as favourable as you will find in Cusco. **Qosqo Service**, *corner of Av Pachacútec and Mayta Cápac*, has *cambio*, postal service and guiding service. **Internet** Yanantin Masintin *Av Imperio de los Incas 119*, US$3 per hr, is part of the *Rikuni* group, as is **Tea House**, which is opposite. Both serve coffees, teas, snacks, etc. The town has electricity 24 hrs. **Post** Serpost (post office), *just off the plaza*, between the Centro Cultural Machu Picchu and *Galería de Arte Tunupa*, and on the

railway line. **Telephone** *Oficina on C Collasuyo*, and there are plenty of phone booths around town. There are lots of places to choose from for exchange, shop around. **Travel agents** Rikuni Tours, *at the old station, Av Imperio de los Incas 123,* T084-211036, rikuni@chaski.unsaac.edu.pe Nydia is very helpful. They change money, have a postal service and sell postcards, maps and books (expensive).

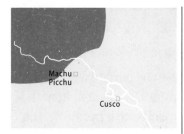

Vilcabamba

Introduction

The lower reaches of the Río Urubamba beyond Machu Picchu are the gateway to regions which are very different from the highlands of Cusco, yet intimately linked to it by history. The most important town is **Quillabamba**, where, they say, it is summer all year round. From here you head north to the end of the Andes and the beginning of the vast jungle, the limit between the two marked by the waterfalls and canyon of the **Pongo de Mainique**, frequently described as one of the most beautiful places on earth. East of Quillabamba is the mysterious last stronghold of the Incas, **Vilcabamba**, long sought after by conquistadores and archaeologists. Now it is the destination of one of Peru's hardest treks.

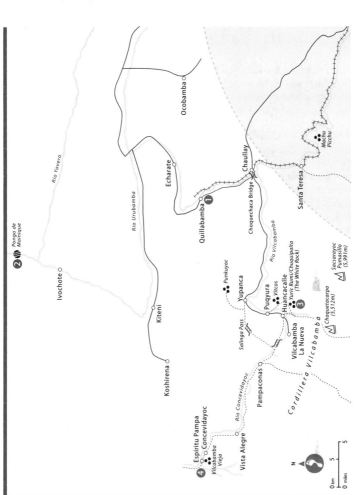

★ Don't miss...

① Quillabamba After some hard travelling or long-distance trekking, rest, relax and enjoy a freshly squeezed fruit juice, see page 180.

② Pongo de Mainique See the Río Urubamba's final, glorious spectacle as it tumbles into the Amazon Basin, see page 180.

③ Yurac Rumi Take a moment to investigate and honour the White Rock, the most sacred site of the Incas, see page 181.

④ Espíritu Pampa This hike allows you to follow in the footsteps of the last Incas and the *conquistadores* who so ruthlessly pursued them. Let your mind stray to images of the heavily armoured and mounted Spaniards and the brutal struggles that must have taken place on the Plain of Ghosts, see page 182.

⑤ Birdwatching Apart from its historical interest, the Vilcabamba region is one of great beauty. The wide range of altitudes and habitats and areas of relatively pristine forest make it ideal for birdwatching, see pages 180, 186 and 187.

Ins and outs

As no trains run beyond Aguas Calientes, the only route to Quillabamba is by road from Cusco via Ollantaytambo. Road transport runs from Quillabamba to Ivochote, for boat transport to the Pongo de Mainique, and Huancacalle, for the start of the hikes in the Vilcabamba region. ▸▸ *For further details see Transport, page 189.*

The road to Quillabamba

After leaving Ollantaytambo, the road passes through **Peña**, a place of great beauty. Once out of Peña, the road climbs on endless zigzags, offering breathtaking views, to reach the **Abra Málaga Pass**, just below the beautiful glaciated peak of Verónica. Here, at 4,000-4,300 m, are some patches of Polylepis woodland, which contain a number of endangered birds. These include the white-browed tit spinetail, the ash-breast tit tyrant and the royal cinclodes. Since it is so accessible, this has become a prime site for birdwatchers, and conservationists are working hard to protect the area. At **Chaullay**, the road meets the old railway to Quillabamba, Machu Picchu and Cusco and continues up the east bank of the river.

Quillabamba → *Phone code: 084. Colour map 2, A2.*

La Ciudad de Eterno Verano (The City of Eternal Summer), as it is known, was once a prosperous town from the sale of coffee. It has now become the overnighting spot for people going to Vilcabamba, Espíritu Pampa and the magnificent Pongo de Mainique, the region's gateway to the Amazon. This delightful market town now survives on the export of fruit, coffee, honey and other produce to Cusco. The tourist season is from June to July, when Peruvian holidaymakers descend on the town to absorb its wonderful warm and sunny climate and relaxed atmosphere. Although Quillabamba has plenty to offer, it's normally overlooked because of the incredibly bumpy, but beautiful ride to get there. The railway from Machu Picchu used to continue for 79 km, through Chaullay, to Quillabamba in the Urubamba Valley, but there are no passenger services on this line any more as much of the track was severely damaged in 1998. There is a Dominican mission here. ▸▸ *For Sleeping, Eating and other listings see pages 188-189.*

Around Quillabamba

For the weary traveller one of the biggest attractions, about 1½ km from Quillabamba, is **Sambaray**, ① *US$0.20. Transport by combi costs US$0.20, taxi US$0.60,* a recreation area with an outdoor swimming pool, restaurant, volleyball and football field. As Sambaray is situated on the Río Alto Urubamba, you can also swim in the river, or, if you're feeling brave, tube down it. Ask locals for the best place to start, as the river can be quite rapid.

Siete Tinajas (Seven Small Baths) is a beautiful waterfall some 45 minutes by combi from town (take the bus from Paradero El Grifo, US$1). It is well worth the trip for the photos, although be careful when climbing to the top, as it can be very slippery. Another waterfall is **Mandor**, also around an hour from Quillabamba. You may go by taxi or walk, although it is advisable to take a guide. Ask at your hotel as there will always be someone willing to take you.

Pongo de Mainique

Before the Río Urubamba enters the vast plain of the Amazon Basin it carves its way through one last wall of foothills and the result is spectacular. The Pongo de Mainique is a sheer rainforest canyon, hundreds of metres deep with the Urubamba surging through its centre and many small waterfalls tumbling in on either side. The Machiguenga people who live in the area believe this to be a portal to the afterlife and it's easy to see why. It is an awe-inspiring journey. The Machiguengas, however, are very private people and do not take kindly to uninvited strangers; if you wish to visit them on their reserve take someone who has contact with them. The jungle surrounding the canyon is home to much wildlife, including many species of macaw. ▶ *For Sleeping, Eating and other listings see pages 188-189.*

To get to the Pongo de Mainique, take a bus from Quillabamba's northern bus 'terminal' (a dusty outdoor affair with many food stalls and the occasional ticket booth) to **Ivochote**, via a new road into the jungle (see Transport, page 189). The road can be in terrible condition in places. En route you'll pass **Kiteni**, a rapidly expanding jungle town. Ivochote is the end of the road, literally, but it develops a party atmosphere on Saturdays, market day in the jungle. Due to the Camisea Natural Gas Project downriver boat traffic is fairly intense. *Lanchas* (boats) head downstream early in the morning on most days during the dry season. In the wet season (roughly December to April) the river may be too dangerous to navigate, especially the rapids in the Pongo itself. Depending on your bargaining ability, passage downriver to the Pongo or to the **Casa de los Ugarte** (see Sleeping, page 188) will set you back between US$6 and US$8.50, providing the captain has trading business downstream. Hiring a boat independently will cost a lot more. To return upstream prices are roughly one third higher, owing to the increased amount of gasoline required to motor against the current.

Two to three hours downstream from the **Casa de los Ugarte**, on the right-hand bank of the river, you pass the Machiguenga community of **Timpia**, home of a high-level ecotourism project and comfortable lodge, run in co-operation with **InkaNatura Travel** (see Tour operators, page 189).

Beyond the Pongo a day's boat travel will bring you to **Malvinas**, centre of the hugely controversial Camisea Natural Gas Project, and on to **Camisea** itself. From the Pongo downstream to Camisea will cost US$6 by boat. Another day downriver and you'll reach **Shepahua**, a largely indigenous village on the edge of the Alto Purus region. This is frontier territory; the forests beyond Shepahua towards the Brazilian border are home to tribes with little contact with the outside world. In recent years this has been a conflict zone between the region's indigenous inhabitants and illegal loggers seeking to profit from the still-pristine forests. Those with time and an adventurous spirit can continue downriver to **Pucallpa** (a journey of several days) and, if the mood takes you, to the Amazon itself.

Huancacalle and around

At **Chaullay**, the historic **Choquechaca Bridge**, built on Inca foundations, was wiped out by a landslide in 1998. It has since been reconstructed and reopened, allowing drivers to cross the river to the village of Huancacalle, a two-street village (no restaurants, but a few shops) between four and seven hours from Quillabamba. Huancacalle is the best base for exploring the nearby Inca ruins of Vitcos and the starting point for the trek to Espíritu Pampa. At **Vitcos** is the palace of the last four Inca rulers from 1536 to 1572, and **Yurac Rumi**, the sacred White Rock of the Incas (also referred to as **Chuquipalta**, see the walking tour, below). Both are now easily accessible and well worth the effort of a visit. Vitcos was discovered by Hiram Bingham in 1911, the same year he discovered Machu Picchu but, unlike that more famous site, it has all the documented historical associations which make a visit particularly interesting and rewarding. The White Rock, once the most sacred site in South America, is very large (8 m high and 20 m wide), with intricate and elaborate carvings. Lichens now cover its whiteness. ▶ *For Sleeping, Eating and other listings see pages 188-189.*

Allow plenty of time for hiking to, and visiting, the ruins. You can also hike up to **Vilcabamba La Nueva** from Huancacalle. It's a three-hour walk through beautiful countryside with Inca ruins dotted around. There is a missionary building run by Italians, with electricity and running water, where you may be able to spend the night.

Walking tour of Vitcos and Yurac Rumi

Vitcos and **Ñustahispanan** lie behind the hill that rises immediately on the far side of the river from Huancacalle. Ñustahispanan is the site of the Yurac Rumi, the White Rock of the Incas (see above). A walk around both sites, taking your time, would take about four hours, but three hours is sufficient for a whirlwind tour. Guides can be hired in Huancacalle for a small fee (US$2-3) for a guided walk to both sites.

Just past the **Hospedaje Sixpac Manco**, cross the bridge on your left. On the far side of the river the trail splits – take the left-hand fork. The right-hand trail leads to the Choquetacarpo pass, and, eventually, to Choquequirao, a magnificent Inca citadel (see page 210). The left-hand track leads you up an impressive restored Inca stairway to a small field. It's a steep climb. Follow the incline of the field and another small restored section of Inca Trail. From this point you will see the beautifully sculpted Yurac Rumi (White Rock). The rock has an intricate system of water channels surrounding it and these run into a finely carved Inca bath, in excellent condition.

Underneath the White Rock on the right-hand side lies a series of 'seats'; local guides claim these to have been used by the Inca's chosen virgins during ceremonies held at the site. Shadows and light play strangely on the rock's finely carved features; take the time if you can to return later in the day and have another look.

From the White Rock continue downhill, following the contour of the hill to the left. As you walk down the valley, Ñustahispanan comes into view – agricultural terraces, another 'sacred rock' and a stone mimicking the shape of the mountains down the valley.

Following the trail on the left-hand side of the valley takes you to Vitcos. The path climbs higher on the left-hand side and very soon Vitcos comes into view, with mountains silhouetted behind. At Vitcos you will find **Manco Inca's Palace**, a beautiful multi-doored building with excellent stonework. The site was being restored at the time of writing. Above the palace is a flat area, perhaps originally used for ceremonial purposes, with fantastic 360° views, from the snowy peaks of the Vilcabamba Range to the verdant valleys below. The entire site is highly defensible, surrounded on three sides by steep drops and accessed by a thin bridge of land on the fourth. To return to Huancacalle, retrace your steps or descend to the road on the far side of the river.

Huancacalle to Espíritu Pampa → *Colour map 2, A1.*

The trek to Espíritu Pampa from Huancacalle takes three days, but would be a more comfortable undertaking in four. Espíritu Pampa itself is quite a large site, and further groups of buildings may still be awaiting discovery in the densely forested mountains surrounding the valley. Give yourself at least a day at the site to soak up the atmosphere before continuing a further six hours to Chanquiri, the starting point for transport to Kiteni and Quillabamba. ▸▸ *For Sleeping, Eating and other listings see pages 188-189.*

Background

In 1536, three years after the fall of the Inca Empire to the Spanish *conquistadores*, Manco Inca led a rebellion against the conquerors. Retiring from Cusco when Spanish reinforcements arrived, Manco and his followers fell back to the remote triangle of Vilcabamba, where they maintained the Inca traditions, religion and government

The last Incas of Vilcabamba

After Pizarro killed Atahualpa in 1532 the Inca Empire disintegrated rapidly, and it is often thought that native resistance ended there. But in fact it continued for 40 more years, beginning with **Manco**, a teenage half-brother of Atahualpa.

In 1536, Manco escaped from the Spanish and returned to lead a massive army against them. He besieged Cusco and Lima simultaneously, and came close to dislodging the Spaniards from Peru. Spanish reinforcements arrived and Manco fled to Vilcabamba, a mountainous forest region west of Cusco that was remote, but still fairly close to the Inca capital, which he always dreamed of recapturing.

The Spanish chased Manco deep into Vilcabamba but he managed to elude them and continued his guerrilla war, raiding Spanish commerce on the Lima highway, and keeping alive the Inca flame. Then, in 1544, Spanish outlaws to whom he had given refuge murdered him, ending the most active period of Inca resistance.

The Inca line passed to his sons. The first, a child too young to rule named **Sayri Túpac**, eventually yielded to Spanish enticements and emerged from Vilcabamba, taking up residence in Yucay, near Urubamba in 1558. He died mysteriously – possibly poisoned – three years later.

His brother **Titu Cusi**, who was still in Vilcabamba, now took up the Inca mantle. Astute and determined, he resumed raiding and fomenting rebellion against the Spanish. But in 1570, Titu Cusi fell ill and died suddenly. A Spanish priest was accused of murdering him. Anti-Spanish resentment erupted, and the priest and a Spanish viceregal envoy were killed. The Spanish Viceroy reacted immediately, and the Spanish invaded Vilcabamba for the third and last time in 1572.

A third brother, **Túpac Amaru** was now in charge. He lacked his brother's experience and acuity, and his destiny was to be the sacrificial last Inca. The Spanish overran the Inca's jungle capital, and dragged him back to Cusco in chains. There, Túpac Amaru, the last Inca, was publicly executed in Cusco's main plaza.

The location of the neo-Inca capital of Vilcabamba was forgotten over the centuries, and the search for it provoked Hiram Bingham's expeditions, and his discovery of Machu Picchu. Bingham also discovered Vilcabama the Old, without realizing it, but the true location at Espíritu Pampa was only pinpointed by Gene Savoy in the 1960s, and was not confirmed irrefutably until the work of Vincent Lee in the 1980s.

outside the reach of the Spanish authorities. Centuries after the eventual Spanish crushing of Inca resistance, it was difficult to locate and identify Manco's capital of Vilcabamba. See the box, page 183.

Guides and supplies

An excellent guide is Jesús Castillo Alveres who can be contacted through the **Hospedaje Sixpac Manco** in Huancacalle (see page 188). Many members of the Cobos family (see page 187) also guide – Juvenal Cobos has guided for BBC documentary teams among others. A good rate of pay for guides/mule drivers is US$5 per day, plus US$5 per mule or horse used. Before you leave be very clear about your exact itinerary and expectations; some guides have been known to leave clients in Espíritu Pampa, half a day's hike from the roadhead in Chanquiri. Always provide sufficient food and a waterproof tent by way of accommodation for your guide on the trail. If you enjoy your trip give your guide a tip; it will be appreciated. Remember, *arrieros* (mule drivers) based in Huancacalle have to walk all the way back along the route, a journey of at least 2½ days, and for this they don't charge. Always take all plastic and non-biodegradable rubbish back to Cusco for more efficient disposal. All supplies must be brought from Huancacalle as even basic supplies are scarce on the trail.

Best time to visit

The best time of year is from May to November, possibly December. Outside this period it is very dangerous as the trails are very narrow and can be thick with mud and very slippery. Insect repellent is essential; there are millions of mosquitoes. Also take pain-killers and other basic medicines; these will be much appreciated by the local people should you need to take advantage of their hospitality.

Day 1 – Huancacalle to Río Chalcha → *Around six or seven hours' walking.*

From **Hospedaje Sixpac Manco** follow the course up the Río Vilcabamba, staying on the right side. Your compass bearing is roughly west and you'll maintain this direction for most of the first day and, indeed, the trek to Espíritu Pampa itself. You're heading towards the Abra Colpapasa (Colpapasa Pass), which lies to the right of the jagged peaks in front of you. Climb up the right bank until you reach the road heading for Vilcabamba La Nueva. Near a slightly Swiss-looking house with a diamond-shaped image of Christ, turn right up the hill. After 70 m or so, turn left off the road up the dirt track. The trail starts edging towards the peaks, beginning to leave the river's course behind. This whole area is a picturesque mix of cloudforest remnants and farmland. Just before another cross and where the stream crosses the trail (you're back on the road again!) turn right and cross the small concrete bridge. On the far side head up this valley, keeping on the left of the stream. After a short period you rejoin the road once more. Turn right and keep ascending the valley. From here to Vilcabamba you can essentially follow the road, electricity wires and river up the valley. Look out for shortcuts cutting out the bends. As you approach Vilcabamba La Nueva the valley floor begins to flatten out into agricultural and grazing land. An Italian-sponsored programme is supporting a carpentry project here, hence the impressive buildings in parts of the village.

When you enter Vilcabamba take the first right at the junction. You want to head up the large valley to the right, **not** the smaller valley rising above the town to your left. You're heading roughly north-northwest at this point. Cross the stream at the bottom of the smaller valley, following the road along the left-hand side of the larger westerly valley. Holding your course up the river valley, you reach the **Abra Colpapasa** at over 4,000 m. Here there's a sign announcing government plans to improve the route to Espíritu Pampa. From the pass, given clear weather (which the author didn't have!) you can see many of the great snow peaks in the Vilcabamba Range, including Salkantay (Savage Mountain) and Pumasillo (Puma's Claw – also marked as Sacsarayoc on many Peruvian maps). Once through, follow the left side of the pass, descending gently. There's a 'road' – possibly work in progress – that follows a high line in early sections of the valley, and several short-cut paths cutting off the bends beneath. You're still heading west. After one hour there's a magnificent set of Inca steps, dropping steeply towards the river and the valley floor. The trail turns to the left slightly, crossing another stream entering the main flow from the left; a nicely constructed wooden bridge, the **Puente Malcachaca**, crosses the stream. Before crossing the bridge two trails come into view on the far side. The higher trail leads to the village of Pampaconas and on to Espíritu Pampa. The lower trail (described below) circumvents the village, following the river directly

Vilcabamba Mountains

Peru's rugged and largely unexplored Vilcabamba Mountains lie to the north and east of the main Andean chain, situated between the canyons of the mighty Apurímac and Urubamba rivers. Extending a mountainous tongue into the Amazon Basin, they rise from tropical rainforest to the freezing glaciers of Nevado Salcantay at 6,271 m, an area of around 30,000 sq km.

Vilcabamba lies in a region of immense biological diversity known as the Tropical Andes Eco-region, the meeting of the Andes and the Amazon which supports the greatest range of animal and plant life on the planet. This diversity is the result of massive variations in altitude, climate and habitat within a relatively small area. Vilcabamba's isolation has also meant that many high-altitude species have been cut off from other populations for thousands, perhaps millions of years, developing separate characteristics and eventually becoming new species, endemic to the region.

In the face of growing threats from oil and gas companies and settlement from the more densely populated mountain regions of Peru, Conservation International and the Smithsonian Institute conducted a 'rapid assessment programme' finding, among others, 12 previously unknown species of amphibian and reptile, plus a very large rodent. These studies aided the recent creation of the Otishi National Park in some of the range's most remote recesses.

In the foothills and surrounding river valleys live four indigenous groups, the Nuhua, Nanti, Kirineri and Machiguenga. Some of these people live in voluntary isolation from the 'outside world'. Sadly, both the people and wilderness are under threat. It's an all-too-familiar story. Shell explored the area in the early 1980s and its encounters with uncontacted tribes led to the deaths of at least 42% of the Nuhua population, largely through introduced diseases to which these people had little or no immunity. Despite improving its social and environmental practices, Shell pulled out of the region in the late 1990s, but the gas field it discovered is still under development.

Construction of a pipeline is progressing rapidly, cutting a swathe of destruction across the Vilcabamba Range. The pipe heads for the coast, where an export terminal and liquefaction plant is proposed in the buffer zone of the Paracas National Reserve, which has some of the most significant bird and marine mammal populations on the entire Pacific Coast of South America. Serious environmental and social risks scared off a number of investors, but in September 2003 the Camisea Consortium received funding worth US$135 million from the Interamerican Development Bank. Meanwhile, in a quietly issued Peruvian Supreme Decree, the Nuhua-Kugakapori Reserve (for uncontacted or little contacted tribal groups) has been opened to oil and gas development. There have been reports of forced relocation of tribes within the reserve.

Deforestation of the Vilcabamba Range's western slope began in Inca times, but the east has remained unaffected by population pressure and cultivation. Conservationists and, increasingly, ecotourism interests are fighting to preserve its treasures. Can they succeed? Only time will tell.

For more information see *Peru: Camisea Natural Gas Project. Independent Assessment of the Environmental and Social Priorities*, by Robert Goodland. Another good source of information is www.amazonwatch.org

Vilcabamba Huancacalle to Espíritu Pampa

to Espíritu Pampa. This route also leads to several beautiful potential campsites by the river, the best of which are another 15 to 20 minutes' walk from the bridge. If you still feel energetic, you could continue to the Pampas just below the tiny settlement of Ututu (see Day 2, below). The river here carries the local name of the **Río Chalcha**. It is generally marked on maps as the **Río Concevidayoc**, but carries local names in several sections.

Day 2 – Río Chalcha to Vista Alegre → *A total of 6½-7 hours' walking.*

From the campsites near the Chalcha, carry on descending further into the valley – and the Amazon Basin. As you advance the vegetation becomes wilder and less disturbed. The hills on the far side of the river are dominated by stands of virgin cloudforest. With the continuing loss in elevation the trees become studded with epiphytes, plants that make their home on the branches of large trees. They lack root systems so obtain all nutrients and moisture directly from the humid atmosphere and thus are indicators of cloudforest and rainforest environments. The path follows the river closely, passing through a patchwork of fields and natural vegetation. You can feel the air become stickier and more humid as you descend. The tiny and idyllic settlement of **Ututu** is reached 1½ hours after the camp. Perhaps only 10 or 20 people call Ututu home and their lifestyle seems little influenced by the modern world. Just beyond Ututu, through picturesque **Pampa** you cross an orange suspension bridge across the Chalcha to its right bank. The path now enters a spectacular stretch of ancient cloudforest, choked with mosses and vines. In many sections the route follows wonderful sections of Inca trail, stairs, etc. All the time the river roars on your left, gathering strength from the many small creeks that join it. This section lasts 1-1½ hours, but serious birdwatchers with a day to spare would be well rewarded. The area abounds in birdlife, with many colourful species of tanagers, among others. Throughout this section of the trail you're heading more or less northeast.

You now come to a second orange suspension bridge, crossing back to the left-hand side of the valley. A brief climb offers splendid views of the densely forested peaks in the Vilcabamba Range, especially on the right side of the river. Sadly, much of the forest on the trail side in this section has been cut or burned to create small farming plots or *chacras*. Walking close to the ridgeline, the river far below, you pass lush secondary forest and scrub before descending to **Vista Alegre** through a more heavily populated area. The Concevidayoc now carries the local name of Río Vista Alegre. Before you reach camp, located in a convenient football field, you cross three bridges. The first is a fragile construction of dubious safety, made with rough-hewn logs balanced against each other in the centre. In the dry season it's possible to wade across the river and this could be a better option. The second bridge, Cedrochaka, and the third, Puente Vista Alegre, just before the field, are simple log affairs, but secure. A new suspension bridge was being built at Vista Alegre at the time of writing.

Day 3 – Vista Alegre to Espíritu Pampa → *About 7 hours' walking.*

Carry on downstream. After a couple of minutes you'll cross a stony riverbed – a stream entering the Río Vista Alegre. A few logs form a rough bridge which may be impassable in heavy rain. The path continues on the far side, towards a junction – take the right-hand path. The trail follows the river's left bank, largely surrounded by forest, heading roughly north-northeast. After an initial alternation between forest and stony beaches the track enters the largest stretch of primary forest on the route. For the next four or five hours, the forest is broken only by the tiny dwellings of five or six families who live in the area. The route ascends and descends many times between feeder streams entering the main river. You've now returned to your northwesterly course. There are great views of the jungle from various viewpoints on the route.

Again, this is a great area for birding, this time in the transition zone between the cloudforest and the lowland tropical forest. The area seems especially rich in examples of the trogon family, with quetzals very much in evidence. As the trail continues the river drops further and further beneath you. You're walking high on the left slope of the valley. After two hours you reach the tiny settlement of **Urpipata**, set on a hilltop. The **Río Tunqimayo**, 15 minutes further on, is crossed by a spectacular wooden bridge. There are crystal-clear pools in the river, ideal for a refreshing dip. This could be a good campsite if you have time, though space for tents is very limited. A second bridge, 1½ hours further on, crosses the **Río Yuquemayo**.

The dispersed settlement of **Concevidayoc** comes into view 5½ hours from the start of the day's trek. The river below now carries the same name. After another hour you come to the **Puente Pumachaca**, crossing another of the Concevidayoc's tributaries. Around Concevidayoc there are many small side trails leading to houses and fields, but the main trail is obvious. You pass the small ruin of the house of Don Cobos on the left-hand side. If you don't want to proceed further this would be a good camping spot. The Cobos family has been instrumental in the most significant explorations of the Espíritu Pampa area and still guide today, based at the **Hospedaje Sixpac Manco** in Huancacalle.

Shortly after the Cobos' house the trail splits, but a blue arrow indicates the higher trail and route to Espíritu Pampa. Finally you reach the **Abra Tucuiricco** and the foundations of a small but well-constructed Inca house, perhaps built as a lookout to warn of approaching enemies. From here you can look down on Espíritu Pampa and Manco's Vilcabamba Vieja. A set of restored Inca stairs leads downhill and 20 minutes later you come to the small settlement of **Espíritu Pampa**. A large sign announces the restoration of Espíritu Pampa and Vilcabamba. There's a modest shop in the village run by the wife of Américo, Vilcabamba's caretaker. The shop has a pretty limited selection of goods, but sells biscuits, rice, eggs and, of course, Coca Cola. In front of the houses themselves is a small field which is perfect for camping.

Day 4 – Espíritu Pampa

A trail leads up behind the houses to the ruins of Vilcabamba Vieja, a mere 10 minutes' walk away. Some of the lower ruins are currently being restored at the start of what is projected to be a five-year project. The ruins on higher ground are still romantically consumed by the jungle, with vines and the huge root systems of forest giants wrapped around the remains of finely built houses. What is also apparent is how different this city is, compared with others in the Inca Empire, set as it is in a low valley, on the edge of the Amazon Basin. This is a city and a civilization out of its element, the Incas far from their beloved mountains, forced to the very edge of their empire by the European invaders. For birdwatchers there are several leks (display ground) of the Andean cock-of-the-rock, Peru's national bird. The bird's strange calls echo throughout the ruins.

Day 5 – Espíritu Pampa to Chanquiri → *About 5 hours' walking.*

To leave Espíritu Pampa, follow the path that crosses directly in front of the houses, leaving from the north side of the field. The path then crosses the **Río Santa Isabel** after 10 to 15 minutes on a suspension bridge carrying the same name. You are now heading east-northeast, swinging more to the north as you continue. You're now on the left bank of the Santa Isabel, following the river downstream towards its confluence with the Río Concevidayoc. The valley is quite densely populated here, with much slash and burn agriculture and consequent forest clearance. After an hour or so you pass **Chuntabamba**, a small settlement with a school, small shop, etc. There are many little side trails leading to fields and houses in this area, but the main trail is always obvious. You're still heading north at this point. The Santa

Isabel merges with the Río Concevidayoc after two-2½ hours and enters a steep forested canyon. You follow the trail to the left in a picturesque valley of a tributary entering from the west, crossing the **Puente Santa Victoria**, before returning back to the course of the main river. You now descend steeply to the river and cross the **Azulmayo** (or Asolmayo) suspension bridge.

The route begins to climb steeply on the far side. At a split in the trail turn left (north) – if you've taken the correct turn you'll come to a small concrete bridge over a stream five minutes after the turn. It's a very tough, steep climb for one or 1½ hours. **Chanquiri** comes into view in the valley below from the highest point of the climb, high on the side of the hill (but below the summit). This small town lies on the right-hand side of the valley that joins the Santa Isabel, just below the confluence of the two. The valley is that of the **Río San Miguel**. Following the hill into the San Miguel Valley, cross the sturdy **Puente La Resistencia**. Head up the opposite bank until it meets with a road. The road is impassable for vehicles in the higher section, because of many landslides. Some 30 minutes later you arrive in Chanquiri.

● Sleeping

Quillabamba p180

D **Hostal Quillabamba**, *Prolongación y M Grau, just behind the main market, T084-281369, hostalquillabamba@ latinmail.com* Highly kitsch design reminds you of some 1960's Californian motel, marooned on the edge of the Amazon Basin. This is one of the largest hostels in Quillabamba, all rooms have private bath, TV (local channels only) and telephone. There's a swimming pool, which occasionally has water in it, a restaurant and parking facilities. Less appealing is the small zoo with several inadequately housed species of macaw and toucan. They also have a cockfighting school for the championship, which is held every year in late Jul.

D **Lira**, *Jr La Convención 200, T084-281324*. All rooms with bath, a bit noisy and not very clean.

E **Hostal Alto Urubamba**, *Jr 2 de Mayo 333, T084-281131, altourub@ec-red.com* Rooms with shared bath cheaper. Spotlessly clean, pleasant hotel, 1 block from the Plaza de Armas. Staff are friendly and knowledgeable. Small local restaurant attached and there are great views over the town from the roof. Highly recommended.

E **Hostal Don Carlos**, *Jr Libertad 566, T084-281371*. Clean and simple, all rooms have private shower with generally hot water. There is a bar and restaurant.

G There are other accommodations around the main market.

Pongo de Mainique p180

F **Hostal Pongo de Mainique**, *Ivochote, just behind the Señor de Huanca*. This is the nicer of the 2 *hostales*, although both are basic.

F **Señor de Huanca**, *Ivochote, on the right once over the footbridge*.

F-G **Hostales**, *Kiteni*. There are several cheap *hostales* along the main street, but in 2003 these were almost exclusively occupied by workers from the Camisea Gas Project.

G **La Casa de los Ugarte**, *just beyond the Pongo, on the left bank of the river (if heading downstream)*. The small hacienda of Ida and Abel Ugarte. They are very helpful and will let you camp on their land for a small fee. They have a modest general store and basic supplies, fruit and very fresh eggs are available. The forest behind the hacienda is rich in wildlife and the family may be able to arrange expeditions in the jungle, given time to make the arrangements.

Huancacalle p181

F-G **Sixpac Manco** This hostel, managed by the Cobos family, is fairly comfortable and has good beds.

F-G Villagers will accept travellers in their very basic homes (take a sleeping bag).

Chanquiri p187

Chanquiri has no hostel, but you can sleep on someone's floor, perhaps the small restaurant/shop on the west side of the plaza. If they like you and you buy a meal and a couple of drinks they may not charge for accommodation. The main plaza isn't ideal for camping.

⑦ Eating

Quillabamba *p180*
$ **El Gordito**, *on Espinar*. A good place for chicken.
$ **Pub Don Sebas**, *Jr Espinar 235 on Plaza de Armas*. Good, great sandwiches, run by Karen Molero who is very friendly and always ready for a chat.
$ **Pizzería Venecia**, *Jr Libertad 461, on the Plaza de Armas, T084-281582*. Decent pizza, delivery available.
$ **Rolys 2**, *Jr Vilcanota, a little way out of town, near the river)*. Another good option for chicken, but the service is terrible. Go in the afternoon when they're quiet!

There are many *heladerías* (ice cream shops), the best of which are on the west side of the Plaza de Armas. Quillabamba's a great place for freshly squeezed fruit juices – head for the 2nd floor in the main market. **Gabbi's Juice Stall**, on the far right-hand side, is especially recommended.

⑨ Tour operators

Pongo de Mainique *p180*
InkaNatura *In Cusco: Plateros 361, mezzanine, T084-251173; in Lima: Manuel Bañón 461, San Isidro, T01-440 2022, www.inkanatura.com* They run the ecotourism projecy of Timpia.
Ecotrek Peru, *C Choquechaca 229, T084-253653, T974 8058 (mob), www.ecotrekperu.com*, also run tours in the region.

⑧ Transport

Quillabamba *p180*
Bus Most buses leave **Cusco** for Quillabamba from the Terminal Terrestre de Santiago between 1800 and 2000. Journey time is approximately 8 hrs, although expect 14 hrs or more in the rainy season, because of landslides. 4 bus companies on this route are: **Valle de los Incas**, *T084-244787*, **Ben Hur**, *T084-229193*, **Ampay**, *T084-245734*, and **Selva Sur**, *T084-247975*. **Selva Sur** has 2 buses on the route, one of which is quite comfortable, with good reclining seats, perhaps the best bus for the journey. Buy tickets in advance, US$3-4. The bus station in Quillabamba is

on Av 28 de Julio and buses depart for Cusco daily, with buses leaving in the morning around 0700 and in the evening. There are extra services at weekends.

Pongo de Mainique *p180*
Bus From **Quillabamba** buses take 12-14 hrs to reach **Ivochote** and cost around US$4. Ask locals for their opinions on the best companies for this route. Buses (combis) leave Quillabamba for **Huancacalle** daily from Jr San Martín, near Plaza Grau, at 0900 and 1200, US$2.50. The journey takes 4-7 hrs. On Fri they go all the way to Vilcabamba.

Espíritu Pampa *p182*
Bus From **Chanquiri**, at the end of the Espíritu Pampa trail, trucks and buses leave for **Kiteni** and **Quillabamba** on Wed and Sun. It's an 8-12-hr ride, US$2.50. Transport at other times of the week can be problematic.

⑩ Directory

Quillabamba *p180*
Banks BCP, *Jr Libertad*, is good for TCs. Banco Continental, *Av F Bolognesi*, accepts Visa and Cirrus. Banco de la Nación, *Jr Mario Concha, on the plaza*. **Internet** Ciber Master, *Jr Espinar, on the plaza*.

Check out...

WWW...

100 travel guides, 100s of destinations,
5 continents and 1 Footprint...
www.footprintbooks.com

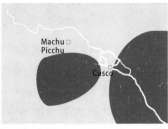

Machu
Picchu

Cusco

East & West of Cusco

Introduction

Most visitors to Cusco, after seeing the city, head to the Sacred Valley and Machu Picchu, but to the east and west are many equally tempting propositions. This part of the country is singularly off the beaten track in relation to the rest of the region. An area of myths, reputed to be where the founders of the Inca dynasty emerged into the world. Along or near the main road from Cusco to Lake Titicaca are a number of archaeological sites, the most prominent of which are **Tipón** and **Raqchi**, while the colonial churches at **Andahuaylillas** and **Huaro** are among the most fascinating in the whole region. There are beautiful lakes, too; four of them are near the village of **Acomayo**, while **Huacarpay** is an excellent place for walking and birdwatching. Also accessible from this road is the majestic Ausangate massif, where you can do some serious high-altitude trekking. And not to be outdone, the western part of the region also boasts its own 'lost city', at **Choquequirao**. As impressive as Machu Picchu, but in comparison hardly ever visited, this is a tremendous site, and getting there requires an expedition of four days or more.

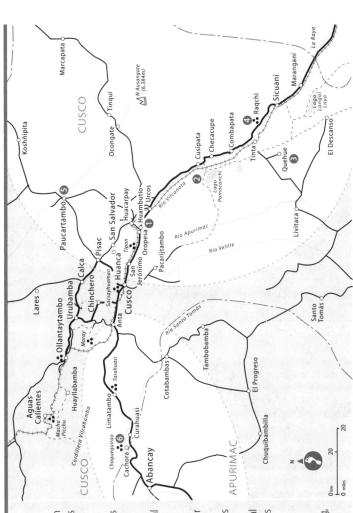

★ Don't miss...

1 Andahuaylillas Visit the Sistine Chapel of the Andes and, nearby, the equally remarkable church at Huaro. For the best view, take a strong torch as they are not lit, see page 202.

2 Acomayo Tired of ruins, churches, roads and people? Then take a trip to the four lakes near this peacefull waterside village, see page 204.

3 Qeswachaka Cross the last Inca suspension bridge, which is rebuilt annually in the only festival of its kind, see page 204.

4 Raqchi This highly spirited place contains the remnants of one of the tallest Inca buildings ever constructed, the temple to the creator god Viracocha. It is now a centre for the local ceramics industry, see page 204.

5 Paucartambo In mid-July the unmissable festival of the Virgen del Carmen is one of the highlights of the Cusco departmental calendar, see page 198.

6 Choquequirao The latest addition to the 'lost cities' trail', only reached by adventurous trekking, see page 210.

East of Cusco

A paved road runs southeast from Cusco to Sicuani, at the southeastern edge of the Department of Cusco. It continues to Puno, on the shores of Lake Titicaca, then on to the border with Bolivia. Combis run every 15-20 minutes between Cusco and Sicuani, and more frequently to the villages and towns in between. ⟩⟩ *For Sleeing, Eating and other listings, see pages 206-209.*

South to Pacarijtambo

Pacarijtambo is a good starting point for the three to four hours' walk to the ruins of **Maukallaqta**, which contain good examples of Inca stonework. From there, you can walk to **Pumaorca**, a high rock carved with steps, seats and a small puma in relief on top. Below this are more Inca ruins.

From Cusco, buses and trucks to Pacarijtambo take four hours, US$2. You can find lodging for the night in Pacarijtambo at the house of the Villacorta family and leave for Cusco by truck the next morning. On the way back, you'll pass the caves of **Tambo Toco**, where a legend says that the four original Inca brothers emerged into the world, in contradiction of the theory that the windows from which the brothers emerged were at Ollantaytambo (see page 148).

▲▲ San Jerónimo to Huanca trek

Leaving Cusco, you will soon pass the condor monument (see page 84) of San Sebastián then enter the old colonial town of **San Jerónimo**, which has become almost a suburb of the sprawling city and is now home to Cusco's wholesale Saturday morning food market. Porters struggle past carrying heavy loads and there is a huge array of colourful fruit and vegetables, as well as campesinos in for the day to sell their produce and wares. Get there for 0800, but be aware that 'gringos' stick out like a sore thumb so take no valuables. San Jerónimo is the starting point for an excellent trek to Huanca.

San Jerónimo to Huaccoto From San Jerónimo, head north along Calle Clorinda Matto de Turner (past the main produce market on the left and the **Andenes de Andrea** restaurant). Further along is the cemetery. The street becomes an unpaved road, swings to the right (east) for 500 m and then left (north) again on its definite course up the mountain. There is a 4WD road which connects San Jerónimo with Huaccotto, laboriously winding its way for 15 km from 3,200 m up to 4,000 m. Much more interesting and worthwhile, is to follow the old Inca and Spanish colonial track, which ascends the *quebrada* (ravine) of the Huacottomayu and is only about half as long and more direct, but also steep in places. This road is wide, very clearly marked and widely travelled. Heading north by northwest, the pedestrian road leaves the narrow streets of the town. On the way out, the road winds past the remains of once great colonial *estancias*.

❢ At least four to five hours should be allowed for the ascent from San Jerónimo to Huaccoto.

The most striking feature of the landscape are the thousands of eucalyptus trees covering the slopes of all the surrounding hillsides. Few truly old trees remain (the eucalyptus was first introduced to this region in the 1870s and 1880s). There are large groves of 20- to 40-year-old trees growing out of older and thicker stumps, harvested around the mid-20th century, interspersed with extensive patches much younger trees. The air is dense with that most envigorating and promising aroma of menthol.

Below you can see the red-tiled roofs of San Jerónimo and the broader expanse of the valley of the Río Huatanay, gradually making its way southeast toward its confluence with the Río Urubamba – only 20 km away – whose waters will eventually flow into the Amazon region and on to the Atlantic Ocean.

The broad trail climbs the mountainside, intersecting the many turns and twists of the little-used track. The walking trail pretty much follows the course of a fast flowing *acequía* (irrigation channel), no doubt originally channelled by the Incas or their predecessors, the Huari-Tiahuanacos, who built Piquillacta (see page 198). There are other canals and aqueducts, which distribute the water from the numerous *puquios* (natural springs), that sprout from the slopes and gullies of **Cerro Pachatusan** (the pillar, or pivot of the world), which, although its main peak and summit are not yet visible, we have been ascending since San Jerónimo.

As the eucalyptus groves begin to thin out, the ridgeline and highlands finally become visible. Due north is the prominent, pyramidal summit of **Pikol**, a minor *apu* (mountain) but an important landmark. Its name is clearly carved on its slopes. To the right of it, at roughly two o'clock, a short segment of jagged dark grey boulders and rocks can clearly be seen. This is the first hint of the **Huaccoto** quarries and the principal reference point to head for. In Inca times, remaining so throughout the colonial and republican periods, Huaccoto was the site of an important stone quarry and a principal source of the building materials for the Inca temples and Spanish colonial mansions of Cusco. To the immediate right is the gully formed by the **Río Huaccotomayu**, which will somehow vanish into the mountain slope a few hundred metres beyond and above.

The treeline is at about 3,700 or 3,800 m. You emerge from it into an altogether different world. The panorama is wide and very luminous (assuming, of course, that the weather is fine). The landscape is composed of rolling hills, dotted with tarns that can swell into flooding lakes during the rainy season. Although the ever-growing African kikuyo grass (introduced to the area in the early 20th century) has already made headway into this last pocket of native highland flora, it is the native grasses – the *ichu* and its nearest relatives – which predominate, but only briefly. Soon is a landscape devoid of trees, with cushion plants growing low to preserve heat and moisture. The most common is the *yareta*, a bright green bubble-like growth, reminiscent of coral, but often, incorrectly, referred to as tundra. Beyond the foreground of rolling hills of yareta and tarn are several *cordilleras* of great mountain peaks.

Huaccoto to Huanca From Huaccoto it is possible to make a detour to the summit of **Pachatusan**, heading for the first of its many false summits (east, then south along the slope of the mountain), though this is only for experienced climbers. Instead,

San Jerónimo to Huanca Trek

continue on the same well-worn path that brought you to this point. A gentle climb of a few more metres and 1 km further, veering slightly east by northeast, sets course towards an obvious breach between Pachatusan and its northwestern extension, known as **Cerro Quellomina**. This pass and a winding trail descend through a maze of impregnable crags, all the way down to the green valley of the Urubamba, which makes its way from southeast to northwest, splaying out into various branches and channels, creating islets and sand banks which disappear in the rainy season.

Along the crest, close to the pass, are numerous wooden crosses draped in long, flowing, veil-like cloths, many of them well over 3 m tall. These have been erected by pilgrims and devotees and each year they are clad in fresh garments. A few hundred metres along the pass, on the left, is the entrance to what were once the famous **Yanantín** gold mines, belonging to the Marqués de Valleumbroso, which now yield only copper. The entire area was once known as the 'Marquesado de Oropeza'. The trail, very wide and easily recognizable, twists down through the rock spires. Another 200 m beyond is a small Inca fortress perched on one of the buttresses. Closer inspection reveals the remains of other observation points and Inca constructions among the rock towers. Just below this point, another major trail branches off to the left (northwest), climbing up to a well-marked pass. This is an original Inca road, leading back up to Ccoricocha and eventually Huchuy Cusco and on to Chinchero.

Soon, although still far below your present position, a large, relatively flat area with many buildings and cereal cultivation, as well as groves of very tall, old eucalyptus trees, comes into view. This green belt of fertility amid the seemingly relentless precipices of Pachatusan's northeastern face is **Huanca**, site of the famous sanctuary, one of the great religious shrines of the Andes. Its fame spreads far beyond its immediate vicinity. Devotees, belonging to branches and brotherhoods, come from as far as Ecuador and Bolivia.

Sanctuary of El Señor de Huanca

The Sanctuary of El Señor de Huanca stands above the clouds, surrounded by flower-filled gardens and trees of many kinds. It is a great gathering place of so many hopes and wishes for goodness, protected by the great misty crag, Pachatusan. From Huaccoto, three hours' hiking, not counting the unavoidable stops to appreciate the scenery, should bring you to the grounds of the sanctuary. The Mercedarian fathers, though fewer than in the past, are still there to greet visitors. The father in charge, whose title is Comendador Capellán, requests that all hikers descending from Huaccoto past the springs pick up all the garbage they can, as a contribution to the conservation of the sanctuary grounds. Lodging and meals are avilable for pilgrims and hikers (see Sleeping, page 206). There is also a public telephone. Note that there is always a ride available from the sanctuary, as the priests are more than willing to help the faithful who need transport. Ring the bell of the private quarters of the sanctuary and the resident priest will assist. The priests have their own private transport, which can be rented for a ride to the closest point for transport to Cusco or Pisac. Of course, a contribution to the sanctuary will be appreciated.

History of the sanctuary We know from Spanish chroniclers of the mid-16th century, such as Pedro de Cieza de León and Juan Polo de Ondegardo, that the Apu Pachatusan was a major *huaca* (shrine) long before the conquest. It was the origin of the ashlars and stone used for building Imperial Cusco of Pachacútec. It had numerous springs, on both its western and eastern slopes. Last but not least, as the later exploitation of the rich mines of the Marqués de Valleumbroso confirmed, it was a source of gold, silver and copper, all of great importance in pre-Columbian Peru, but of much greater value to the piratical economy of 16th-century Europe. The town of Oropesa (where the gold is weighed), some 10 km beyond San Jerónimo and close to Piquillacta, founded by the Spaniards in the boom years of the late 16th century, was aptly named. Even before the

Incas and Spaniards (as well as the Huari-Tiahuanacos of Piquillacta), two fundamental elements characterized the mountain: the abundance of fresh water springs and a large population of puma. Today the puma have disappeared, but the deer that must have constituted their prey can still be seen in groups in more isolated parts of the mountain.

Instead of succumbing to the more zealous approach of the early, crusading *conquistadores*, Pachatusan's sacredness was absorbed and adapted in the more enlightened approach of 'religious syncretism' that prevailed in the mid-17th to late 18th century. How else was the Marqués de Valleumbroso going to get the locals to work the mines? At Huanca, the necessary Christian miracle took place in 1675, 25 years after the great earthquake of 1650. It was a time when miracles, no matter their provenance, were universally required.

In May that year, one Diego Quispe, a simple Indian from Chincheros working in the Yanantín mines, committed some grave disciplinary error for which he was to be dealt severe punishment the next day. He fled into the crags and gullies of Apu Pachatusan, trusting more in the justice of the earth than that of his overlords. He crept into the furthest depths of an overhang and began to pray. As night fell and Quispe prepared to resume his flight to freedom, the miracle took place. Jesus appeared to him, wearing the crown of thorns and bleeding from the lashes on his back. And He spoke the words: "Diego, I have chosen this site to be a volcano of love and a pure spring of regeneration and forgiveness. Go to your home and let the local priest and all your people know. I shall await you here." Diego took a silver chain from his neck and laid it at the base of the rock where the apparition occurred (the first of many centuries of gifts and tributes to El Señor de Huanca).

Diego's life was spared, and more miracles followed. In the course of the next two generations, the boulder acquired a painting of Christ being whipped by a stylized, Moorish-looking ruffian (an ironic echo of the treatment inflicted upon the mineworkers by the Marqués de Valleumbroso). In time, ownership of the land passed to the religious order of La Merced of Cusco (Mercedarios). A large sanctuary was built over the original boulder and among the devotees whose generosity contributed to its construction are various South American presidents, the elder Alessandri of Chile prominent among them.

Today, the boulder and traces of the painting are partially visible through glass. Nearly 400 years' accumulation of plaques, icons and messages are everywhere. People come on foot, horse and by car to fill empty coke bottles and glass jars with the magic water that flows out of Apu Pachatusan just above the sanctuary.

To Huambutío and Paucartambo

Southeast from San Jerónimo the valley begins to narrow as you reach **Saylla**, famous for its *chicharrones* – deep-fried pieces of pork. Between here and Oropesa are the extensive ruins of **Tipón**. They include baths, terraces, irrigation systems and a temple complex, accessible from a path leading from just above the last terrace, all in a fine setting. From Tipón village it's an hour's climb to the ruins; or take a taxi. At the Tipón ruins, if you head to the left at the back, there is a small pathway. Follow the trail round to where you will see more small ruins. From there you will find an amazing Inca road with a deep irrigation channel, which can be followed to Cerro Pachatusan (see San Jerónimo to Huanca trek, above). You can do a walk of two or three days to Pachatusan.

Further on is **Oropesa**, which has been known as Cusco's breadbasket since colonial times and is the national capital of this staple diet. Try the large, delicious circular bread. The church has a fine ornately carved pulpit. Next comes the village of **Huacarpay**, near the shores of Laguna de Huacarpay, in the Piquillacta Archaeological Park. For details of Inca ruins and walks around this area, see below and on page 200.

At **Huambutío**, north of Huacarpay, the road divides: northwest to Pisac (see page 136) and north to Paucartambo, on the eastern slope of the Andes. The road from Huambutío northwest to Pisac (about 20 km) is fully paved. This is an access road for the first river-rafting section on the Río Urubamba, which also connects with another rafting route from Piñipampa. In the rainy season, and for less experienced rafters, the Huambutío (Piñipampa) to Pisac river section is safer to run. The rapids are Class II to III. The rafting trip is 30-35 km long with spectacular views of the Urubamba valley that are not seen in a conventional valley tour. This part of the river offers views of the Sanctuary of El Señor de Huanca (see above)

Paucartambo

This once remote town, 80 km east of Cusco, is on the road to Pilcopata, Atalaya and Shintuya. This is now the overland route used by tour companies from Cusco into Manu National Park. Consequently, it has become a popular tourist destination. On 15-17 July, the **Fiesta of the Virgen del Carmen** is a major attraction and well worth seeing. Masked dancers enact rituals and folk tales in the streets (see box).

Since colonial times this was on the route for produce brought from the jungle to the sierra and thence to the coast. King Carlos III of Spain had a stone bridge built across the river here in the 18th century to replace the previous rope bridge. The locals claimed that the reason the king lost such a large proportion of the *diezmos reales* (tithes, or one-tenth tax on annual produce) due to him from the area was that the mule loads were too heavy for the original bridge. The stone bridge may have solved his tax problem, but it also furthered his aim of promoting the development of Paucartambo and encouraging scientific and exploratory expeditions in the region.

You can walk from Paucartambo to the *chullpas* of **Machu Cruz** in about an hour, or to the *chullpas* of **Pijchu** (take a guide). You can also visit the Inca fortress of **Huatojto**, which has fine doorways and stonework. A car will take you as far as Ayre, from where the fortress is a two-hour walk. From Paucartambo, in the dry season, you can go 44 km to **Tres Cruces**, along the Pilcopata road, turning left after 25 km. Señor Cáceres in Paucartambo will arrange this trip for you. Tres Cruces gives a wonderful view of the sunrise in June and July: peculiar climactic conditions make it appear as if three suns are rising. Tour operators in Cusco (see page 113) can arrange transport and lodging.

Around Laguna de Huacarpay

The **Piquillacta Archaeological Park** is 30 km southeast of Cusco, with an area of 3,421 ha. Its nucleus is the remains of a lake, the Laguna de Huacarpay, now smaller than in ancient times when it was called Muyna. It is also known as **Laguna de Lucre**. The basin of the lake lies at an altitude of 3,200 m and is surrounded by several hills no higher than 3,350-3,400 m. Its shape is roughly circular and its circumference is presently about 8 km. Around it are many pre-Columbian archaeological remains, of which the principal ones are: Piquillacta, Choquepuquio, Kañaraqay, Urpicancha and Rumicolca.

Sections of the lake are overgrown with thick beds of totora reeds and other

Around Laguna de Huacarpay

N

0 km (approx) 1

0 miles (approx) 1

To Huambutío

Choquepuquio

To Cusco

Huacarpay

Piquillacta

To Andahuaylillas, Huaro & Urcos

Laguna de Huacarpay

Rumicolca

Urpicancha

Kañarakay

Cerro Combayoc

Lucre

The fiesta of the Virgen del Carmen

In the village of Paucartambo, 80 km east of Cusco, a pagan-Christian festival celebrates the Virgen del Carmen annually on 15-17 July. Her feast days are in the Quechua month of "Earthly Purification".

There are two popular myths surrounding the history of the Virgen del Carmen. The first tells how the Virgin appeared in Paucartambo. The story goes that a rich Ccollao woman called Felipa Begolla came to Paucartambo to trade goods. One day she was unloading her wares, when, in one of her earthenware pots, the head of a beautiful woman appeared and a sweet voice spoke to her, "Do not be afraid, my dear, my name is Carmen". The head shone like the rays of the sun. Felipa contracted a great cabinet maker in the town to carve a body made of fine wood on which to place that beautiful head. She brought the statue of the Virgin into the town's church and all the Ccollas celebrated since the Virgin had arrived in a pot from the Ccollao, an area beginning 150 km southeast of Cusco, beyond the Ausangate massif, covering the enormous highland plateau which includes Titicaca and stretching as far as northern Argentina. The inhabitants of this area, the Ccolla, swore to come every year on July 16 so that the Virgin would not feel sad at being away from her own land. The Virgin del Carmen festival became popular and so, each year, dancing groups dressed in colourful costumes with decorated masks came to re-enact the old folk tales. (Sra Betty Yabar, Testimonio de Cheqec, 1971)

In the other popular myth, the Chontakirus, a tribe of jungle Indians, tell that the Ch'unchos, who in history and fables embody profanity and contempt for sacred things, stole the statue of the Virgin from the Ccollas of Puno who were taking it to Paucartambo for the Corpus celebrations. During the confrontation the Ch'unchos killed the Ccollas and threw the statue into the Río Amaru (river of the serpent). From that day, the river was renamed the Madre de Dios, after the Mother of God. The statue was rescued from the waters and taken to the church in Paucartambo, where she remains. Scars from the arrows in her chest can still be seen. (Sra Alfonsina Barrionuevo, Cusco Màgico, 1968)

For the festival, the church is decorated, with the Mamacha Carmen dressed in fine clothes and she is visited by the dancing Comparsas. Some travel from far away, such as the Negritos who, in colonial times, came to dance for the Virgin, praying for their freedom. The Ch'unchos, her captors, are her main dancers and they guard her along the route of the procession. The party continues for the next two days with lots of dancing and music. Each dancing group has its own station in town and every year important people are named as Carguyocs, who are in charge of a particular dancing group at every ceremony. The Carguyocs cover all the costs of the festivity for the dancers and for all the people who visit. They provide lodging, food and drink.

The Mamacha Carmen is taken out on her final procession to the colonial stone bridge (built by King Carlos III of Spain in the 18th century). She then blesses the four Suyos, or cardinal points. The Saqras (demons) scurry over the rooftops trying to tempt her, but the Virgin with her kindness makes them repent. In the afternoon, a re-enactment of the battle between the Ccollas and the Ch'unchos, called the Guerrilla, takes place. The whole town gets involved. During these events, the music, dancing and drinking continue.

East & West of Cusco Around Laguna de Huacarpay

Andean lakeside vegetation. As the lake is gradually drying up, the reeds are spreading and fragmenting the open water, but several large sections of water remain. Water levels fluctuate between the so-called 'dry' and 'rainy' seasons and in other climatic events, such as El Niño. The village of Huacarpay, on its northern shore, can be subjected to damaging floods.

The Laguna de Huacarpay is habitat to a variety of birdlife. In the open water, flocks of puna teals, pochards and pintails, as well as more scattered individual Andean ruddy ducks, with their conspicuous blue beaks, can be seen. The totora reed banks are home to several varieties of gallinules and coots, the giant and the red-fronted being most noticeable. Along the shores of the lake and the neighbouring marshlands live puna ibis (though not in large numbers) and sometimes white-faced ibis; also some herons and occasional egrets. There are also lapwings, terns and Andean gulls. Most of these are present year-round. Huacarpay is the most readily accessible area from Cusco in which to observe a typical Andean highland lake environment.

▲ The lake circuit

A good way to see all this is to hike or cycle around the lake, on 8 km of level, paved secondary road, which few motor vehicles use. The main focus of this basic circuit is birdwatching and only two or three secondary archaeological sites, but the hike can be lengthened to include the majority of the archaeological sites built on the surrounding hills. Some can be visited independently, but on an anticlockwise circuit of the lake basin they can easily be taken in.

Starting from a point about 3-4 km due south of the Lucre turn-off on the main Cusco-Urcos highway, heading due south, you reach the southern end of the lake. The road begins to swing slightly to the left (east) and soon splits: right to the town of Lucre and left around the lake. **Lucre** has been associated with textiles from Inca times. In the 1850s and 1860s, the area was owned by the Garmendia family who pioneered the first industrial production of textiles (worsteds, tweeds, alpaca and vicuña finished cloth) in this area, maybe in all Peru. To do this they imported a complete textile mill from England, the whole works, including the engineers and mechanics. It was shipped to Mollendo, thence to Arequipa and on over the Andes by mule. For many years it played a significant part in the local economy. But today, there is no sign of it.

The left-hand fork continues east and shortly begins to climb a little and heads northeast. Here a really nice hike starts. On some maps this is marked Morada de Huascar, but its true name is **Kañarakay**. From this point, angling away and above the modern road, following the gently rising crest and the various converging trails and footpaths, you begin to glimpse the layers of history of this area. Looking north, some 5 km across the lake, as if moulded onto its hill, lies the rectilinear grid of Piquillacta. West of it and slightly lower are the less regular, but taller walls of Choqepuquio, while slightly lower but close by are the remains of a colonial hacienda, also named Choqepuquio. Much further away, 20-30 km north, is the unusual, stark profile of Cerro Pachatusan. Looking east from Piquillacta the gates of Rumicolca are visible, the irrigation canals contouring the mountains from distant, forgotten sources. Also visible is the unmistakable architectural harmony between structure and environment which characterizes Inca building, in this case, the terraces of Urpicancha. That's the entire hike which lies ahead.

Start hiking northeastward. What at first sight appears to be arid, rocky country interspersed with crumbling ridges and strewn with loose rocks and scree, is in fact the remnants of a vast network of roads, passageways, buildings, retaining walls and stairways. Several cities lie scattered here, successively inhabited, abandoned and repopulated. This is also the realm of the cacti: *opuntia predominate*, but also thin, elongated prickly pears, enormously tall flat nopales, small barrel cacti, some with huge bright scarlet and yellow flowers. There are seven-pointed San Pedro cacti, with lily-white flowers which bud at dawn, blossom at noon and wither by sunset. Epyphitic bromeliads, most of them *tsillandsias* with bushy crowns of long thin leaves armed with sharp thorns, cling to ancient walls and grow in empty windows. There are also aloes and agave, and almost everywhere are blankets of Spanish moss. The fauna is limited to lizards and rodents, which keep the insect population under control. Most common are black widow spiders, which live under stones (it best to leave rocks where they are and watch carefully where you sit down for a break!). Kestrels and hawks streak overhead, but the most typical of local birds are the Andean flicker, a large bright yellow-greenish speckled ground woodpecker, fond of lizards, and the giant hummingbirds – Patagonia gigas – with their nests strategically placed among the thick branches of a thorny cactus.

After 1 km of this jumble of stone, you come to the ruins of **Urpicancha** (Urpi meaning dove, and cancha an enclosed field). Some legends say this was the birthplace of the Inca Huáscar, who waged war with his half-brother Atahualpa. Urpicancha is like a small oasis in the middle of the dusty environment surrounding the lake. It consists of a succession of a terraced hillside, descending almost to the lakeshore. At its base are two partial enclosures, made of well-fitted rocks which have acquired a striking orange hue from the lichen. A freshwater spring descends the hillside, partially piped, and there's an old colonial house, closed for some years now. It's a shady spot, with eucalyptus, willows and some mature elderberry trees (*sauco*).

From here, the hike climbs up to Rumicolca. Several paths meander along the western slope of the large hill called Cerro Combayoc. All these trails will lead to Rumicolca. The closer to Urpicancha, or from Urpicancha itself, that you head up Combayoc, the more scenic the hike will be. The entire Muyna basin can be seen, and the eastern side of Combayoc, including 40 km of the Vilcanota river valley, Andahuaylillas and sections of the quarries of Rumicolca.

Rumicolca

Back on the main road to Sicuani and Puno, shortly after the turn-off to Piquillacta, you will see, on the right, the huge gateway of Rumicolca. You can walk around it for free. This was a Huari aqueduct, built across this narrow stretch of the valley, which the Incas clad in fine stonework to create this gateway. If you look at the top you can see the original walls, four tiers high. It is now being 'restored' which in Cusco means rebuilt; a highly controversial topic.

Rumicolca itself (the name means depository or storage site for rocks) was a control point and parallel set of gateways through which in Inca times all traffic between Cusco and Collasuyo (the southeastern quarter of the Inca dominions) had to pass. It is very imposing. The wall through which the gates pass is of common enough composition, rough-hewn rock bound by a hardened clay mortar. There is evidence that this was covered in stucco and painted in ochres and reds. The gateways, though, are some of the finest Inca masonry. Large, perfectly cut, polished andesite ashlars fit together exactly, without mortar, of a quality equal to anything in Cusco, Ollantaytambo or Pisac. The finely dressed gateways probably date from the 14th century, contemporary with the monumental phase of Inca architecture in the era of Pachacútec or his successor Túpac Yupanqui. The wall which the gateway crosses is 600 to 800 years older and supported a Huari aqueduct which brought water to Piquillacta.

Piquillacta

ⓘ *0700-1730, entry by BTU tourist ticket (see page 71). Buses to Urcos from Av Huáscar in Cusco will drop you at the entrance on the north side of the complex, though this is not the official entry.*

Rumicolca is a few metres from the modern Cusco to Puno road. On the other side of the road, less than 50 m away, lies the entrance to the Huari adobe wall ruins of Piquillacta (which translates as the City of Fleas). Piquillacta is a large site, with some reconstruction in progress. It was an administrative centre at the southern end of the Huari Empire. The Huari, contemporaneous with the Tiahuanaco culture (AD 600-1000), were based near present-day Ayacucho in the Central Highlands, almost 600 km by road north of Cusco.

◆ The church is likely to be locked. For the giant key, look for Sr Pablo Ticuña t 2 de Mayo 367, a block away. He will show you around for US$0.85 per person (he only speaks Spanish).

Huari influence covered most of what we now know as Peru, from Cajamarca and the Pacific coast in the north to the borders of the Tiahuanaco in the south. Their system of regional storehouses, irrigation, roads and government was similar to, and was adopted by, the Incas. Archaeological evidence from Piquillacta is confusing, but mostly suggests that this was not a place for permanent residents, more for storing supplies, for housing itinerant groups of workers, for tribute gathering and distribution and for ceremonies. The whole site is surrounded by a wall, there are many enclosed compounds with buildings of over one storey and it appears that the walls were plastered and finished with a layer of lime.

From Piquillacta, head west into a valley through which runs the paved road from Cusco to Paucartambo. Cross it and continue for about 50 m until you come to the remains of the old dirt road which runs parallel to the modern one for a short stretch and then veers left, crossing an old bridge. Over the bridge head west by southwest, past the site of a lime crusher (some houses, a small adobe factory). On the right is a marshy extension of Huacarpay lake. Here is some of the best birdwatching in the entire trek. Follow the main (or any secondary) path up the side of the valley, gaining the first ridge about 100 m beyond. Look south and see the dark walls of **Choquepuquio**, perhaps the most mysterious of the archaeological sites on the trek. The walls suggest two-storeyed houses, but also a redoubt, built to withstand siege and attack.

Choquepuquio was erected as a stronghold in insecure times. Its drama derives from it not being restored (as are most of the other sites in the park, a controversial topic, eg at Rumicolca). It is unkempt, there are thistles and brambles to deal with and, when seen up close, its walls appear even taller and more enigmatic than at first glance. From Choqepuquio follow any of the paths leading to the road which goes to Cusco. You will emerge directly opposite the Lucre turn-off where the hike began.

Southeast to Urcos

Andahuaylillas
Continuing southeast towards Urcos you reach Andahuaylillas and the first of three fascinating 17th-century churches. This is a simple structure, but it has been referred to as the Andean Sistine Chapel because of its beautiful frescoes, and internal architecture. Go in, wait for your eyes to adjust to the darkness, then turn to look at the two pictures either side of the splendid door. On the right is the path to heaven, which is narrow and thorny; on the left the way to hell, which is wide and littered with flowers. They are attributed to the artist Luis de Riaño. Above is the high choir, built in local wood, where there are two organs. Craning your neck further you will see the remarkable painted and carved ceiling. The main altar is gilded in 24-carat gold leaf and has symbols from both the Quechua and Christian religions, such as the sun and the lamb, respectively. Many of the canvases depict the lives of the church's patron saints, St Peter and St Paul. Ask for Sr Eulogio; he is a good guide, but speaks Spanish only.

Outside, around the peaceful plaza, are massive trees dripping with red seeds and hanging moss. These are Pisonay trees.

Huaro and Urcos
Before the next major town of Urcos is the quiet village of Huaro; turn left off the main road to reach the appalling main plaza, dominated by a concrete lookout tower. The

church on this plaza is stunning inside. Walking in takes your breath away. The walls are plastered with frescoes used to evangelize the illiterate. Grinning skeletons compete with dragons and devils ushering the living into the afterlife and punishing them thereafter. Although finished in 1802 by Tadeo Escalante, they are now mostly in a sad state of repair. Tour groups come here, but there is precious little money being spent on preservation. The first fresco on the right as you enter shows the torment of sinners in hell. A liar has his tongue torn out with pliers, a drunk has boiling alcohol poured down his throat through a funnel and others are impaled on a wheel. The torture is not confined to the masses. In a boiling cauldron, among the tortured, writhing, naked bodies are a priest, a cardinal and a bishop, identified by their hats.

Looking left of the door there is a priest giving absolution at the death of a girl in a poor house while below, a rich house plays host to a sumptuous banquet (with roasted guinea pig on the menu, of course). A woman here is choking and being led away by the skeleton of Death. The moral is clear. Right of the entrance, below another portrait of rich people having a feast, is the Tree of Life with good versus evil as Death wields an axe and Jesus sounds a bell.

To the right of this, on the left wall, is Judgement Day at its grimmest. Centre stage is a graveyard, the coffins of which are being yanked open by skeletons to drag the dead to either the underworld on the right (entered via the mouth of a dragon) or heaven (complete with Pearly Gates and musicians playing trumpets).

On the left are people being pulled from flames by angels. This is Purgatory and its inhabitants are those who have committed minor sins. Having paid their dues they will now be allowed into heaven. The democracy of the Catholic vision again allows these sinners to include cardinals and bishops.

To the right of this painting we see that Death is never far away. A huge skeleton containing the body of a woman (for we are all born of woman) has at its feet the paraphernalia of the rich, which cannot be taken into the next life. More skeletons stand behind people ignorant of their destiny. An angel sounds a trumpet from the top of a pillar at the moment of death. Meanwhile, the devil can be seen lurking under the bed of a person being given absolution. Again, look up at the wonderful ceiling.

Beyond Huaro is **Urcos**. There are lodgings here, but they're basic to say the least.

Ausangate and Tinqui → *Colour map 2, B4.*

A spectacular road from Urcos crosses the Eastern Cordillera to Puerto Maldonado in the jungle (see page 226). Some 47 km after passing the snow-line Hualla-Hualla pass, at 4,820 m, the super-hot thermal baths of **Marcapata**, ⓘ *US$0.10*, 173 km from Urcos, provide a relaxing break. Some 82 km from Urcos, on the road to Puerto Maldonado, at the base of **Nevado Ausangate** (6,384 m), is the town of **Ocongate**, which has two hotels on the Plaza de Armas.

Beyond Ocongate is Tinqui, the starting point for hikes around Ausangate (6,372 m), the highest mountain in southeastern Peru, in the Cordillera Vilcanota. On the flanks of the Nevado Ausangate is **Q'Olloriti**, where a church has been built close to the snout of a glacier. This place has become a place of pilgrimage (see page 107).

▲ Hiking around Ausangate

The hike around the mountain of Ausangate takes five to six days. It is spectacular, but quite hard, with three passes over 5,000 m, so you need to be acclimatized. Alternatively, a shorter and easier return trek can be made from Ausangate down the beautiful **Pitumarca Valley** to the town of the same name and the Sacred Valley. It is recommended to take a guide or *arriero*. *Arrieros* and muleteers have formed a union and as such they are much more organized than in recent years. An *arriero* charges US$7 per day, US$6 per day for each mule, more for a saddle horse. A chief *arriero* takes along one to two assistants (US$5 per day per assistant). *Arrieros* expect foodstuffs (noodles, sugar, rice, coca leaves), plus cigarettes, alcohol, and kerosene to be provided for a well-planned expedition. *Arrieros* and mules can be hired in Tinqui. A recommended *arriero* is Enrique Mandura, who also rents out equipment. **South American Explorers** (who can supply all the latest advice) recommend Theo. Make sure you sign a contract with full details. Buy all food supplies in Cusco. Maps are available at the **Instituto Geográfico Militar** in Lima or **South American Explorers**. Some tour companies in Cusco have details about the hike (see page 113).

Southeast from Urcos

Southeast from Urcos, the main road passes through Cusipata, with an Inca gate and wall. Here the ornate bands for the decoration of ponchos are woven. Close by is the Huari hilltop ruin of Llallanmarca.

Acomayo and the Inca bridge

Beyond Cusipata on the main road is **Checacupe** which has a fine church with good paintings and a handsome carved altar rail. Between these two towns a road branches west up what soon becomes a dirt road. At the first fork, just before a beautiful mountain lake, turn right to travel past a small community and on to Acomayo, a pretty village which has a chapel with mural paintings of the 14 Incas.

From Acomayo, you can walk to Huáscar, which takes one hour, and from there to **Pajlia**; a climb which leads through very impressive scenery. The canyons of the upper Apurímac are vast beyond imagination. Great cliffs drop thousands of metres into dizzying chasms and huge rocks balance menacingly overhead. The ruins of Huajra Pucará lie near Pajlia. They are small, but in an astonishing position.

From Acomayo, return down the same road, past the lake again until you reach the fork where you earlier turned right. Take a sharp right here to travel further along the lake. You will travel past three more beautiful lakes. If you are lost ask for Tungasuca via the *circuito de las cuatro lagunas*. Stop awhile by the fourth. It is absolutely quiet here and a great place to recharge your soul. Set against the pale green grass banks, serene waters reflect the red soil of the hills behind. The only sound is the occasional splash and hoot of a white-beaked Andean coot. The air is thin, clear and crisp.

The road continues to Yanaoca, where you'll find basic accommodation and restaurants. From here it is possible to continue on to Sicuani, but a side trip to **Qeswachaka** and the grass Inca bridge 30 km away is well worth the effort. Turn right just before you leave the village to join a road which, at times, is very rough. The way is marked with kilometre signs and you must turn right just after Km 22 where another road begins, marked with a Km 0. You will find steps down to the bridge shortly before Km 31, two bends from the bright orange road bridge.

The footbridge has been rebuilt every year for the past 400 years during a three-day festival. This starts on June 10 and is celebrated by the three communities who use the bridge. It is built entirely of *pajabrava* grass, woven and spliced to make six sturdy cables which are strung across the 15-m chasm. Look in the water at the far side and you will probably see the remains of the previous year's effort; the work lasts five months, after which the fibres deteriorate and you should not attempt to cross.

Another side trip is to the **Carañawi Cave** (at 4,100 m), about two hours before Qeswachaka. From Yanaoca find transport towards Livitaca and ask locals where to get off for Carañawi. There is also a large sign. You may only enter the cave between June and October as there is too much water at other times of the year. Camping is possible, but be prepared for extreme cold; there is no water available. It is certainly also possible to drive here in a rented car, but the road is terrible so taking a 4WD is a good idea.

Tinta and Raqchi → *Colour map 2, B4.*

ⓘ *Entrance to the site is US$1.75. There is a basic shop at the site. The school next door greatly appreciates donations of books and materials.*

After Combapata on the main road, 23 km before Sicuani, is Tinta, whose church has a brilliant gilded interior and an interesting choir vault. Further on, about 120 km south-east of Cusco in the province of Canchis, in a fertile tributary valley of the Vilcanota, is the colonial village of **San Pedro de Cacha**. Although unremarkable in itself, the village stands within one of the most important archaeological sites in Peru, Raqchi.

A few hundred metres beyond the village are the principal remains, the once great **Temple of Viracocha**, the pan-Andean god, creator of all living creatures. This is one of the only remaining examples of a two-storey building of Inca architecture. It was 90 m long and 15 m high and was probably the largest roofed building ever built by the Incas. Above walls of finely dressed masonry 3-4 m high – stonework equal to that found in Cusco or Machu Picchu – rise the remains of another 5-6 m high wall of adobe brickwork of which only isolated sections remain. Similarly, of the 22 outer columns, which supported great sloping roofs, just one or two remain complete, the others being in various states of preservation. There are numerous other constructions, including *acllahuasi* (houses of chosen women, spinners and weavers of ceremonial cloth), barracks, granaries, reservoirs, baths and fountains. The burial

South to Sicuani

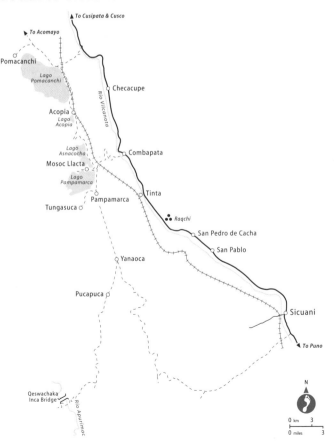

site includes round *chullpa* tombs of the sort found around Lake Titicaca. Much of it was damaged and demolished in search of treasure during or after the Spanish conquest. According to some accounts, the temple was built by Inca Viracocha in the late 14th century, but some chronicles attribute it to Pachacútec.

Archaeological research has shown that Raqchi was always a place associated with religious and ceremonial activity. This predates not only the Inca, but also the Canches (an ethnic group which flourished in the middle horizon of Tiahuanaco), who were conquered and incorporated into the Inca Empire. Since Raqchi was the principal religious site of the Canches, it was natural that the Incas should dedicate their own temple on their allies' hallowed ground. Perhaps the most significant reason behind the choice of this as a sacred site is that Raqchi stands on the slopes of the only dormant volcano in the Cusco region, Kimsachata. The name in Quechua means 'three-cornered' or 'triplets'. Various myths of Viracocha's travels in the area tell of a hostile reception by local inhabitants resulting in their destruction by fire and brimstone invoked by Viracocha, others show him taming and overcoming a devastating eruption of Kimsachata.

On the volcano's slopes are pure water springs and sulphurous thermal springs, salt and rich clay deposits. The clay provides the region's principal industry, pottery and ceramics (whence its other name, Raqchi, which in Quechua is a large vessel or pot used in the preparation of *chicha*), as well as building materials such as tiles and particularly strong bricks. ➤➤ *For information on local festivals, see page 207.*

Sicuani → *Phone code: 084. Colour map 2, B4. Altitude: 3,690 m.*

Sicuani is an important agricultural centre and an excellent place for items of llama and alpaca wool and skins. They are sold at the railway station and at the excellent Sunday morning market. The plaza is not as bad as the aberrations found in villages in the nearby mountains, but it is flanked along one entire side by a mirror-glass-fronted, purple-painted concrete monstrosity. On the other side are examples of what might have been much more appropriate colonial-style, balconied buildings. Around the plaza are several shops selling local hats.

● Sleeping

Sanctuary of El Señor de Huanca *p196*
G Lodging and meals are avilable for pilgrims and hikers: US$5.75 for bed and board, free for somewhere to sleep only (but you can cook). Both include full use of bath and toilet.

Paucartambo *p198*
G **Albergue Municipal Carmen de la Virgen**. Fairly basic.
G **Quinta Rosa Marina**, *near the bridge*. Similarly basic.

Andahuaylillas *p202*
E **La Casa del Sol**, *close to the central plaza on Garcilaso*. Relaxing, clean and bright hostel. Well-decorated rooms set around a courtyard, this is excellent value. Owned by Dr Gladys Oblitas, the hostel funds her project to provide medical services to poor *campesinos*. While staying you can take a course or take part in workshops on natural

and alternative medicine. She also has a practice in Cusco, *Procuradores 42, T084-227264, medintegral@hotmail.com*

Huaro and Urcos *p202*
G **Hostal Luvic**, on the plaza, Urcos, cheap and basic.
G **Hostal Señor de Qoillurrit'i**, *on the main road on the central plaza*. Best of a bad bunch. Dormitory rooms are very basic but clean; there is also a private double of similar quality. Showers are cold in a separate block outside.
Hotel Laterraza, which may look upmarket from the outside, should be avoided if at all possible.

Ausangate and Tinqui *p203*
G **Ausangate**, *Tinqui*, very basic but warm, friendly atmosphere. Sr Crispin (or Cayetano), the owner, is knowledgeable and can arrange guides, mules, etc. He and his brothers can be contacted in Cusco on

F084-227768. All have been recommended as reliable sources of trekking and climbing information, for arranging trips and for being very safety conscious.

G **Hostal Tinqui Guide**, *on the right-hand side as you enter the village*, friendly, meals available, the owner can arrange guides and horses.

Acomayo and the Inca bridge *p204*
There are many places to camp wild by the lakes. Take warm clothing for night time and plenty of water. At Qeswachaca there's good camping downstream, but take water.

Tinta and Raqchi *p205*
G **Casa Comunal**, *Tinta*. Clean dormitory accommodation and good food.

Sicuani *p206*
The bus terminal is in the newer part of town, which is separated from the older part and the Plaza de Armas by a pedestrian walkway and bridge. At the new' end of the bridge, but also close to the centre of town, are several *hostales* advertising hot water and private bathrooms.
E **Hotel Obada**, *Jr Tacna 104, T084-351214*, has seen better days. There are large, clean rooms with hot showers.
E **Royal Inti**, *Av Centenario 116, T084-352730*, on the west side of the old pedestrian bridge across the river, is modern, clean and friendly.
E **Samariy**, *Av Centenario 138 (next to Royal Inti), T084-352518*. Offers good value rooms with bathrooms.
G **Hostal Obada**, *2 de Mayo, close to hotel of the same name*. Basic dormitory accommodation with separate bathrooms.
G per person **José's Hostal**, *Av Arequipa 143, T084-351254*. Rooms with bath, clean and good.

🍴 Eating

Huaro and Urcos *p202*
$ **Restaurante Pollería**, *on the main plaza in Urcos*, is acceptable and cheap.

Sicuani *p206*
$ **2 de Mayo**, running northeast from the plaza, there are several cafés which are good for snacks and breakfasts.
$ **El Fogón**, *C Zevallos, the main drag down*

from the plaza, smart, painted pink, on the left heading down. Serves up good chicken and chips for US$1.70.
$ **Mijuna Wasi**, *Jr Tacna 146*. Closed Sun. One of several *picanterías* which prepares typical dishes such as *adobo* served with huge glasses of *chicha* in a delapidated but atmospheric courtyard. Recommended.
$ **Pizzería Bon Vino**, *2 de Mayo 129, 2nd floor, off the east side of the plaza*, is good for an Italian meal.
$ **Viracocha**, *on the west side of the plaza, left of the concrete monstrosity*, is OK.

🍸 Bars and clubs

Sicuani *p206*
Piano Bar, *just off the first block of 2 de Mayo*, is the best nightspot in town.

🎡 Festivals and events

Acomayo and the Inca bridge *p204*
Jun 10 a 3-day festival is celebrated for the rebuilding of the grass Inca footbridge at **Qeswachaka**.

Raqchi *p205*
Raqchi is still a venue for ceremonial events. The **Wiracocha** festivities in San Pedro and neighbouring San Pablo start on **24 Jun**. This date marks the dual Andean celebration of the ancient Inca festival of the sun, **Inti Raymi**, and the Christian feast day of **San Juan Bautista**, closely associated with water, streams and bathing, as well as being the patron saint of cattle and cattle breeders. It is the time of branding. On the eve of the fiesta, bonfires are lit across the Andes and fortunes are divined. Dancers come to Raqchi from all over Peru and through music and dance they illustrate everything from the ploughing of fields to bull fights. This leads into the feast of **San Pedro and San Pablo** on 29 Jun.

🚌 Transport

Lucre *p200*
Bus Buses too Lucre leave from the bus station on Calle Huáscar, in Wanchac district, on a side street ½ block from the market, 1 hr. Fare from Cusco to **Oropesa** is US$0.30 (passing by San Sebastián, San Jerónimo, Saylla, Huasao, Tipón); fare

Cusco-Lucre is US$0.45. Small cars wait at the start of the 8-km circuit around the Huacarpay lake charging US$1.50 (Ruperto Valencia and Ernesto Arredondo are recommended drivers).

San Jerónimo *p194*

Bus ET León de San Jerónimo from Puquín District (on the road to Chinchero) to San Jerónimo; catch this minibus on the corner of C Ayacucho and Av Sol 3rd block. It goes through the downtown area, Wanchac district, Av de la Cultura all the way to San Jerónimo (final stop beyond the plaza, at the corner of the Fe y Alegría and Santa Bernardita schools).

Santiago Express from plaza of Santiago district, a few blocks from La Virgen de Belén and the Antonio Lorena Hospital. Board this bus on 3rd block of Av Sol (near the post office); it turns left to Wanchac, then follows Av de la Cultura to San Jerónimo's main plaza. US$ 0.15.

Chaska from Villa El Sol-Independencia in the Santiago district above Cusco to Jr Arica at the plaza in San Jerónimo. Best place to catch it in central Cusco is the corner of C Ayacucho and Av Sol (3rd block). US$0.15. All services run from 0530 to 2200. All pass in front the San Jerónimo police station, from which C Clorinda Matto de Turner, for the start of the trek, is 1½ blocks away (this is the street where the San Jerónimo main market is located, as well as the cemetery at the very end).

Sanctuary of El Señor de Huanca *p196*

About 3 km beyond **Oropesa** is a turning to the left; the higher road, called Carretera Carmen Bonita, goes to **Paucartambo** and on to Manu. To the left, following the river bank, the road passes **Huambutío, Vilcabamba, San Salvador** and ends at **Pisac**, connecting with the road to the Sacred Valley of the Urubamba and the road back to Cusco via Sacsayhuaman.

Bus Transport from Cusco leaves from the Coliseo Cerrado and the back of the Social Security Hospital compound, 2 blocks from the Hospital Regional main bus stop; to the right on Av de la Cultura going southeast. Buses run on weekends and daily during the Señor de Huanca celebrations, 14-21 Sep, and the following pilgrimage season which

goes on throughout Oct. Departs 0700 until midday and returns from midday to 1600.

Empresa de Transportes Paucartambo y Pitusiray, Av Tullumayo 202 (lower part), southeast part of Cusco. Relevant schedules are: Mon-Sat, Cusco to **San Salvador**, 1½ hrs, 0640 and 1300, US$0.75; San Salvador to Cusco 0800 and 1330, and from San Salvador to **Pisac** at 1400, 45 mins-1 hr, US$0.60.

Taxis Available to the Sanctuary of El Señor de Huanca for about US$10 one way, with waiting time and return trip US$20-25.

Paucartambo *p198*

Private car hire for a round trip from Cusco on 15-17 Jul costs US$30. Tour operators in Cusco can arrange this. A minibus leaves for Paucartambo from Av Huáscar in Cusco, every other day, US$4.50, 3-4 hrs; alternate days Paucartambo-Cusco. Trucks and a private bus leave from the Coliseo, behind Hospital Segura in Cusco; 5 hrs, US$2.50.

Andahuaylillas *p202*

To Andahuaylillas take a taxi, or the **Oropesa** bus from Av Huáscar in Cusco, via Tipón, Piquillacta and Rumicolca.

Huaro and Urcos *p202*

Transportes Vilcanota depart from the terminal on Av de la Cultura, Cusco, at the Paradero Hospital Regional (on a side street), and run to **San Jerónimo, Saylla, Huasao, Tipón, Oropesa, Piquillacta/ Huacarpay, Andahuaylillas** and on to **Urcos**. These buses run from 0500 to 2100, fare US$ 0.72 to Urcos.

Ausangate and Tinqui *p203*

Buses These leave for Tinqui from Cusco Mon-Sat at 1000 (6-7 hrs, US$3.50) from C Tomasatito Condemayta, near the Coliseo Cerrado.

Acomayo and the Inca bridge *p204*

To get to Acomayo, take a Cusco-Sicuani bus or truck (US$1, 1½ hrs), then a truck or bus to **Acomayo** (3 hrs, same price). Alternatively, get off at Checacupe and take a truck on to Acomayo. To visit the 4 beautiful mountain lakes and Inca bridge, it would be worthwhile renting a 4WD for 2 days (**Kantu Perú Tours** in Cusco can organize this as well as a driver/guide for US$280, see p113). Giving locals a lift is both fun and helpful – they will make sure you take the right road. Alternatively, hire a vehicle with a driver. It is just as feasible by combi, if you have more time. The bridge can also be reached from Combapata on the main Cusco-Sicuani-Puno road. Combis and colectivos leave for the 30-km trip when full from the plaza for **Yanaoca** (US$0.50). Then hitchhike to **Quehue** (no accommodation), a 1½-hr walk from Qeswachaka, or to **Qeswachaka** itself, on the road to Livitaca. Be prepared for long waits on this road. On Wed and Sat there are direct buses to **Livitaca** from Cusco with the **Warari** and **Olivares** companies which pass the site, returning on Mon and Thu.

Tinta and Raqchi *p205*
There are frequent buses and trucks to and from Cusco, or you can take the train.

Sicuani *p206*
Combis run every 15-20 mins between Cusco and Sicuani (137 km, US$1.25). It is 250 km to **Puno**. 38 km beyond the town is La Raya pass (4,321 m), the highest on this route, which marks the divide between Cusco Department and the altiplano which stretches to Lake Titicaca. It is impossible to buy unleaded petrol in this town.

❶ Directory

Sanctuary of El Señor de Huanca *p196*
Telephone There is a public telephone at the Sanctuary.

Sicuani *p206*
Banks Banco de la Nación has a branch on the plaza as does Banco de Crédito, but the one cash machine takes only local cards.

West of Cusco

West of Cusco is the road to the city of Ayacucho in the Central Highlands. Branching off this road at the town of Abancay (195 km from Cusco) is the principal overland route to Lima, via Nasca – of the famous Lines – and the coastal city of Pisco – the famous booze of the same name comes from near here. There are enough Inca sites on or near this road in the Department of Cusco, and also to the south of the city, to remind us that the empire's influence spread to all four cardinal points. Add to this some magnificent scenery, especially in the canyon of the Río Apurímac, and you have the makings of some fascinating excursions away from the centre. One, to the ruins of Choquequirao, is a tough but rewarding trip. ►► *For Sleeping and Eating, see page 216.*

Anta to Curahuasi → *Colour map 2, B2.*

The Cusco-Machu Picchu train follows the road west from the city through the Anta canyon for 10 km, and then, at a sharp angle, the Urubamba Canyon, and descends along the river valley, flanked by high cliffs and peaks. In the town of **Anta**, felt trilby hats are on sale.

Some 76 km from Cusco, beyond Anta on the Abancay road, and 2 km before Limatambo, are the ruins of **Tarahuasi**. A few hundred metres from the road there is a very well-preserved Inca temple platform, with 28 tall niches, and a long stretch of fine polygonal masonry. The ruins are impressive, enhanced by the orange lichen which give the walls a beautiful honey colour. Near here the Spanish *conquistadores* on their push towards the Inca capital of Cusco suffered what could have been a major setback. Having crossed the Río Apurímac, the expeditionary force under the command of Hernando de Soto encountered an Inca army at Vilcaconga. On the first day of the battle, de Soto's men were almost routed, although only five were killed, but in the night reinforcements led by Almagro arrived. The following morning the Incas were demoralized to see a larger force than the one they had defeated the day before and, after renewed fighting, left the field to the Spaniards.

One hundred kilometres from Cusco along the Abancay road is the exciting descent into the **Apurímac Canyon**, near the former Inca suspension bridge that inspired Thornton Wilder's *The Bridge of San Luis Rey* (see Books, page 294). The bridge itself was made of rope and was where the royal Inca road crossed the river. When the *conquistadores* reached this point on the march to Cusco, they found the bridge destroyed. But luck was again on their side since, it being the dry season, the normally fierce Apurímac was low enough for the men and horses to ford. In colonial times the bridge was rebuilt several times, but it no longer exists. Thornton Wilder (1897-1975), whose novel won the 1928 Pulitzer prize, uses an episode in the bridge's history to meditate upon individual destiny. On 20 July 1714, five travellers are on the bridge when its ropes snap and it plummets into the river. A monk, Brother Juniper, witnesses their death and investigates the lives of each, trying to understand the role of divine providence in their demise. Three of the characters are fictional, but the other two are the son and teacher of La Perricholi, the most famous actress in Peru at the time and one-time mistress of the Viceroy Amat. For his efforts, and for his questioning of God's purpose, Juniper's book is declared heretical by the Inquisition and both book and author are burned at the stake.

Also along the road to Abancay from Cusco, near **Curahuasi** (126 km from Cusco), famous for its aromatic anise herb, is the stone of **Saihuite**, ① *US$1.45*, carved with animals, houses, etc, which appears to be a relief map of an Indian village. Unfortunately, 'treasure hunters' have defaced the stone. There are other interesting carvings in the area around the Saihuite stone.

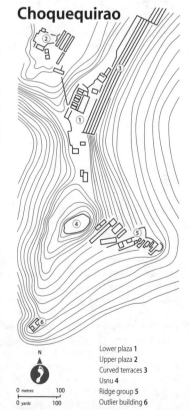

Choquequirao

Choquequirao → *Colour map 2, B2.*
Choquequirao is another 'lost city of the Incas', built on a ridge spur almost 1,600 m above the Apurímac. Its Inca name is unknown, but research has shown that it was built during the reign of Inca Pachacútec. Although only 30% has been uncovered, it is believed to be a larger site than Machu Picchu, but with fewer buildings. The stonework is different from the classic Inca construction and masonry, simply because the preferred granite and andesite are not found in this region. A number of high-profile explorers and archaeologists, including Hiram Bingham, researched the site, but its importance has only recently been recognized. And now tourists are venturing in there, too. With new regulations being applied to cut congestion on the Inca Trail, Choquequirao is destined to replace the traditional hike as the serious trekker's alternative.

The main features of Choquequirao include the **Lower Plaza**, considered by most experts to be the focal point of the city. Double-jammed doorways and high-quality stonework suggest that the buildings were used by high-ranking

N

0 metres 100
0 yards 100

Lower plaza 1
Upper plaza 2
Curved terraces 3
Usnu 4
Ridge group 5
Outlier building 6

Upper Plaza, reached by a huge set of steps or terraces, has what are possibly ritual baths. Some have speculated that this area was occupied by the priesthood of Choquequirao. The lesser quality of the stonework and the absence of double-jammed doorways suggest slightly lower status than the Lower Plaza. A beautiful set of slightly **curved agricultural terraces** run for over 300 m east-northeast of the Lower Plaza. The Usnu is a levelled hilltop platform, ringed with stones and giving awesome 360-degree views. Perhaps it was a ceremonial site, or was used for solar and astronomical observations. The Ridge Group, still shrouded in vegetation, is large collection of buildings some 50-100 m below the Usnu. Unrestored, with some significant hall-like structures, this whole area makes for great exploring. Perhaps this extensive and complex set of buildings formed the living quarters for the site's residents. The Outlier Building, isolated and surrounded on three sides by sheer drops of over 1½ km into the Apurímac Canyon, possesses some of the finest stonework within Choquequirao. The Outlier's separation from other structures must also be significant, but exactly why, like so many other questions regarding the Incas and their society, remains a mystery.

Capuliyoc, nearly 500 m below the Lower Plaza, is a great set of agricultural terraces, visible on the approach from the far side of the valley. These terraces enabled the Incas to cultivate plants from a significantly warmer climate in close geographical proximity to their ridge-top home.

There are three ways to reach Choquequirao. None is a gentle stroll. The shortest way is from **Cachora**, a village on the south side of the Apurímac, reached by a side road from the Cusco-Abancay highway, shortly after Saihuite. It is four hours by bus from Cusco to the turn-off, then a three-hour descent from the road to Cachora (from 3,695 m to 2,875 m). Buses run from Abancay to Cachora, but none arrive after 1100. Accommodation, guides (Celestino Peña is the official guide) and mules are available in Cachora. Details of this route are given below.

The second and third routes take a minimum of eight days and require thorough preparation. Both cross the watershed of the Cordillera Vilcabamba between the Urubamba and Apurímac rivers. The second hike (see route description below) uses the same route from Cachora as the first trek, then continues from Choquequirao to the Yanama river valley before continuing to Santa Teresa or Machu Picchu itself. The third route splits from the second in the Yanama Valley and goes to Huancacalle (see page 181), via the pass of Choquetacarpo, 4,600 m high. From Huancacalle it's possible to continue on to Espíritu Pampa on the edge of the rainforest. Either route can be undertaken in reverse. Both pass the mines of La Victoria and both involve an incredible number of strenuous ascents and descents. En route you are rewarded with fabulous views of the Sacsarayoc massif (also called Pumasillo), Salkantay, other snow peaks, and the deep canyons of the Río Blanco and the Apurímac. You will also see condors and meet very friendly people, but the highlight is Choquequirao itself.

▲▲ Vilcabamba traverse trek

Described below is a trek across the mountains from Cachora to Choquequirao and on to Machu Picchu. The full route via the Yanama and Santa Teresa valleys crosses the entire Vilcabamba range, between the mighty canyons of the Apurímac and Urubamba rivers, connecting two of the most impressive archaeological sites in South America. For those with time this is an excellent alternative to the classic Inca Trail and in places follows well-preserved examples of Inca road. Alternatively, you can follow the first part of the route only, from Cachora to Choquequirao, and return via the same trail.

The Vilcabamba range was the last refuge of the Inca Empire and, under Manco Inca and his sons, resistance endured for decades after the initial conquest.

66 99 Roughly translated from Quechua, Apurímac means 'the river that speaks'. The roaring rapids along its course give ample justification for this title.

Hemmed in between two great rivers, the mountains form a natural fortress and Inca ruins, many little known and unrestored, lie scattered across the entire region. It is recommended that you hire a guide, either locally in Cachora or in Cusco. Not only will you obtain local knowledge of the area and route, but also you will be helping to bring employment to an extremely isolated region of Peru and at the same time give an incentive to preserve the region's cultural and environmental resources. The Peruvian 1:100,000 IGN Sheet *Machu Picchu* completely covers the route, although in some places accuracy is not great. Maps are available at the **Instituto Geográfico Nacional** in Lima or at **South American Explorers** in Cusco. Some agencies in Cusco are beginning to offer organized treks on these routes.

Day 1

From Cachora take the road heading down, out of the village, through lush cultivated countryside and meadows. On a clear day you should have good views of the snow peak of **Padrayoc**, roughly to the north, on the far side of the Apurímac Canyon. There are many trails close to the village; if uncertain of the trail, ask, the locals are very friendly. After 15 minutes' of descent a sign for Choquequirao points to a left-hand path, initially following the course of a small stream. Follow the trail and cross a footbridge to the other side of a large stream. From here the trail becomes more obvious, with few trails diverging from the main route. The trail tracks along the left side of the valley, more or less flat, passing an old hacienda on the right-hand side. To your right is the Apurímac Canyon, the river flowing far beneath (although difficult to see at this point), and the Vilcabamba range.

After 9 km, 2-2½ hours from the start of the trek, is the wonderful *mirador* (viewpoint) of **Capuliyoc**, at 2,800 m, with fantastic vistas of the Apurímac Canyon and the snowy Vilcabamba range across the river. With a pair of binoculars it's just possible to recognize Choquequirao, etched into the forested hills to the west. Condors are sometimes seen in this area. Beyond Capuliyoc the trail begins to descend towards the river. Here, away from the village, there exist some excellent examples of dry forest, largely devoid of leaves in the dry season. Further down the valley lies **Cocamasana**, a rest spot with a rough covered roof. From this point the river is clearly visible, running emerald green when the water level is low, a rushing white torrent during the rains. At Km 16 is **Chiquisca** (1,930 m), a lovely wooded spot and home to a local family. Chiquisca has a good, fairly clean water supply, so it's an opportunity to fill bottles. If you don't want to continue any further on the first day, this is a good campsite, although please respect the wishes of the local family whose land this is. Another 45-minute to one-hour descent leads you to the suspension bridge crossing the Río Apurímac (1,500 m). Currents are strong on the river, but a few sheltered spots are good for a refreshing dip. Roughly translated from Quechua, Apurímac means 'the river that speaks'. The roaring rapids along its course give ample justification for this title.

Crossing the bridge the path ascends very steeply for 1½ hours. **Santa Rosa**, a good area for camping, again near the property of a local family, is just after the Km 21 sign. Clean water is available. If this area is occupied, another larger site is available 10 minutes further up the hill. Ask residents for directions.

From Santa Rosa continue uphill on a steep zigzag for two hours to the *mirador* of **Marampata**. The **Huanpaca** waterfall can be seen on the far side of the valley. From Marampata the trail flattens out, following the right side of the canyon, downstream, towards Choquequirao. At the time of writing no charge was being made to enter the site, however a guard post/control was being built, suggesting that this situation could change in the very near future. In the valley below the guard post and underneath the main site, you can see some newly excavated agricultural terraces. Far below, in a different warmer microclimate, these terraces enabled the inhabitants to cultivate lower-altitude fruits and vegetables in close proximity to their highland staples. After 1½ hours on this flatter trail you enter some beautiful stretches of cloudforest, before a final short climb and arrival at **Choquequirao** itself. In July 2003 most groups camped on the great set of terraces reached upon arrival at the site. At an altitude of 3,000 m the nights can be cold. If coming from Santa Rosa you should have the afternoon free to explore the complex. There is much more to Choquequirao than first appears, so, given time, you could easily allow an extra day here. Many find the unrestored buildings below the main plaza particularly enchanting, with remains of terraces and living quarters, still smothered in dense forest. They also give an impression of what the site must have looked like when first rediscovered, a great contrast to the restored Lower and Upper Plaza areas. **To return to Cachora** at this point, simply retrace the route, possibly camping at Chiquisca, which would nicely break the two-day return trek.

Day 3

The third day, if completed in one day (as described below), is almost certainly the toughest on the trek. It will keep you walking pretty much all day, and there's a steep ascent to the campsite, just to add to your pleasure! Climb to the Upper Plaza complex roughly to the northwest of the Main Plaza and terraces. There are spectacular vistas of the canyon, surrounding peaks, including Ampay to the west and also over the central areas of Choquequirao itself. A rough and sometimes overgrown trail climbs steeply up the hill behind, following sections of old Inca trail and drainage channels, and passing some small ruins. The route traverses cloudforest, festooned with mosses, around the left side of the mountain for one hour, with some precipitous drops on the left. Beyond Choquequirao many sections of trail will prove a challenge to those with severe vertigo! The path then emerges into an area of alpine grassland and starts to descend steeply, zigzagging into the valley of the **Quebrada Victoria**. Towards the lower section of the grassland is a green glade, used to graze pack animals. It's possible to camp here, but water could be a problem in the dry season.

East & West of Cusco Vilcabamba traverse trek

Vilcabamba traverse trek

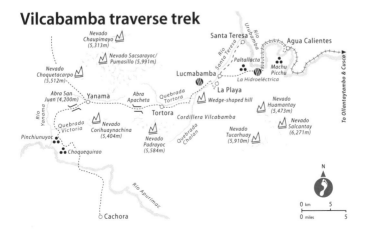

After the glade the path continues its descent, once again entering scrub and then dry forest. Note the contrast between the dry vegetation on this side of the valley, which receives sun for most of the day, and the damp and green forest on the far side of the valley, often in shadow. This is vivid illustration of how mountain ranges such as the Vilcabamba create a vast range of microclimates, and therefore biodiversity, in an extremely limited geographical area. After 30 minutes the trail passes close to the unrestored houses and terraces of **Pinchiunuyoc**. It's possible to obtain water here as the original Inca water channels are still flowing. After another 1½ or two hours of steep descent you reach the Quebrada Victoria at around 2,000 m. The climate here is subtropical and, except for the large numbers of sandflies, this is a great spot for lunch and a bracing dip in the river. In the wet season or during flash floods the Quebrada Victoria could be impossible to cross; seek local information.

Continue downstream along the right-hand bank of the *quebrada* (ravine) for perhaps 200 m and you'll come to the beginning of the trail leading up the other side of the *quebrada*, running almost entirely through thick forest. This is a brutal ascent, climbing for three or four hours until reaching the campsite at roughly 3,500 m. The campsite, which has a limited water supply, is, once again, on the land of a local family who live perched on the edge of the abyss, with the forest and towering glacial peak of Corihuaynachina as a backdrop. Several trails branch off the main route near the family's land and potentially this could be confusing. Perhaps the surest way to locate your home for the night is to listen for the sounds of domestic animals, the barking of dogs and crowing of cockerels coming from the family's home. It's a magnificent campsite, but cold at night. Enjoy the view from your tent!

Day 4

Carry on up the trail from camp, following the left side of the valley, roughly in the direction of Corihuaynachina. The **Abra San Juan** (San Juan Pass) is to the left of this peak. Continue through cloudforest for 2½ hours. The trail can be very muddy in places. There are some beautiful examples of mountain cedar in the area and the valley supports much wildlife, including spectacled bears. Birdlife is prolific and diverse, with many species of mountain tanager, solitary eagles in the valleys lower reaches, mountain caracaras, and sometimes condors soaring above the peaks. The route passes several abandoned mine shafts dating from the last century and these are possible to explore (at your own risk) with flashlights.

After the initial 2½ or 3 hours' hiking from camp the forest fades, replaced by high Andean *puna* (grassland), studded with flowers, and, in places, a strange blood-red lichen covering the rocks. The path follows a section of original Inca trail, arriving at the Abra San Juan (4,200 m) roughly four hours after leaving camp. On a clear day there are magnificent views of the Nevados (snowy peaks) of Sacsarayoc (also known as Pumasillo) and Choquetacarpo. Below the peaks is the valley of the Río Yanama. The alternative route to Huancacalle can be seen to the north on the far side of the Yanama. Follow the path roughly east-northeast, descending for 2½ or three hours, and this will bring you to the small, traditional village of **Yanama**, at around 3,500 m. On the way down to Yanama some of the drop-offs are very steep. The valley is full of wildflowers. In the village it's usually possible to camp in front of the school buildings and to buy basic food (potatoes, etc). It may be possible to hire mules and guides in the village. Yanama has no road connection to the outside world and traditional cultures are still strong. Please respect these peoples' ways and don't offer children sweets, etc. Note the excellent quality of the stonework in many of the traditional dwellings, and also the fine grass roofing.

Day 5

Ascend the Yanama Valley for 1½ hours, following the course of the Río Yanama, which runs on your left. Waterfalls can be seen on either side, snowmelt from glaciers

high above. Towards the head of the valley the trail starts to veer away from the river
to the right, beginning the ascent to the 4,800-m **Abra Apacheta** (Apacheta Pass). It's
a hard climb of around three hours and the altitude can take its toll. The mountain to
the right of Apacheta is Padrayoc, the mountain visible from Cachora, towering above
the Apurímac. From the pass, in clear weather, it's possible to see **Salcantay**, at
6,271 m the highest peak in the Vilcabamba range. The descent from the pass is long
and some trails lead away from the main route to houses and farms – be careful,
especially in foggy conditions. The path tends to veer to the right and leads into the
valley of the **Quebrada Tortora**. This area is badly marked on the IGN 1:100,000 sheet,
and a stream that you keep on your left, and that runs into the Quebrada Tortora,
appears not to be marked. Once into the Tortora Valley you follow the Río Tortora for
about an hour until crossing to the other side via a small bridge just before a metal-
roofed house. Continue with the river on your right until you reach a flat, grassy area
with several houses. This is **Hornopampa**. From here you can see Tortora village, 1 km
or so down the valley. Tortora appears to be marked too far up the valley in the IGN
1:100,000 sheet, which could cause confusion. In Tortora you can camp near the
medical post. The biting insects here can be awful! To make up for the bugs, the are
lovely views of many tall peaks, including **Huamantay**, visible down the valley.

Day 6

Walk downhill through forest for two hours, staying on the right side of the river. Just
before you come to a big wedge shaped hill at the bottom of the valley cross to the
other side. Tortora bridge lies just below a series of grassy meadows in this region.
The trails in this area are often affected by landslides, so seek local information. On
crossing the bridge follow the gently sloping trail through fairly undisturbed sections
of forest for four or five hours until reaching the small community of **La Playa** where it
is possible to camp. You may want to camp slightly before the village, for greater
privacy. La Playa has a run-down feel, and doesn't give the most welcoming
impression for the passing hiker. The town centre and the road (see below) are both
located across the bridge on the right side of Río Santa Teresa. You can obtain basic
supplies at a couple of small stores in the town centre. About halfway between the
Tortora Bridge and La Playa the trail crosses a rocky streambed, the path doesn't
continue directly on the other side. Climb about 50 m up the rocky streambed and
you'll see the trail continuing on the right. A short distance after this a beautiful
waterfall tumbles across the trail, perhaps 100 m high. Next to the trail, under the fall
is a pool, perfect for bathing and a (very!) refreshing shower.

La Playa marks the beginning of a rough road that runs to Santa Teresa.
Camiones (trucks) leave for Santa Teresa at 0600 on most days. The road may be
closed in the wet season.

Day 7

To continue the hike from La Playa you have two options: for both cross to the right
side of the river. From here you can simply follow the road downhill to Santa Teresa, or
catch the early morning *camión* if you're feeling lazy. The second, more interesting
route is to follow the road for 30 minutes to the tiny settlement of **Lucmabamba**. On
the right-hand side a restored section of Inca trail leads into the hills. Follow this trail
uphill, towards the ruins of **Paltallacta**, which lie over the ridge in the next valley. From
the road it's 2½ or three hours' climb through scrubby bush and sections of
cloudforest until reaching the pass. The restored section of Inca road runs out (in July
2003) after about 1 km and a narrow but clear trail takes its place. In one or two places
it's possible to see small sections of the original Inca trail. At the summit of the hill is a
magnificent area of virgin cloudforest, worth the climb in itself. Once you begin to
descend on the other side it's possible, weather conditions allowing, to view Machu
Picchu from a very interesting perspective, encircled by hills, and behind, the snow

covered peaks of the Urubamba range. The large waterfall you can see, spilling out from the mountain in front of Machu Picchu is La Hidroeléctrica, designed to generate power for the surrounding area. Half an hour below the summit you reach the dispersed ruins of **Paltallacta**, unrestored walls and terraces that must have once represented a substantial settlement. Recent expeditions in the area have uncovered many new finds, including one originally described by Hiram Bingham and subsequently lost for almost a century. Who knows what remains to be discovered? Just below the ruins, to the left of the trail, are some grassy areas which give a wonderful perspective on the whole scene.

From Paltallacta, a one- or 1½-hour steep descent leads to **Ahobamba Valley** and a cable bridge crossing the Río Ahobamba. Take care crossing the bridge as the wooden planks have been known to break. Once on the other side follow the path along the river, past the waterfall (La Hidroeléctrica), keeping to the right, past some fenced facilities, presumably associated with the hydroelectric project. You're now in the valley of the **Río Urubamba**, having crossed the entire Vilcabamba range! From here there should be plenty of people to ask directions. There are two levels of railway track in the area. To get the local train back to Aguas Calientes you need to climb up the bank to reach the main, higher track. Here there is a small railway station from which trains normally leave once a day, between 1400 and 1600 for Aguas Calientes. Alternatively you can walk to Aguas Calientes, 9 km and two hours' walk, simply by following the railway tracks. At several points along the tracks are good views of Machu and Huayna Picchu, towering above the Urubamba. Be careful of speeding trains! Near the Hidroeléctrica train station are the well preserved ruins of an Inca temple (ask the locals for directions). This site features an intricately carved sacred rock, similar to that at Machu Picchu, which almost perfectly mirrors the contour of the mountain on the other side of the valley. If you still have energy this is certainly worth a look before returning to Aguas Calientes.

● Sleeping

Anta to Curahuasi *p209*
G **Hostal Central**, *Jirón Jaquijahuanca 714, Anta*, a basic, friendly, place with motorbike parking; beware of water shortages.
G **Hostal Rivera**, *near the river, at Limatambo*, an old stone house built round a courtyard, clean, quiet and full of character.
G **Hostal San Cristóbal**, *Curahuasi*, clean, nice decor, pleasant courtyard, shared bath, cold shower (new bathroom block being built).
Camping in Curahuasi is possible on the football pitch, but ask the police for permission.

Choquequirao *p210, map p210*
G **Hospedaje Judith Catherine**, *Cachora, T084-320202*. Price per bed.

● Eating

Anta to Curahuasi *p209*
$ **Tres de Mayo**, *Anta*, is very good and popular, with top service.
$ **Restaurant**, *Limatambo*, hidden from the road by trees, is a good option.
$ **La Amistad**, *Curahuasi*, is the best restaurant in town, is popular, with good food and moderate prices, but has poor service.

● Transport

Anta to Curahuasi *p209*
The bus fare to Anta from Cusco is US$0.30.

Machu
Picchu
Cusco

Southern Jungle

Introduction

The immense Amazon Basin covers a staggering 4 million square kilometres, an area roughly equivalent to three quarters the size of the United States. But despite the fact that 60% of Peru is covered by this green carpet of jungle, less than 6% of its population lives there. This lack of integration with the rest of the country makes it difficult to get around easily but it does mean that much of Peru's rainforest is still intact.

The Peruvian jungles are home to a diversity of life unequalled anywhere on earth, and it is this great diversity which makes the Amazon Basin a paradise for nature lovers, be they scientists or simply curious amateurs. Overall, Peru's jungle lowlands contain some 10 million living species, including 2,000 species of fish and 300 mammals. They also contain over 10% of the world's 8,600 bird species and, together with the adjacent Andean foothills, 4,000 butterfly species.

The southern part of Peru's Amazon jungle contains the **Manu National Biosphere Reserve** (2.2 million hectares), the **Tambopata National Reserve** (254,358 hectares) and the **Bahuaja-Sonene National Park** (1.1 million hectares); three great protected areas in the Department of Madre de Dios, which adjoins the eastern edge of the Department of Cusco and extends to the borders of Brazil and Bolivia.

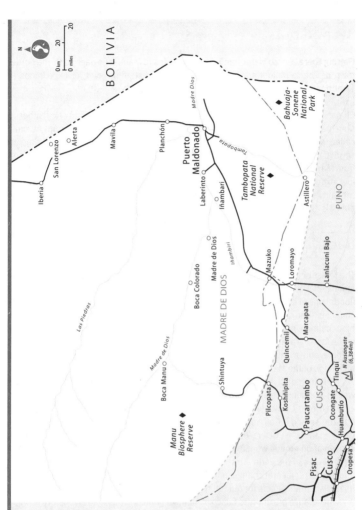

Southern Jungle

★ Don't miss...

① **Collpa** See the multitude of macaws and parrots getting their essential minerals from one of these macaw licks.

② **Ox-bow lakes** You may catch a glimpse of giant otters if you take a trip on one of the many *cochas* (ox-bow lakes).

③ **Ants** Watch the fearsome fire ants or the even scarier bullet ants and sample some juicy jungle grub.

④ **Dawn chorus** Listen to the birds singing in the forest canopy and the chatter of the monkeys going about their business.

⑤ **The forest** The first memorable sight from the plane of the expanse and flatness of the forest as you leave the mountains behind.

⑥ **The night sky** After your cold shower and dinner by the light of an oil lamp, go outside and marvel at the night sky, with its shooting stars, and the fireflies in the bushes; but be careful – it's a jungle out there.

Ins and outs

Getting there Cusco is the starting point for trips to Manu (see page 221). The border town of Puerto Maldonado (see page 207) is the starting point for expeditions to Tambopata and is only a 30-minute flight from Cusco. ▶▶ *For further information see Transport, page 234.*

Climate The climate is warm and humid, with a rainy season from November to March and a dry season from April to October. Cold fronts from the South Atlantic, called *friajes*, are characteristic of the dry season, when temperatures drop to 15-16°C during the day, and 13°C at night. The best time to visit is in the dry season from May to the end of November, when there are fewer mosquitoes and the rivers are low, exposing the beaches. Trips, especially lodge-based, can also be planned during the rainy season. The dry season is a good time to see birds nesting and to view the animals at close range, as they stay close to the rivers and are easily seen.

Background

The forest of this lowland region is technically called Subtropical Moist Forest, which means that it receives less rainfall than tropical forest and is dominated by the floodplains of its meandering rivers. One of the most striking features is the former river channels that have become isolated as *cochas* (ox-bow lakes). These are home to black caiman, giant otter and a host of other living organisms. Other rare species living in the forest are jaguar, puma, ocelot and tapir. There are also capybara, 13 species of primate and many hundreds of bird species. If you include the cloudforests and highlands of the Manu Biosphere Reserve, the bird count almost totals 1,000.

This incredible biological diversity brings with it an acute ecological fragility. As well as containing some of the most important flora and fauna on earth, the region also harbours gold-diggers, loggers and hunters. For years, logging, gold prospecting and the search for oil and gas have endangered the unique rainforest. Fortunately, though, the destructive effect of such groups has been limited by the various conservation groups working to protect it. Ecologists consider the Amazon rainforest as the lungs of the earth – the Amazon Basin produces 20% of the earth's oxygen – and any fundamental change in its constitution, or indeed its disappearance, could have disastrous effects for our future on this planet.

The relative proximity to Cusco of Manu in particular has made it one of the prime nature-watching destinations in South America. Despite its reputation, Manu is heavily protected, with visitor numbers limited and a large percentage of the park inaccessible to tourists. Nevertheless, there is no need to worry that this level of management is going to diminish your pleasure. There is more than enough in the way of birds, animals and plants to satisfy the most ardent wildlife enthusiast. There is a town in the vicinity of Tambopata, Puerto Maldonado, and until recently the whole area was under threat from exploitation and settlement. However, the suspension of oil exploration in 2000 led to a change of status for a large tract of this area, giving immediate protection to another of Peru's zones of record-breaking diversity.

In 2003 the new emerging threat to the forests of Madre de Dios was the planned construction of the *Transoceánica*, a road linking the Atlantic and Pacific oceans via Puerto Maldonado and Brazil. The paving of this road system, creating a high speed link between the two countries, will certainly bring more uncontrolled colonization in the area, as seen so many times in the Brazilian Amazon, placing the forests of the Tambopata region under further pressure. Uncontrolled colonization along Bahuaja-Sonene's southern border, in the Tambopata headwaters area, is another cause of growing concern, which, at the time of writing had failed to be addressed by either the government or local conservation groups. For further information regarding the *Transoceánica* see the June 2003 edition of *National Geographic*, 'Peru's Long Haul – Highway to Riches or Ruin?' by Ted Conover.

Manu Biosphere Reserve → *Colour map 2, A3/4.*

The Manu Biosphere Reserve covers an area of almost 2.25 mn ha (almost half the size of Switzerland) and is one of the largest conservation units on earth, encompassing the complete drainage of the Manu River, with an altitudinal range from 200 m to 4,100 m above sea level. No other rainforest can compare with Manu for the diversity of life forms. The reserve is one of the great birdwatching spots of the world; a magical animal kingdom which offers the best chance of seeing giant otters, jaguars, ocelots and several of the 13 species of primates which abound in this pristine tropical wilderness. The more remote areas of the reserve are home to uncontacted indigenous tribes and many other indigenous groups with very little knowledge of the outside world. ▸▸ *For Sleeping, Eating and other listings see pages 229-236.*

Ins and outs

Getting there There is an **airstrip** at Boca Manu, but no regular flights from Cusco. These are arranged the day before, usually by Manu tour operators, if there are enough passengers. The journey can also be done by truck or by bus. **Getting around** From Pilcopata there are trucks to Atalaya (one hour, US$8) and Shintuya (four hours, US$10). Trucks leave in the morning between 0600 and 0900. Make sure you go with a recommended truck driver. Only basic supplies are available after leaving Cusco, so take all your camping and food essentials, including insect repellent. Transport can be disrupted in the wet season because the road is in poor condition (tour operators have latest details). Tour operators usually use their own vehicles for the overland trip from Cusco to Manu. ▸▸ *For further information see Transport, page 234.*

The park areas

The Biosphere Reserve formerly comprised the **Manu National Park** (1,692,137 ha), where only government sponsored biologists and anthropologists are allowed to visit with permits from the Ministry of Agriculture in Lima; the **Manu Reserved Zone** (257,000 ha), set aside for applied scientific research and ecotourism; and the **Cultural Zone** (92,000 ha), containing acculturated native groups and colonists, where the locals still employ their traditional way of life.

In 2003 the former Manu Reserved Zone was absorbed into the Manu National Park, increasing its protected status. Ecotourism activities have been allowed to continue in specially designated tourism and recreational zones along the course of the Lower Manu River. These tourism and recreational areas are accessible by permit only. Entry is strictly controlled and visitors must visit the area under the auspices of an authorized operator with an authorized guide. Permits are limited and reservations should be made well in advance, though it is possible to book a place on a trip at the last minute in Cusco. In the former Reserved Zone there are two lodges, the rustic **Casa Machiguenga** (see page 229) run by the Machiguenga communities of Tayakome and Yomibato with the help of a German NGO, and the upmarket **Manu Lodge** (see page 229). In the Cocha Salvador area, several companies have tented safari camp infrastructures, some with shower and dining facilities, but all visitors sleep in tents. Some companies have installed walk-in tents with cots and bedding.

The Cultural and Multiple Use Zones are accessible to anyone and several lodges exist in the area (see page 229). It is possible to visit these lodges under your own steam. Among the ethnic groups in the Multiple Use Zone (a system of buffer areas surrounding the core Manu area) are the Harakmbut, Machiguenga and Yine in the Amarakaeri Reserved Zone, on the east bank of the Río Alto Madre de Dios. They have set up their own ecotourism activities, entirely managed by local indigenous people. Associated with Manu are other areas protected by conservation groups, or local people (for example the Blanquillo reserved zone and a new conservation concession in the adjacent Los Amigos river system) and some cloudforest parcels along the road. The **Nuhua-Kugapakori Reserved Zone** (443,887 ha), set aside for these two nomadic native groups, is the area between the headwaters of the Río Manu and headwaters of the Río Urubamba, to the north of the Río Alto Madre de Dios.

Birdwatching in Manu
Much of the Manu National Park is totally unexplored and the variety of birds is astounding: about 1,000 species, significantly more than the whole of Costa Rica and over a tenth of all the birds on earth. Although there are other places in the Manu area where you can see Manu's bird life and an astonishing variety of other wildlife, an excellent place for the visiting birder with limited time is the **Manu Wildlife Centre**.

Manu Biosphere Reserve

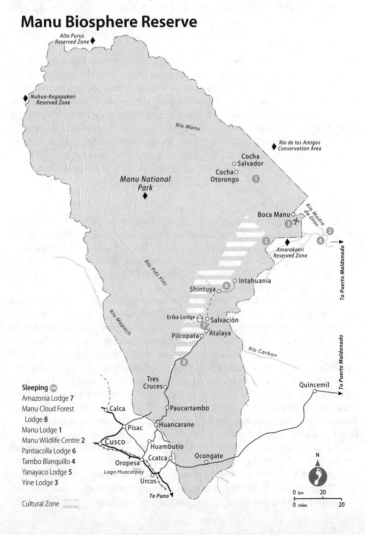

Sleeping
Amazonia Lodge 7
Manu Cloud Forest Lodge 8
Manu Lodge 1
Manu Wildlife Centre 2
Pantiacolla Lodge 6
Tambo Blanquillo 4
Yanayaco Lodge 5
Yine Lodge 3

Cultural Zone

⦂ The giant otters of Río Madre de Dios

Giant otters (*Pteronura brasiliensis*) are the largest and most spectacular of the world's 13 otter species, sometimes reaching 1.8 m (6 ft) in length. The otters live and hunt in family groups and local people call them lobos del río or 'wolves of the river', as a mark of respect for their supreme hunting abilities.

The giant otters in Lago Sandoval are endangered. The species as a whole has been pushed to the very edge of extinction by the skin trade, and now perhaps less than 2,000 remain in South America, the only continent in which they occur.

Despite legal protection the otters now face a new threat, this time from uncontrolled tourism. Only a few years ago a family of nine giant otters lived in Lago Sandoval; today only three or four remain. This is almost certainly due to excessive tourist activity – wildlife viewing canoes and catamarans – on the lake. These boats, either through ignorant guides anxious to earn tips or tourist pressure, approach the otters too closely.

Giant otters are highly territorial and sensitive animals that require large areas of pristine lake and river habitat to survive. This habitat is shrinking fast owing to human encroachment and areas such as Tambopata and Manu offer the best chance of the species' survival. According to studies carried out by the Frankfurt Zoological Society you should always maintain a distance of at least 70 m (230 ft) from giant otters. Keep quiet and move slowly. Approaching or chasing giant otters causes stress, which eventually can lead to the death of pups or otters leaving the lake entirely.

As a tourist visiting Lago Sandoval or *cochas* (ox-bow lakes) in the forest beyond, you MUST share the responsibility to preserve these magnificent predators. If your guide or other tourists in the group wish to approach the otters, please insist that they adhere to the above conditions and keep your distance – if you explain why, most tourists will be happy with your decision. By keeping to these simple rules you will be making a small but very significant contribution to the survival of giant otters in the wild.

For more information the Frankfurt Zoological Society's website is a good start: www.giantotters.com

A typical trip starts in Cusco and takes in the wetlands of Huacarpay Lakes (to the south of the city (see page 198) where a variety of Andean waterfowl and marsh birds can be seen. Here, the endemic and beautiful bearded mountaineer hummingbird can be seen feeding on tree tobacco. Then the route proceeds to the cloudforest of the eastern slopes of the Andes. Driving slowly down the road through the cloudforest, every 500 m loss in elevation produces new birds. This is the home of the Andean cock-of-the-rock, and a visit to one of their leks (they are common here) is one of the world's top ornithological experiences. These humid montane forests are home to a mind-boggling variety of multicoloured birds and a mixed flock of tanagers, honeycreepers and conebills turns any tree into a Christmas tree! There are two species of quetzal here, too.

Levelling out onto the forested foothills of the Andes, the upper tropical zone is then reached. This is a forest habitat that in many parts of South America has disappeared and been replaced by tea, coffee and coca plantations. In Manu, the forest is intact, and special birds such as Amazonian umbrellabird and blue-headed and military macaws can be found.

Tours to Manu

There are about 15 authorized agencies in Cusco (see page 119) offering tours to Manu. Prices vary considerably, from as little as US$600 per person for a six-day tour up to US$1,000-1,500 per person with the more expensive, usually lodge-based tours.

The cheaper tours usually travel overland there and back, which takes at least three full days (in the dry season), meaning you'll spend much of your time on a bus or truck and will end up exhausted. Another important factor to consider is whether or not your boat has a canopy, as it can be very uncom-fortable sitting in direct sunlight or rain for hours on end. Also the quality of guides varies a lot – you might want to meet your guide before deciding on a trip if you are in Cusco. Beware of pirate operators on the streets of Cusco who offer trips to the former Reserved Zone of Manu and end up halfway through the trip changing the route 'due to emergencies', which, in reality means they have no permits to operate in the area. For a full list of all companies who are allowed access to the former Reserved Zone, contact the Manu National Park office (see Directory, page 235). You can only enter the Zone with a recognized guide who is affiliated to an authorized tour company. Take finely woven, long-sleeved and long-legged clothing and effective insect repellent. Note that for independent travellers, only the Cultural and Multiple Use Zones are an option. Lodge reservations should be made at the relevant offices in Cusco as these lodges are often not set up to receive visitors without prior notice.

Eco-tour Manu, a non-profit-making organization made up of tour operators, assures quality of service and actively supports conservation projects in the area. When you travel with an Eco-tour member you are ensuring that you support tropical rainforest conservation projects. Eco-tour Manu comprises *Manu Expeditions*, *Manu Nature Tours*, *Pantiacolla Tours*, *InkaNatura Travel*, *Aventuras Ecológicas Manu* and *Expedicones Vilca*. Contact any member company for information.

Good places to be based for upper tropical birding and an introduction to lowland Amazon species are **Amazonia, Erika** and **Pantiacolla** lodges , all on the Río Alto Madre de Dios. From here on, transport is by river and the beaches are packed with nesting birds in the dry season. Large-billed terns scream at passing boats and Orinoco geese watch warily from the shore. Colonies of hundreds of sand-coloured nighthawks roost and nest on the hot sand.

As you leave the foothills behind and head into the untouched forests of the western Amazon, you are entering forest with the highest density of birdlife per square kilometre on earth. Sometimes it seems as if there are fewer birds than in an English woodland; only strange calls betray their presence. Then a mixed flock comes through, containing maybe 70-plus species, or a brightly coloured group of, say, rock parakeets dashes out of a fruiting tree.

This forest has produced the highest day-list ever recorded anywhere on earth and it holds such little-seen gems as black-faced cotinga and rufous-fronted ant-thrush. Antbirds and ovenbirds creep in the foliage and give tantalizing glimpses until, eventually, they reveal themselves in a shaft of sunlight. Woodcreepers and woodpeckers climb tree-trunks and multicoloured tanagers move through the rainforest canopy. To get to this forest is difficult and not cheap, but the experience is well worth it.

Some good places for lowland birding are the **Manu Wildlife Centre** and **Tambo Blanquillo**, both of which are located close to a large *collpa* (macaw lick) and to *cochas* (ox-bow lakes) crammed with birds. There's an excellent walk-up canopy tower at the Manu Wildlife Center where rainforest canopy species can be seen with ease. There are many excellent areas; the entire **Lower Manu River** is superb, and Cocha Salvador, deep inside the pristine forests of the national park, is hard to beat.

> *You can't arrange trips to the tourist zones of the national park from Shintuya; all arrangements must be made in Cusco.*

A trip to Manu is one of the ultimate birding experiences and topping it off with a *collpa* is a great way to finish; hundreds of brightly coloured macaws and other parrots congregate to eat the clay essential to their digestion in one of the world's great wildlife spectacles.

The road to Manu

The arduous trip over the Andes from Cusco to the end of the road at Shintuya takes a whole day by local truck (16-24 hours in the dry, 20-40 hours in the wet season). It is a long and uncomfortable journey, but, throughout the route, you will see some spectacular scenery.

From Cusco you climb up to the Huancarani Pass before **Paucartambo** (3½ hours), and then drop down to this picturesque mountain village in the Mapacho Valley (for details of accommodation, etc, in Paucartambo, see page 206). You can make detour to **Tres Cruces**, 44 km from Paucartambo, for a great view of the sunrise over the Amazon. The road then ascends to the Ajcanacu Pass (cold at night), after which it goes down to the cloudforest and then the rainforest, reaching **Pilcopata** at 650 m (12 hours). One hour more – the route is hair-raising and breathtaking – and you are in **Atalaya**, which is the jump-off point for river trips further into the Manu. On the way, you pass **Manu Cloudforest Lodge**, **Cock of the Rock Lodge** and the **San Pedro Biological Station** (see page 229). Atalaya, the first village on the Río Alto Madre de Dios, consists of a few houses and some basic accommodation. Even in the dry season this part of the road is appalling and trucks often get stuck. In Atalaya, boats are available to take you across the river to *Amazonia Lodge* (see page 229). The route continues to **Salvación**, where a Manu park office is situated and there are a few basic hostels and restaurants.

Shintuya

The end of the road is Shintuya, the starting point for river transport. It is a commercial and social centre, as wood from the jungle is transported from here to Cusco. There are two Shintuyas: one is the port and mission and the other is the native village. You can find a boat in the native village or down on the beach (port); if waiting for a local trading boat to head down river you may be hanging around for some time, perhaps one or two days; ask for Diego Ruben Sonoco or Miguel Vise, they may be able to help. There are a few basic restaurants, but supplies here tend to be expensive.

Boca Colorado

From Shintuya you can catch one of the infrequent cargo boats that sail down river to the gold-mining centre of Boca Colorado on the Río Madre de Dios, via Boca Manu, and pass several ecotourism lodges en route including **Pantiacolla Lodge** and **Manu Wildlife Centre** (for details see page 229). The trip takes around nine hours, and costs US$15; to Boca Manu is three to four hours, US$12. From Boca Colorado there are plenty of boats to Laberinto (six to seven hours, US$20). From Laberinto there are regular combis to Puerto Maldonado (see page 226), 1½ hours. Boca Colorado has some very basic accommodation, but it is not recommended for single women travellers.

Boca Manu is the connecting point between the Alto Madre de Dios, Manu and Madre de Dios rivers. It has a few houses, an airstrip and some well-stocked shops. It is also the entrance to the Manu Reserve and to go further you must be part of an organized group. The entrance fee to the Reserved Zone is 150 soles per person (about US$40) and is included in package tour prices. The park ranger station is located in **Limonal**, 20 minutes by boat from Boca Manu. You need to show your permit here and, provided you have a permit, camping is allowed.

Blanquillo

Between Boca Manu and Colorado is this private reserve (10,000 ha). Bring a good tent with you and all food if you want to do it yourself, or alternatively accommodation is available at the Tambo Blanquillo. Wildlife is abundant, especially macaws and parrots at the macaw lick near **Manu Wildlife Centre** (see page 229). There are occasional boats to Blanquillo from Shintuya; US$10, 6-8 hrs.

To the Reserved Zone

Upstream on the Río Manu you pass **Manu Lodge** (see page 229), on the Cocha Juárez, three or four hours by boat. You can continue to Cocha Otorongo, 2½ hours and Cocha Salvador, 30 minutes, the biggest lake with plenty of wildlife where **Casa Machiguenga Lodge** is located and several companies have safari camp concessions. From here it is two hours to **Pakitza**, the entrance to the National Park Zone. This is only for biologists with a special permit.

Puerto Maldonado and around → *Phone code: 082. Colour map 2, A6.*

Puerto Maldonado is an important starting point for visiting the rainforest, or for departing to Brazil or Bolivia. Still, most visitors won't see much of the place because they are whisked through town on their way to a lodge on the Río Madre de Dios or the Río Tambopata. The city dwellers aren't too pleased about this and would like tourists to spend some time in town, but it's a hot, humid place where nothing much happens.

Ins and outs

Getting there The vast majority of people fly to Puerto Maldonado from Lima or Cusco. Combis to the airport run along Avenida 2 de Mayo, 10-15 minutes, US$0.60. A *mototaxi* from town to the airport is US$1.50. A yellow fever vaccination is offered free at the airport on arrival, but check that a new needle is used. Also under Transport are details of the road trip from the Sierra and of boats in the region. **Getting around** Scooters and mopeds can be hired from **San Francisco**, on the corner of Puno and González Prada for US$1.15 per hour or US$10 per day. No deposit is required but your passport and driving licence need to be shown.➠ *See Transport, page 234 for details.*

Sights

Overlooking the confluence of the Ríos Tambopata and Madre de Dios, Puerto Maldonado is a major logging and brazil nut processing centre. From the park at the end of Jirón Arequipa, across from the Capitanía, you get a good view of the two rivers, the ferries across the Madre de Dios and the lumber at the dockside. The brazil nut harvest is from December to February and the crop tends to be good on alternate years. Nuts are sold on the street, plain or coated in sugar or chocolate. **El Mirador**, ⓘ *Av Fitzcarrald and Av Madre de Dios, 1000-1600, US$0.30*, is a 30-m high tower with three platforms giving fine views over the city and surrounding rainforest. There is also a toilet at the top – no curtains – from which there is an equally fine view over the city! ▸▸ *For Sleeping, Eating and other listings see pages 229-236.*

Around Puerto Maldonado

Lago Sandoval, ① *US$5, you must go with a guide; this can be arranged by the boat driver,* is a beautiful and tranquil lake one-hour boat ride along the Río Madre de Dios, and then a 5-km walk into the jungle. There are two jungle lodges at the lake (see page 231). It is sometimes possible to see giant river otters early in the morning and several species of monkey, macaw (especially the smaller red-bellied macaws, which maintain a large breeding population near the lake) and hoatzin. At weekends, especially on Sundays, the lake gets quite busy. Boats can be hired at the port for about US$20 a day – plus petrol – to go to Lago Sandoval, but don't pay the full cost in advance.

Upstream from Lago Sandoval, towards Puerto Maldonado, is the wreck of a boat that resembles the *Fitzcarrald*. The steamer (a replica of Fitzcarrald's boat) lies a few metres from the Río Madre de Dios in the bed of a small stream. The German director, Werner Herzog, was inspired to make his famous film of the same name by the story of Fitzcarrald's attempt to haul a boat across the watershed from the

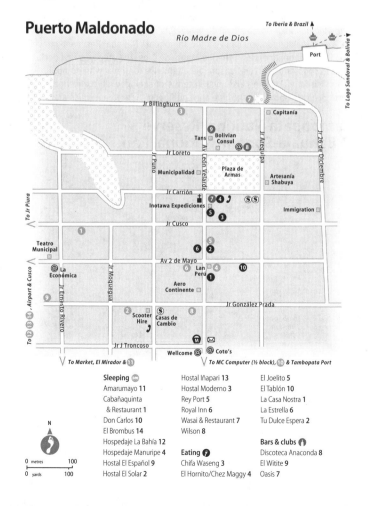

Puerto Maldonado

Southern Jungle Puerto Maldonado & around

Sleeping ⬤	Hostal Iñapari 13	El Joelito 5
Amarumayo 11	Hostal Moderno 3	El Tablón 10
Cabañaquinta	Rey Port 5	La Casa Nostra 1
& Restaurant 1	Royal Inn 6	La Estrella 6
Don Carlos 10	Wasai & Restaurant 7	Tu Dulce Espera 2
El Brombus 14	Wilson 8	
Hospedaje La Bahía 12		**Bars & clubs** 🍸
Hospedaje Manuripe 4	**Eating** 🍴	Discoteca Anaconda 8
Hostal El Español 9	Chifa Waseng 3	El Witite 9
Hostal El Solar 2	El Hornito/Chez Maggy 4	Oasis 7

Ucuyali to the Madre de Dios drainage basin (this happened in what is now the Manu National Park).

If you are interested in seeing a gold rush, a trip to **Laberinto** is suggested. There is one hotel and several poor restaurants. Combis and trucks leave from Puerto Maldonado, 1½ hours, US$2.50, and return in the afternoon daily. Boats leave from here to Manu (see above).

At Km 13 on the Cusco road is a pleasant recreational centre with a restaurant and natural pools where it's possible to swim. It gets busy at weekends. It's US$2 each way by *mototaxi* from town.

Trips can be made to **Lago Valencia**, 60 km away near the Bolivian border – four hours there, six hours back. It is a *cocha* (ox-bow lake) with lots of wildlife. Many excellent beaches and islands are located within an hour's boat ride. It is possible to stay overnight with local families.

Tambopata National Reserve → *Colour map 2, A6.*

ⓘ *US$8 per person if staying at a lodge, or US$19 per person if camping at Lago Sandoval, US$30-40 if camping elsewhere in the park. If staying at a lodge, they will organize the payment of the fee, otherwise, you need to visit the INRENA office in Puerto Maldonado, Jr Cusco 165, T084-573278.*

From Puerto Maldonado you can visit the Tambopata National Reserve by travelling up the Río Tambopata or down the Río Madre de Dios. The area was first declared a reserve in 1990 and is a very reasonable alternative for those who do not have the time to visit Manu. It is a close rival in terms of seeing wildlife and boasts some superb *cochas* (ox-bow lakes). There are a number of lodges here which are excellent

Tambopata National Reserve & Bahuaja-Sonene National Park

Sleeping 🛏		
Casa de Hospedaje Mejía 5	Explorers Inn 4	Sandoval Lake Lodge 10
Cuzco Tambo Lodge 1	Picaflor Research Centre 6	Tambopata Jungle Lodge 11
Eco Amazonia Lodge 2	Posada Amazonas Lodge 7	Tambopata Research
El Corto Maltés 3	Reserva Amazónica Lodge 8	Centre 12
	Sachavaca Inn 9	Wasai Lodgel 13

for lowland rainforest birding. **Explorers' Inn** is perhaps the most famous, but the 229 **Posada Amazonas/Tambopata Research Centre** and **Tambopata Lodge** are also good. In a new initiative, to try to ensure that more tourism income stays in the area, several local families have established their own small-scale Casas de Hospedaje. These offer more basic facilities and make use of the nearby forest but are cheaper and may well lead to a more intimate forest experience.

The **Bahuaja-Sonene National Park** runs from the Río Heath, which forms the Bolivian border, across to the Río Tambopata, 50-80 km upstream from Puerto Maldonado. It was expanded to 1,091,416 ha in August 2000 when the **Tambopata National Reserve** (254,358 ha) was created to form a buffer zone. The park is closed to visitors though those visiting the *collpa* on the Tambopata or river rafting down the Río Tambopata will travel through it.

Most of the lodges in the Tambopata area use the term 'ecotourism', or something similar, in their publicity material, but this is applied pretty loosely. **Posada Amazonas** and the **Heath River Wildlife Center** collaborate with the local communities in the area and in this sense are fairly unusual. Fortunately, no lodge offers trips where guests hunt for their meals and only one or two may offer an inappropriate visit to a local community. See Responsible tourism, page 36, for points to note. Long-term researchers should be aware that leishmaniasis (see Health, page 57) exists in this area.

● Sleeping

Lodges in the Southern Jungle are usually included as part of a package run by tour operators from Cusco, see p119.

The road to Manu *p225*
F **Albergue Eco Turístico Villa Carmen**, *Pilcopata, www.business.com.pe/villa-carmen* A fairly pleasant place to stay.
F **Gallito de las Rocas**, *Pilcopata, opposite the police checkpoint*, is clean. Price per person.
F **Sra Rubella**, *Pilcopata*, an unnamed place, very basic, but friendly.

Shintuya *p225*
G **The Mission** The priest will let you stay in the dormitory rooms at the mission and you can camp (beware of thieves).

Manu Biosphere Reserve *p221, map p222*
Amazonia Lodge, *in Cusco at Matará 334, T084-231370, amazonia1@correo.dnet.com.pe* On the Río Alto Madre de Dios just across the river from Atalaya, an old tea hacienda run by the Yabar family, famous for its bird diversity and fine hospitality, a great place to relax, contact Santiago in advance and he'll arrange a pick-up.
Boca Manu Lodge, *opposite the Boca Manu airstrip*, a comfortable lodge run by Sr Carpio.
Cock of the Rock Lodge, *on the road from Paucartambo to Atalaya, at 1,500 m*, next to a cock-of-the-rock lek, run by the **Perú Verde** group (see below). Double rooms with shared bath and 7 private cabins with en suite bath.
Manu Cloud Forest Lodge, *located at Unión at 1,800 m on the road from Paucartambo to Atalaya*. Owned by **Manu Nature Tours**, 6 rooms with 4 beds.
Pantiacolla Lodge, *30 mins downstream from Shintuya*. Book through **Pantiacolla Tours**. Owned by the Moscoso family. This lodge is located underneath the Pantiacolla Mountains, which, due to the large altitudinal range in a small area, boasts great biological diversity, particularly with birds. Good trail system.
Tambo Amana, *30 mins from Shintuya on foot, tamboamana@yahoo.com* Run by the indigenous Chinipa family, this is a cultural as opposed to wildlife-watching tour, learning about Harakmbut culture, plant uses, how to shoot bows and arrows, etc. If you make your own way there, this is a very economical jungle trip at US$190 for 5 days/4 nights for those prepared to rough it a bit. Jessica Bertram de Sasari helps the Chinipa family with marketing and is a good source of information. You can contact her at *Hospedaje Mario's, C Choquechaca 469, Cusco, T084-225500, jessicabertrampe@yahoo.com* **Perudiscovery**, *www.perudiscovery.com*, and **Culturas Perú**, *www.culturasperu.com*, can

both arrange a stay here. If contacting the Chinipa family direct, you need to speak Spanish (or Harakmbut!).

Yine Lodge, *next to Boca Manu airport*. This is a new co-operative project, also managed by **Pantiacolla**, between the company and the native Yine community of Diamante.

Manu Lodge, run by **Manu Nature Tours** and only bookable as part of a full package deal with transport, is situated on the Manu River, 3 hrs upriver from Boca Manu towards Cocha Salvador. It's in a fine location overlooking Cocha Juárez, an ox-box lake which often plays host to a family of giant otters. The lodge has an extensive trail system, and stands of mauritia palms near the lake provide nesting sites for colonies of blue and yellow macaws.

Manu Wildlife Centre, book through **Manu Expeditions** or **InkaNatura**. 2 hrs down the Río Madre de Dios from Boca Manu, near the Blanquillo macaw lick. There's also a tapir lick and walk-up canopy tower. 22 double cabins, all with private bathroom and hot water. Also canopy towers for birdwatching (see p222).

Yanayaco Lodge, book through **Expediciones Vilca** in Cusco. 1 hr upriver from Diamante village. A new lodge located close to a small parrot lick.

Puerto Maldonado *p226, map p227*

A **Wasai**, *Billinghurst opposite the Capitanía, T082-572290, www.wasai.com (or Plateros 320, Cusco T084-221826, cuzco@wasai.com)*. Price includes breakfast, a/c, TV, shower. In a beautiful location overlooking the Río Madre de Dios, with forest surrounding cabin-style rooms which are built on a slope down to the river, small pool with waterfall, good restaurant if slightly expensive (local fish a speciality). You may be able to negotiate lower prices for longer stays. Recommended, but service can be stretched if the hotel is full. They can organize local tours and also have a lodge on the Río Tambopata (see below).

C **Don Carlos**, *Av León Velarde 1271, T082-571029, T/F082-571323*. With a nice view over the Río Tambopata; rooms have a/c, TV and phone, good. Restaurant.

C-D **Cabañaquinta**, *Cusco 535, T082-571864, cabanaquinta@webcusco.zzn.com* Rooms with bathroom, fan and cable TV, very comfortable. The restaurant is good and there

is a lovely garden. Airport transfer is arranged and the staff are friendly. The more expensive rooms have hot water. Recommended.

D **Amarumayo**, *Libertad 433, 10 mins from the centre, T082-573860*. Comfortable lodging, with pool and garden. Good restaurant. Recommended.

D **El Brombus**, *4.5 km from Puerto Maldonado, halfway to the airport, T082-573230*. A small rustic lodge with a very good restaurant, overlooking the Río Madre de Dios. Owned by Fernando Rozemberg, who speaks English and runs good tours.

D **Royal Inn**, *Av 2 de Mayo 333, T082-571048*. Modern and clean, the best of the mid-range hotels, rooms at the back are less noisy.

E **Hostal El Español**, *González Prada 644, T082-572381*. Very clean, comfortable rooms in a nice building. The *hostal* is set back from the road, in a quiet part of town, so this is one place where you don't have motorcycles driving past your window every 10 seconds!

E **Hospedaje La Bahía**, *Av 2 de Mayo 710, T082-572127*. Cheaper without bath or TV, new, large clean rooms. The best of the cheaper options.

E **Hostal El Solar**, *González Prada 445, T082-571571*. With bathroom, cheaper without. Basic but clean, rooms have fan.

E **Hostal Iñapari**, *4 km from centre, 5 mins from the airport, T082-572575, joaquin@lullitec.com.pe* Run by a Spanish couple, Isabel and Javier, the price (per person) includes breakfast and dinner, excellent food, very relaxing, friendly and clean. They also have a rustic camping facility in the rainforest on the remote Río Pariamanu, a tributary of the Las Piedras river system, upriver from Puerto Maldonado.

E **Rey Port**, *Av León Velarde 457, T082-571177*. Room rate includes bath, clean, fan, good value and friendly.

E **Wilson**, *Jr González Prada 355, T082-572838*. Rooms with bath, clean but basic.

F **Hostal Moderno**, *Billinghurst 357, T082-571063*. Brightly painted, clean, quiet and friendly, another good cheap hotel but little privacy.

G **Hospedaje Manuripe**, *Av 2 de Mayo 287, T082-573561*. Price per person, basic but clean, rooms with shared bath, has a travel agency for day tours to Lago Sandoval and longer tours to the Tambopata region.

Tambopata National Reserve *p228, map p228.*

Río Madre de Dios
Cuzco Tambo Lodge, *book through Cusco-Maldonado Tour, Pasaje de Harinas 177, T084-244054, Cusco, tamblod@terra.com.pe* Bungalows 15 km out on the northern bank of the Río Madre de Dios. 2-, 3- and 4-day jungle programmes available, from US$90 per person in low season, tours visit Lago Sandoval.
Eco Amazonia Lodge, *book through their office in Cusco: Portal de Panes 109, oficina 6, T084-236159, ecolodge@qenqo-unsaac.edu.pe* On the Río Madre de Dios, 1 hr downriver from Puerto Maldonado. Room for up to 80 in basic bungalows and dormitories, good for birdwatching with viewing platforms and tree canopy access, has its own Monkey Island with animals taken from the forest, US$150 for 3 days/2 nights.

El Corto Maltés, *Billinghurst 229, Puerto Maldonado, T084-573831, cortomaltes@terra.com.pe* On the south side of the Río Madre de Dios, halfway to Sandoval, the focus of most visits. Hot water, huge dining room, well run. Attracts a lot of French groups.
C **Casa de Hospedaje Mejía**, *to book T084-571428, visit Mejía Tours, L Velarde 333, or just turn up.* An attractive rustic lodge on Lago Sandoval, with 10 double rooms, full board can be arranged, canoes are available.
Reserva Amazónica Lodge, *to book, visit Inkaterra, Andalucía 174, Lima 18, T01-610 0404, Plaza las Nazarenas 211, Cusco, T084-245314, Puerto Maldonado T082-572283, www.inkaterra.com* 45 mins by boat down the Río Madre de Dios. Jungle tours available with multilingual guides, the lodge is surrounded by its own 10,000 ha but most tours are to Lago Sandoval. Tastefully redecorated, a hotel in the jungle with 6 suites for those who need a little more luxury (US$240 for 3 days/2 nights), and 38 rustic bungalows with private bathrooms, solar power, friendly staff, very good food in a huge dining room supported by a big tree.

TAMBO TOURS

ADVENTURE TRIPS TO THE TAMBOPATA RESERCH CENTER & AMAZON

Daily departures for groups & individuals.

Offices in the US & CUZCO Experience since 1988

toll free: US & Canada... **1-888-2GO-PERU** (246-7378)

www.**2GOPERU**.com e-mail · tambo@tambotours.com

TAMBO TOURS PO BOX 60541· HOUSTON, TEXAS 77205

International: 001-281-528-9448 fax: 281-528-7378

US$160 per person (double occupancy) for 2-day/1-night package, rising to US$370 for 5 days/4 nights, a naturalists' programme is also provided, negotiable out of season. **Reserva Amazónica Lodge** boasts the largest number of ant species recorded in a single location: 342. The lodge has a Monkey Island (Isla Rolín) for the recovery of primates, which are readapted to their natural environment.

Sandoval Lake Lodge, *book through InkaNatura, Manuel Bañón 461, San Isidro, Lima, T01-440 2022, www.inkanatura.com (see also Cusco Tour operators, page 113).* 1 km beyond **Mejía** on Lago Sandoval, usually accessed by canoe across the lake after a 3-km walk or rickshaw ride along the trail, can accommodate 50 people in 25 rooms, huge bar and dining area, electricity, hot water. There is a short system of trails nearby, guides are available in several languages. Prices start at US$140 per person (double occupancy) for 2 days/1 night, to US$250 double for 4 days/3 nights. They also have a small lodge on the Río Heath, the **Heath River Wildlife Center**, consisting of 6 cabins which can accommodate 12 people. Each cabin has a toilet and hot and cold shower. This lodge is a cooperative project with the traditional Ese'eja community of Sonene. A further hour upriver from the HRWC is a large macaw and parrot lick, providing excellent birdwatching opportunities. Río Heath runs close to a large area of savannah, known as Pampas del Heath (an extension of the vast Beni savannas in Bolivia). This very distinct ecosystem, unique in Peru, with many specialist species such as the stilt-legged maned wolf, was difficult to reach from the lodge at the time of writing, however access may improve in the future. Wildlife viewing in the area is good, and should improve with time as protection of the area develops.

Upper Amazon Lodge, *www.geocities.com/upperamazon* A small, new, rustic lodge at the start of the trail to Lake Sandoval.

Río Tambopata

Lodges on the Tambopata are reached by vehicle to Bahuaja port, 15 km upriver from Puerto Maldonado by the community of Infierno, then by boat.

Explorers Inn, *book through Peruvian Safaris, Alcanfores 459, Miraflores, Lima, T01-447 8888, or Plateros 365, T084-235342, Cusco, safaris@amauta.rcp.net.pe* The office in Puerto Maldonado is at *Fitzcarrald 136, T082-572078.* The lodge is located adjoining the Tambopata National Reserve, in the part where most research work has been done, 58 km from Puerto Maldonado. It's a 2½-hr ride up the Río Tambopata (1½ hrs return, in the early morning, so take warm clothes and rain gear), one of the best places in Peru for seeing jungle birds (580 plus species have been recorded here), butterflies (1,230 plus species), also giant river otters, but you probably need more than a 2-day tour to benefit fully from the location. Offers tours through the adjoining community of La Torre to meet local people and find out about their farms (*chacras*) and handicrafts. The guides are biologists and naturalists from around the world who undertake research in the reserve in return for acting as guides. They provide interesting wildlife treks, including one to the macaw lick (*collpa*). US$180 for 3 days/2 nights, US$165 in the low season.

Picaflor Research Centre, *Casilla 105, Puerto Maldonado, T082-572589, www.picaflor.org* A small lodge located just before Tambopata Jungle Lodge. Guiding in English, visits are made to Lago Condenado. US$190 for 3 days/2 nights with discounts for longer stays; they also offer birdwatching and researcher programmes at US$20 per night and a volunteer programme, minimum of 10 nights, US$10 per day, in return for 3 hrs assistance each day marking trails, etc.

Posada Amazonas Lodge, *book through Rainforest Expeditions, Aramburú 166, of 4B, Miraflores, Lima 18, T01-421 8347, F01-421 8183, or Portal de Carnes 236, Cusco, T084-246243, or Arequipa 401, Puerto Maldonado, T082-571056, or through www.perunature.com* (winners of Conservation International's Ecotourism Excellence Award in 2000). On the Río Tambopata, 2 hrs upriver from Puerto Maldonado. A collaboration between a tour agency the local native community of Infierno. Large attractive rooms with bathroom, cold showers, visits to Lake Tres Chimbadas, with good birdwatching opportunities including the Tambopata *collpa*. Offers trips to a nearby indigenous primary health care project where a native healer gives guided tours of the medicinal plant garden. Tourist income has helped the centre become self-funding. Service and guiding is very good. Recommended. Prices start at US$190 for a 3 day/2 night package, or US$522 for 5 days/4 nights including the **Tambopata Research Centre (TRC)**, the company's older, more intimate, but comfortable lodge. Rooms are smaller than **Posada Amazonas**, shared showers, cold water. The lodge is next to the famous Tambopata macaw clay lick. The area surrounding the TRC is pristine primary rainforest with excellent wildlife viewing. Primates are abundant and other large mammals, such as tapir and jaguar, are often seen, especially in the dry season.

Sachavaca Inn, *to book, Puerto Maldonado, T082-571045, www.webcusco.com/ sachavacasinn* 2 bungalows for up to 20 people, located between **Explorer's Inn** and **Tambopata Jungle Lodge**. Visits are made to Lago Sachavacayoc.

Tambopata Jungle Lodge, *make reservations at Av Pardo 705, Cusco, T084-225701, postmast@patcusco.com.pe* Trips on the Río Tambopata, usually go to Lake Condenado, some to Lake Sachavacayoc, and to the Collpa de Chuncho (macaw lick), guiding mainly in English and Spanish, usual package US$160 per person for 3 days/2 nights (US$145 in the low season), naturalists' programme provided.

Wasai Lodge, *same owners and web address as Hotel Wasai in Puerto Maldonado (see above)*. On the Río Tambopata, 80 km (3½ hrs) upriver from Puerto Maldonado, 1½ hrs return, small lodge with 3 bungalows for 30 people, 15 km of trails around the lodge, guides in English and Spanish. The Collpa de Chuncho, one of the biggest macaw licks in the world, is only 1 hr upriver; 3-day trips US$160, 7 days US$500.

Fundo Buenaventura, *contact in advance, T082-571646, or buenaventura50@hotmail. com* There is usually a representative to meet incoming flights at Puerto Maldonado airport. Part of the tourist intiative by long-term colonists living along the Río

Tambopata, 50-75 km upriver from Puerto Maldonado, 5-6 hrs by *peque-peque*. Accommodation for up to 10 in basic, rustic facilities, provides an insight into local lifestyles, minimum of 2 nights, from US$20-35 per person, includes transport to/from Tambopata dock, all food, mosquito net and Spanish-speaking guide, check if the package includes a trip to a *collpa*, in which case you'll also need a tent.

Amazon Rainforest Conservation Center (**ARCC**), *contact Pepe Moscoso, T082-573655, or www.jungleodyssey.com* This lodge, run by **Jungle Odyssey**, was just being completed at the time of writing and is situated 6 hrs upstream on the remote Río Las Piedras, next to an ox-bow lake, Lago Solidad. Few details were available, but it is claimed that giant otters and other rare wildlife inhabit the area. If true, this would be an interesting alternative to lodge-based tours in the Tambopata area.

TReeS *UK– c/o J Forrest, PO Box 33153, London NW3 4DR. USA – W Widdowson, PO Box 5668, Eureka, CA 95502.* Some of the lodges mentioned above also offer guiding and research placements to biology and environmental science graduates. For more details send them a SAE to the above address.

⊘ Eating

The road to Manu *p225*
$ **Las Palmeras**, *Pilcopata*, a good option.

Atalaya *p225*
$ **Rosa and Klaus**, *Atalaya*, are very friendly people; meals are available at their home, where you can camp.

Puerto Maldonado *p226, map p227*
$$ **Chifa Waseng**, *Cusco 244*. Chinese (not very authentic), open 1200-1400, 1800-2300, but closed Mon lunchtime.
$$ **La Estrella**, *Av León Velarde 474*. The smartest and the best of the *pollos a la brasa* places around.
$$ **El Hornito/Chez Maggy**, *on the plaza*. Good pizzas served in a cosy atmosphere.

Southern Jungle Eating

● *For an explanation of sleeping and eating price codes used in this guide, see inside the*
● *front cover. Other relevant information is found in Essentials, see pages 42-47.*

This is a popular meeting place for travellers, conservationists and researchers.

$$ **El Joelito**, *Av León Velarde 328*, and *El Califa, Piura 266, (recommended)*. Often have bushmeat, mashed banana and palm hearts on the menu.

$$ **El Tablón**, *Av 2 de Mayo 253, T082-572355*. *Pollo a la brasa*, Argentine barbecue and karaoke bar! Huge portions and they even deliver.

$ **La Casa Nostra**, *Av León Velarde 515*. The best place for snacks and cakes.

$ **Tu Dulce Espera**, *Av León Velarde 469*. Does serve good *tamales*, but some of the other lunch options are nothing special.

$ **Pío Chickens**, *González Prada 347*. Great for smoothies and juices.

🍸 Bars and clubs

Puerto Maldonado *p226, map p227*
Bar Oasis, *on the south side of the plaza, next to Chez Maggy*.
Billiard hall, *Puno 520*.
La Chosa del Candamo, *Av Avelino Cáceres, on the way to the airport, near El Brombus*. Good for Brazilian music.
Discoteca Anaconda, *side of the plaza*.
El Witite, *Av León Velarde 153*. A popular and good disco which plays mostly Latin music and charges US$1.50 after 2300, open only Fri and Sat.

🛍 Shopping

Puerto Maldonado *p226, map p227*
Artesanía Shabuya, *Plaza de Armas 279, T082-571856*. The best shop in town if you are looking for handicrafts.
Inotawa Expediciones, *Av León Velarde 315, T082-572511 (Lima T02-467 4560), www.inotawaexpeditions.com* This is a travel agency which also sells handicrafts.

🧭 Tour operators

Puerto Maldonado *p226, map p227*
The Guides Association, contact through association secretary and guide Joselín Vizcarra Yatto, *Av 26 de Diciembre 472, junglejosi@hotmail.com* The association seeks to promote higher guiding standards and regulation in the Maldonado area. Guides within the association charge US$25

per day, excluding expenses (boat hire, fuel, food, etc).

All guides should have a *carnet* issued by the Ministry of Tourism (DRITINCI), which verifies them as suitable guides for trips to Lago Sandoval and other places and confirms their identity. Here is a selection: **Javier Huayaban Troncoso**, *javierhuay@hotmail.com*, is an excellent and recommended guide. Other reputable guides are **Hernán Llave Cortez**, Celso Centeno, the **Mejía brothers** and the **Valarezo** brothers, all of whom can be contacted on arrival at the airport, if available. Also **Javier Salazar** of Hostal Iñapari, who specializes in trips up the remote Río Las Piedras.

Many independent expeditions now focus on the Río Las Piedras, an area that, despite lack of official protection and the activities of selective logging operations, still maintains large populations of Amazonian fauna. Boat hire can be arranged through the **Capitán del Puerto (Río Madre de Dios)**, *T082-573003*.

Tambopata Nature Reserve *p228, map p228*
Tambo Tours, *PO Box 60541, Houston, Texas 77205, and 23115 Calico Corners, Suite 1001, Spring, TX 77373, USA, T1-800-997 7378/1-888-246 7378, T001-281-528 9448, www.2GOPERU.com* Customized trips to the Amazon and archaeological sites of Peru for groups and individuals. Daily departures.

🚌 Transport

Manu Biosphere Reserve *p221, map p222*
Air A private flight will set you back around US$750 one-way (this cost can be divided between the number of passengers). Contact **Transandes**, *T084-224638*, or **Aerocóndor**, *T084-252774*. Both airlines have offices in the Cusco airport terminal. Flights, which use small propeller-engined aircraft, can sometimes be delayed by bad weather.
Road Trucks leave every Mon, Wed and Fri from the Coliseo Cerrado in Cusco at about 1000 (be there by 0800) to **Pilcopata** and **Shintuya** (passing Atalaya). The journey can take at least 24 hrs and is rough and uncomfortable. They return the following day, but there is no service on Sun.

There is also a **bus** service, which leaves from the same place to **Pilcopata**, on Mon and Fri and returns on Tue and Sat. The journey takes 12 hrs in the dry season and costs US$8-10.

Puerto Maldonado *p226, map p227*
Air There are more flights to Maldonado in the high season, but during this time flights can be booked up 3 weeks or more in advance, especially the cheaper seats. Book as early as possible. Flight details below refer to the high season. In theory **Tans** fly daily to Puerto Maldonado, normally at around 1100, however they aren't very dependable and flights are often delayed or cancelled. **Aerocontinente** fly every day from Lima via Cusco, leaving Cusco at around 0915, making this the earliest and sometimes most convenient flight if transfering to jungle lodges. The flights return to Cusco and Lima at 1130. **Lan Perú** fly from Lima via Cusco on Tue, Thu and Sat, leaving Cusco at 1115; the return flight leaves Maldonado at 1240.
River To Boca Manu and Shintuya, via Colorado. Take a combi to Laberinto (see p228) and take a cargo boat from there to Colorado; several daily, US$12. You can get a daily cargo boat from there to Boca Manu and Shintuya, 9-10 hrs, US$15. From Shintuya trucks go to Pilcopata and Cusco (see above under Manu).
Road The road from the cold of the high Andes to the steamy heat of the Amazon jungle can only be described as a challenge. You should take a mosquito net, repellent, sunglasses, sunscreen, a plastic sheet, a blanket, food and water.

From Cusco take a bus to **Urcos**; 1 hr, US$2.25 (see also p 208). Trucks leave from here for **Mazuko** around 1500-1600, arriving around 2400 the next day; 33 hrs, US$6.65. Catch a truck early in the morning from here for Puerto Maldonado, US$4.50, 13-14 hrs. It's a painfully slow journey on an appalling road. Trucks frequently get stuck or break down. The road passes through Ocongate and Marcapata, where there are hot thermal springs, before reaching **Quincemil**, 240 km from Urcos (15-20 hrs), a centre for alluvial gold-mining with many banks. (Accommodation is available in F **Hotel Toni**, friendly, clean,

cold shower, good meals.) Ask the food-carriers to take you to visit the miners washing for gold in the nearby rivers. Quincemil marks the halfway point and the start of the all-weather road. Gasoline is scarce in Quincemil because most road vehicles continue on 70 km to Mazuko, which is another mining centre, where they fill up with the cheaper gasoline of the jungle region. The whole journey takes 50-55 hrs. The road is 99 km long, unpaved and the journey is very rough, but the changing scenery is magnificent and worth the hardship and discomfort. This road is impossible in the wet season. Make sure you have warm clothing for travelling through the Sierra. The trucks only stop 4 times each day, for meals and to allow a short sleeping period for the driver.

An alternative route from Cusco goes via Paucartambo, Pilcopata and Shintuya, and from there by boat to Puerto Maldonado (see The road to Manu, p225).

ⓘ Directory

Manu Biosphere Reserve *p221, map p222*
Conservation organizations
Asociación Peruana para la Conservación de la Naturaleza (Apeco), *Parque José Acosta 187, 2nd floor, Magdalena del Mar, Lima 17, T01-264 0094, www.apeco.org* **Pronaturaleza**, *In Lima: Av Alberto de Campo 417, Lima 17, T01-264 2736 and in Puerto Maldonado: Puerto Jr Cajamarca, cuadra 1 s/n, T082-571585. www.pronaturaleza.org* **Perú Verde**, *Ricaldo Palma J-1, Santa Mónica, Cusco, T084-243408, www.peruverde.org* A local NGO that can help with information and has free video shows about Manu National Park and Tambopata National Reserve. They are friendly and helpful and also have information on programmes and research in the jungle area of Río Madre de Dios. **Manu National Park Office**, *Av Micaela Bastidas 310, (Casilla Postal 591), Cusco T084-240898, pqnmanu@terra.com.pe* 0800-1400. They issue a permit for the former Reserved Zone (see Boca Manu p226 for the cost). Another contact point is **ProManu**, *Urb Magisterial, 2da etapa G-3, Cusco, T084-252937, www.promanu.org*

Airline offices Aero Continente/ Aviandina, *Av León Velarde 584, T572004, F082-571971.* **Lan Perú**, *Av León Velarde y 2 de Mayo, T082-573677.* **Tans**, *Av León Velarde 160, T082-571429.*

Banks and money exchange BCP, cash advances with Visa, no commission on TCs. **Banco de la Nación**, cash on Mastercard, quite good rates for Tcs. *Both are on the south side of the Plaza.* The best rates for cash are at the *casas de cambio*/gold shops on Puno 6th block, eg *Cárdenas Hnos*, Puno 605.

Embassies and consulates Bolivian Consulate, *on the north side of the plaza.*

Immigration Peruvian immigration, *26 de Diciembre 356, 1 block from the plaza.*

Get your exit stamp here.

Internet There are 3 on *Av León Velarde 7th* block, Coto's, **Wellcome**, and MC Computer (*No 756*). *La Económica, 2 de Mayo y E Rivero, opposite the Teatro Municipal. Another on the north side of the Plaza.* All charge between US$1.15 and US$1.40/hr.

Language schools Tambopata Language Centre, *T082-572610, www.geocities.com/tambopata_language* You can now learn Spanish while living close to the rainforest, a cheaper option than studying in Cusco. **Post** Serpost, *Av León Velarde, cuadra 6.* **Telephone** Telefónica, *Puno cuadra 7.* A phone office on the plaza, next to El Hornito, where you can buy all phone cards for national and international calls.

Introduction

It's a well-established cliché to call Lima a city of contradictions, but it's difficult to get beyond that description. Here you'll encounter grinding poverty and conspicuous wealth in abundance. The 8,000,000 inhabitants of this great, sprawling metropolis will defend it to the hilt and, in their next breath, tell you everything that's wrong with it. The hardships of the poor are all too evident in the lives of those struggling to get by in the crowded streets and frantic bus lanes. The rubbish-strewn districts between the airport and the city and, even more so, the shanty towns on the outskirts emphasize the vast divisions within society.

Most visitors, though, have the option of heading for Miraflores or San Isidro, whose chic shops, bars and cafés would grace any major European city. Here, smart restaurants and elegant hotels rub shoulders with pre-Inca pyramids; neat parks and the Larcomar shopping centre, built into a cliff, overlook the ocean; and parapenters fly on the Pacific winds.

★ Don't miss...

1 Plaza de Armas Enclosed wooden balconies and a great cathedral. Seek out a colonial mansion, such as the Palacio Torre Tagle, to see the opulence of Spanish secular architecture, see page 243.

2 Museo de la Nación Housed in a spectacular modern building, it has the most complete overview of precolonial Peruvian culture, see page 249.

3 Museo Arqueológico Rafael Larco Herrera Some excellent exhibitions and lovely gardens, see page 250.

4 Circuito de Playas If the sea and sky aren't merging into one on a cloudy day, late afternoon would be a good time to do this drive or taxi ride along the foot of the cliffs beside the Pacific, see page 250.

5 Barranco Spend all evening in this suburb, where restaurants, bars, peñas and discotheques are all within walking distance, especially on Bolognesi, see page 249.

6 Huaca Pucllana For top-quality dining with a difference (setting and menu) try this restaurant at the foot of the pyramid, in Miraflores. Cheaper and more relaxed is Dalmacia, on Calle San Fernando, which has a Spanish feel, see page 255.

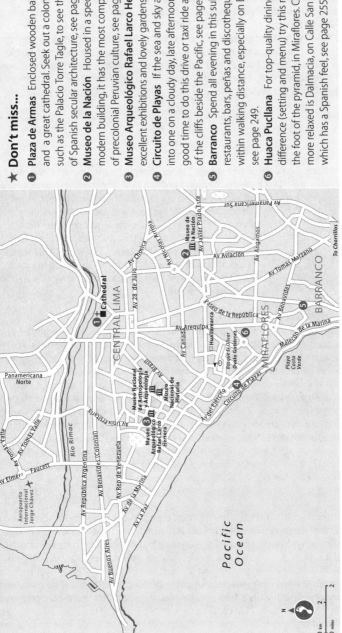

Lima

Lima → *Phone code: 01. Population: 8,000,000.*

While Lima has the ability to incite frustration, fear and despair in equal measure it can also, given the chance, entertain, excite and inform. It has some of the finest historical monuments and museums in the country. The colonial centre, with its grand Plaza de Armas, fine churches and beautiful wooden balconies, is one of Peru's 10 UNESCO World Heritage sites. The city's cuisine has earned it the title 'Gastronomic Capital of the Americas' and the bars, discos and peñas of Barranco and Miraflores ring to the sounds of techno and traditional music, and everything in between. Scratch beneath that coating of grime and decay and you'll find one of the most vibrant and hospitable cities in the world.

Ins and outs

Getting there

All international flights land at Jorge Chávez Airport, some 16 km west of the centre of the city. It is a little further to Miraflores and Barranco. Transport into town is easy if a bit expensive. Tickets for official taxis are bought inside the airport building; the cheaper option are the taxis waiting outside the airport building, but within the airport perimeter fence.

❦ *Routes on any public transportation vehicle are posted on windshields with coloured stickers. Destinations written on the side of any vehicle should be ignored.*

If you arrive in Lima by bus, it is likely you'll pull into the main terminal at Jirón Carlos Zavala, just south of the historical centre of Lima. It is essential that you take a taxi to your hotel even if it's close, as this area is not safe day or night. Most of the hotels are to the west.

Getting around

Downtown Lima can be explored on foot in the daytime, but take all the usual precautions. The central hotels are fairly close to many of the tourist sites. At night taxis are a safer option. Miraflores is about 15 km south of the centre. Many of the better hotels and restaurants are located here and in neighbouring San Isidro.

The Lima public transportation system, at first glance very intimidating, is actually quite good. There are three different types of vehicles that will stop whenever flagged down: buses, combis, and colectivos. They can be distinguished by size; big and long, mid-size and mini-vans, respectively. The flat-rate fare for any of these three types of vehicle is US$0.35. Note that on public holidays, Sundays and from 2400 to 0500 every night, a small charge is added to the fare. Always try to pay with change to avoid hassles, delays and dirty looks from the *cobrador* (driver's assistant). ▶▶ *See also Getting around, page 38 and Transport, page 259.*

Best time to visit

Only 12° south of the equator, you would expect a tropical climate, but Lima has two distinct seasons. The winter is from May to November, when a damp *garúa* (sea mist) hangs over the city, making everything look greyer than it is already. It is damp and cold, 8° to 15°C. The sun breaks through around November, revealing bright blue skies, and temperatures rise as high as 30°C. This is beach weather for all Limeños, when weekends become a very crowded raucous mix of sun, sea, salsa and *ceviche* at the city's more popular coastal resorts. Note that the temperature in the coastal suburbs is lower than the centre because of the sea's influence. You should protect yourself against the sun's rays when visiting the beaches around Lima, and elsewhere in Peru.

i perú has offices at *Jorge Chávez International Airport, T01-574 8000, open 24 hrs a day; Casa Basadre, Av Jorge Basadre 610, San Isidro, T01-421 1227/1627, Mon-Fri 0900-1830; Larcomar shopping centre, Módulo 14, Plaza Gourmet, Miraflores,* Monday-Wednesday 1130-2000, Thursday-Sunday 1130-2100. **Info Perú,** *Jr de la Unión (Belén) 1066, of 102, T01-424 7963, infoperu@qnet.com.pe* Monday-Friday 0930-1800, Saturday 0930-1400. A very helpful office with lots of good advice, English and French spoken. Ask for the helpful, free, *Peru Guide* published in English by Lima Editora, *T-01-444 0815,* available at travel agencies or other tourist organizations.

As much an agency as tourist office, but highly recommended nonetheless, is Siduith Ferrer Herrera, CEO of **Fertur Peru,** *Jr Junín 211 (main office) at the Plaza de Armas, T01-427 1958, fertur@terra.com.pe* 0900-1900. Fertur also has a satellite at *Hostal España, Jr Azangaro 105, T01-427 9196.* Her agency not only offers up to date, correct tourist information on a national level, but also great prices on national and international flights, discounts for those with ISIC and youth cards and **South American Explorers** members (of which she is one). Other services include flight reconfirmations, hotel reservations and transfers to and from the airport or bus stations.

South American Explorers, *Piura 135, Miraflores (Casilla 3714, Lima 100), T01-445 3306, limaclub@saexplorers.org* SAE is the best place to get the most up-to-date information regarding everything from travel advisories to volunteer opportunities. Opening hours are Monday-Friday 0930-1700 (till 2000 on Wednesday) and Saturday 0930-1300. A yearly membership is currently US$50 per person and US$80 per couple. Services include access to member-written trip reports, a full map room for reference, an extensive library in English and a book exchange. Members are welcome to use the SAE's PO Box for receiving post and can store luggage as well as valuables in their very secure deposit space. SAE sells official maps from the Instituto Geográsfico Nacional, SAE-produced trekking maps, used equipment and a large variety of Peruvian crafts. Note that all imported merchandise sold at SAE is reserved for members only, no exceptions. They host regular presentations on various topics ranging from jungle trips to freedom of the press. SAE also offers a discount in membership fees to researchers, archaeologists and scientists in exchange for information and/or presentations. If you're looking to study Spanish in Peru, hoping to travel down the Amazon or in search of a quality Inca Trail tour company, they have the information you'll need to make it happen. SAE, apart from the services mentioned above, is simply a great place to step out of the hustle and bustle of Lima and delight in the serenity of a cup of tea, a magazine and a good conversation with a fellow traveller. The SAE Headquarters are located in the USA: *126 Indian Creek Rd, Ithaca, NY, 14850, T607-2770488, F607-2776122, ithacaclub@saexplorers.org For information and travel tips on-line: www.saexplorers.org Representatives in UK: Bradt Publications, 19 High St, Chalfont St Peters, Bucks, SL9 9QE, T01753-893444, Info@bradt-travelguides.com* If signing up in UK please allow four to six weeks for receipt of membership card.

Background

Lima, originally named *La Ciudad de Los Reyes*, The City of Kings, in honour of the Magi, was founded on Epiphany in 1535 by Francisco Pizarro. From then until the independence of the South American republics in the early 19th century, it was the chief city of Spanish South America. The name Lima, a corruption of the Quechua name *Rimac* (speaker), was not adopted until the end of the 16th century.

At the time of the Conquest, Lima was already an important commercial centre. It continued to grow throughout the colonial years and by 1610, the population was 26,000, of whom 10,000 were Spaniards. This was the time of greatest prosperity. The

Lima Background

commercial centre of the city was just off the Plaza de Armas in the Calle de Mercaderes (first block of Jirón de la Unión) and was full of merchandise imported from Spain, Mexico and China. All the goods from the mother country arrived at the port of Callao, from where they were distributed all over Peru and as far away as Argentina.

There were few cities in the Old World that could rival Lima's wealth and luxury, until the terrible earthquake of 1746. The city's notable elegance was instantly reduced to dust. Only 20 of the 3,000 houses were left standing and an estimated 4,000 people were killed. Despite the efforts of the Viceroy, José Manso de Velasco, to rebuild the city, Lima never recovered her former glory.

During the 19th century, the population dropped from 87,000 in 1810 to 53,000 in 1842, after the Wars of Independence, and the city suffered considerable material damage during the Chilean occupation which followed the War of the Pacific.

By the beginning of the 20th century the population had risen to 140,000 and the movement of people to the coastal areas meant that unskilled cheap labour was available to man the increasing numbers of factories. Around this time, major improvements were made to the city's infrastructure in the shape of modern sanitation, paved streets, new markets and plazas. For the entertainment of the burgeoning middle classes, a modern race track was opened in what is now the Campo de Marte, as well as the municipal theatre, the Teatro Segura. Large-scale municipal

Lima orientation

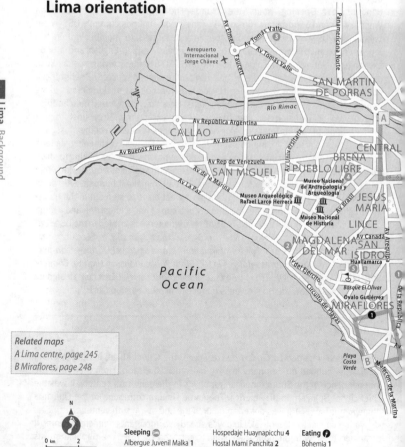

Related maps
A Lima centre, page 245
B Miraflores, page 248

N

0 km 2
0 miles 2

Sleeping
Albergue Juvenil Malka 1
Country Club & Libertador 5

Hospedaje Huaynapicchu 4
Hostal Mami Panchita 2
Hostal Residencial Victor 3

Eating
Bohemia 1

improvements continued under the dictatorship of Augusto Leguía and the presidency 243
of Oscar Benavides, who focused on education for the masses, housing facilities for
workers and cheap restaurants in the slum areas which were growing up around Lima.

Lima, a city of over 8,000,000 people, continues to struggle to live up to its former
reputation as the City of Kings. It is seriously affected by smog for much of the year and
is surrounded by *pueblos jóvenes*, or shanty settlements of squatters who have
migrated from all parts of Peru in search of work and higher education. Villa El Salvador,
a few miles southeast of Lima, may be the world's biggest 'squatters' camp' with
350,000 people building up an award-winning self-governing community since 1971.

The city has changed drastically in the last few years. The commercial heart of
Lima has begun to move away from the centre of town and has taken root in more
upmarket districts such as Miraflores and San Isidro. Amid the traditional buildings
which still survive soar many skyscrapers that have changed the old skyline.

Central Lima

Plaza de Armas
One block south of the Río Rímac lies the Plaza de Armas, which has been declared a
World Heritage site by UNESCO. The plaza used to be the city's most popular meeting point and main market. In the centre of the plaza is a bronze fountain dating from 1650.

Palacio de Gobierno (Government Palace), on the north side of the plaza, stands on the site of the original palace built by Pizarro. When the Viceroyalty was founded it became the official residence of the representative of the crown. Despite the opulent furnishings inside, the exterior remained a poor sight throughout colonial times, with shops lining the front facing the plaza. The façade was remodelled in the second half of the 19th century, then transformed in 1921, following a terrible fire. In 1937, the palace was totally rebuilt. The changing of the guard is at 1200. In order to take a tour of the palace you must register a day in advance at the office of public relations, next door (ask a guard for directions). Tours are given in Spanish and English and last between one and 1½ hours; there is no charge (on a 1030 tour you get to see the changing of the guard from inside the palace).

The **cathedral** ⓘ *Open to visitors Mon-Sat 1000-1430, all-inclusive entrance ticket is US$1.50*, stands on the site of two previous buildings. The first, finished in 1555, was partly paid for by Francisca Pizarro on the condition that her father, the *conquistador*, was buried there. A larger church, however, was soon

Lima Central Lima sights

required to complement the city's status as an Archbishopric. In 1625, the three naves of the main building were completed while work continued on the towers and main door. The new building was reduced to rubble in the earthquake of 1746 and the existing church, completed in 1755, is a reconstruction on the lines of the original.

The interior is immediately impressive, with its massive columns and high nave. Also of note are the splendidly carved stalls (mid-17th century), the silver-covered altars surrounded by fine woodwork, the mosaic-covered walls bearing the coats of arms of Lima and Pizarro and an allegory of Pizarro's commanders, the 'Thirteen Men of Isla del Gallo'. The assumed remains of Francisco Pizarro lie in a small chapel on the right of the entrance, in a glass coffin, though later research indicates that they reside in the crypt.

There is a **Museo de Arte Religioso** in the cathedral, with free guided tours (English available, give tip); ask to see the picture restoration room.

Next to the cathedral is the **Archbishop's Palace**, rebuilt in 1924, with a superb wooden balcony. On the opposite side of the plaza is the **Municipalidad de Lima**, just behind which is **Pasaje Ribera el Viejo**, a pleasant place to hang out with several good cafés with huge terraces. ▶▶ *For Sleeping, Eating and other listings, see pages 250-262.*

Around the centre

From the plaza, passing the Palacio de Gobierno on the left, straight ahead is the Central Railway's **Estación de los Desamparados**. The name, which means 'station of the helpless ones', comes from the orphanage and church that used to be nearby. The station now holds temporary, but long-running exhibitions.

The **Puente de Piedra**, behind the Palacio de Gobierno, is a Roman-style stone bridge built in 1610. Until about 1870 it was the only bridge strong enough to take carriages across the Río Rímac to the district of the same name. Though this part of the city enjoyed considerable popularity in colonial times, it could no longer be considered fashionable.

The **Alameda de los Descalzos** was designed in the early 17th century as a restful place to stroll and it soon became one of the city's most popular meeting places. On the Alameda is the **Convento de los Descalzos** ① *T01-481-0441. Daily 1000-1300 and 1500-1800 except Tue. US$1, by guided tour only, 45 mins in Spanish, but worth it.* Founded in 1592, it contains over 300 paintings of the Cusco, Quito and Lima schools which line the four main cloisters and two ornate chapels. The chapel of El Carmen was constructed in 1730 and is notable for its baroque gold leaf altar. A small chapel dedicated to Nuestra Señora de la Rosa Mística has some fine Cusqueña paintings. The museum shows the life of the Franciscan friars during colonial and early republican periods. The cellar, infirmary, pharmacy and a typical cell have been restored.

▪ *Most of Lima's major museums are outside the central area. We list the most important which have relevance to Cusco, see Suburbs page 249.*

Santo Domingo church and monastery ① *Jr Camaná, 1 block northwest from the Plaza de Armas past the post office, T01-427 6793, Mon-Sat 0900-1300, 1500-1800; Sun and holidays, mornings only, US$0.75,* were built in 1549. the church is still as originally planned, with a nave and two aisles covered by a vaulted ceiling, though the present ceiling dates from the 17th century. The cloister is one of the most attractive in the city and dates from 1603. There is a second, much less elaborate cloister. A chapel, dedicated to San Martín de Porres, one of Peru's most revered saints, leads off from a side corridor. Between the two cloisters is the Chapter House (1730), which was once the premises of the Universidad de San Marcos. Beneath the sacristy are the tombs of San Martín de Porres and Santa Rosa de Lima (first saint of the Americas and patron saint of Lima). In 1669, Pope Clement presented the alabaster statue of Santa Rosa in front of the altar.

Behind Santo Domingo is the **Gran Parque Chabuca Granda**, named after one of Peru's most famous singers and composers. Every afternoon musicians and artists give free shows and you can sample Peruvian dishes and sweets.

San Francisco baroque church ⓘ *Jr Lampa, corner of Ancash, 1st block northeast of the Plaza de Armas, T01-427 1381, daily 0930-1745, US$1.50, US$0.50 children, guided tours only*, which was finished in 1674, was one of the few edifices to withstand the 1746 earthquake. The nave and aisles are lavishly decorated in the Moorish, or Mudéjar, style. The choir, which dates from 1673, is notable for its

Lima centre

Sleeping 🛏

El Balcón Dorado **1**
Europa **2**
Familia Rodríguez **3**
Hostal de las Artes **10**
Hostal España **4**
Hostal Iquique **11**
Hostal La Posada del
   Parque **9**

Hostal Roma &
   Café Carrara **5**
Maury **6**
Pensión Ibarra **7**
Plaza Francia Inn **8**

Eating 🍴

Chun Koc Sen &
   Wa Lok **1**

Cordano **2**
Govinda **9**
Heydi **3**
L'Eau Vive & Antaño **4**
Machu Picchu **6**
Manhatten **8**
Natur **5**
Salon Capon **7**

beautifully carved seats in Nicaraguan hardwood and its Mudéjar ceiling. There is a valuable collection of paintings by the Spanish artist, Francisco de Zuburán (1598-1664), which depict the apostles and various saints.

The **monastery** is famous for the Sevillian tilework and panelled ceiling in the cloisters (1620). The 17th-century *retablos* in the main cloister are carved from cedar and represent scenes from the life of San Francisco, as do the paintings. A broad staircase leading down to a smaller cloister is covered by a remarkable carved wooden dome dating from 1625. Next to this smaller cloister is the Capilla de la Soledad where a café is open to the public. The catacombs under the church and part of the monastery are well worth seeing. This is where an estimated 25,000 Limeños were buried before the main cemetery was opened in 1808.

Two blocks down Ancash, at No 536, is the **Casa de las Trece Monedas**, built in 1787 by Counts from Genoa. It still has the original doors and window grills.

Turn right down Avenida Abancay to the **Museo del Tribunal de la Santa Inquisición** ① *Plaza Bolívar, C Junín 548, near the corner of Av Abancay, Mon-Sun 0900-1700. Free. Students offer to show you round for a tip; good explanations in English.* The main hall, with a splendidly carved mahogany ceiling, remains untouched. The Court of Inquisition was first held here in 1584, after being moved from its first home opposite the church of La Merced. From 1829 until 1938 the building was used by the Senate. In the basement there is an accurate recreation in situ of the gruesome tortures. The whole tour is fascinating, if a little morbid. A description in English is available at the desk.

San Pedro church and monastery ① *Jr Ucayali, 3rd block from Paza de Armas. Mon-Sat 0700-1200, 1700-1800,* is different from any other in the city. The church, finished by Jesuits in 1638, has an unadorned façade. In one of the massive towers hangs a five-tonne bell called *La Abuelita* (the grandmother), first rung in 1590, which sounded the Declaration of Independence in 1821. The contrast between the sober exterior and sumptuous interior couldn't be more striking. The altars are marvellous, in particular the high altar, attributed to the skilled craftsman, Matías Maestro. The church also boasts Moorish-style balconies and rich, gilded wood carvings in the choir and vestry, all tiled throughout. The most important paintings in the church are hung near the main entrance. In the monastery, the sacristy is a beautiful example of 17th-century architecture. Also of note are La Capilla de Nuestra Señora de la O and the penitentiary. Several viceroys are buried below.

he **Palacio Torre Tagle** ① *Jr Ucayali 363, Mon-Fri during working hours, visitors may enter the patio only,* is the city's best surviving specimen of secular colonial architecture. It was built in 1735 for Don José Bernardo de Tagle y Bracho, to whom King Philip V gave the title of First Marquis of Torre Tagle. The house remained in the family until it was acquired by the government in 1918. Today, it is still used by the Foreign Ministry, but visitors are allowed to enter courtyards to inspect the fine, Moorish-influenced wood-carving in the balconies, wrought iron work, and a 16th-century coach complete with commode. From the palace, turn right, then left to return to the Plaza de Armas.

Jirón de La Unión, the main shopping street, runs southwest from the Plaza de Armas. It has been converted into a pedestrian precinct which teems with life in the evening. In the two blocks south of Jirón Unión, known as Calle Belén, several shops sell souvenirs and curios. The newer parts of the city are based on **Plaza San Martín**, south of Jirón de la Unión, with a statue of San Martín in the centre. The plaza has been restored and is now a nice place to sit and relax. **Plaza Dos de Mayo** is 1¼ km to the west. About 1 km due south of this again is the circular **Plaza Bolognesi**, from which many major avenues radiate.

La Merced church and monastery ① *Plazuela de la Merced, Unión y Huancavelica, T01-427 8199, 0800-1200, 1600-2000 daily (church), 0800-1200, 1500-1730 daily (monastery).* The first mass in Lima was said here on the site of the first church to be built. At Independence the Virgin of La Merced was made a Marshal of the Peruvian army. The restored colonial façade is a fine example of baroque architecture. Inside are some magnificent altars and the tilework on some of the walls is noteworthy. A door from the right of the nave leads into the monastery where you can see some 18th-century religious paintings in the sacristy. The cloister dates from 1546.

Museo de Arte

① *9 de Diciembre (Paseo Colón) 125. T01-423 4732. Tue-Sun 1000-1700. US$2.30.*
The Museo de Arte, in the Palacio de la Exposición, was built in 1868 in Parque de la Exposición. More than 7,000 exhibits give a chronological history of Peruvian cultures and art from the Paracas civilization up to the present day. It includes excellent examples of 17th- and 18th-century Cusco paintings, a beautiful display of carved furniture, heavy silver and jewelled stirrups and also pre-Columbian pottery. Guides are free and signs are in English. The *Filmoteca* (movie club) is on the premises and shows films just about every night. See the local paper for details, or look in the museum itself.

San Isidro → *There are many good hotels and restaurants in San Isidro.*

The district of San Isidro combines some upscale residential areas, many of Lima's fanciest hotels and important commercial zones with a huge golf course smack in the middle. Along Avenida La República is **El Olivar**, an old olive grove planted by the first Spaniards, now a beautiful park. It's definitely worth a stroll by day or night.

At Avenida Rosario and Avenida Rivera are the ruins of **Huallamarca**, or **Pan de Azúcar** ① *US$1.75*, a restored adobe pyramid of the Maranga culture, dating from about AD 100-500. There is a small site museum on the premises.➤➤ *For Sleeping, Eating and other listings see pages 250-262.*

Miraflores

Miraflores, apart from being a nice residential part of Lima, is also full of fashionable shops, cafés, discotheques, fine restaurants and good hotels and guesthouses. In the centre of all this is the beautiful Parque Central de Miraflores – **Parque Kennedy** – located between Avenida Larco and Avenida Oscar Benavides (locally known as Avenida Diagonal). This extremely well-kept park has a small open-air theatre with performances from Thursday to Sunday, ranging from Afro-Peruvian music to rock'n'roll. Towards the bottom of the park is a nightly crafts market open from 1700 to 2300. Just off Avenida Diagonal across from the park is Pasaje San Ramón, better known as **Calle de las Pizzas** (Pizza Street). This small pedestrian walkway is full of outdoor restaurants/bars/discotheques open until the small hours of the morning. A very popular place to see and be seen.

At the end of Avenida Larco and running along the Malecón de la Reserva is the renovated **Parque Salazar** and the very modern shopping centre called **Centro Comercial Larcomar**. Here the shopping centre's terraces, which have been carved out of the cliff, contain expensive shops, hip cafés and restaurants, an open-air internet café and discos. The balustrades have a beautiful view of the ocean and sunset. The 12-screen cinema is one of the best in Lima and even has a 'cine-bar' in the twelfth theatre. Don't forget to check out the Cosmic Bowling Alley with its black lights and fluorescent balls. A few hundred metres to the north is the renovated Parque Champagnat and then, across the bridge over the gorge, the famous **Parque del Amor** where on just about any night of the week you'll see at least one wedding party taking photos of the happy couple. Peruvians are nothing if not romantic.

Lima Miraflores

At the intersection of **Calles Borgoña y Tarapacá**, near the 45th block of Avenida Arequipa, is the **Huaca Pucllana**, a 5th-8th-century ceremonial and administrative centre of the pre-Inca, Lima culture. The small adobe-brick pyramid is 23 m high. Guided tours only in Spanish are available. It has a site museum. ▸▸ *For Sleeping, Eating and other listings see pages 250-262.*

Barranco

South of Miraflores is Barranco, which was already a seaside resort by the end of the 17th century. During Spanish rule, it was a getaway for the rich who lived in or near the

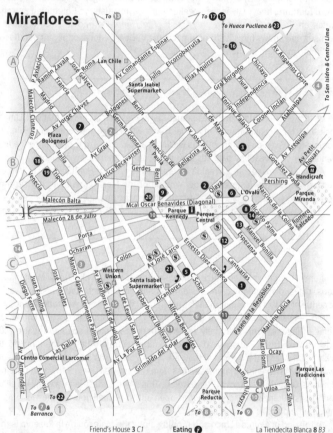

Miraflores

0 metres 50
0 yards 50

Sleeping
Albergue Turístico
  Juvenil Internacional **1** *D3*
Antigua Miraflores **2** *B1*
Ariosto **11** *D2*
Casa de la Sra Jordan **14** *C1*
Friend's House **3** *C1*
Hospedaje Atahualpa **4** *A3*
Hospedaje José Luis **9** *D3*
Hostal Bellavista de
  Miraflores **5** *B2*
Hostal La Castellana **6** *D2*
Hostal Torreblanca **13** *A2*
La Hacienda **15** *C1*
Miraflores Park **7** *D1*
San Antonio Abad **10** *D3*
Sipán **8** *D2*

Eating
Astrid y Gaston **12** *C3*
Bircher Benner **1** *C3*
Café Café **2** *B2*
Café Voltaire **3** *B3*
C'est Si Bon **15** *A2*
Curich **19** *B1*
Dalmacia **22** *D1*
Dino's Pizza **17** *A2*
El Paraíso **5** *C2*
Haiti **6** *B3*
Huaca Pucllana **23** *A3*
Las Brujas de Cachiche **7** *B1*
La Tiendecita Blanca **8** *B3*
La Trattoria **13** *C3*
Madre Natura **16** *A3*
Pardo's Chicken **4** *D2*
Pizza Street **9** *B2*
Ricota & Café Tarata **21** *C2*
Tomar e Irse **20** *B2*
Torero Sí Señor **18** *B1*
Vivaldi **14** *C3*

Bars & clubs
Media Naranja **10** *C2*
Murphys **11** *C3*

centre. Nowadays, Barranco is something of an intellectual haven where a number of artists have their workshops.

The attractive public library, formerly the town hall, stands on the delightful plaza. Nearby is the interesting *Bajada*, a steep path leading down to the beach, where many of Lima's artists live. The **Puente de los Suspiros** (Bridge of Sighs) leads towards the Malecón, with fine views of the bay.

Barranco is a quiet, sleepy suburb during the day but comes alive at night when the city's young flock here to party at weekends. Squeezed into a few streets are dozens of good bars and restaurants. No visit to Lima would be complete without a tour of Barranco's 'sights'. ▶▶ *For Sleeping, Eating and other listings see pages 250-262.*

San Borja

Museo de la Nación

ⓘ *Av Javier Prado Este 2465 T01-476 9875/9878. Tue-Sun 1000-1700. US$1.75, 50% discount with ISIC card.*

This is the anthropological and archaeological museum for the exhibition and study of the art and history of the aboriginal races of Peru. There are good explanations in Spanish and English on Peruvian history, and ceramics, textiles and displays of many ruins in Peru. It is arranged so that you can follow the development of Peruvian precolonial history through to the time of the Incas. A visit is recommended before you go to see the archaeological sites themselves. There are displays of the tomb of the Señor de Sipán, artefacts from Batán Grande near Chiclayo (Sicán culture), reconstructions of the friezes found at Huaca La Luna and Huaca El Brujo, near Trujillo, and of Sechín and other sites. Also included is the **Museo Peruano de Ciencias de la Salud**, which has a collection of ceramics and mummies, plus an explanation of pre-Columbian lifestyle, divided into five sections: *micuy* (Quechua for food), *hampi* (medicine), *onccoy* (disease), *hampini* (healing) and *causay* (life). Temporary exhibitions are held in the basement, where there is also an Instituto de Cultura bookshop.

From Avenida Garcilaso de la Vega in downtown Lima take a combi with a window sticker that says 'Javier Prado/Aviación'. Get off at the 21st block of Javier Prado at Avenida Aviación. From Miraflores take a bus down Avenida Arequipa to Avenida Javier Prado (27th block), then take a bus with a window sticker saying 'Todo Javier Prado' or 'Aviación'. A taxi from downtown Lima or from the centre of Miraflores costs US$2. The museum has a cafetería.

Pueblo Libre

Museo Nacional de Antropología, Arqueología e Historia

ⓘ *Plaza Bolívar (not to be confused with Plaza Bolívar in the centre). T01-463 5070. Tue-Sat 0915-1700, Sun and holidays 1000-1700. US$3. Photo permit US$5. Guides are available.*

On display are ceramics of the Chimú, Nasca, Mochica and Pachacámac cultures, various Inca curiosities and works of art, and interesting textiles. The museum houses the Raimondi Stela and the Tello obelisk from Chavín, and a reconstruction of one of the galleries at Chavín. It also has a model of Machu Picchu. Take any public public transport on Avenida Brasil with a window sticker saying 'Tdo Brasil'. Get off at the 21st block called Avenida Vivanco. Walk about five blocks down Vivanco and the museum will be on your left. Taxi from downtown Lima costs US$1.50; from Miraflores US$2.

Museo Nacional de Historia, ⓘ *Plaza Bolívar, next to the Museo de Antropología y Arqueología*, is in a mansion built by Viceroy Pezuela and occupied by San Martín

(1821-22) and Bolívar (1823-26). The exhibits comprise colonial and early republican paintings, manuscripts, portraits, etc. The paintings are mainly of historical episodes.

Museo Arqueológico Rafael Larco Herrera

ⓘ *Av Bolívar 1515, T01-461 1312, www.museolarco.perucultural.org.pe Daily 0900-1800. US$4.50 (half price for students). Disabled access. Photography not allowed.*

Located in an 18th-century mansion, itself built on a 7th-century pre-Columbian pyramid, this museum has a collection which gives an excellent overview on the development of Peruvian cultures through their pottery. It has the world's largest collection of Moche, Sicán and Chimú pieces. There is a Gold and Silver of Ancient Peru pavilion, a magnificent textile collection and a fascinating erotica section. Texts are in Spanish, English and French. It is surrounded by beautiful gardens. Take any bus to the 15th block of Avenioda Brasil. Then take a bus down Avenida Bolívar. A taxi from downtown, Miraflores or San Isidro, takes 15 minutes, and costs US$2-3. Follow the 'blue line' marked on the pavement to the Museo Nacional de Antropología, Arqueología e Historia (see above), a 10-minute walk.

Lima beaches

Lima sits next to an open bay, with its two points at **La Punta** (Callao) and **Punta La Chira** (Chorrillos). During the summer (December-March), beaches get very crowded on weekdays as much as weekends even though all the beaches lining the Lima coast

❗ *The beach, although not safe to walk at night, has a great view of the whole Lima coastline from Chorrillos to La Punta.*

have been declared unsuitable for swimming. A stroll on the beach is pleasant during daylight hours, but when the sun goes down, the thieves come out and it becomes very dangerous. Needless to say, camping is a very bad idea.

The **Circuito de Playas**, which begins with **Playa Arica** (30 km from Lima) and ends with **San Bartolo** (45 km from Lima), has many great beaches for all tastes. If you want a beach that is always packed with people, there's **El Silencio** or **Punta Rocas**. Quieter options are **Señoritas** or **Los Pulpos**. **Punta Hermosa** has frequent surfing and volleyball tournaments.

🛏 Sleeping

All hotels and restaurants in the upper price brackets charge 19% state tax and 10% service on top of prices. Neither is included in the prices below, unless indicated otherwise. The more expensive hotels charge in dollars according to the parallel rate of exchange at midnight. Many first-time visitors prefer to stay in the centre, close to the colonial heart of the capital. The area is unsafe at night and not entirely safe by day. Less risky, more comfortable and enjoyable is Miraflores, with a good mix of places to stay, great ocean views, bookstores, restaurants and cinemas. You can then commute to the centre by bus (30 to 45 mins) or by taxi (20 to 30 mins).

Central Lima *p243, map p245*

A **Maury**, *Jr Ucayali 201, T01-428 8188, hotmaury@amauta.rcp.net.pe* Breakfast included. Fancy, secure, very clean, most luxurious hotel in the historical centre.
B **El Balcón Dorado**, *Jr Ucayali 199, T01-427 6028, balcondorado@hotmail.com* Price includes tax, service and continental breakfast. Centrally located, very friendly, café.
C **Hostal Roma**, *Jr Ica 326, T01-427 7572, www.hostalroma.8m.com* With bathroom (D without), hot water all day, safe to leave luggage, basic but clean, often full, motorcycle parking (**Roma Tours**, helpful for trips, reservations, flight confirmations, Dante Reyes speaks English). Highly recommended.

D-E Hostal de las Artes, *Jr Chota 1460, T01-433 0031, http://arteswelcome.tripod.com* Price with bathroom, (F without; no singles with bath; G per person in dormitory), Dutch-owned, English spoken, clean, safes in rooms and safe luggage store, friendly, nice colonial building with small garden in patio, solar hot water system, friendly, book exchange, airport transfer US$12. Recommended.

D-E Hostal Iquique, *Jr Iquique 758, Breña, T01-423 3699, http://barrioperu.terra.com.pe/hiquique* With bathroom (E without). Discount for SAE members. Clean but noisy and draughty, friendly, use of kitchen, warm water, storage facilities, rooms on the top floor at the back are best. Repeated recommendations.

D Plaza Francia Inn, *Jr Rufino Torrico 1117 (blue house, no sign, look for 'Ecología es vida' mural opposite), near 9th block of Av Garcilaso de la Vega (aka Wilson), T01-330 6080, T9454260 (mob), franciasquareinn@yahoo.com* Dormitory E, very clean and cosy, hot water 24 hrs, safety box in each room for each bed, kitchen and laundry facilities,

airport pick-up for up to 4 people US$12 (send flight details in advance), discounts for ISIC cardholders, SAE members and readers of this Handbook, same owners as **Posada del Parque**. Highly recommended.

F Hostal España, *Jr Azángaro 105, T01-427 9196, www.hotelespanaperu.com* E with private bath (3 rooms), G per person in dormitory, fine old building, shared bathroom, hot showers possible either very early or very late, friendly, run by a French-speaking Peruvian painter and his Spanish wife, English spoken, internet service, motorcycle parking, luggage store (free), laundry service, don't leave valuables in rooms, roof garden, good café, can be very busy and attention suffers.

F Familia Rodríguez, *Av Nicolás de Piérola 730, 2nd floor, T01-423 6465, jotajot@terra.com.pe* With breakfast, clean, friendly, popular, some rooms noisy, stores luggage, also has dormitory accommodation with only 1 bathroom (same price), transport to airport US$10 per person for 2 people, US$4 per person for 3 or more, offers good information, secure. Recommended.

251

Lima Sleeping

4starSouthAmerica

Great destinations...

...in great style!

Internet-Specials Now Available!

Argentina • Bolivia • Brazil • Chile • Ecuador • Paraguay • Peru • Uruguay

Have your vacation customized or join one of over 400 escorted scheduled Tours

Free Tour Brochure!
Flight Consolidator Fares!

Toll free 1-800-747-4540
Europe: +49(700)4444-7827
UK: 0871-711-5370

Tour-Info: www.4starSouthAmerica.com **Flights**: www.4starFlights.com

252 F **Pensión Ibarra**, *Av Tacna 359, 14th-16th floor, (no sign), T01-427 8603, pensionibarra@ekno.com* Breakfast US$2, discount for longer stay. Use of kitchen, balcony with views of the city, clean, friendly, very helpful owner, hot water, full board available (good small café next door). Highly recommended.

F-G **Europa**, *Jr Ancash 376, T01-427 3351, opposite San Francisco church*. Good, clean rooms with shared bathrooms, excellent hot showers, also dormitory accommodation, great value, friendly, popular with backpackers. Keep valuables secure.

G **Hospedaje Huaynapicchu**, *Jr Pedro Ruiz 703 y Pasaje Echenique 1108, Breña, access from 11th block of Av Brazil, T01-431 2565, huaynapicc@business.com.pe* Price per person, includes breakfast, shared bathroom, hot water all day. Welcoming family, English spoken, internet access, laundry service, secure, very clean, great value.

G **Hostal Machu Picchu**, *Av Juan Pablo Fernandini 1015 (block 10 of Av Brasil), Breña, T01-424 3479*. Price per person. Family-run, rooms with shared bathroom only, hot water, cheap, friendly, kitchen facilities, cable TV, laundry service, excellent value.

San Isidro *p247, map p242*

LL **Country Club**, *Los Eucaliptos 590, T01-611 9000, www.accesoperu.com/countryclub* Excellent service, luxurious rooms, safes in rooms, cable TV, free internet for guests, good bar and restaurant, classically stylish.

L **Libertador**, *Los Eucaliptos 550, T01-421 6666, www.libertador.com.pe* Member of the Golden Tulip chain, overlooking the golf course, full facilities for the business traveller, comfortable rooms, bar, gym, sauna, jacuzzi, fine service, good restaurant. Recommended.

AL **Garden Hotel**, *Rivera Navarrete 450, T01-442 1771, reservas@gardenhotel.com.pe* Price includes tax, breakfast and internet access. Good, large beds, shower, small restaurant, ideal for business visitors,. Recommended.

F **Albergue Juvenil Malka**, *Los Lirios 165 (near 4th block of Av Javier Prado Este), T01-442 0162, hostelmalka@terra.com.pe* Youth hostel, 20% discount with ISIC card, dormitory style, 4-8 beds per room, English spoken, cable TV, laundry, kitchen, nice café, climbing wall. Highly recommended.

Miraflores *p247, map p248*

LL **Miraflores Park**, *Av Malecón de la Reserva 1035, T01-242 3000, mirapark@peruorientexpress.com.pe* Price (over US$300 a night) includes tax, beautiful ocean view, excellent service and facilities, the top of the range in Lima, check with the hotel for monthly offers. Highly recommended.

L **La Hacienda**, *28 de Julio 511 y Av Larco, T01-444 4346, reservas@bwlahacienda.com* Breakfast and taxes included. English spoken, excellent service, has casino.

AL **Antigua Miraflores**, *Av Grau 350 at C Francia, T01-241 6116, www.peru-hotels-inns.com* A beautiful, small and elegant hotel in a quiet but central location, very friendly service, tastefully furnished and decorated, gym, cable TV, good restaurant. Recommended.

AL **Ariosto**, *Av La Paz 769, T01-444 1414, ariosto@chavin.rcp.net.pe* Price includes tax and buffet breakfast. Friendly, 24-hr medical assistance and all other services, airport transfer. Recommended.

A **Hostal La Castellana**, *Grimaldo del Solar 222, T01-444 3530*. Price includes tax. Pleasant, good value, nice garden, safe, restaurant, laundry, English spoken, 10% discount for South American Explorers (SAE) members. Recommended.

A **San Antonio Abad**, *Ramón Ribeyro 301, T01-447 6766, www.hotelsanantonioabad.com* Clean, secure, quiet, good service, welcoming, tasty breakfasts, 1 free airport transfer with reservation. Recommended.

A **Hostal Torreblanca**, *Av José Pardo 1453, near the seafront, T01-447 0142, hostal@torreblancaperu.com* Price includes breakfast and airport pick-up. Quiet, safe, laundry, restaurant and bar, friendly, cosy rooms, will help with travel arrangements. Recommended.

B **Hostal Bellavista de Miraflores**, *Jr Bellavista 215, T01-445 7834, hostalbellavista@terra.com.pe* Price includes tax, breakfast and internet access. Excellent location, quiet, pleasant, all rooms with cable TV, can be noisy from outside at weekends.

B **Sipán**, *Paseo de la República 6171, T01-447 0884, reservas@hotelsipan.com* Breakfast and tax included in price. Very pleasant, in a residential area, with bath, cable TV, fridge, security box, internet access. Free airport transfers available.

C **Hospedaje Atahualpa**, *Atahualpa 646c,
T01-447 6601*. Price includes breakfast.
Cheaper without bath. Parking, hot water,
cooking and laundry facilities, luggage
stored, taxi service.

D **Casa de La Sra Jordan**, *Porta 724, near
Parque del Amor, T01-445 9840*. Price per
person. 8 rooms, reservations required,
family home, friendly, quiet.

D **Hospedaje José Luis**, *Francisco de Paula
Ugarriza 727, San Antonio, T01-444 1015,
www.hoteljoseluis.com.pe* Price includes
breakfast. Rooms with bath, hot water,
safe, quiet, clean, internet, kitchen facilities,
friendly, English spoken.

E **Albergue Turístico Juvenil Internacional**,
*Av Casimiro Ulloa 328, San Antonio between
San Isidro and Miraflores, T01-446 5488,
hostellinginternational@terra.com.pe*
Youth hostel, dormitory accommodation.
Price per person, C in a double private r
oom, US$2.50 discount for IHA card holders.
Basic cafeteria for breakfasts, travel
information, lounge with cable TV, cooking
(minimal) and laundry facilities, swimming
pool often empty, extra charge for
kitchen facilities, clean and safe, situated
in a nice villa. Recommended.

E **Friend's House**, *Jr Manco Cápac 368,
T01-446 6248*. Hot water, cable TV,
use of kitchen at no cost, very popular
with backpackers, near Larcomar
shopping centre. Highly recommended.

Barranco *p248, map p242*

E **The Point**, *Malecón Junín 300, T01-247
7997, www.thepointhostel.com* Quickly
becoming popular with backpackers,
internet, cable TV, welcomes gay and
lesbian travellers.

F **Mochileros Hostal**, *Av Pedro de
Osma 135, 1 block from main plaza, T01-477
4506, www.backpackersperu.com* Price
per person. Beautiful house but a bit scruffy,
friendly English-speaking owner, shared
rooms or C for double bed, good pub
on the premises, stone's throw from
Barranco nightlife.

Elsewhere

Santa Beatriz *map p245*
B **Hostal La Posada del Parque**, *Parque
Hernán Velarde 60, near 2nd block of Av Petit
Thouars, T01-433 2412, www.incacountry.com*
Run by Sra Mónica Moreno and her husband
Leo Rovayo who both speak good English, a
charmingly refurbished old house in a safe
area, excellent bathrooms, cable TV,
breakfast US$3 extra, airport transfer (24 hrs)
US$14 for up to 3 passengers. Highly
recommended as excellent value.

San Miguel *map p242*
C **Hostal Mami Panchita**, *Av Federico Callese
198, T01-263 7203, raymi_travels@perusat.
net.pe* Dutch-Peruvian owned, English,
French, Dutch, Spanish and German spoken,
includes breakfast and welcome drink,
comfortable rooms with bath, hot water,
living room and bar, patio, email service,
book exchange, have their own **Raymi
Travel** agency (good service), 15 mins from
airport, 15 mins from Miraflores, 20 mins
from historical centre. Recommended.
Several chicken places and *chifas* nearby
around Mercado Magdalena.

Near the airport, *map p242*
There are lots of places to stay on **Av
Tomás Valle**, the road from the airport
to the Panamericana Norte, but they are
almost without exception short stay
and unsafe.

B **Hostal Residencial Victor**, *Manuel Mattos
325, Urb San Amadeo de Garagay, Lima 31,
T01-567 5107, hostalvictor@terra.com.pe*
5 mins from the airport by taxi, or phone or
email in advance for free pick-up. Clean,
large comfortable rooms, with bath, hot
water, cable TV, free luggage store, American
breakfast, evening meals can be ordered
from local pizza or chicken places, *chifa*
nearby, very helpful, owner Víctor Melgar
has a free reservation service for Peru and
Bolivia. Recommended.

Lima Sleeping

🍴 Eating

Central Lima *p243, map p245*

$$ Antaño, *Ucayali 332, opposite the Torre Tagle Palace, T01-426 2372, limadeantano@ yahoo.com* Good, typical Peruvian food, nice patio. Recommended.

$$ L'Eau Vive, *Ucayali 370, also opposite Torre Tagle Palace, T01-427 5612*. Run by nuns, open Mon-Sat, 1230-1500 and 1930-2130, fixed-price lunch menu, Peruvian-style in interior dining room, or à la carte in either of the dining rooms that open on to the patio, excellent, profits go to the poor. Ave Maria is sung nightly at 2100.

$$ Manhatten, *Jr Miró Quesada 259, T01-428 2117*. Open Mon-Fri 0700-1900, low end executive-type restaurant, local and international food, good.

$ Café Carrara, *Jr Ica 330, attached to Hostal Roma*. Open daily until 2300, multiple breakfast combinations, pancakes, sandwiches, nice ambience, good.

$ Cordano, *Jr Ancash 202, T01-427 0181*. Typical old Lima restaurant/watering hole, slow service and a bit grimy but full of character. Definitely worth the time it takes to drink a few beers.

$ Govinda, *Av Garcilaso de la Vega 1670, opposite Gran Parque de Lima*. Vegetarian food and natural products, good.

$ Heydi, *Puno 367*. Good, cheap seafood, open daily 1100-2000, popular.

$ Machu Picchu, *Jr Ancash 312, near Hostal Europa*. Huge portions, grimy bathrooms (to say the least), yet very popular, closed for breakfast.

$ Natur, *Moquegua 132, 1 block from Jr de la Unión, T01-427 8281*. The owner, Humberto Valdivia, is also president of the South American Explorers' board of directors, the casual conversation, as well as his vegetarian restaurant, is certainly highly recommended.

Chinatown

There are many excellent *chifas* in the district of Barrios Altos.

$ Chun Koc Sen, *Jr Paruro 886, T01-427 5281*. Open daily 0900-2300.

$ Kin Ten, *Ucayali y Paruro*. Excellent vegetarian options.

$ Salon Capon, *Jr Paruro 819 (also in Larcomar)*. Good dim sum, though cakes when you pay the bill are not as good as those at **Wa Lok**.

$Wa Lok, *Jr Paruro 864, T01-427 2656*. Good dim sum, cakes and fortune cookies (when you pay the bill). Owner Liliana Com speaks fluent English, very friendly.

San Isidro *p247, map p242*

$$$ Antica Pizzería, *Av Dos de Mayo 728, T01-222 8437*. Very popular, great ambience, excellent food, Italian owner. (Also in *Barranco at Alfonso Ugarte 242, T01-247 3443*, and an excellent bar with a limited range of food at *Av Conquistadores cuadra 6, San Isidro*.) Very good value, fashionable, get there early for a seat.

$$$ Le Bistrot de mes Fils, *Av Conquistadores 510, T01-422 6308*. Cosy French Bistrot, great food.

$$$ Valentino, *C Manuel Bañon 215, T01-441 6174*. One of Lima's best international restaurants.

$$ El Segundo Muelle, *Av Conquistadores 490, T01-421 1206, Av Canaval y Moreyra (aka Corpac) 605, T01-224 3007, and Malecón Miraflores, by Parque del Amor*. Excellent *ceviche*, younger crowd. Highly recommended.

$ Delicass, *C Miguel Dasso 133, T01-445 7917*. Great deli with imported meats and cheeses, open late, slow service. Recommended.

$ Qubba, *Av Salaverry 3230, next to Swiss Embassy*. Delicious set lunches for US$3.30, crowded after 1300.

$ If you want to snack for free, go to a supermarket and take advantage of the free tastings (eg Wong on Tue)

Cafés

Café Olé, *Pancho Fierro 115 (1 block from Hotel Olivar), T01-440 7751*. Huge selection of entrées and desserts.

Café Positano/Café Luna, *Miguel Dasso 147*. Popular with politicians, café and bistro.

News Café, *Av Santa Luisa 110, T01-421 6278*. Great salads and desserts, popular and expensive. Also in Larcomar.

$$$ **Astrid y Gaston**, *C Cantuarias 175, T01-444 1496*. Excellent local and international cuisine, one of the best.

$$$ **Las Brujas de Cachiche**, *Av Bolognesi 460, T01-447 1883, www.brujasdecachiche. com.pe* An old mansion converted into bars and dining rooms, beautifully decorated, traditional food (menu in Spanish and English), best *lomo saltado* in town, buffets 1230-1430 daily except Sat, live *criollo* music. Highly recommended.

$$$ **Café Voltaire**, *Av Dos de Mayo 220, T01-447 4807*. International cuisine with emphasis on French dishes, beautifully cooked food, pleasant ambience, good service. Closed Sun.

$$$ **Huaca Pucllana**, *Gral Borgoña cuadra 8 s/n, alt cuadra 45 Av Arequipa, T01-445 4042*. Facing the archaeological site of the same name, contemporary Peruvian fusion cooking, very good food in an unusual setting.

$$$ **Rosa Náutica**, *Espigón No 4, Lima Bay, T01-445 0149*. Built on an old British-style pier. Delightful opulence, finest fish cuisine, experience the atmosphere by buying an expensive beer in the bar at sunset, 1230-0200 daily. Highly recommended.

$$$ **La Trattoria**, *C Manuel Bonilla 106, 1 block from Parque Kennedy, T01-446 7002*. Italian cuisine, popular, serving the best cheesecake in Lima.

$$ **Bohemia**, *Av Santa Cruz 805, on the Ovalo Gutiérrez, T01-445 0889*. Large menu of international food, great salads and sandwiches. Highly recommended. Also at *Av El Polo 706, 2nd floor, T01-435 9924 and at Pasaje Nicolás de Rivera 142, opposite the main post office near the Plaza de Armas, Lima centre, T01-427 5537*.

$$ **Curich**, *Bolognesi 755*. Run by painter and musician Tony Curich, great home-made food, lunch specials, piano concerts nightly, poetry readings, traditional atmosphere, an institution.

$$ **Dalmacia**, *C San Fernando 401, T01-445 7917*. Spanish-owned, casual gourmet restaurant, excellent. Highly recommended.

$$ **Torero Sí Señor**, *Av Angamos Oeste 598, T01-446 5150*. Spanish food, fun, loud. Also at *Bolognesi 706, T01-445 3789*. Mexican version of same restaurant.

$ **Bircher Benner**, *Diez Canseco 487 y Grimaldo del Solar, T01-444 4250*. Closed Sun, natural food store inside, slow service, good cheap vegetarian menu.

$ **Café Tarata**, *Pasaje Tarata 260*. Good atmosphere, family-run, good varied menu.

$ **Dino's Pizza**, *Av Comandante Espinar 374 (and many other branches), T01-242 0606, www.pizza.com.pe* Great pizza at a good price, delivery service.

$ **Pardo's Chicken**, *Av Benavides 730, T01-446 4790*. Chicken and chips, very good and popular (branches throughout Lima).

$ **Ricota**, *Pasaje Tarata 248, T01-445 2947*. Charming café on a pedestrian walkway, with a huge menu, big portions and very friendly. Recommended.

$ **Madre Natura**, *C Chiclayo 815, T01-445 2522*. Great natural foods shop with a vegetarian café at the back, quiet, beautiful courtyard. Highly recommended.

$ **El Paraíso**, *C Alcanfores 416, 2 blocks from Av Benavides*. Natural foods/snacks, fruit salads and juices. Highly recommended.

$ There are various small restaurants good for a cheap set meal along *C Los Pinos y Av Schell*, at the bottom of Parque Kennedy. *C San Ramón*, more commonly known as **Pizza St** (across from Parque Kennedy), is a pedestrian walkway lined with restaurants specializing in Italian food. Very popular and open all night at weekends.

Cafés

Café Café, *Martín Olaya 250, near the Parque Kennedy roundabout*. Very popular, good atmosphere, over 100 different blends of coffee, good salads and sandwiches, very popular with 'well-to-do' Limeños. Also at *Alvarez Calderón 194, San Isidro*, and in Larcomar (good sea views).

Café Zeta, *José Gálvez y Diagonal, past Parque Kennedy, T01-446 5922*. American-owned, excellent Peruvian coffee, teas, hot chocolate, and the best home-made cakes away from home, cheap too.

C'est si bon, *Av Comandante Espinar 663, T01-446 9310*. Excellent cakes by the slice or whole, best in Lima.

Haiti, *Av Diagonal 160, Parque Kennedy*. Open almost round the clock daily, large terrace, decent food and coffee, great for people-watching, frequented by politicians, journalists and artists.

Lima Eating

Pin Poini, *small kiosk on Parque del Amor.*
Good place to watch the ocean and sip real
Italian coffee.
La Tiendecita Blanca, *Av Larco 111 on
Parque Kennedy, T01-445 9797.* One of
Miraflores' oldest, expensive, good
people-watching, very good cakes,
European-style food and delicatessen.
Tomar e Irse, *Mcal Oscar R Benavides 598.*
Cool new place with innovative design and
beans from around the world.
Vivaldi, *Av Ricardo Palma 258, 1 block from
Parque Kennedy, T01-446 1473.* Also at
Conquistadores 212, San Isidro. Good, pricey.

Barranco *p248, map p242*

$$$ **La Costa Verde**, *Barranquito beach,
T01-247 1244.* Excellent fish and wine,
expensive but recommended as the best by
Limeños, 1200-2400 daily, Sun buffet.
$$$ **Naylamp**, *Av 2 de Mayo 239, T01-467
5011.* Good seafood and *ceviche*, fashionable,
and expensive.
$$ **Festín**, *Av Grau 323, T01-247 7218.* Huge
menu, typical and international food.
$$ **Las Mesitas**, *Av Grau 341, T01-477 4199.*
Creole food and old sweet dishes which you
won't find anywhere else. Recommended.

Bars and clubs

Lima has excellent nightlife, with a lot of
variety. Often there is a cover charge ranging
from US$3-10 per person.

Central Lima *p243, map p245*

Estadio Futbol Sports Bar, *Av Nicolás de
Piérola 926 on the Plaza San Martín, T01-428
8866.* Beautiful bar with a discotheque on
the bottom floor, international football
theme, serving good food. Recommended.
Piano Bar Munich, *Jr de la Unión 1044
(basement).* Small and fun.
Queirolo Bar, *Jr Camaná 900 at Jr Quilca.*
Excellent for local colour.
El Rincón Cervecero, *Jr de la Unión (Belén)
1045.* German pub without the beer, fun.

Miraflores *p247, map p248*

Bars
Barra Brava, *Av Grau 192, T01-241 5840.* Lots
of fun, sports bar(ish).
Diogreeks Pub, *Av Dos de Mayo 385, T01-447
7958.* Nice pub with Greek decor.
Media Naranja, *C Schell 130, at the bottom of
Parque Kennedy.* Brazilian bar.
Murphys, *C Schell 627.* Great Irish pub now
doing food such as fish and chips.
Rey David, *Av Benavides 567, Centro
Comercial Los Duendes.* Small café/bar.

Clubs
There are many discotheques on Pizza St by
Parque Kennedy.

Cocodrilo Verde, *Francisco de Paula 226 near
corner with Bellavista.* Relaxed, stylish bar,
slightly pricey but worth it for the Wed night
jazz, and live music at weekends, can charge
cover for music at weekends.
Ministry, *Altos de D'Onofrio, opposite Parque
Kennedy, T01-938 9231.* Good music, and
demonstrations of dance, exhibitions,
tattooing, entry US$3. Recommended.
Santa Sede, *Av 28 de Julio 441.* Very popular,
great music, fun crowd. Recommended.
Satchmo, *Av La Paz 538, T01-442 8425.* Live
jazz, creole and blues shows.

Barranco *p248, map p242*

Barranco is the centre of Lima nightlife. Pasaje
Sánchez Carrión, right off the main plaza, used
to be the heart of it all, lined with bars and
discos, although the crowds are driving
people elsewhere. Some places have been
closed for safety reasons following a fatal fire
in an overcrowded nightclub, **Utopia**, where
safety rules were ignored. Av Grau, across the
street from the plaza, is lined with bars. and
there are many bars around Plaza Raimondi, 1
block from Bolognesi. Many of the bars in this
area turn into discotheques later on.

Bars
Backpacker's Inn, *Av Pedro de Osma 135,
inside the Mochileros Hostal.* Often has live
music, such as salsa.
Bosa Nova, *Bolognesi 660,* is a chilled
student-style bar with good music.

La Estación, *Av Pedro de Osma 112*. Live music, older crowd.
Juanitos, *Av Grau, opposite the park*. Barranco's oldest bar, and the perfect start to the evening.
Kitsch Bar, *Bolognesi 743*. The name says it al:flock wallpaper, dolls, religious icons, after midnight it becomes unbearably packed, but great dancing.
La Noche, *Bolognesi 307, at Pasaje Sánchez Carrión*. A Lima institution. Live music, Mon is jazz night, kicks off around 2200 (also in Central Lima – see above).
La Posada del Mirador, *near the Puente de* los Suspiros (Bridge of Sighs). Beautiful view of the ocean, but you pay for the privilege.
Sargento Pimienta, *Bolognesi 755*. Live music, always a favourite with Limeños.
Trinidad, *Bolognesi, opposite Sargento Pimienta*, is relaxed.

Clubs
El Dragón, *N de Piérola, near corner with Grau*. Popular dancing venue.
My Place, *C Domeyer 122*.
De Parranda, *Av Grau*. Once Lima's most popular discotheque, large and modern.
Las Terrazas, *Av Grau 290*.

⊕ Entertainment

Cinemas

The newspaper *El Comercio* lists cinema information in the section called *Luces*. Tue is reduced price at most cinemas. Most films are in English with subtitles and cost US$2 in the centre and around US$4-5 in Miraflores. The best cinema chains in the city are Cinemark, Cineplanet and UVK Multicines.

Miraflores *p247, map 248*
Cine Romeo y Julieta, *Pasaje Porta 115, at the bottom of Parque Kennedy, T01-447 5476*.
Multicine Starvision El Pacífico, *on the Ovalo by Parque Kennedy, T01-445 6990*.

Peñas

Central Lima *p243, map p245*
Las Brisas de Titicaca, *Pasaje Walkuski 168, at the 1st block of Av Brasil near Plaza Bolognesi, T01-332 1881*. A Lima institution.

Miraflores *p247, map p248*
De Cajón, *C Merino 2nd block, near 6th block* of *Av del Ejército*. Good *música negra*.
Sachun, *Av del Ejército 657, T01-441 0123*. Great shows during the week as well as at weekends.

Barranco *p248, map p242*
Casa Vieja, *Salaverry 139*. Standard *peña* in a converted theatre, nice atmosphere.
Del Carajo, *San Ambrosio 328, T01-247 7977*. All types of traditional music.
Don Porfirio, *C Manuel Segura 115, T01-447 3119*. Traditional *peña*. Recommended.
La Estación de Barranco, *Pedro de Osma 112, T01-477 5030*. Good, family atmosphere, varied shows.
Las Guitarras, *C Manuel Segura 295, 6th block of Av Grau, T01-247 3924*. Recommended.
Los Balcones, *Av Grau across from main plaza*. Good, noisy and crowded.
Manos Morenas, *Av Pedro de Osma 409, T01-467 0421*. Also a restaurant, older crowd, great shows beginning at 2230.
Peña Poggi, *Av Luna Pizarro 578, T01-247 5790*. 30 years old, traditional. Recommended.

● Festivals and events

18 Jan celebrates the anniversary of the founding of Lima, with a Peruvian music festival on the previous night (17 Jan), culminating in the Plaza de Armas.
Semana Santa, or Holy Week, is a colourful spectacle with processions.

28-29 Jul, Independence, has music and fireworks in the Plaza de Armas.
Oct is the month of **Our Lord of the Miracles** with impressive processions starting from Las Nazarenas church on the 4th block of Av Tacna.

◯ Shopping

Crafts

Parque Kennedy, the main park of Miraflores, has a daily crafts market open 1700-2300.

There are crafts markets on **Av Petit Thouars** in Miraflores near Parque Kennedy. Av Petit Thouars runs parallel to Av Arequipa. Its 54 blocks end at Av Ricardo Palma, a few blocks from Parque Kennedy. At the 51st block there's a crafts market area with a large courtyard and small flags. This is the largest crafts arcade in Miraflores. From here to C Ricardo Palma the street is lined with crafts markets. One of the newer ones has a small café. All are open daily until late(ish).

Markets

On C García Naranjo, La Victoria, just off Av Grau in the centre of town is **Polvos Azules**, the official black market of Lima. The normal connotations of a 'black market' do not apply here as this is an accepted part of Lima society, condoned by the government and used by people of all backgrounds. It's good for cameras, hiking boots, music and an extensive selection of walkmans. Be careful, this is not a safe area, so be alert and put your money in your front pockets.

Supermarkets

Lima has 3 supermarket chains: **Santa Isabel**, **E Wong** and **Metro**. They all are well stocked and carry a decent supply of imported goods (*Marmite*, Tesco products, etc).The **Santa Isabel**, *Av Benavides y Av Alcanfores in Miraflores*, is open 24 hrs.

◔ Tour operators

For international tour operators, such as **4 Star South America**, see Essentials, p13. **South American Explorers**, *www.SAexplorers.org* are also an excellent source of information and advice.
Cóndor Travel, *Mayor Armando Blondet 249, San Isidro, T01-615 3000, www.condortravel.com.pe*, also in Cusco.
Coltu, *Av José Pardo 138, Miraflores, T01-241 5551, www.coltur.com.pe* Very helpful and well organized. Also has an office in Cusco.
Dasatour, *Jr Francisco Bolognesi 510, Miraflores, T01-447 7772, Pardo 589, T084-223341, www.dasatour.com.pe* Also has an office in Cusco.
Explorandes, *C San Fernando 320, T01-445 8683, Av Garcilaso 316-A, T084-245700, www.explorandes.com.pe* Offers a wide range of adventure and cultural tours, experienced, high-end company with award-winning environmental practices. Also has an office in Cusco.

KinjyoTravel, *Las Camelias 290, San Isidro, T01-442 4000, postmast@kinjyo.com.pe* Also has an office in Cusco.
Lima Tours, *Jr Belén 1040, Lima centre, T01-424 5110, and at Av Pardo y Aliaga 6908, T01-222 2525*. Recommended throughout Peru. Also has offices in Cusco.
Peru Bike, *Urb Nueva Castilla, Calle A, D-7, Surco, Lima 33, T01-449 5234, www.perubike.com* Experienced agency leading tours of varying length, specializing in the Andes, professional guiding.
Peru Expeditions, *Av Arequipa 5241-504, Miraflores, Lima, T01 447-2057, www.peru-expeditions.com* Expeditions, tours, low-cost flights, transfers and hotels.
South American Tours, *Av Miguel Dasso 117, piso 14, San Isidro*.
Viracocha Turismo, *Av Vasco Núñez de Balboa 191, Miraflores, Lima, T01-445 3986, F01-447 2429*. Cultural and mystical tours. Also hiking, rafting and birdwatching for outdoor types.

● Transport

Air

For all information on international flight arrivals and departures, see Touching down (p32). For all information on domestic flights, see Getting around (p38). To enquire about arrivals or departures, *T01-575 1712* (international), or *T01-574 5529* (domestic). For airport facilities and transport to and from Lima airport, see Touching down p32.

Airlines

Domestic Aero Continente, *Av José Pardo 605, Miraflores, T01-241 4816, www.aero continente.com.pe* Flights to most major destinations in Peru. **Aviandina**, is a subsidiary of Aero Continente. **Lan Perú**, *Av José Pardo 513, Miraflores, T01-213 8200/8300, www.lanperu.com* Flights from Lima to Arequipa, Chiclayo, Cusco, Juliaca, Puerto Maldonado and Trujillo. **Tans**, *Jr Belén 1015, Lima Centre, Av Arequipa 5200, Miraflores, T01-213 6000/6030, www.tans.com.pe* Flights to most major destinations in Peru. **Taca Perú**, *Av Comandante Espinar 331, Miraflores, T01-213 7000, www.grupotaca.com* Flights between Lima and Cusco. **Star Up**, *Av José Pardo 269, Miraflores, T01-445 6032*. Flights to Ayacucho, Cusco, Huánuco, Andahuaylas and Tingo María.

International Aerolíneas Argentinas, *Av José Pardo 805, 3rd floor, Miraflores, T01-241 332*. **AeroMéxico**, *Centro Empresarial Camino Real, San Isidro, T01-421 3500*. **Air France**, *Av José Pardo 601, Miraflores, T01-444 9285*.

American Airlines, *Av Canaval y Moreyra 380, San Isidro, and in Hotel Las Américas, Av Benavides y Av Larco, Miraflores, T01-211 7000*. **Avianca**, *Av Paz Soldán 225, oficina C5, San Isidro, T01-221 7822*. **Continental**, *C Victor Belaúnde 147, oficina 101, San Isidro, and in the Hotel Marriott, 13th block of Av Larco, Miraflores, T01-221 4340*. **Copa**, *Av Dos de Mayo 741, Miraflores, T01-444 7815*. **Delta**, *Centro Empresarial Camino Real, San Isidro, T01-211 9211*. **Iberia**, *Av Camino Real 390, 9th floor, San Isidro, T01-421 4616*. **KLM**, *Av José Pardo 805, 6th floor, Miraflores, T01-242 1240*. **Lacsa**, *2 de Mayo 755, Miraflores, T01-444 7818*. **Lan Chile**, *Av José Pardo 513, Miraflores, T01-213 8200*. **Lloyd Aéreo Boliviano**, *Av José Pardo 231, Miraflores, T01-241 5510*. **Lufthansa**, *Av Jorge Basadre 1330, San Isidro, T01-442 4455*. **Varig**, *Av Camino Real 456, 8th floor, San Isidro, T01-442 4207*.

Bus

Local

Lima Centre-Miraflores: Av Arequipa runs 52 blocks between downtown Lima and Parque Kennedy in Miraflores. There is no shortage of public transport on this avenue; they have 'Todo Arequipa' on the windscreen. When heading towards downtown from Miraflores the window sticker should say 'Wilson/Tacna'. To get to Parque Kennedy from downtown look on the windshield for 'Larco/Schell/Miraflores', 'Chorrillos/Huaylas' or 'Barranco/Ayacucho'.

Vía Expresa: Lima's only urban freeway runs from Plaza Grau in the centre of town, to the

Lima Transport

SOUTH AMERICAN EXPLORERS
http://www.SAexplorers.org

Want to VOLUNTEER, STUDY, TRAVEL or EXPLORE?

JOIN the SOUTH AMERICAN EXPLORERS now!

Visit our clubhouses in Lima & Cusco (Peru) and Quito (Ecuador)

Call us at 800-274-0568 or 607-277-0488. You may also visit us at www.SAexplorers.org or email us at info@SAexplorers.org northern tip of the district of **Barranco**. This 6-lane thoroughfare, locally known as *El Zanjón* (the Ditch), with a separate bus lane in the middle, is the fastest way to cross the city. In order from Plaza Grau the 8 stops are: 1) **Av México**; 2) **Av Canadá**; 3) **Av Javier Prado**; 4) **Corpac**; 5) **Av Aramburu**; 6) **Av Angamos**; 7) **Av Ricardo Palma**, for Parque Kennedy; 8) **Av Benavides**. Buses downtown for the Vía Expresa can be caught on Av Tacna, Av Wilson (also called Garcilaso de la Vega), Av Bolivia and Av Alfonso Ugarte. These buses, when full, are of great interest to highly skilled pickpockets who sometimes work in groups. If you're standing in the aisle be extra careful

Long distance

Although Lima is home to a seemingly never-ending list of bus companies, only a small percentage are actually recommended. Companies that offer a service between Cusco and Lima are given in the Cusco Transport section, page 122. Confirm that the bus leaves from same place that the ticket was purchased.

One company that is recommended for service to all parts of Peru is **Cruz del Sur**, *Jr Quilca 531, Lima Centre, T01-224 6200, www.cruzdelsur.com.pe* This terminal has routes to many destinations in Peru with *Ideal* service, meaning quite comfortable buses and periodic stops for food and bathroom breaks, a cheap option with a quality company. Its other terminal is at *Av Javier Prado Este 1109, San Isidro, T01-225 6163*. This terminal offers the *Imperial* service (luxury buses), more expensive and direct, with no chance of passengers in the aisle, and *Cruzero* service (super luxury buses). They go to Cusco, to other parts of the country and to La Paz. Another company with services to Cusco is **Expreso Molina**, *Jr Ayacucho 1141, Lima Centre, T01-428 0617.*

Taxi

Taxi colectivos: Regular private automobiles charging US$0.50 make this a faster, more comfortable option than public transportation. There are 3 routes: 1) between Av Arequipa and Av Tacna which runs from Miraflores to the centre of Lima; 2)

between Plaza San Martín and Callao; 3) between the Vía Expresa and the district of Chorrillos. Look for the coloured sticker posted on the windshield. These cars will stop at any time to pick people up. When full (usually 5 or 6 passengers) they only stop for someone getting off, then the process begins again to fill the empty space.

Taxis: Meters are not used, so the fare should be agreed upon before you get in. Tips are not expected. The South Korean company Daewoo introduced their model 'Tico' a few years back and this has become the taxi of choice. They are quick, clean and invariably yellow, but most importantly, they have seatbelts that work. Whatever the size or make, yellow taxis are usually the safest since they have a number, the driver's name and radio contact. A large number of taxis are white, but as driving a taxi in Lima (or for that matter, anywhere in Peru) simply requires a windshield sticker saying 'Taxi', they come in assorted colours and sizes.

The following are taxi fares for some of the more common routes, give or take a sol. **From downtown Lima to**: Parque Kennedy (Miraflores), US$2; **Museo de la Nación**, US$2; **South American Explorers**, US$2; **Archaeology Museum**, US$2; **Immigration**, US$1.15.

From Miraflores (Parque Kennedy) to: Museo de la Nación, US$2. Archaeology Museum, US$3. Immigration, US$2. For prices to and from the airport, see Touching down, p32).

Official taxi companies, registered with the Municipality of Lima, are without a doubt the safest option but cost much more than just picking one up in the street. Hourly rates possible. Companies include: Taxi América, *T01-265 1960*; Moli Taxi, *T01-479 0030*; Taxi Real, *T01-470 6263*; Taxi Tata, *T01-274 5151*; TCAM, run by Carlos Astacio, *T01-983 9305*, safe, reliable.

Recommended, knowledgeable drivers: Hugo Casanova Morella, *T01-485 7708* (he lives in La Victoria), for city tours, travel to airport, etc. Mónica Velásquez Carlich, *T01-425 5087, T943 0796 (mob), vc_monica@hotmail.com* For airport pick-ups, tours, speaks English, most helpful.

● Directory

Banks and money exchange

Banks BCP (formerly **Banco de Crédito**), *Jr Lampa 499, Lima Centre (main branch), Av Pardo 425 and Av Larco at Pasaje Tarata, Miraflores, Av Pardo y Aliaga at Av Camino Real, San Isidro.* Mon-Fri 0900-1800, Sat 0930-1230. Accepts and sells American Express TCs only, accepts Visa card and branches have Visa ATM. **Banco de Comercio,** *Av Pardo 272 and Av Larco 265, Miraflores, Jr Lampa 560, Lima Centre (main branch).* Mon-Fri 0900-1800, Sat 0930-1200. Changes and sells American Express TCs only, ATM accepts Visa/Plus. **Banco Continental,** *corner of Av Larco and Av Benavides and corner of Av Larco and Pasaje Tarata, Miraflores, Jr Cusco 286, Lima Centre near Plaza San Martín.* Mon-Fri 0900-1800, Sat 0930-1230. TCs (American Express). Visa ATM. **Banco Financiero,** *Av Ricardo Palma 278, near Parque Kennedy (main branch).* Mon-Fri 0900-1800, Sat 0930-1230. TCs (American Express), ATM for Visa/Plus. **Banco Santander Central Hispano (BSCH),** *Av Pardo 482 and Av Larco 479, Miraflores, Av Augusto Tamayo 120, San Isidro (main branch).* Mon-Fri 0900-1800, Sat 0930-1230. TCs (Visa and Citicorp). ATM for Visa/Plus. **Banco Wiese Sudameris,** *Av Diagonal 176 on Parque Kennedy, Av José Pardo 697, Miraflores, Av Alfonso Ugarte 1292, Breña, Miguel Dasso 286, San Isidro.* Mon-Fri 0915-1800, Sat 0930-1230. TCs (American Express only), ATM for Visa/Plus. **Citibank,** *in all Blockbuster stores, and at Av 28 de Julio 886, Av Benavides 23rd block and Av Emilio Cavenecia 175, Miraflores, Av Las Flores 205 and branch in Centro Comercial Camino Real, Av Camino Real 348, San Isidro.* Blockbuster branches open Sat and Sun 1000-1900. Changes and sells Citicorp cheques. **Interbank,** *Jr de la Unión 600, Lima Centre (main branch).* Mon-Fri 0900-1800. Also *Av Pardo 413, Av Larco 690 and in Larcomar, Miraflores, Av Grau 300, Barranco, Av Pezet 1405 and Av Pardo y Aliaga 634, San Isidro,* and supermarkets Wong and Metro. Accepts and sells American Express TCs only, ATM for Mastercard.

Casas de cambio There are many *casas de cambio* on and around Jr Ocoña off the Plaza San Martín. Repeatedly recommended is **LAC Dolar**, *Jr Camaná 779, 1 block from Plaza San Martín, 2nd floor, T01-428 8127/427 3906.* Also at *Av La Paz 211, Miraflores, T01-242 4069.* Mon-Sat 0900-1900, Sun and holidays 0900-1400, good rates, very helpful, safe, fast, reliable, 2% commission on cash and TCs (Amex, Citicorp, Thomas Cook, Visa), will come to your hotel if you're in a group. Also recommended is **Virgen P Socorro**, *Jr Ocoña 184, T01-428 7748.* Daily 0830-2000, safe, reliable and friendly.

Cambistas On the corner of Ocoña and Jr Camaná you'll no doubt see the large concentration of cambistas (street changers) with huge wads of dollars and soles in one hand and a calculator on the other. They should be avoided. Changing money on the street should only be done with official street changers wearing an identity card with a photo. Keep in mind that this card doesn't automatically mean that they are legitimate but most likely you won't have a problem. Around Parque Kennedy and down Av Larco in Miraflores are dozens of official *cambistas* with ID photo cards attached to their usually blue, sometimes green vest. There are also those who are independent and are dressed in street clothes, but it's safer to do business with an official money changer.

American Express Office, *Av Belén 1040 in the Lima Tours office, near Plaza San Martín.* Official hours are Mon-Fri 0900-1700, Sat 0900-1300, but there is always someone there in case of emergencies. Services are as follows: replaces lost or stolen American Express TCs of any currency in the world. Can purchase Amex TCs with Amex card only. Also at Also at *Camino Real 698, San Isidro, T01-222 2525,* for travel services. **Mastercard**, *Porta 111, 6th floor, Miraflores, T01-242 2700.*

Embassies and consulates

Australia, *Av Víctor Belaúnde 147, no 1301, San Isidro, T01-222 8281.* 0900-1200. **Austria**, *Av Central 643, 5th floor, San Isidro, T442 0503, lima-ob@bmaa.gv.at* 0900-1200. **Belgium**, *Angamos Oeste 380, Miraflores, T01-241 7566, LIMA@DIPLOBEL.ORG* 0830-1200. **Bolivia**, *Los Castaños 235, San Isidro, T01-440 2095,*

jemis@emboli.attla.com.pe 0900-1300.
Canada, *Libertad 130, Miraflores, T01-444
4015, lima@dfait-maeci.gc.ca* Mon, Tue, Thu,
Fri 0800-1700, Wed 0800-1300. **Denmark**,
*Bernardo Monteagudo 201, Magdalena,
T01-264 4040*. Mon-Fri 0930-1230,
1530-1730. **France**, *Arequipa 3415, San Isidro,
T01-215 8420, FRANCE.EMBAJADA@terra.
com.pe* 0900-1300. **Germany**, *Av Arequipa
4210, Miraflores, PO Box (Casilla) 18-0504,
T01-212 5016, F01-212 4194*. 0900-1200.
Israel, *Natalio Sánchez 125, 6th floor, Santa
Beatriz, T01-433 4431, emisrael@terra.com.pe*
Mon-Fri 1000-1300. **Italy**, *Av G Escobedo 298,
Jesús María, T01-463 2727, embajada@
italembperu.org.pe* Mon-Fri 0830-1100.
Japan, *Av San Felipe 356, Jesús María, T01-218
1130, F01-463 0302*. Mon-Fri 0900-1200.
Netherlands, *Av Principal 190, Santa Catalina,
La Victoria, T01-476 1069 www.hys.com.pe/nl/*
Mon-Fri 0900-1200. **New Zealand**, *Av
Camino Real 390, Torre Central, 17th floor
(Casilla 3553), San Isidro, T01-221 0475,
2012527@POL.com.pe* Mon-Fri 0830-1300,
1400-1700. **South African Consulate**, *Av
Natalio Sánchez 125, Santa Beatriz, T01-422
2280, saemb@amauta.rcp.net.pe* **Spain**,
*Jorge Basadre 498, San Isidro, T01-440 6998,
embesppa@correp.mae.es* Mon-Fri
0900-1300. **Sweden**, *Camino Real 348, Torre
El Pilar, 9th floor, San Isidro, T01-212 5800,
swedemb@mail.cosapidata.com.pe* 0800-
1200. **Switzerland**, *Av Salaverry 3240, San
Isidro, T01-264 0305, Vertretung@lim.rcp.
admin.ch* Mon-Fri 0900-1300. **UK**, *Torre
Parque Mar, Av José Larco 1301, 22nd floor,
T01-617 3000, www.britemb.org.pe* Dec-Apr
1300-2130 (Mon and Fri 1300-1830),
Apr-Nov 1300-2130 (Fri 1300-1830). **USA**, *Av
Encalada block 17, Monterrico, Surco, T01-434
3000, http://usembassy.state.gov/lima/*
0800-1200, for emergencies after hours
T01-434 3032, the consulate is located in the
same building.

Internet and email

Lima is completely inundated with internet
cafés, so you will have absolutely no problem
finding one regardless of where you are. An
hour will cost you around US$0.85-1.50.

Police and immigration

Tourist police, *Jr de la Unión, block 10,
Lima, T01-424 2053*. You should come here if
you have had property stolen. They are
friendly, helpful and speak English and some
German. **Administrative office**: *Moore 268,
 Magdalena at the 38th block of Av Brasil,
T01-460 1060/460 0844*, open daily 24 hrs.
Police (PNP, Policía Nacional del
Perú) *T01-475 2995, Lima*. They have
stations in every town. **Immigration**, *Av
España 700 y Jr Huaraz, Breña*, 0830-1500, but
they only allow people to enter until 1330.
See Getting in, page 23, for procedures on
visa extensions. Provides new entry stamps if
passport is lost or stolen.

Post offices

Central Post Office, *Jr Camaná 195*, near
the Plaza de Armas. Mon-Fri 0s730-1900,
Sat 0730-1600. **Poste Restante** is in the
same building but is considered unreliable.
Miraflores Post Office is on *Av Petit Thouars
5201*. There are many more small branches
scattered around Lima, but are less reliable.

Telephone

Telefónica There are many offices all
over Lima. Most allow collect calls but
some don't. All offer fax service (sending
and receiving). There are **payphones** all
over the city. Some accept coins, some
only phone cards and some honour both.
Phone cards can often be purchased in
the street near these booths. Some
Telefónica offices are: *Pasaje Tarata 280,
Miraflores (near Av Alcanfores); Av Bolivia
347, Lima Centre; C Porta 139, Miraflores
(near the bottom of Parque Kennedy)*.
There are also many independent
phone offices all over the city. For
full details on phone operation, see
Essentials, page 64.

Background

History

Inca Dynasty

The origins of the Inca Dynasty are shrouded in mythology. The best-known story reported by the Spanish chroniclers talks about Manco Cápac and his sister rising out of Lake Titicaca, created by the Sun as divine founders of a chosen race. This was in approximately AD 1200. Over the next 300 years the small tribe grew to supremacy as leaders of the largest empire ever known in the Americas, the four territories of Tawantinsuyo, united by Cusco as the umbilicus of the universe. The four quarters of Tawantinsuyo, all radiating out from Cusco, were: 1 Chinchaysuyo, north and northwest; 2 Cuntisuyo, south and west; 3 Collasuyo, south and east; 4 Antisuyo, east.

At its peak, just before the Spanish Conquest, the Inca Empire stretched from the Río Maule in central Chile, north to the present Ecuador-Colombia border, containing most of Ecuador, Peru, western Bolivia, northern Chile and northwest Argentina. The area was roughly equivalent to France, Belgium, Holland, Luxembourg, Italy and Switzerland combined (980,000 sq km).

The Incas, under their first ruler, Manco Cápac, migrated north to the fertile Cusco region, settling between the rivers Saphi and Tullumayo (marked today by the two Cusco streets which still bear their names). Here, they established Cusco as their capital. They were initially a small group of *ayllus*, or family-based clans, devoted to agriculture. They began their expansion gradually, by forging links over a long period of time with other ethnic groups in the area in order to acquire more land for cultivation. Successive generations of rulers were fully occupied with overcoming local rivals, such as the Colla and Lupaca to the south, and the Chanca to the northwest. The Incas had had a long-running dispute with the Chanca, a powerful people based around Ayacucho, whose lands adjoined theirs. The Inca oral histories recorded by the Spanish recount that, towards the end of the reign of Viracocha, the Chanca finally felt strong enough to launch an all-out attack on Cusco itself and that the people of Cusco emerged victorious under the command of a young general called Cusi Yupanqui, who would later take the name Inca Pachacútec (Earth changer). The hero was subsequently crowned as the new ruler.

From the start of Pachacútec's own reign in 1438, barely 100 years before the arrival of the Spanish, imperial expansion grew in earnest, the defeat of the Chanca being the trigger. With the help of his son and heir, Túpac, territory was conquered from the Titicaca Basin south into Chile, and all the north and central coast down to the Lurin Valley. The Incas also subjugated the Chimú, the highly sophisticated rival empire who had re-occupied the abandoned Moche capital at Chan Chán, in the north, near present-day Trujillo. Typical of the Inca method of government, some of the Chimú skills were assimilated into their own political and administrative system, and some Chimú nobles were even given positions in Cusco.

Perhaps the pivotal event in Inca history came in 1527 with the death of the ruler, Huayna Cápac. Civil war broke out in the confusion over his rightful successor. One of his legitimate sons, Huáscar, ruled the southern part of the empire from Cusco. Atahualpa, Huáscar's half-brother, governed Quito, the capital of Chinchaysuyo. In 1532, soon after Atahualpa had won the civil war, **Francisco Pizarro** arrived in Tumbes with 179 *conquistadores*, many on horseback. Atahualpa's army was marching south, probably for the first time, when he clashed with Pizarro at Cajamarca, in the northeastern Peruvian Andes.

This was one of the biggest cities in the Inca Empire and was where the Incas and

The children of the sun

Like any agrarian society, the Incas were avid sky watchers, but their knowledge of astronomy was naturally limited to what could be of practical use to them with regard to their farming activities. In common with other cultures throughout the world, they realized that the seasons on which their subsistence depended were governed by the apparent movement of the sun, who they called Inti, and placed at the head of their pantheon of gods. As the Inca Garcilaso de la Vega explains in his Royal Commentaries (1609), the Incas gave the name huata to the sun's annual motion, which in Quechua can mean either 'year', or 'to attach'. They believed that the sun had been created by the supreme creator god Viracocha, who caused it to rise from an island on Lake Titicaca now known as Isla del Sol, and that the moon goddess, the sun's sister, called Mama Killa, rose from the nearby island of Coatí (known today as the Island of the Moon). Lake Titicaca is central to the creation legends of the Incas, having also been the birthplace of the first two Incas (also brother and sister) and the scene of a great flood sent, it is said, by Viracocha, to punish mankind for having disobeyed his teachings. Colourful as they may seem, such myths were also central to the political structure of the Inca State, in that they established the Inca's divine right to rule, as a direct descendant of the sun god Inti and, therefore, his representative on earth.

Any agrarian society learns over time when to sow and harvest its crops by observing the cycle of nature around it. But in a planned, centralized economy governed by a self-proclaimed elite, the seasons of the year must be anticipated and, if it is to remain in power, that elite must be seen to monopolize the knowledge required for such predictions. The Incas, therefore, recruited the high priests, or tarpuntaes, who made astronomical observations from the empire's many temples dedicated to the sun, from the ranks of their own nobility, who were essentially the Inca's extended family. These priests observed solar and lunar eclipses, which were variously interpreted as the sexual union of the two astral bodies or, more calamitously, manifestations of their anger with their chosen people, a warning of the imminent death of a public figure, or indications that they themselves were under attack.

These astronomer-priests divided the year into twelve lunar months, which they themselves realized fell short of the solar year. They corrected this discrepancy by carefully following the course of the sun using cylindrical stone columns erected on the hills around the city of Cusco and measuring their shadows to calculate the solstices, placing their new year at the time of the summer solstice and their greatest celebration, Inti Raymi, during the winter solstice (June in the modern calendar). The equinoxes were calculated using a single stone pillar placed in the centre of each temple dedicated to the sun. At noon, when the stone barely cast a shadow, Inti was said to be sitting 'with all his light on the column'. As the Incas extended their empire towards present-day Ecuador, they realized that at the new temples they established, the further north they went, the more the shadow cast by the stones they erected was reduced. Quito's temple, therefore, just 22 km south of the equator, where the sun casts no shadow at midday, was held to be the favourite resting place of Inti, thereby rivalling the importance of the oldest and most venerated shrine in the empire at Qoricancha, in Cusco.

Spanish had their first showdown. Here Pizarro ambushed and captured Atahualpa and slaughtered his guards. Despite their huge numerical inferiority, the heavily armed Spaniards took advantage of an already divided Inca Empire to launch their audacious attack. The Incas attempted to save their leader by collecting the outrageous ransom demanded by Pizarro for Atahualpa's release. This proved futile as the Spanish, fearing a mobilization of Inca troops, executed the Inca leader once the treasure had been collected. There was no army coming to Atahualpa's rescue. Pizarro and his fellow *conquistador*, Diego de Almagro, had reacted hastily to a false rumour and their fatal decision was criticized at the time, including by Emperor Charles V. Pushing on to Cusco, Pizarro was at first hailed as the executioner of a traitor: Atahualpa had ordered the death of Huáscar in 1533, while himself a captive of Pizarro, and his victorious generals were bringing the defeated Huáscar to see his half-brother. Panic followed when the *conquistadores* set about sacking the Inca capital and they fought off with difficulty an attempt by Manco Inca to recapture Cusco in 1536.

Inca society

The people we call the Incas were a small aristocracy numbering only a few thousand, centred in the highland city of Cusco. They rose gradually as a small regional dynasty, similar to others in the Andes of that period, starting around AD 1200. Then, suddenly, in the mid-1400s, they began to expand explosively under Pachacútec, a sort of Andean Alexander the Great, and later his son, Túpac. Less than 100 years later, they fell before the rapacious warriors of Spain. The Incas were not the first dynasty in Andean history to dominate their neighbours, but they did it more thoroughly and went further than anyone before them.

Empire building

Enough remains today of their astounding highways, cities and agricultural terracing for people to marvel and wonder how they accomplished so much in so short a time. They seem to have been amazingly energetic, industrious and efficient – and the reports of their Spanish conquerors confirm this hypothesis.

They must also have had the willing cooperation of most of their subject peoples, most of the time. In fact, the Incas were master diplomats and alliance-builders first, and military conquerors only second, if the first method of expansion failed. The Inca skill at generating wealth by means of highly efficient agriculture and distribution brought them enormous prestige and enabled them to 'out-gift' neighbouring chiefs in huge royal feasts involving ritual outpourings of generosity, often in the form of vast gifts of textiles, exotic products from distant regions, and perhaps wives to add blood ties to the alliance. The 'out-gifted' chief was required by the Andean laws of reciprocity to provide something in return, and this would usually be his loyalty, as well as a levy of manpower from his own chiefdom.

Thus, with each new alliance the Incas wielded greater labour forces and their mighty public works programmes surged ahead. These were administered through an institution known as *mit'a*, a form of taxation through labour. The state provided the materials, such as wool and cotton for making textiles, and the communities provided skills and labour.

Mit'a contingents worked royal mines, royal plantations for producing coca leaves, royal quarries and so on. The system strove to be equitable, and workers in such hardship posts as high altitude mines and lowland coca plantations were given correspondingly shorter terms of service.

Organization

Huge administrative centres were built in different parts of the empire, where people and supplies were gathered. Articles such as textiles and pottery were produced there in large workshops. Work in these places was carried out in a festive manner, with

All roads lead to Cusco

There was a time when roads of colossal dimensions and magnificent construction crossed the difficult Andean terrain, thousands and thousands of kilometres in the most amazing network ever seen in antiquity. Through the building and management of this complex system, the Inca empire achieved both its expansion and its consolidation.

Cusco, navel of the world and capital of the powerful Tawantinsuyo, was where these roads began and ended. From the city's civic arena, Huacaypata (today's Plaza de Armas), the four trunk roads set out to each of the four (*tahua*) quarters (*suyus*) into which the empire was divided: **Chinchaysuyo** to the northwest as far as Quito and the Columbian border; **Collasuyu** to the south, incorporating the altiplano as far as Argentina and Chile; **Cuntisuyu** to the west, bound by the Pacific Ocean; and **Antisuyu** to the east and the Amazon lowlands.

The limits presented by sea and jungle made the roads to north and south into a great axis which came to be known as **Capaq Ñan** (Royal, or Principal Road). They became the Incas' symbol of power over men and over the sacred forces of nature. So marvellous were these roads that the Spaniards who saw them at the height of their glory said there was nothing comparable in all Christendom and that, for example, a young girl from court could run their length barefoot as they were even swept clean. Amazement was not the sole preserve of the Europeans, as an early chronicle reveals. A settler who lived a long way from the capital reached the road in his district and said, "At last, I have seen Cusco."

Imperial life revolved around these roads. Via them the produce of the coastal valleys and Amazonia were collected in tribute, to be exchanged prudently with those of the sierra, or to be stored for times of shortage. Whole communities were moved along these roads, to keep rebellion in check or to take the skills they possessed to another corner of the empire. These people had been conquered by armies thousands strong who advanced, unstoppable, along the roads, their supplies guaranteed at the *tambos* (storehouses) that were placed at regular intervals. News and royal decrees travelled with all haste, delivered by the famous *chasquis*, a race of men dedicated exclusively to running in relay along the roads.

While the roadbuilding did not happen all at once, the speed with which Pachacútec and his successors transformed the Andean world was incredible. In scarcely a century the most important civilization of the southern hemisphere had been created, only to be destroyed as the Spaniards capitalized on the fratricidal war between Huáscar and Atahualpa. What happened to the roads after that parallels what happened to the civilization itself. For a while the Spaniards used the very same roads which had been used to feed this immense body, only to leave it weakened and lifeless. Then, the large populations which the roads connected were exiled to live in reductions in the valleys where they could be controlled more easily and the roads, now running from one ghost town to the next, faded into oblivion.

The Incas, however, built for eternity. Many sections of the great network can be found today, not only in good condition but still in use, like the Inca Trail to Machu Picchu. Many other sections are lost under vegetation. But today Inca roads are considered of national importance and there is a hope that work will begin on their conservation, especially the singularly important Capaq Ñan.

plentiful food, drink and music. Here was Andean reciprocity at work: the subject supplied his labour, and the ruler was expected to provide generously while he did so.

Aside from *mit'a* contributions there were also royal lands claimed by the Inca as his portion in every conquered province, and worked for his benefit by the local population. Thus, the contribution of each citizen to the state was quite large, but apparently, the imperial economy was productive enough to sustain this.

Another institution was the practice of moving populations around wholesale, inserting loyal groups into restive areas, and removing recalcitrant populations to loyal areas. These movements of *mitmakuna*, as they were called, were also used to introduce skilled farmers and engineers into areas where productivity had to be raised.

Communications

The huge empire was held together by an extensive and highly efficient highway system. There were an estimated 30,000 km of major highway, most of it neatly paved and drained, stringing together the major Inca sites. Two parallel highways ran north to south, along the coastal desert strip and the mountains, and dozens of east-west roads crossing from the coast to the Amazon fringes. These roadways took the most direct routes, with wide stone stairways zigzagging up the steepest mountain slopes and rope suspension bridges crossing the many narrow gorges of the Andes.

Every 12 km or so there was a *tambo*, or way station, where goods could be stored and travellers lodged. The *tambos* were also control points, where the Inca state's accountants tallied movements of goods and people. Even more numerous than *tambos*, were the huts of the *chasquis*, or relay runners, who continually sped royal and military messages along these highways.

The Inca state kept records and transmitted information in various ways. Accounting and statistical records were kept on skeins of knotted strings known as *quipus* (see box, page 270). Numbers employed the decimal system, and colours indicated the categories being recorded. An entire class of people, known as *quipucamayocs*, existed whose job was to create and interpret these. Neither the Incas nor their Andean predecessors had a system of writing as we understand it, but there may have been a system of encoding language into *quipus*.

Archaeologists are studying this problem today. History and other forms of knowledge were transmitted via songs and poetry. Music and dancing, full of encoded information which could be read by the educated elite, were part of every major ceremony and public event information was also carried in textiles, which had for millennia been the most vital expression of Andean culture.

Textiles

Clothing carried insignia of status, ethnic origin, age and so on. Special garments were made and worn for various rites of passage. It has been calculated that, after agriculture, no activity was more important to Inca civilization than weaving. Vast stores of textiles were maintained to sustain the Inca system of ritual giving. Armies and *mit'a* workers were partly paid in textiles. The finest materials were reserved for the nobility, and the Inca emperor himself displayed his status by changing into new clothes every day and having the previous day's burned.

Most weaving was done by women and the Incas kept large numbers of 'chosen women' in female-only houses all over the empire. Among their duties was to supply textiles to the elite and the many deities, to whom the weavings were frequently given as burned offerings. These women had other duties, such as making *chicha* – the Inca corn beer which was consumed and sacrificed in vast quantities on ceremonial occasions. They also became wives and concubines to the Inca elite and loyal nobles. And some may have served as priestesses of the moon, in parallel to the male priesthood of the sun.

Religious worship

The Incas have always been portrayed as sun-worshippers, but it now seems that they were just as much mountain-worshippers. Recent research has shown that Machu Picchu was at least partly dedicated to the worship of the surrounding mountains, and Inca sacrificial victims have been excavated on frozen Andean peaks at 6,700 m. In fact, until technical climbing was invented, the Incas held the world altitude record for humans.

Human sacrifice was not common, but every other kind was, and ritual attended every event in the Inca calendar. The main temple of Cusco was dedicated to the numerous deities: the Sun, the Moon, Venus, the Pleiades, the Rainbow, Thunder and Lightning, and the countless religious icons of subject peoples which had been brought to Cusco, partly in homage, partly as hostage. Here, worship was continuous and the fabulous opulence included gold cladding on the walls, and a famous garden filled with life-size objects of gold and silver. Despite this pantheism, the Incas acknowledged an overall Creator God, whom they called Viracocha. A special temple was dedicated to him, at Raqchi, about 100 km southeast of Cusco. Part of it still stands today.

Military forces

The conquering Spaniards noted with admiration the Inca storehouse system, still well-stocked when they found it, despite several years of civil war among the Incas. Besides textiles, military equipment, and ritual objects, they found huge quantities of food. Like most Inca endeavours, the food stores served a multiple purpose: to supply feasts, to provide during lean times, to feed travelling work parties, and to supply armies on the march.

Inca armies were able to travel light and move fast because of this system. Every major Inca settlement also incorporated great halls where large numbers of people could be accommodated, or feasts and gatherings held, and large squares or esplanades for public assemblies.

Inca technology is usually deemed inferior to that of contemporary Europe. Their military technology certainly was. They had not invented iron-smelting and basically fought with clubs, palmwood spears, slings, wooden shields, cotton armour and straw-stuffed helmets. They did not even make much use of the bow and arrow, a weapon they were well aware of. Military tactics, too, were primitive. The disciplined formations of the Inca armies quickly dissolved into melees of unbridled individualism once battle was joined.

This, presumably, was because warfare constituted a theatre of manly prowess, but was not the main priority of Inca life. Its form was ritualistic. Battles were suspended by both sides for religious observance. Negotiation, combined with displays of superior Inca strength, usually achieved victory, and total annihilation of the enemy was not on the agenda.

Architecture

Other technologies, however, were superior in every way to their 16th-century counterparts: textiles, settlement planning and agriculture in particular with its sophisticated irrigation and soil conservation systems, ecological sensitivity, specialized crop strains and high productivity under the harshest conditions.

Unlike modern cities, Inca towns, or *llaqtas*, were not designed to house large, economically active populations. Inca society was essentially agrarian and, among the common people, almost everyone worked and lived on the land. The towns and cities that the Incas did build were meant to serve as residential areas for the state's administrative and religious elite. Throughout Tawantinsuyo, the *llaqtas* were divided into two zones, along blood lines, between the two principal *ayllus*, of Hanan and Urin. The streets were laid out in a simple grid pattern, with the whole forming a trapezoid. The trapezoid was the fundamental basis of Inca architecture,

Quipus: holding the strings of empire

Despite their extraordinary advances in the fields of government, agriculture, architecture, astronomy and engineering, it is generally agreed that the Incas never developed a written language. But given the phenomenal degree to which the Inca State was centrally planned and governed, it should come as no surprise to learn that they did employ a complex mnemonic device for the keeping of state records.

The *quipu* consisted of a series of strings with knots tied in them. Those *quipus* found so far by archaeologists vary in length from just a few centimetres to more than a metre. By varying the colour of the strings, and the position and type of knot, the Incas were able to record vast amounts of information related to the affairs of the empire in a series of censuses of its entire population of more than 10 million.

The *quipucamayocs*, an hereditary group trained in the art of compiling and deciphering the *quipus*, were charged with keeping a complete demographic record from births and deaths to age groups, the number of men-under-arms, marriages, and the material wealth of the empire, which comprised great storehouses like those discovered by the Spanish when they reached Cusco in 1533. These huge rectangular sheds contained everything that was grown or manufactured in an empire where private ownership was almost unknown, including grain, cloth, military equipment, coca, metal, shoes and items of clothing. All of this vast treasure, which the gold-hungry Spanish completely ignored, would have been precisely documented using *quipus*.

The Inca social system of *ayllus*, or clans, was based on groups of multiples of 10, and its arithmetical system was therefore also decimal. Apparently the concept of zero was understood but had no symbol; on those *quipus* deciphered by researchers it is represented by the absence of a knot. The data recorded on a *quipu* was calculated using an abacus, or *yupana*, which was fashioned from a rectangular tablet divided into smaller rectangular blocks, upon which grains of quinoa and corn of different colours were used to add, subtract, multiply and divide complex sums. The Spanish chronicler José de Acosta (1590) was astonished by the dexterity and exactitude of the Incas' *yupanacamayocs*, who he claimed never made a mistake and were much faster and more accurate than the Spanish accountants who used pen and paper.

While most scholars maintain that *quipus* were only used to record numbers, some others assert that they were also utilized to record other kinds of information, and that they were therefore effectively written records, or books. Recent research has suggested that the Incas employed a decimal alphabet in which consonants were represented by numbers and vowels were omitted, enabling them to communicate, and conserve, abstract concepts like poetry and storytelling on both their *quipus* and in the geometric designs of their weavings.

If such theories can be proved, they would make the Incas the inventors of written language in South America, and the *quipucamayocs* their court historians and Peru's first chroniclers.

The Incas fell short of their Andean predecessors in the better-known arts of ancient America – ceramics, textiles and metalwork – but it could be argued that their supreme efforts were made in architecture, stoneworking, landscaping, roadbuilding, and the harmonious combination of these elements. These are the outstanding survivals of Inca civilization, which still remain to fascinate the visitor: the huge, exotically close-fit blocks of stone, cut in graceful, almost sensual curves; the astoundingly craggy and inaccessible sites encircled by great sweeps of Andean scenery; the rhythmic layers of farm terracing that provided land and food to this still-enigmatic people. The finest examples of Inca architecture can be seen in the city of Cusco and throughout the Sacred Valley.

Ruling elite

The ruling elite lived privileged lives in their capital at Cusco. They reserved for themselves and privileged insiders certain luxuries such as the chewing of coca, the wearing of fine vicuña wool, and the practice of polygamy. But they were an austere people, too. Everyone had work to do, and the nobility were constantly being posted to state business throughout the empire. Young nobles were expected to learn martial skills, besides being able to read the *quipus*, speak both Quechua and the southern language of Aymara, and know the epic poems.

The Inca elite belonged to royal clans known as *panacas*, which each had the unusual feature of being united around veneration of the mummy of their founding ancestor – a previous Inca emperor, unless they happened to belong to the *panaca* founded by the Inca emperor who was alive at the time. Each new emperor built his own palace in Cusco and amassed his own wealth rather than inheriting it from his forebears, which perhaps helps to account for the urge to unlimited expansion.

This urge ultimately led the Incas to overreach themselves. Techniques of diplomacy and incorporation no longer worked as they journeyed farther from the homeland and met ever-increasing resistance from people less familiar with their ways. During the reign of Huayna Cápac, the last emperor before the Spanish invasion, the Incas had to establish a northern capital at Quito in order to cope with permanent war on their northern frontier. Following Huayna Cápac's death came a devastating civil war between Cusco and Quito, and immediately thereafter came the Spanish invasion. Tawantisuyo, the empire of the four quarters, collapsed with dizzying suddenness.

Conquest and after

Peruvian history after the arrival of the Spaniards was not just a matter of *conquistadores* versus Incas. The vast majority of the huge empire remained unaware of the conquest for many years. The Chimú and the Chachapoyas cultures of northern Peru were powerful enemies of the Incas. The Chimú developed a highly sophisticated culture and a powerful empire stretching for 560 km along the coast from Paramonga south to Casma. Their history was well recorded by the Spanish chroniclers and continued through the conquest possibly up to about 1600. The Kuelap/Chachapoyas people were not so much an empire as a loose-knit 'confederation of ethnic groups with no recognized capital' (Morgan Davis *Chachapoyas: The Cloud People*, Ontario, 1988). But the culture did develop into an advanced society with great skill in roads and monument building. Their fortress at Kuelap, in the northeast, where the Andes meet the Amazon, was known as the most impregnable in Tawantinsuyo. It remained intact against Inca attack and Manco Inca even tried, unsuccessfully, to gain refuge here against the Spaniards.

Exploration of the Vilcabamba

The Peruvian Vilcabamba remained virtually unexplored until the 20th century, both because of its geographical isolation and a lack of interest. The few travellers who went there, like the **Comte de Sartiges** in 1833, concentrated on the southwestern fringes and the site of Choquequirao.

Then in 1910 **Sir Clements Markham**, the President of the Royal Geographical Society, published *The Incas of Peru*, which focused attention on the late 'neo-Inca' period when they fled from Cusco deep into the Vilcabamba heartland after the Spanish invasion. This whetted the interest of a young American academic from Yale called **Hiram Bingham**.

Bingham's subsequent reporting of Machu Picchu in 1911 is so famous that it has at times obscured the other discoveries he made in the area: Vitcos, which the last Incas used as their capital in exile for 35 years after the Spanish had conquered the rest of their empire; and another mysterious site down below in the jungle, whose significance evaded Bingham at the time, in an area called Espíritu Pampa which he evocatively translated as 'the Plain of Ghosts'.

Over the course of two subsequent expeditions, in 1912 and 1914-15, he went on to report many other sites and cover an awe-inspiring amount of ground. It is fair to say that almost a century later, many explorers and archaeologists are still just adding footnotes and elucidations to Bingham's pioneering work.

Another less heralded but important contribution came from the mining prospector **Christian Bües**, who roamed the area in the 1920s and left a meticulously detailed map which is still used by today's explorers. He was the first to visit the remote and well-preserved ruin of Inca Wasi in the Puncuyoc hills.

Significant discoveries were made in 1941 by an American expedition led by the film-maker and anthropologist **Paul Fejos**, which investigated the Inca Trail. They found the dramatic site of Wiñay Wayna ('forever young'), which was named after an orchid found locally, and the nearby Inti Pata. The expedition was accompanied by a young scholar called **John H Rowe**, who went on over a long career to become the most influential Andeanist of his generation.

Gene Savoy made a swashbuckling entrance into the exploring world in 1964 with his discovery that the Espíritu Pampa site Bingham had partially found down in the jungle 50 years before was actually far larger than had been suspected. It could now be properly identified as the site of Old Vilcabamba, the city the Incas escaped to right at the end of their 'kingdom in exile' when they were driven out of Vitcos. The Spanish burnt and looted it in 1572 before capturing Túpac Amaru.

Savoy's methods were often unorthodox and his work at Espíritu Pampa was cut short when a *denuncia* was issued against him by the local community. A search party was sent down from Lima to apprehend him, led by an American archaeologist called **Gary Ziegler**. Savoy escaped and has since concentrated very successfully on exploring Chachapoyas in the north.

In the 1980s, an architect and ex-Marine called **Vince Lee** retraced much of Savoy's route and made positive identifications of many old Inca fortresses along the way. Lee brought draughtsmanship and some much-needed humour to the study of Inca ruins in the area, as the title of his entertaining book *Sixpac Manco* exemplifies.

My own introduction to exploration in the area came at roughly the same time, when I joined some of the reconnaissance groups organized by the Cusichaca Project, run by British archaeologist Ann Kendall, who reported on the area around the Aobamba and Santa Teresa valleys.

The Vilcabamba became difficult to travel in during the height of the Sendero Luminoso years and it was not until 2002 that interest in the area was reawakened with the discovery of a hill-top Inca site on Cerro Victoria by a National Geographic team led by Peter Frost and Gary Ziegler – the same Ziegler who had chased after Gene Savoy several decades before.

This was followed in the same year by the discovery of another site by Ziegler and myself called Cota Coca, which lies in the lower Yanama Valley and has been concealed for many years because the sides of that valley have collapsed.

In 2003, another Thomson – Ziegler Research Expedition, this time supported by the Royal Geographical Society, used thermal imaging cameras to fly over the cloudforest and find the outlines of stone buildings beneath the vegetation. The main Inca site under investigation was called Llactapata - appropriately one of the very sites Bingham had first reported partially on, in 1912. As with Espíritu Pampa, Llactapata was found to be far larger than Bingham had initially realized.

The above is a short summary only of the many expeditions that have been made into the Vilcabamba. Unlike mountaineering and the climbing of summits, there is no 'registered log' for the discovery of Inca sites and, while I have tried to attribute each successive discovery in the area to the correct team, there may be some unpublished explorers of whom I am unaware. I apologize to anyone who may have been inadvertently omitted as a result. In the words of Vince Lee: "I don't know who you are. I wish I did."

Why are discoveries still being made here when the rest of the world is so well mapped? It is partly because the Vilcabamba is such a dense quadrant of twisting river canyons and thick cloudforest, making it easy to pass within 10 ft of a ruin and miss it.

Both for aesthetic and strategic reasons, the Incas chose to build on remote, isolated sites, as even the most casual visitor to Machu Picchu can observe. They also often built settlements in sectors scattered at different levels on a hillside, so that while one sector may have been found, others remain hidden.

All these factors mean that it is highly likely more ruins will be found in the years to come. The Vilcabamba has by no means given up all its secrets.

For more information see Hugh Thomson's book *The White Rock: An Exploration of the Inca Heartland* Phoenix (UK) / Overlook Penguin (USA) and the website www.thewhiterock.co.uk, which has up-to-date links with the most recent discoveries.

© Hugh Thomson 2003

In 1535, wishing to secure his communications with Spain, Pizarro founded Lima, near the ocean, as his capital. The same year Diego de Almagro set out to conquer Chile. Unsuccessful, he returned to Peru, quarrelled with Pizarro, and in 1538 fought a pitched battle with Pizarro's men at the salt pits, near Cusco. He was defeated and put to death. Pizarro, who had not been at the battle, was assassinated in his palace in Lima by Almagro's son three years later.

For the next 27 years each succeeding representative of the Kingdom of Spain sought to subdue the Inca successor state of Vilcabamba, north of Cusco, and to unify the fierce Spanish factions. Francisco de Toledo (appointed 1568) solved both problems during his 14 years in office: Vilcabamba was crushed in 1572 and the last reigning Inca, Túpac Amaru, put to death.

For the next 200 years the Viceroys closely followed Toledo's system, if not his methods. The Major Government – the Viceroy, the *Audiencia* (High Court), and *corregidores* (administrators) – ruled through the Minor Government – Indian chiefs in charge of large groups of natives – an approximation to the original Inca system.

Towards Independence

The Indians rose in 1780, under the leadership of an Inca noble who called himself Túpac Amaru II. He and many of his lieutenants were captured and put to death under torture at Cusco. Another Indian leader in revolt suffered the same fate in 1814, but this last flare-up had the sympathy of many of the locally born Spanish, who resented their status, inferior to the Spaniards born in Spain, the refusal to give them anything but the lowest offices, the high taxation imposed by the home government, and the severe restrictions upon trade with any country but Spain.

Help came to them from the outside world. José de San Martín's Argentine troops, convoyed from Chile under the protection of Lord Cochrane's squadron, landed in southern Peru on 7 September 1820. San Martín proclaimed Peruvian Independence at Lima on 28 July 1821, though most of the country was still in the hands of the Viceroy, José de La Serna. Bolívar, who had already freed Venezuela and Colombia, sent Antonio José de Sucre to Ecuador where, on 24 May 1822, he gained a victory over La Serna at Pichincha.

San Martín, after a meeting with Bolívar at Guayaquil, left for Argentina and a self-imposed exile in France, while Bolívar and Sucre completed the conquest of Peru by defeating La Serna at the battle of Junín (6 August 1824) and the decisive battle of Ayacucho (9 December 1824). For over a year there was a last stand in the Real Felipe fortress at Callao by the Spanish troops under General Rodil before they capitulated on 22 January 1826. Bolívar was invited to stay in Peru, but left for Colombia in 1826.

Modern Peru

Political developments

19th century

Independence from Spanish rule meant that power passed into the hands of the Creole elite with no immediate alternation of the colonial social system. The *contribución de indígenas*, the colonial tribute collected from the native peoples was not abolished until 1854, the same year as the ending of slavery. For much of the period since Independence Peruvian political life has been dominated by these traditional elites. Political parties have been slow to develop and the roots of much of the political conflict and instability which have marked the country's history lie in personal ambitions and in regional and other rivalries within the elite.

The early years after Independence were particularly chaotic as rival *caudillos* (political bosses) who had fought in the Independence wars vied with each other for power. The increased wealth brought about by the guano boom (the manure of seabirds had become an important fertilizer in Europe) led to greater stability, though political corruption became a serious problem under the presidency of **José Rufino Echenique** (1851-54) who paid out large sums of the guano revenues as compensation to upper-class families for their (alleged) losses in the Wars of Independence. Defeat by Chile in the War of the Pacific discredited civilian politicians even further and led to a period of military rule in the 1880s.

Early 20th century

Even though the voting system was changed in 1898, this did little to change the dominance of the elite. Voting was not secret so landowners herded their workers to the polls and watched to make sure they voted correctly. Yet voters were also lured by promises as well as threats. One of the more unusual presidents was **Guillermo Billinghurst** (1912-14) who campaigned on the promise of a larger loaf of bread for five cents, thus gaining the nickname of 'Big Bread Billinghurst'. As president he proposed a publically funded housing programme, supported the introduction of an eight hour day and was eventually overthrown by the military who, along with the elite, were alarmed at his growing popularity among the urban population.

The 1920s was dominated by **Augusto Leguía**. After winning the 1919 elections Leguía claimed that Congress was plotting to prevent him from becoming president and induced the military to help him close Congress. Backed by the armed forces, Leguía introduced a new constitution which gave him greater powers and enabled him to be re-elected in 1924 and 1929. Claiming his goal was to prevent the rise of communism, he proposed to build a partnership between business and labour. A large programme of public works, particularly involving building roads, bridges and railways, was begun, the work being carried out by poor rural men who were forced into unpaid building work. The Leguía regime dealt harshly with critics: opposition newspapers were closed and opposition leaders arrested and deported. His overthrow in 1930 ended what Peruvians call the *Oncenio* (11-year period).

The 1920s also saw the emergence of a political thinker who would have great influence in the future, not only in Peru but elsewhere in Latin America. **Juan Carlos Mariátegui**, a socialist writer and journalist, argued that the solution to Peru's problems lay in the reintegration of the Indians through land reform and the breaking up of the great landed estates.

Another influential thinker of this period was **Víctor Raúl Haya de la Torre**, a student exiled by Leguía in 1924. He returned after the latter's downfall to create the **Alianza Popular Revolucionaria Americana** (APRA), a political party calling for state control of the economy, nationalization of key industries and protection of the middle classes, which, Haya de la Torre argued, were threatened by foreign economic interests.

In 1932 APRA seized control of Trujillo; when the army arrived to deal with the rising, the rebels murdered about 50 hostages, including 10 army officers. In reprisal the army murdered about 1,000 local residents suspected of sympathizing with APRA. APRA eventually became the largest and easily the best-organized political party in Peru, but the distrust of the military and the upper class for Haya de la Torre ensured that he never became president.

A turning point in Peruvian history occurred in 1948 with the seizure of power by **General Manuel Odría**, backed by the coastal elite. Odría outlawed APRA and went on to win the 1950 election in which he was the only candidate. He pursued policies of encouraging export earnings and also tried to build up working-class support by public works projects in Lima. Faced with a decline in export earnings and the fall in world market prices after 1953, plus increasing unemployment, Odría was forced to stand down in 1956.

In 1962 Haya de la Torre was at last permitted to run for the presidency. However, although he won the largest percentage of votes he was prevented from taking office by the armed forces who seized power and organized fresh elections for 1963. In these the military obtained the desired result: Haya de la Torre came second to **Fernando Belaúnde Terry**. Belaúnde attempted to introduce reforms, particularly in the landholding structure of the sierra; when these reforms were weakened by landowner opposition in Congress, peasant groups began invading landholdings in protest.

At the same time, under the influence of the Cuban revolution, guerrilla groups began operating in the sierra. Military action to deal with this led to the deaths of an estimated 8,000 people. Meanwhile Belaúnde's attempts to solve a long-running dispute with the International Petroleum Company (a subsidiary of Standard Oil) resulted in him being attacked for selling out to the unpopular oil company and contributed to the armed forces' decision to seize power in 1968.

The 1968 coup and its legacy

This was a major landmark in Peruvian history. Led by **General Juan Velasco Alvarado**, the Junta had no intention of handing power back to the civilians. A manifesto issued on the day of the coup attacked the 'unjust social and economic order' and argued for its replacement by a new economic system 'neither capitalist nor communist'. Partly as a result of their experiences in dealing with the guerrilla movement, the coup leaders concluded that agrarian reform was a priority.

Wide-ranging land reform was launched in 1969, during which large estates were taken over and reorganized into cooperatives. By the mid-1970s, 75% of productive land was under cooperative management. The government also attempted to improve the lives of shanty-town dwellers around Lima, as well as attempting to increase the influence of workers in industrial companies. At the same time attempts were made to reduce the influence of foreign companies with the nationalization of several transnationals.

Understandably, opposition to the Velasco government came from the business and landholding elite. The government's crack-down on expressions of dissent, the seizure of newspapers and taking over of TV and radio stations all offended sections of the urban middle class. Trade unions and peasant movements found that, although they agreed with many of the regime's policies, it refused to listen and expected their passive and unqualified support. As world sugar and copper prices dropped, inflation rose and strikes increased. Velasco's problems were further increased by opposition within the armed forces and by his own ill health. In August 1975 he was replaced by **General Francisco Morales Bermúdez**, a more conservative officer, who dismantled some of Velasco's policies and led the way to a restoration of civilian rule.

Belaúnde returned to power in 1980 by winning the first elections after military rule. His government was badly affected by the 1982 debt crisis and the 1981-83 world recession, and inflation reached over 100% a year in 1983-84. His term was also marked by the growth of the Maoist guerrilla movement **Sendero Luminoso** (Shining Path) and the smaller **Túpac Amaru** (MRTA).

Initially conceived in the University of Ayacucho, Shining Path gained most support for its goal of overthrowing the whole system of Lima-based government from highland Indians and migrants to urban shanty towns. The activities of Sendero Luminoso and Túpac Amaru (MRTA) frequently disrupted transport and electricity supplies, although their strategies had to be reconsidered after the arrest of both their leaders in 1992. Víctor Polay of MRTA was arrested in June and Abimael Guzmán of Sendero Luminoso was captured in September and sentenced to life imprisonment. Although Sendero did not capitulate, many of its members took advantage of the Law of Repentance, which guaranteed lighter sentences in return for surrender, and freedom in exchange for valuable information. Meanwhile, Túpac Amaru was thought to have ceased operations (see below).

In 1985 APRA, in opposition for over 50 years, finally came to power. With Haya de la Torre dead, the APRA candidate **Alan García Pérez** won the elections and was allowed to take office by the armed forces. García attempted to implement an ambitious economic programme intended to solve many of Peru's deep-seated economic and social problems. He cut taxes, reduced interest rates, froze prices and devalued the currency. However, the economic boom which this produced in 1986-87 stored up problems as increased incomes were spent on imports. Moreover, the government's refusal to pay more than 10% of its foreign debt meant that it was unable to borrow. In 1988 inflation hit 3,000% and unemployment soared. By the time his term of office ended in 1990 Peru was bankrupt and García and APRA were discredited.

Fujimori and after

In presidential elections held over two rounds in 1990, **Alberto Fujimori** of the Cambio 90 movement defeated the novelist **Mario Vargas Llosa**, who belonged to the Fredemo (Democratic Front) coalition. Fujimori, without an established political network behind him, failed to win a majority in either the senate or the lower house. Lack of congressional support was one of the reasons behind the dissolution of congress and the suspension of the constitution on 5 April 1992.

President Fujimori declared that he needed a freer hand to introduce market reforms and combat terrorism and drug trafficking, at the same time as rooting out corruption. Initial massive popular support, although not matched internationally, did not evaporate. In elections to a new, 80-member Democratic Constituent Congress (CCD) in November 1992, Fujimori's Cambio 90/Nueva Mayoría coalition won a majority of seats. A new constitution drawn up by the CCD was approved by a narrow majority of the electorate in October 1993. Among the new articles were the immediate re-election of the president (previously prohibited for one presidential term), the death penalty for terrorist leaders, the establishment of a single-chamber congress, the reduction of the role of the state, the designation of Peru as a market economy and the favouring of foreign investment. As expected, Fujimori stood for re-election on 9 April 1995 and the opposition chose as an independent to stand against him former UN General Secretary, Javier Pérez de Cuéllar. Fujimori was re-elected by a resounding margin, winning about 65% of the votes cast. The coalition that supported him also won a majority in Congress.

The government's success in most economic areas did not appear to accelerate the distribution of foreign funds for social projects. Rising unemployment and the austerity imposed by economic policy continued to cause hardship for many, despite the government's stated aim of alleviating poverty.

Dramatic events on 17 December 1996 thrust several of these issues into sharper focus: 14 Túpac Amaru guerrillas infiltrated a reception at the Japanese Embassy in Lima, taking 490 hostages. Among the rebels' demands were the release of their imprisoned colleagues, better treatment for prisoners and new measures to raise living standards. Most of the hostages were released and negotiations were pursued during a stalemate that lasted until 22 April 1997. The president took sole responsibility for the successful, but risky assault which freed all the hostages (one died of heart failure) and killed all the terrorists.

The popularity that Fujimori garnered from not yielding to Túpac Amaru deflected attention from his plans to stand for a third term following his unpopular manipulation of the law to persuade Congress that the new constitution did not apply to his first period in office. By 1998, opposition to Fujimori standing again had gained a substantial following, but not enough to dissuade the president or his supporters. Until the last month of campaigning for the 2000 presidential elections, Fujimori had a clear lead over his two main rivals, ex-mayor of Lima Alberto Andrade and former social security chief Luis Castaneda. Meanwhile, the popularity of a fourth candidate,

Alejandro Toledo, a former World bank official of humble origins, surged to such an extent that he and Fujimori were neck and neck in the first poll. Toledo, a pro-marketeer given to left-wing rhetoric, and his supporters claimed that Fujimori's slim majority was the result of fraud, a view echoed in the pressure put on the president, by the US government among others, to allow a second ballot.

The run-off election, on 28 May 2000, was also contentious since foreign observers, including the Organization of American States, said the electoral system was unprepared and flawed, proposing a postponement. The authorities refused to delay. Toledo boycotted the election and Fujimori was returned unopposed, but with scant approval. Having won, he proposed "to strengthen democracy".

This pledge proved to be utterly worthless following the airing of a secretly shot video on 14 September 2000 of Fujimori's close aide and head of the National Intelligence Service (SIN), Vladimiro Montesinos, handing US$15,000 to a congressman, Alberto Kouri, to persuade him to switch allegiances to Fujimori's coalition. Fujimori's demise was swift. His initial reaction was to close down SIN and announce new elections, eventually set for 8 April 2001, at which he would not stand.

Montesinos was declared a wanted man and fled to Panama, where he was denied asylum. He returned to Peru in October, prompting First Vice-president Francisco Tudela to resign in protest over Montesinos' continuing influence. Fujimori personally led the search parties to find his former ally and Peruvians watched in amazement as this game of cat-and-mouse was played out on their TV screens.

While Montesinos himself successfully evaded capture, investigators began to uncover the extent of his empire, which held hundreds of senior figures in its web. His activities encompassed extortion, money-laundering, bribery, intimidation, probably arms and drugs dealing and possibly links with the CIA and death squads. Swiss bank accounts in his name were found to contain about US$70 million, while other millions were discovered in accounts in the Cayman Islands and elsewhere.

Meanwhile, Fujimori, apparently in pursuit of his presidential duties, made various overseas trips, including to Japan. Here, on 20 November, he sent Congress an email announcing his resignation. Congress rejected this, firing him instead on charges of being 'morally unfit' to govern. An interim president, Valentín Paniagua, was sworn in, with ex-UN Secretary General Javier Pérez de Cuéllar as Prime Minister, and the government set about uncovering the depth of corruption associated with Montesinos and Fujimori. Further doubt was cast over the entire Fujimori period by suggestions that he may not have been born in Peru, as claimed, but in Japan. If he was indeed Japanese by birth as well as ancestry, he should never have been entitled to stand for the highest office in Peru.

In the run-up to the 2001 elections, the front-runner was Alejandro Toledo, but with far from a clear majority. Ex-President Alan García emerged as Toledo's main opponent, forcing a second ballot on 3 June. Toledo won with 52% of the vote. He pledged to heal the wounds that had opened in Peru since his first electoral battle with the disgraced Fujimori, but his first year in office was marked by slow progress on both the political and economic fronts. With the poverty levels still high, few jobs created and riots in the south over the mishandling of the sale of electricity companies in 2002, Toledo's popularity began to nosedive. Voters regarded his desire to be democratic as indecisive, but he did recoup some approval points by admitting paternity of an illegitimate daughter. A series of strikes by farmers, teachers and government workers forced the president to declare a state of emergency in May 2003 to restore order.

❧ *The word coca comes from the Aymara word q'oka, which translates as 'food for travellers and workers'.*

The ancient leaf

Coca flourishes in the subtropical valleys of the eastern Andes, as well as in the Sierra Nevada de Santa Marta in Colombia, and for millennia it has been central to the daily life and religious rituals of many of the indigenous cultures of South America. The coca plant (*Erythroxylum coca*) is an evergreen shrub found in warm, fertile valleys. Its leaves are oval , 3 to 5 cm long and resemble laurel or bay leaves. Chewed with lime, which acts as a catalyst, the leaf releases a mild dose of cocaine alkaloid, numbing the senses, dulling both hunger and pain and even providing some vitamins otherwise absent in the starch-heavy diet of the highland people.

Under the Incas, the use of coca was restricted to ceremonies involving the nobility and priesthood. After the conquest the Spanish promoted it among the half-starved slaves of the mines of Huancavelica and Potosí. It wasn't until 1862 that an Austrian chemist refined the leaf to produce pure cocaine, which was subsequently marketed as a cure for opium addiction, a local anaesthetic, a tonic and (as Coca Cola) a headache remedy. In the 1970s, with the drug's growth in popularity in the US and Europe, cocaine became big business, funding entire guerrilla movements and creating multi-billion dollar fortunes for men like Colombia's Pablo Escobar.

Some ethnobiologists estimate that coca has been cultivated in the Andes for at least 4,000 years and in Ecuador archaeological discoveries from the Valdivia Period (1500 BC) seem to provide early evidence of the use of coca: ceramic figurines have been found representing men whose most outstanding features are the bulges in the cheeks characteristic of the coca chewer. The traditional consumption of coca remains an important symbol of ethnic identity for the indigenous peoples of the highlands.

Under the Incas, coca was revered as a gift from the gods and was strictly controlled by the state. It was used in religious rites and burials and for divination. After the conquest, the role of coca in indigenous religious practices and divination provoked the Catholic extirpators of idolatry to ban its use. Diego de Robles began the Western-led demonization of coca which continues to this day when he declared that it was "a plant that the devil invented for the total destruction of the natives", and it was condemned outright at the first ecclesiastical council of Lima in 1551.

However, it did not take the Spanish long to recognize the enormous business potential. As the Uruguayan historian Eduardo Galeano writes: "In the mines of Potosí in the 16th century as much was spent on European clothing for the oppressors as on coca for the oppressed. In Cusco, 400 Spanish merchants made their living from trafficking coca, one hundred thousand baskets, containing a million kilos of coca leaves, entered the silver mines of Potosí annually. The Church extracted taxes from the traffic. Inca Garcilaso de la Vega tells us, in his *Royal Commentaries*, that the greater part of the income of the bishop, canons and other church ministers came from the tithe on coca... With the few coins that they received for their work, the Indians bought coca leaves... chewing the leaves they could stand better... the inhuman tasks imposed upon them".

Today coca continues to play an important role in the lives of Peru's indigenous highlanders. The act of chewing coca is a form of social bonding; it can stave off hunger and fatigue, relieve the effects of altitude, help divine the future, or appease Mother Earth in ceremonies as old as the cultures that have guarded them so jealously through the centuries.

Background Modern Peru

In July 2002 Montesinos was convicted of usurping power and sentenced by the Peruvian anti-corruption court to nine years and four months in prison. His trial on other counts continued. In the meanwhile, Peru's Truth and Reconciliation Commission compiled its report on the violence of the 1980-2000 period. It concluded in August 2003 that at least 69,000 people, twice as many as previously estimated, died at the hands of the rebels and military forces.

Society

The most remarkable thing about Peru, population 26.5 million in 2002, is its people. For most Peruvians life is a daily struggle to survive in the face of seemingly insurmountable problems. But most people do get by, through a combination of ingenuity, determination and sheer hard work.

Peru may not be the poorest country in South America, but recent estimates put the number of poor at 49% of the population, while almost a fifth of people live in extreme poverty. Over a third of homes have no electricity or running water and a third of children suffer from chronic malnutrition.

Health

There have been major improvements in health care in recent years, but almost a third of the population have no access to public health services. The infant mortality rate is high – 37 deaths per 1,000 births – and the figure rises steeply in some rural areas where one in ten infants die within a year of birth.

Though health services are free, people still have to pay for prescribed medicines, which are very expensive, and so rarely finish a course of treatment. Lack of health education and limited primary health care also means that many women die in childbirth. Abortion is illegal in Peru, but those with cash can always find a private doctor. Those without the means to pay for a doctor run the risk of death or infection from botched abortions.

Education

Education is free and compulsory for both sexes between six and 14. There are public and private secondary schools and private elementary schools. There are 32 state and private universities, and two Catholic universities. But resources are extremely limited and teachers earn a pittance. Poorer schoolchildren don't have money to buy pencils and notebooks and textbooks are few and far between in state schools. Furthermore, many children have to work instead of attending school; a quarter of those who start primary school don't finish. This is also due to the fact that classes are taught in Spanish and those whose native tongue is Quechua, Aymara or one of the Amazonian languages find it difficult and give up.

Migration

The structure of Peruvian society, especially in the coastal cities, has been radically altered by internal migration. This movement began most significantly in the 1950s and 1960s as people from all provinces of Peru sought urban jobs in place of work on the land. It was a time of great upheaval as the old system of labour on large estates was threatened by the peasant majority's growing awareness of the imbalances between the wealthy cities and impoverished sierra. The process culminated in the agrarian reforms of the government of General Juan Velasco (1968-75). Highland-to-city migration was given renewed impetus during the war between the state and Sendero Luminoso in the 1980s. Many communities which were depopulated in that decade are now beginning to come alive again.

Culture

People

Peru has a substantial indigenous population, only smaller as a percentage of the total than Bolivia and Guatemala of the Latin American republics. The literacy rate of the indigenous population is the lowest of any comparable group in South America and their diet is 50% below acceptable levels. The highland Indians bore the brunt of the conflict between Sendero Luminoso guerrillas and the security forces, which caused thousands of deaths and mass migration from the countryside to provincial cities or to Lima. Many indigenous groups are also under threat from colonization, development and road-building projects. Long after the end of Spanish rule, discrimination, dispossession and exploitation is still a fact of life for many native Peruvians.

Quechua

According to Inca legend, the dynasty's forebears were a small group who originally lived near Lake Titicaca. They later moved to Cusco, from where they expanded to create the Inca Empire. Their culture soon covered an area from the southernmost edge of present-day Colombia, through Quito and Ecuador, Peru and Bolivia to northern Chile and Argentina. Out of this rapid expansion grew the myth that the Quechua language originated with the Incas and spread along with their influence. But linguistic evidence points to Quechua being spoken in northern and central Peru long before the Incas arrived on the scene, even though the precise starting point of the language cannot be pinpointed. So the common idea that Quechua equals Inca is misleading (for more information on this issue, visit www.shef.ac.uk/q/quechua/).

Quechua is spoken widely throughout the Andes by people of a predominantly agricultural society, growing potatoes and corn as their basic diet, largely outside the money economy. This society ranges from Bolivia to Ecuador (where the language is known as Quichua). According to some estimates, about two million Quechua-speakers cannot converse in Spanish, but there are many more Indians who now speak only Spanish. Though recognized as an official language, little effort is made to promote Quechua nationally. It is only the remoteness of many Quechua speakers which has preserved it in rural areas. This isolation has also helped preserve many ancient traditions and beliefs. See also Festivals, on page 288.

Aymara

High up in the Andes, in the southern part of Peru, lies a wide, barren and hostile plateau, the altiplano. Prior to Inca rule Tiahuanaco on Lake Titicaca was a highly organized centre for one the greatest cultures South America has ever witnessed: the Aymara people. Today, the shores of this lake and the plains that surround it remain the homeland of the Aymara. The majority live in Bolivia, the rest are scattered on the southwestern side of Peru and northern Chile. The climate is so harsh on the altiplano that, though they are extremely hard-working, their lives are very poor. They speak their own language, Aymara.

Amazonian peoples

Before the arrival of the Europeans, an estimated six million people inhabited the Amazon Basin, comprising more than 2,000 tribes or ethnic-linguistic groups who managed to adapt to their surroundings through the domestication of a great variety of animals and plants, and to benefit from the numerous nutritional, curative, narcotic and hallucinogenic properties of thousands of wild plants.

⁞ The family that weaves together...

Nowadays, and presumably for at least the last 200 to 300 years, the women weave most of the men's garments and the men weave the women's, or at least a very important part of them: the men weave the women's skirts. It works like this: the women weave the fine warp-faced pieces like *llicllas* (*mantas*), ponchos, *chumpis* (belts), *ch'uspas*, and similar items. But the plainer elements, men's pantaloons, women's skirts, the colourful wide *golones* (the decorative edging attached to them) are woven by men on large treadle looms, imported from Europe soon after the conquest. The men also weave the thick blankets, but on heavier versions of the traditional backstrap loom (or waist loom). The men are also the knitters and crochet makers. There are a few elements of Andean garb that are not woven at all, the most important being the *chullo* (the classic wool cap with the earl flaps), but there are also *chullos* for children of either sex and, in some areas like Pitumarca, for young girls until puberty. All of these are knitted, the preferred alternative to the standard knitting needles being the spokes of bicycle wheels.

It's not easy to determine the precise origin of these aboriginal people. What is known, however, is that since the start of colonial times this population slowly but constantly decreased, mainly because of western diseases such as influenza and measles. This demographic decline reached dramatic levels during the rubber boom of the late 19th and early 20th centuries as a result of forced labour and slavery.

Today, at the basin level, the population is calculated at no more than two million inhabitants making up 400 ethnic groups, of which approximately 200,000 to 250,000 live in the Peruvian jungle. Within the basin it is possible to distinguish at least three large conglomerates of aboriginal societies: the inhabitants of the *varzea*, or seasonally flooded lands alongside the large rivers (such as the Omagua, Cocama and Shipibo people); the people in the interfluvial zones or firm lands (such as the Amahuaca, Cashibo and Yaminahua) and those living in the Andean foothills (such as the Amuesha, Ashaninka and Matsigenka).

The Amazonian natives began to be decimated in the 16th century, and so were the first endangered species of the jungle. These communities still face threats to their traditional lifestyles, notably from timber companies, gold miners and multinational oil giants. There appears to be little effective control of deforestation and the intrusion of colonists who have taken over native lands to establish small farms. And though oil companies have reached compensation agreements with local communities, previous oil exploration has contaminated many jungle rivers, as well as exposing natives to risk from diseases against which they have no immunity.

Criollos and mestizos

The first immigrants were the Spaniards who followed Pizarro's expeditionary force. Their effect, demographically, politically and culturally, has been enormous. They intermarried with the indigenous population and the children of mixed parentage were called mestizos. The Peruvian-born children of Spanish parents were known as *criollos*, though this word is now used to describe people who live on the coast, regardless of their ancestry, and coastal culture in general.

Afro-Peruvians

Peru's black community is based on the coast, mainly in Chincha, south of Lima, and also in some working-class districts of the capital. Their forefathers were originally imported into Peru in the 16th century as slaves to work on the sugar and cotton plantations on the coast. Though small – between 2% and 5% of the total population – the black community has had a major influence on Peruvian culture, particularly in music and dancing and cuisine.

Asian immigrants

There are two main Asian communities in Peru, the Japanese and Chinese. Large numbers of poor Chinese labourers were brought to Peru in the mid-19th century to work in virtual slavery on the guano reserves on the Pacific Coast and to build the railroads in the central Andes. The culinary influence of the Chinese can be seen in the many *chifas* found throughout the country.

The Japanese community, now numbering some 100,000, established itself in the first half of the 20th century. The normally reclusive community gained prominence when Alberto Fujimori, one of its members, became the first president of Japanese descent outside Japan anywhere in the world. During Fujimori's presidency, many other Japanese Peruvians took prominent positions in business, central and local government. Despite the nickname 'chino', which is applied to anyone of Oriental origin, the Japanese and Japan are respected for their industriousness and honesty (well, most of them, anyway).

Europeans

Like most of Latin America, Peru received many emigrés from Europe seeking land and opportunities in the late 19th century. The country's wealth and political power remains concentrated in the hands of this small and exclusive class of whites, which also consists of the descendants of the first Spanish families. There still exists a deep divide between people of European descent and the old colonial snobbery persists.

Religion

The Inca religion (described on page 269) was displaced by Roman Catholicism from the 16th century onwards, the conversion of the inhabitants of the 'New World' to Christianity being one of the stated aims of the Spanish *conquistadores*. Today, official statistics state that 92.5% of the population declares itself Catholic.

One of the first exponents of Liberation Theology, under which the Conference of Latin American Bishops in 1968 committed themselves to the 'option for the poor', was Gustavo Gutiérrez, from Huánuco. This doctrine caused much consternation to orthodox Catholics, particularly those members of the Latin American church who had traditionally aligned themselves with the oligarchy. Gutiérrez, however, traced the church's duty to the voiceless and the marginalized back to Fray Bartolomé de las Casas.

The Catholic Church faced a further challenge to its authority when President Fujimori won the battle over family planning and the need to slow down the rate of population growth. Its greatest threat, however, comes from the proliferation of evangelical Protestant groups throughout the country. Some 5.5% of the population now declare themselves Protestant and one million or more people belong to some 27 different non-Catholic denominations.

Although the vast majority of the population ostensibly belongs to the Roman Catholic religion, in reality religious life for many Peruvians is a mix of Catholic beliefs imported from Europe and indigenous traditions based on animism, the worship of deities from the natural world such as mountains, animals and plants. Some of these ancient indigenous traditions and beliefs are described throughout this section.

Arts and crafts

Peru is exceptionally rich in handicrafts. Its geographic division into four distinct regions – coast, mountains, valleys and Amazon Basin – coupled with cultural differences, has resulted in numerous variations in technique and design. Each province, even each community, has developed its own style of weaving or carving.

The Incas inherited 3,000 years of skills and traditions: gold, metal and precious stonework from the Chimú; feather textiles from the Nasca; and the elaborate textiles of the Paracas. All of these played important roles in political, social and religious ceremonies. Though much of this artistic heritage was destroyed by the Spanish conquest, the traditions adapted and evolved in numerous ways, absorbing new methods, concepts and materials from Europe while maintaining ancient techniques and symbols.

Textiles and costumes

Woven cloth was the most highly prized possession and sought after trading commodity in the Andes in pre-Columbian times. It is, therefore, not surprising that ancient weaving traditions have survived. **The Incas** inherited this rich weaving tradition. They forced the Aymaras to work in *mit'as* or textile workshops. The ruins of some enormous *mit'as* can be seen at the temple of Raqchi, south of Cusco (see page 205). Inca textiles are of high quality and very different from coastal textiles, being warp-faced, closely woven and without embroidery. The largest quantities of the finest textiles were made specifically to be burned as ritual offerings – a tradition which still survives. The Spanish, too, exploited this wealth and skill by using the *mit'as* and exporting the cloth to Europe.

Prior to Inca rule Aymara men wore a tunic (*llahua*) and a mantle (*llacata*) and carried a bag for coca leaves (*huallquepo*). The women wore a wrapped dress (*urku*) and mantle (*iscayo*) and a belt (*huaka*); their coca bag was called an *istalla*. The *urku* was fastened at shoulder level with a pair of metal *tupu*, the traditional Andean dress-pins.

The Inca men had tunics (*unkus*) and a bag for coca leaves called a *ch'uspa*. The women wore a blouse (*huguna*), skirts (*aksu*) and belts (*chumpis*), and carried foodstuffs in large, rectangular cloths called *llicllas*, which were fastened at the chest with a single pin or a smaller clasp called a *ttipqui*. Women of the Sacred Valley now wear a layered, gathered skirt called a *pollera* and a *montera*, a large, round, red Spanish type of hat. Textiles continue to play an important part in society. They are still used specifically for ritual ceremonies and some even held to possess magical powers.

Textile materials and techniques

The Andean people used mainly alpaca or llama wool. The former can be spun into fine, shining yarn when woven and has a lustre similar to that of silk, though sheep's wool came to be widely used following the Spanish conquest.

A commonly used technique is the drop spindle. A stick is weighted with a wooden wheel and the raw material is fed through one hand. A sudden twist and drop in the spindle spins the yarn. This very sensitive art can be seen practised by women while herding animals in the fields. Spinning wheels were introduced by Europeans and are now prevalent owing to increased demand. Pre-Columbian looms were often portable and those in use today are generally similar. A woman will herd her animals while making a piece of costume, perhaps on a backstrap loom, or waist loom, so-called because the weaver controls the tension on one side with her waist with the other side tied to an upright or tree. The pre-Columbian looms are usually used for personal costume while the treadle loom is used by men for more commercial pieces.

The skills of **dyeing** were still practised virtually unchanged even after the arrival of the Spanish. Nowadays, the word *makhnu* refers to any natural dye, but originally was the name for cochineal, an insect which lives on the leaves of the nopal cactus. These dyes were used widely by pre-Columbian weavers. Today, the biggest centre of production in South America is the valleys around Ayacucho. Vegetable dyes are also used, made from the leaves, fruit and seeds of shrubs and flowers and from lichen, tree bark and roots.

Pottery

Inca ceramic decoration consists mainly of small-scale geometric and usually symmetrical designs. One distinctive form of vessel which continues to be made and used is the *arybola*. This pot is designed to carry liquid, especially *chicha*, and is secured with a rope on the bearer's back. It is believed that *arybolas* were used mainly by the governing Inca elite and became important status symbols. Today, Inca-style is very popular in Cusco and Pisac.

With the Spanish invasion many indigenous communities lost their artistic traditions, others remained relatively untouched, while others still combined Hispanic and indigenous traditions and techniques. The Spanish brought three innovations: the potter's wheel, which gave greater speed and uniformity; knowledge of the enclosed kiln; and the technique of lead glazes. The enclosed kiln made temperature regulation easier and allowed higher temperatures to be maintained, producing stronger pieces. Today, many communities continue to apply prehispanic techniques, while others use more modern processes.

Jewellery and metalwork

Some of the earliest goldwork originates from the Chavín culture – eg the *Tumi* knife found in Lambayeque. These first appeared in the Moche culture, when they were associated with human sacrifice. Five centuries later, the Incas used *Tumis* for surgical operations such as trepanning skulls. Today, they are a common motif.

The Incas associated gold with the sun. However, very few examples remain as the Spanish melted down their amassed gold and silver objects. They then went on to send millions of Indians to their deaths in gold and silver mines.

During the colonial period gold and silver pieces were made to decorate the altars of churches and houses of the elite. Metalworkers came from Spain and Italy to develop the industry. The Spanish preferred silver and strongly influenced the evolution of silverwork during the colonial period. A style known as Andean baroque developed around Cusco embracing both indigenous and European elements. Silver bowls in this style – *cochas* – are still used in Andean ceremonies.

Woodcarving

Wood is one of the most commonly used materials. Carved ceremonial objects include drums, carved sticks with healing properties, masks and the Incas' *keros* – wooden vessels for drinking *chicha*. *Keros* come in all shapes and sizes and were traditionally decorated with scenes of war, local dances, or harvesting coca leaves. The Chancay, who lived along the coast between 100 BC and AD 1200, used *keros* carved with sea birds and fish. Today, they are used in some Andean ceremonies, especially during **Fiesta del Cruz**, the Andean May festival.

Glass mirrors were introduced by the Spanish, although the Chimú and Lambayeque cultures used obsidian and silver plates, and Inca *chasquis* (messengers) used reflective stones to communicate between hilltop forts. Transporting mirrors was costly, therefore they were produced in Lima and Quito. Cusco and Cajamarca then became centres of production. In Cusco the frames were carved, covered in gold leaf and decorated with tiny pieces of cut mirror. Cajamarca artisans, meanwhile, incorporated painted glass into the frames.

Gourd-carving, or *mate burilado*, as it is known, is one of Peru's most popular and traditional handicrafts. It is thought even to predate pottery – engraved gourds found on the coast have been dated to some 3,500 years ago. During the Inca empire gourd-carving became a valued art form and workshops were set up and supported by the state. Gourds were used in rituals and ceremonies and to make *poporos* – containers for the lime used while chewing coca leaves.

Music and dance

The music of Peru can be described as the very heartbeat of the country. Peruvians see music as something in which to participate, and not as a spectacle. Just about everyone, it seems, can play a musical instrument or sing. Just as music is the heartbeat of the country, so dance conveys the rich and ancient heritage that typifies much of the national spirit. Peruvians are tireless dancers and dancing is the most popular form of entertainment. Unsuspecting travellers should note that once they make that first wavering step there will be no respite until they collapse from exhaustion.

Each region has its own distinctive music and dance that reflects its particular lifestyle, its mood and its physical surroundings. The music of the sierra, for example, is played in a minor key and tends to be sad and mournful, while the music of the lowlands is more up-tempo and generally happier. Peruvian music divides at a very basic level into that of the highlands (*Andina*) and that of the coast (*Criolla*).

Highlands When people talk of Peruvian music they are almost certainly referring to the music of the Quechua- and Aymara-speaking Indians of the highlands which provides the most distinctive Peruvian sound. The highlands themselves can be very roughly subdivided into some half dozen major musical regions, of which perhaps the most characteristic are Ancash and the north, the Mantaro Valley, Cusco, Puno and the Altiplano, Ayacucho and Parinacochas.

Urban and other styles Owing to the overwhelming migration of peasants into the barrios of Lima, most types of Andean music and dance can be seen in the capital, notably on Sundays at the so-called *Coliseos*, which exist for that purpose. This flood of migration to the cities has also meant that the distinct styles of regional and ethnic groups have become blurred. One example is **Chicha music**, which comes from the *pueblos jóvenes*, and was once the favourite dance music of Peru's urban working class. *Chicha* is a hybrid of Huayno music and the Colombian cumbia rhythm – a meeting of the highlands and the tropical coast.

Another recent phenomenon is **tecno-cumbia**, which originated in the jungle region with groups such as **Rossy War**, from Puerto Maldonado, and **Euforia**, from Iquitos. It is a vibrant dance music which has gained much greater popularity across Peruvian society than *chicha* music ever managed. There are now also many exponents on the coast such as **Agua Marina** and **Armonía 10**. Many of the songs comment on political issues and Fujimori used to join **Rossy War** on stage.

Música criolla, the music from the coast, could not be more different from that of the sierra. Here the roots are Spanish and African. The immensely popular **Valsesito** is a syncopated waltz that would certainly be looked at askance in Vienna and the **Polca** has also undergone an attractive sea change.

Reigning over all, though, is the **Marinera**, Peru's national dance, a splendidly rhythmic and graceful courting encounter and a close cousin of Chile's and Bolivia's *Cueca* and the Argentine *Zamba*, all of them descended from the *zamacueca*. The Marinera has its *Limeña* and *Norteña* versions and a more syncopated relative, the *Tondero*, found in the northern coastal regions, is said to have been influenced by slaves brought from Madagascar.

All these dances are accompanied by guitars and frequently the *cajón*, a resonant wooden box on which the player sits, pounding it with his hands. Some of the great names of *música criolla* are the singer/composers **Chabuca Granda** and **Alicia Maguiña**, the singer **Jesús Vásquez** and the groups **Los Morochucos** and **Hermanos Zañartu**.

Afro-Peruvian Also on the coast is the music of the small but influential black community, the *Música Negroide* or *Afro-Peruano*, which had virtually died out when it was resuscitated in the 1950s, but has since gone from strength to strength, thanks to **Nicomedes and Victoria Santa Cruz** who have been largely responsible for popularizing this black music and making it an essential ingredient in contemporary Peruvian popular music. It has all the qualities to be found in black music from the Caribbean – a powerful, charismatic beat, rhythmic and lively dancing, and strong percussion provided by the *cajón* and the *quijada de burro*, a donkey's jaw with the teeth loosened. Its greatest star is the Afro-Peruvian diva **Susana Baca**. Her incredible, passionate voice inspired Talking Head's David Byrne to explore this genre further and release a compilation album in 1995, thus bringing Afro-Peruvian music to the attention of the world. Another notable exponent is the excellent **Perú Negro**, one of the best music and dance groups in Latin America.

Musical instruments Before the arrival of the Spanish in Latin America, the only instruments were wind and percussion. Although it is a popular misconception that Andean music is based on the panpipes, guitar and *charango*, anyone who travels through the Andes will realize that these instruments only represent a small aspect of Andean music. The highland instrumentation varies from region to region, although the harp and violin are ubiquitous. In the Mantaro area the harp is backed by brass and wind instruments, notably the clarinet. In Cusco it is the *charango* and *quena* and on the altiplano the *sicu* panpipes.

The *quena* is a flute, usually made of reed, characterized by not having a mouthpiece to blow through. As with all Andean instruments, there is a family of *quenas* varying in length from around 15 cm to 50 cm. The *sicu* is the Aymara name for the *zampoña*, or panpipes. It is the most important prehispanic Andean instrument, formed by several reed tubes of different sizes held together by knotted string. Virtually the only instrument of European origin is the *charango*. When stringed instruments were first introduced by the Spanish, the indigenous people liked them but wanted something that was their own and so the *charango* was born. Originally, they were made of clay, condor skeletons and armadillo or tortoise shells.

Dances

The highlands are immensely rich in terms of music and dance, with over 200 dances recorded. Every village has its fiestas and every fiesta has its communal and religious dances. *Comparsas* are organized groups of dancers who perform for spectators dances following a set pattern of movements to a particular musical accompaniment, wearing a specific costume. These dances have a long tradition, having mostly originated from certain contexts and circumstances and some of them still parody the ex-Spanish colonial masters.

Many dances for couples and/or groups are danced spontaneously at fiestas throughout Peru. These include indigenous dances which have originated in a specific region and ballroom dances that reflect the Spanish influence. One of the most popular of the indigenous dances is the **Huayno**, which originated on the altiplano but is now danced throughout the country. It involves numerous couples, who whirl around or advance down the street, arm-in-arm, in a *pandilla*. During fiestas, and especially after a few drinks, this can develop into a kind of uncontrolled frenzy.

Festivals

Fiestas (festivals) are a fundamental part of life for most Peruvians, taking place up and down the length and breadth of the country and with such frequency that it would be hard to miss one, even during the briefest of stays. This is fortunate, because arriving in any town or village during these inevitably frenetic celebrations is one of the great Peruvian experiences.

While Peru's festivals can't rival those of Brazil for fame or colour, the quantity of alcohol consumed and the partying run them pretty close. What this means is that, at some point, you will fall over, through inebriation or exhaustion, or both. After several days of this, you will awake with a hangover the size of the Amazon rainforest and probably have no recollection of what you did with your backpack.

The object of the fiesta is a practical one, such as the success of the coming harvest or the fertility of animals. Thus the constant eating, drinking and dancing serves the purpose of giving thanks for the Sun and Rain that makes things grow and for the fertility of the soil and livestock, gifts from *Pachamama* (Mother Earth), the most sacred of all gods. So, when you see a Peruvian spill a little *chicha* (maize beer) every time they refill, it's not because they're sloppy but because they're offering a *ch'alla* (sacrifice) to Pachamama.

Literature

The fact that the Incas had no written texts in the conventional European sense and that the Spaniards were keen to suppress their conquest's culture means that there is little evidence today of what poetry and theatre was performed in pre-conquest times. It is known that the Incas had two types of poet, the *amautas* – historians, poets and teachers who composed works that celebrated the ruling class' gods, heroes and events – and *haravecs* – who expressed popular sentiments. Written Quechua today is less common than works in the oral tradition. Although Spanish culture has had some influence on Quechua, the native stories, lyrics and fables retain their own identity. Not until the 19th century did Peruvian writers begin seriously to incorporate indigenous ideas into their art, but their audience was limited. Nevertheless, the influence of Quechua on Peruvian literature in Spanish continues to grow.

Colonial period
In 16th-century Lima, headquarters of the Viceroyalty of Peru, the Spanish officials concentrated their efforts on the religious education of the new territories and literary output was limited to mainly histories and letters.

Chroniclers such as **Pedro Cieza de León** (*Crónica del Perú*, published from 1553) and **Agustín de Zárate** (*Historia del descubrimiento y conquista del Perú*, 1555) were written from the point of view that Spanish domination was right. Their most renowned successors, though, took a different stance. **Inca Garcilaso de la Vega** was a mestizo, whose *Comentarios reales que tratan del origen de los Incas* (1609) were at pains to justify the achievements, religion and culture of the Inca Empire. He also commented on Spanish society in the colony. A later work, *Historia general del Perú* (1617), went further in condemning Viceroy Toledo's suppression of Inca culture. Through his work, written in Spain, many aspects of Inca society, plus poems and prayers have survived.

Writing at about the same time as Inca Garcilaso was **Felipe Guaman Poma de Ayala**, whose *El primer nueva corónica y buen gobierno* (1613-15) is possibly one of the most reproduced of Latin American texts (eg on T-shirts, CDs, posters and carrier bags). Guaman Poma was a minor provincial Inca chief whose writings and illustrations, addressed to King Felipe III of Spain, offer a view of a stable pre-conquest Andean society (not uniquely Inca), in contrast with the unsympathetic colonial society that usurped it.

In the years up to Independence, the growth of an intellectual elite in Lima spawned more poetry than anything else. As *criollo* discontent grew, satire increased both in poetry and in the sketches which accompanied dramas imported from Spain. The poet **Mariano Melgar** (1791-1815), who wrote in a variety of styles, died in an uprising against the Spanish but played an important part in the Peruvian struggle from freedom from the colonial imagination.

After Independence

After Independence, Peruvian writers imitated Spanish *costumbrismo*, sketches of characters and lifestyles from the new Republic. The first author to transcend this fashion was **Ricardo Palma** (1833-1919), whose inspiration, the *tradición*, fused *costumbrismo* and Peru's rich oral traditions. Palma's hugely popular *Tradiciones peruanas* is a collection of pieces which celebrate the people, history and customs of Peru through sayings, small incidents in mainly colonial history and gentle irony.

Much soul-searching was to follow Peru's defeat in the War of the Pacific. **Manuel González Prada** (1844-1918), for instance, wrote essays fiercely critical of the state of the nation: *Páginas libres* (1894), *Horas de lucha* (1908). **José Carlos Mariátegui**, the foremost Peruvian political thinker of the early 20th century, said that González Prada represented the first lucid instant of Peruvian consciousness.

20th century

Mariátegui himself (1895-1930), after a visit to Europe in 1919, considered deeply the question of Peruvian identity, writing about politics, economics, literature and the Indian question from a Marxist perspective (see *Siete ensayos de interpretación de la realidad peruana*, 1928). Other writers had continued this theme. **Clorinda Matto de Turner** (1854-1909), with *Aves sin nido* (1889), was the forerunner by several years of the 'indigenist' genre in Peru and the most popular of those who took up González Prada's cause. Other prose writers continued in this vein at the beginning of the 20th century, but it was **Ciro Alegría** (1909-67) who gave major, fictional impetus to the racial question. Of his first three novels, *La serpiente de oro* (1935), *Los perros hambrientos* (1938) and *El mundo es ancho y ajeno* (1941), the latter is his most famous.

Contemporary with Alegría was **José María Arguedas** (1911-69), whose novels, stories and politics were also deeply rooted in the ethnic question. Arguedas, though not Indian, had a largely Quechua upbringing and tried to reconcile this with the hispanic world in which he worked. This inner conflict was one of the main causes of his suicide. His books include *Agua* (short stories, 1935), *Yawar fiesta* (1941), *Los ríos profundos* (1958) and *Todas las sangres* (1964).

In the 1950s and 1960s, there was a move away from the predominantly rural and indigenist to an urban setting. At the forefront were, among others, **Mario Vargas Llosa**, **Julio Ramón Ribeyro**, **Enrique Congrains Martín**, **Oswaldo Reynoso**, **Luis Loayza**, **Sebastián Salazar Bondy** and **Carlos E Zavaleta**. They explored all aspects of the city, including the influx of people from the sierra. These writers incorporated new narrative techniques in the urban novel, which presented a world where popular culture and speech were rich sources of literary material, despite the difficulty in transcribing them.

Alfredo Bryce Echenique (born 1939) has enjoyed much popularity following the success of *Un mundo para Julius* (1970), a satire on the upper and middle classes of Lima. Other contemporary writers of note are **Sergio Bambarén**, whose 1995 debut novel, *The Dolphin – story of a dreamer,* was written in English and became a bestseller when published in Spanish, and **Jaime Bayly**, who is also a journalist and TV presenter. His novels include *Fue ayer y no me acuerdo, Los últimos días de la* prensa and *La noche es virgen*. Without doubt, the most important poet in Peru, if not Latin America, in the first half of the 20th century, was **César Vallejo**, born in 1892 in Santiago de Chuco (Libertad). In 1928 he was a founder of the Peruvian Socialist Party, then he joined the Communist Party in 1931 in Madrid. From 1936 to his death in Paris in 1938 he opposed the fascist takeover in Spain. His first volume was *Los heraldos negros* in which the dominating theme of all his work, a sense of confusion and inadequacy in the face of the unpredictability of life, first surfaces. *Trilce* (1922), his second work, is unlike anything before it in the Spanish language. *Poemas humanos* and *España, aparta de mí este cáliz* (written as a result of Vallejo's experiences in the Spanish Civil War) were both published posthumously, in 1939.

Painting

The Catholic Church was the main patron of the arts during the colonial period. The innumerable churches and monasteries that sprang up in the newly conquered territories created a demand for paintings and sculptures, met initially by imports from Europe of both works of art and of skilled craftsmen, and later by home-grown products. An essential requirement for the inauguration of any new church was an image for the altar and many churches in Lima preserve fine examples of sculptures imported from Seville during the 16th and 17th centuries. But sculptures were expensive and difficult to import, and as part of their policy of relative frugality the Franciscan monks tended to favour paintings. The Jesuits, too, tended to commission paintings and several major works by Sevillian artists can be seen in Lima's churches.

Painters and sculptors soon made their way to Peru in search of lucrative commissions including several Italians who arrived during the later 16th century. The Jesuit **Bernardo Bitti** (1548-1610), for example, trained in Rome before working in Lima, Cusco, Juli and Arequipa. European imports, however, could not keep up with demand and local workshops of creole, mestizo and Indian craftsmen flourished from the latter part of the 16th century. As the Viceregal capital and the point of arrival into Peru, the art of Lima was always strongly influenced by European, especially Spanish models, but the old Inca capital of Cusco became the centre of a regional school of painting which developed its own characteristics. A series of paintings of the 1660s, now hanging in the Museo de Arte Religioso in Cusco, commemorate the colourful Corpus Christi procession of statues of the local patron saints through the streets of Cusco. These paintings document the appearance of the city and local populace, including Spanish and Inca nobility, priests and laity, rich and poor, Spaniard, Indian, African and mestizo. Many of the statues represented in this series are still venerated in the local parish churches. They are periodically painted and dressed in new robes, but underneath are the original sculptures, executed by native craftsmen. Some are of carved wood while others use the pre-conquest technique of maguey cactus covered in sized cloth.

One of the most successful native painters was **Diego Quispe Tito** (1611-81) who claimed descent from the Inca nobility and whose large canvases, often based on Flemish engravings, demonstrate the wide range of European sources that were available to Andean artists in the 17th century. But the **Cusco School** is best known for the anonymous devotional works where the painted contours of the figures are overlaid with flat patterns in gold, creating highly decorative images with an underlying tension between the two- and three-dimensional aspects of the work. The taste for richly decorated surfaces can also be seen in the 17th- and 18th-century frescoed interiors of many Andean churches, as in Chinchero, Andahuaylillas and Huaro, and in the ornate carving on altarpieces and pulpits throughout Peru.

Land and environment

Geography

Peru is the third largest South American country, the size of France, Spain and the United Kingdom combined, and presents formidable difficulties to human habitation. Virtually all of the 2,250 km of its Pacific Coast is desert. From the narrow coastal shelf the Andes rise steeply to a high plateau dominated by massive ranges of snow-capped peaks and gouged with deep canyons. The heavily forested and deeply ravined Andean slopes are more gradual to the east. Further east, towards Brazil and Colombia, begin the vast jungles of the Amazon Basin.

Highlands

The highlands, or sierra, extend inland from the coastal strip some 250 km in the north, increasing to 400 km in the south. The average altitude is about 3,000 m and 50% of Peruvians live there. Essentially, it is a plateau dissected by dramatic canyons and dominated by some of the most spectacular mountain ranges in the world.

In spite of these ups and downs which cause great communications difficulties, the presence of water and a more temperate climate on the plateau has attracted people throughout the ages. Present day important population centres in the Highlands include Cajamarca in the north, Huancayo in central Peru and Cusco in the south, all at around 3,000 m. Above this, at around 4,000 m, is the 'high steppe' or *puna*, with constant winds and wide day/night temperature fluctuations. Nevertheless, fruit and potatoes (which originally came from the *puna* of Peru and Bolivia) are grown at this altitude and the meagre grasslands are home to the ubiquitous llama.

Eastern Andes and Amazon Basin

Almost half of Peru is on the eastern side of the Andes and about 90% of the country's drainage is into the Amazon system. It is an area of heavy rainfall with cloudforest above 3,500 m and tropical rainforest lower down. There is little savanna, or natural grasslands, characteristic of other parts of the Amazon Basin.

There is some dispute on the Amazon's source. Officially, the mighty river begins as the Marañón, whose longest tributary rises just east of the Cordillera Huayhuash. However, the longest journey for the proverbial raindrop, some 6,400 km, probably starts in southern Peru, where the headwaters of the Apurímac (Ucayali) flow from the snows on the northern side of the Nevado Mismi, near Cailloma.

With much more rainfall on the eastern side of the Andes, rivers are turbulent and erosion dramatic. Although vertical drops are not as great – there is a whole continent to cross to the Atlantic – valleys are deep, ridges narrow and jagged and there is forest below 3,000 m. At 1,500 m the Amazon jungle begins and water is the only means of surface transport available, apart from three roads which reach Borja (on the Marañón), Yurimaguas (on the Huallaga) and Pucallpa (on the Ucayali), at about 300 m above the Atlantic which is still 4,000 km or so downstream. The vastness of the Amazon lowlands becomes apparent and it is here that Peru bulges 650 km northeast past Iquitos to the point where it meets Colombia and Brazil at Leticia. Oil and gas have recently been found in the Amazon, and new finds are made every year, which means that new pipelines and roads will eventually link more places to the Pacific Coast.

Climate

In the highlands, April to October is the dry season. It is hot and dry during the day, around 20° to 25°C, and cold and dry at night, often below freezing. From November to April is the wet season, when it is dry and clear most mornings, with some rainfall in the afternoon. There is a small temperature drop (18°C) and not much difference at night (15°C). In the Amazonian lowlands April to October is the dry season, with temperatures up to 35°C. In the jungle areas of the south a cold front can pass through at night. November to April is the wet season. It is humid and hot, with heavy rainfall at any time.

Wildlife and vegetation

Peru is a country of great biological diversity. It contains 84 of the 104 recognized life zones and is one of the eight 'mega-diverse countries' on earth. The fauna and flora are to a large extent determined by the influence of the Andes, the longest uninterrupted mountain chain in the world, and the mighty Amazon river, which has by far the largest volume of any river in the world.

Andes

From the desert rise the steep Andean slopes. In the deeply incised valleys Andean fox and deer may occasionally be spotted. Herds of llamas and alpacas graze the steep hillsides. Mountain caracara and Andean lapwing are frequently observed soaring, and there is always the possibility of spotting flocks of mitred parrots or even the biggest species of hummingbird in the world (*Patagonia gigas*).

The Andean zone has many lakes and rivers and countless swamps. Exclusive to this area short-winged grebe and the torrent duck which feeds in the fast flowing rivers, and giant and horned coots. Chilean flamingo frequent the shallow soda lakes.

The *puna*, a habitat characterized by tussock grass and pockets of stunted alpine flowers, gives way to relict elfin forest and tangled bamboo thicket in this inhospitable windswept and frost-prone region. Occasionally the dissected remains of a *Puya* plant can be found; the result of the nocturnal foraging of the rare spectacled bear. There are quite a number of endemic species of rodent including the viscacha, and it is the last stronghold of the chinchilla. Here also pumas roam preying on the herbivores which frequent these mountain-pudu, Andean deer or guemal and the mountain tapir.

Tropical Andes

The elfin forest gradually grades into mist enshrouded cloudforest at about 3,500 m. In the tropical zones of the Andes, the humidity in the cloudforests stimulates the growth of a vast variety of plants particularly mosses and lichens. The cloudforests are found in a narrow strip that runs along the eastern slopes of the spine of the Andes. It is these dense, often impenetrable, forests clothing the steep slopes that are important in protecting the headwaters of all the streams and rivers that cascade from the Andes to form the mighty Amazon as it begins its long journey to the sea.

This is a verdant world of dripping epiphytic mosses, lichens, ferns and orchids which grow in profusion despite the plummeting overnight temperatures. The high humidity resulting from the 2 m of rain that can fall in a year is responsible for the maintenance of the forest and it accumulates in puddles and leaks from the ground in a constant trickle that combines to form a myriad of icy, crystal-clear tumbling streams that cascade over precipitous waterfalls.

In secluded areas the flame-red Andean cock-of-the-rock give their spectacular display to females in the early morning mists. Woolly monkeys are also occasionally sighted as they descend the wooded slopes. Mixed flocks of colourful tanagers are commonly encountered, and the golden-headed quetzal and Amazon umbrella bird are occasionally seen.

At about 1,500 m there is a gradual transition to the vast lowland forests of the Amazon Basin, which are warmer and more equable than the cloudforests clothing the mountains above. The daily temperature varies little during the year with a high of 23° to 32°C falling slightly to 20° to 26°C overnight. This lowland region receives some 2 m of rainfall per year most of it falling from November to April. The rest of the year is sufficiently dry, at least in the lowland areas to inhibit the growth of epiphytes and orchids which are so characteristic of the highland areas. For a week or two in the rainy season the rivers flood the forest. The zone immediately surrounding this seasonally flooded forest is referred to as *terre firme* forest.

The vast river basin of the Amazon is home to an immense variety of species. The environment has largely dictated the lifestyle. Life in or around rivers, lakes, swamps and forest depend on the ability to swim and climb and amphibious and tree-dwelling animals are common. Once the entire Amazon Basin was a great inland sea and the river still contains mammals more typical of the coast, eg manatees and dolphins.

Here, in the relatively constant climatic conditions, animal and plant life has evolved to an amazing diversity over the millennia. It has been estimated that 3.9 sq km of forest can harbour some 1,200 vascular plants, 600 species of tree, and 120 woody plants. In these relatively flat lands, a soaring canopy some 50 m overhead is the power-house of the forest. It is a habitat choked with strangling vines and philodendrons among which mixed troupes of squirrel monkeys and brown capuchins forage. In the high canopy small groups of spider monkeys perform their lazy aerial acrobatics, whilst lower down, clinging to epiphyte-clad trunks and branches, groups of saddle-backed and emperor tamarins forage for blossom, fruit and the occasional insect prey.

The most accessible part of the jungle is on or near the many great meandering rivers. At each bend of the river the forest is undermined by the currents during the seasonal floods at the rate of some 10 m or 20 m per year leaving a sheer mud and clay bank, whilst on the opposite bend new land is laid down in the form of broad beaches of fine sand and silt.

A succession of vegetation can be seen. The fast growing willow-like *tessaria* first stabilizes the ground enabling the tall stands of *caña brava gynerium* to become established. Within these dense almost impenetrable stands the seeds of rainforest trees germinate and over a few years thrust their way towards the light. The fastest growing is a species of *cercropia* which forms a canopy 15 m to 18 m over the *caña* but even this is relatively short-lived. The gap in the canopy is quickly filled by other species. Two types of mahogany outgrow the other trees forming a closed canopy at 40 m with a lush understory of shade-tolerant *heliconia* and ginger. Eventually even the long-lived trees die off to be replaced by others providing a forest of great diversity.

Jungle wildlife

The meandering course of the river provides many excellent opportunities to see herds of russet-brown capybara – a sheep-sized rodent – peccaries and brocket deer. Of considerable ecological interest are the presence of ox-bow lakes, or *cochas*, since these provide an abundance of wildlife which can be seen around the lake margins.

The best way to see the wildlife is to get above the canopy. Ridges provide elevated viewpoints for excellent views over the forest. From here, it is possible to look across the lowland flood plain to the very foothills of the Andes, possibly some 200 km away. Flocks of parrots and macaws can be seen flying between fruiting trees and noisy troupes of squirrel monkeys and brown capuchins come very close.

The lowland rainforest of Peru is particularly famous for its primates and giant otters. Giant otters were once widespread in Amazonia but came close to extinction in the 1960s owing to persecution by the fur trade. The giant otter population in Peru has since recovered and is now estimated to be at least several hundred. Jaguar and other

Background Land and environment

predators are also much in evidence. Although rarely seen their paw marks are commonly found along the forest trails. Rare bird species are also much in evidence, including fasciated tiger-heron and primitive hoatzins.

The (very) early morning is the best time to see peccaries, brocket deer and tapir at mineral licks (*collpa*). Macaw and parrot licks are found along the banks of the river. Here at dawn a dazzling display arrives and clambers around in the branches overhanging the clay lick. At its peak there may be 600 birds of up to six species (including red and green macaws, and blue-headed parrots) clamouring to begin their descent to the riverbank where they jostle for the mineral rich clay, a necessary addition to their diet which may also neutralize the toxins in their leaf and seed diet. Rare game birds such as razor-billed curassows and piping guans may also be seen.

A list of over 600 bird species has been compiled. Particularly noteworthy species are the black-faced cotinga, crested eagle, and the spectacular Harpy eagle, perhaps the world's most impressive raptor, easily capable of taking an adult monkey from the canopy. Mixed species flocks are commonly observed containing from 25 to over 100 birds of perhaps more than 30 species including blue dacnis, blue-tailed emerald, bananaquit, thick-billed euphoria and the paradise tanager. Each species occupies a slightly different niche, and since there are few individuals of each species in the flock, competition is avoided. Mixed flocks foraging in the canopy are often led by a white-winged shrike, whereas flocks foraging in the understorey are often led by the bluish-slate ant shrike. (For more information on the birds of Peru, see page 50.)

Books

History and culture

Alden Mason, J, *The Ancient Civilizations of Peru* (1991).
Cáceres Macedo, Justo, *The Prehispanic Cultures of Peru* (1988).
Frost, Peter, *Exploring Cusco*. On Cusco, the Sacred Valley, Inca Trail, Machu Picchu and other ruins.
Hemming, John, *The Conquest of the Incas*. Invaluable for the whole period of the conquest; he himself refers us to Kendall, Ann *Everyday Life of the Incas* (1978) Batsford.
Heyerdahl, T, Sandweiss, DH, and Narváez, A, *Pyramids of Túcume* (1995), Thames & Hudson.
Keatinge, Richard W (editor), *Peruvian Prehistory. An overview of pre-Inca and Inca Society* (1988).
Lee, Vincent R, *Forgotten Vilcabamba* Insights into the Vilcabamba region.
Mosely, Michael E, *The Incas and their Ancestors: The Archaeology of Peru*.
Portal Cabellos, Manuel, *Oro y tragedia de los Incas*. Excellent on the division of the empire, civil war, the conquest and *huaqueros*.
Reinhard, Johan, *The Sacred Center*. Explains Machu Picchu in archaeological terms.

Travel books

Cusco Peru Tourist Guide, Lima 2000. Also recommended for general information on Cusco.
Murphy, Dervla, *Eight Feet in the Andes* (1994). Describes Murphy's journey through highland Peru with her young daughter and a donkey.
Parris, Matthew, *Inca-Kola* (1990), Parris and three friends travel through Peru – adventurous, funny, a great read.
Shah, Tahir, *Trail of Feathers* (2001), Phoenix. Shah goes in search of the truth behind tales of flight in ancient Peru.
Thomson, Hugh, *The White Rock* (2002), Phoenix. Describes Thomson's own travels in the Inca heartland, as well as the journeys of earlier explorers and the history of the region ("the long-awaited, definitive travel book on Peru", John Hemming).
Wright, Ronald *Cut Stones and Crossroads: a Journey in Peru* (1984), Viking. A perceptive mixture of travelogue, history (ancient and modern) and culture.

295

Footnotes

Spanish words and phrases

Volumes of dictionaries, phrase books or word lists will not provide the same enjoyment as being able to communicate directly with the people of the country you are visiting. Learning Spanish is a useful part of the preparation for a trip to Peru and you are encouraged to make an effort to grasp the basics before you go. As you travel you will pick up more of the language and the more you know, the more you will benefit from your stay. The following section is designed to be a simple point of departure.

Whether you have been taught the 'Castilian' pronunciation (z and c followed by i/e/th are pronounced as the th in think) or the 'American' pronunciation (they are pronounced as s), you will encounter little difficulty in understanding either. Regional accents and usages vary, but the basic language is essentially the same everywhere.

Greetings, courtesies

good afternoon/evening/night	*buenas tardes/noches*
good morning	*buenos días*
goodbye	*adiós/chao*
hello	*hola*
How are you?	*¿cómo está?¿cómo estás?*
I do not understand	*no entiendo*
leave me alone	*déjeme en paz/no me moleste*
no	*no*
please	*por favor*
pleased to meet you	*mucho gusto/encantado/encantada*
see you later	*hasta luego*
thank you (very much)	*(muchas) gracias*
What is your name?	*¿cómo se llama? ¿cómo te llamas?*
yes	*sí*
I speak...	*Hablo...*
I speak Spanish	*Hablo español*
I don't speak Spanish	*No hablo español*
Do you speak English?	*¿habla inglés?*
Please speak slowly	*hable despacio por favor*
I am very sorry	*lo siento mucho/disculpe*
I'm fine, thanks	*estoy muy bien gracias*
I'm called...	*me llamo...*
What do you want?	*¿qué quiere?*
I want	*quiero*
I don't want it	*No lo quiero*
long-distance phone call	*una llamada de larga distancia*
good	*bueno*
bad	*malo*

Nationalities and languages

American	*americano/a*	French	*francés/francesa*
Australian	*australiano/a*	German	*alemán/alemana*
Austrian	*austriaco/a*	Irish	*irlandés/irlandesa*
British	*británico/a*	Italian	*italiano/a*
Canadian	*canadiense*	New Zealand	*neozelandés/neozelandesa*
Danish	*danés/danesa*	Norwegian	*noruego/a*
Dutch	*holandés/holandesa*	Portuguese	*portugués/portuguesa*
English	*inglés/inglesa*	Scottish	*escocés/escocesa*

Swedish *sueco/a*
Swiss *suizo/a*

Welsh *galés/galesa*

Basic questions

Have you got a room for two people?
¿Tiene una habitación para dos personas?
How do I get to_? *¿cómo llego a_?*
How much does it cost? *¿cuánto cuesta?*
How much is it? *¿cuánto es?*
When does the bus leave (arrive)? *¿a qué hora sale (llega) el autobús?*

When? *¿Cuándo?*
Where is_? *¿Dónde está?*
Where is the nearest petrol station?
¿dónde está el grifo más cerca?
Why? *¿por qué?*

Basics

bank *el banco*
bathroom/toilet *el baño*
bill *la factura/la cuenta*
cash *el efectivo*
cheap *barato*
church/cathedral *La iglesia/catedral*
exchange house *la casa de cambio*
exchange rate *el tipo de cambio*
expensive *caro*

market *el mercado*
notes/coins *los billetes/las monedas*
police (policeman) *la policía (el policía)*
post office *el correo*
supermarket *el supermercado*
telephone office *el centro de llamadas*
ticket office *la boletería/la taquilla*
travellers' cheques *los travelers/los cheques de viajero*

Getting around

aeroplane/airplane *el avión*
airport *el aeropuerto*
bus station *la terminal de autobús*
bus *el bus/el autobús*
minibus *la combi*
motorcycle taxi *el mototaxi*
bus route *el corredor*
first/second class *primera/segunda clase*
on the left/right *a la izquierda/derecha*

second street on the left *la segunda calle a la izquierda*
ticket *el boleto*
to walk *caminar*
Where can I buy tickets? *¿dónde se puede comprar boletos?*
Where can I park? *¿dónde se puede parquear?*

Orientation and motoring

arrival *la llegada*
avenue *la avenida*
block *la cuadra*
border *la frontera*
fixed route taxi *el colectivo*
corner *la esquina*
customs *la aduana*
departure *la salida*
east *el este, el oriente*
empty *vacío*
full *lleno*
highway, main road *la carretera*
immigration *la inmigración*
insurance *el seguro*
the insured *el asegurado/la asegurada*
to insure yourself against *asegurarse contra*
luggage *el equipaje*

motorway, freeway *el autopista/la carretera*
north *el norte*
oil *el aceite*
passport *el pasaporte*
petrol/gasoline *la gasolina*
puncture *el pinchazo*
south *el sur*
street *la calle*
that way *por allí/por allá*
this way *por aquí/por acá*
tourist card *la tarjeta de turista*
tyre *la llanta*
unleaded *sin plomo*
visa *el visado*
waiting room *la sala de espera*
west *el oeste/el poniente*

air conditioning *el aire acondicionado*
all-inclusive *todo incluido*
blankets *las mantas*
clean/dirty towels *las toallas limpias/sucias*
dining room *el comedor*
double bed *la cama matrimonial*
guesthouse *la casa de huéspedes*
hot/cold water *el agua caliente/fría*
hotel *el hotel*
Is service included? *¿está incluido el servicio?*
Is tax included? *¿están incluidos los impuestos?*
noisy *ruidoso*

pillows *las almohadas*
power cut *el apagón/corte*
restaurant *el restaurante*
room *el cuarto/la habitación*
sheets *las sábanas*
shower *la ducha*
single/double *sencillo/doble*
soap *el jabón*
to clean *limpiar*
toilet *el sanitario*
toilet paper *el papel higiénico*
with private bathroom *con baño privado*
with two beds *con dos camas*

Health

aspirin *la aspirina*
blood *la sangre*
chemist *la farmacia*
condoms *los preservativos, los condones*
contact lenses *los lentes de contacto*
contraceptive *anticonceptivo*
  (pill) *(la píldora anticonceptiva)*
diarrhoea *la diarrea*

doctor *el médico*
fever/sweat *la fiebre/el sudor*
(for) pain *(para) dolor*
head *la cabeza*
period/towels *la regla/las toallas*
stomach *el estómago*
altitude sickness *el soroche*

Time

at one o'clock *a la una*
at half past two *a las dos y media*
at a quarter to three *a cuarto para las tres* or *a las tres menos quince*
it's one o'clock *es la una*
it's seven o'clock *son las siete*
it's six twenty *son las seis y veinte*
it's five to nine *son cinco para las nueve/son las nueve menos cinco*
in ten minutes *en diez minutos*
five hours *cinco horas*
does it take long? *¿tarda mucho?*

Monday *lunes*
Tuesday *martes*
Wednesday *miércoles*
Thursday *jueves*

Friday *viernes*
Saturday *sábado*
Sunday *domingo*

January *enero*
February *febrero*
March *marzo*
April *abril*
May *mayo*
June *junio*
July *julio*
August *agosto*
September *septiembre*
October *octubre*
November *noviembre*
December *diciembre*

Numbers

one *uno/una*
two *dos*
three *tres*
four *cuatro*
five *cinco*
six *seis*
seven *siete*

eight *ocho*
nine *nueve*
ten *diez*
eleven *once*
twelve *doce*
thirteen *trece*
fourteen *catorce*

fifteen *quince*
sixteen *dieciséis*
seventeen *diecisiete*
eighteen *dieciocho*
nineteen *diecinueve*
twenty *veinte*
twenty-one *veintiuno*
thirty *treinta*

forty *cuarenta*
fifty *cincuenta*
sixty *sesenta*
seventy *setenta*
eighty *ochenta*
ninety *noventa*
hundred *cien/ciento*
thousand *mil*

Family

aunt *la tía*
brother *el hermano*
cousin *el/la primo/a*
daughter *la hija*
family *la familia*
father *el padre*
fiancé/fiancée *el novio/la novia*
friend *el amigo/la amiga*
grandfather *el abuelo*

grandmother *la abuela*
husband *el esposo/marido*
married *casado/a*
single/unmarried *soltero/a*
sister *la hermana*
son *el hijo*
uncle *el tío*
wife *la esposa*

Food

Avocado *la palta*
baked *al horno*
bakery *la panadería*
beans *los frijoles/las habichuelas*
beef *la carne de res*
beef steak or pork fillet *el bistec*
boiled rice *el arroz blanco*
bread *el pan*
breakfast *el desayuno*
butter *la mantequilla*
cassava, yucca *la yuca*
casserole *la cazuela*
chewing gum *el chicle*
chicken *el pollo*
chilli pepper or green pepper *el ají*
clear soup, stock *el caldo*
cooked *cocido*
dining room *el comedor*
egg *el huevo*
fish *el pescado*
fork *el tenedor*
fried *frito*
fritters *las frituras*
garlic *el ajo*
goat *el chivo*
grapefruit *el pomelo*
grill *la parrilla*
grilled/griddled *a la plancha*
guava *la guayaba*
ham *el jamón*
hamburger *la hamburguesa*
hot, spicy *picante*

ice cream *el helado*
jam *la mermelada*
knife *el cuchillo*
lime *el limón*
lobster *la langosta*
lunch *el almuerzo*
margarine, fat *la manteca*
meal, supper, dinner *la comida*
meat *la carne*
minced meat *el picadillo*
mixed salad *la ensalada mixta*
onion *la cebolla*
orange *la naranja*
pepper *el pimiento*
plantain, green banana *el plátano*
pasty, turnover *la empanada/el pastelito*
pork *el cerdo*
potato *la papa*
prawns *los camarones*
raw *crudo*
restaurant *el restaurante*
roast *el asado*
salad *la ensalada*
salt *la sal*
sandwich *el bocadillo*
sauce *la salsa*
sausage *la longaniza*
scrambled eggs *los huevos revueltos*
seafood *los mariscos*
small sandwich, filled roll *el bocadito*
soup *la sopa*
spoon *la cuchara*

squash *la calabaza*
squid *los calamares*
supper *la cena*
sweet *dulce*
sweet potato *la batata*
to eat *comer*

toasted *tostado*
turkey *el pavo*
vegetables *los legumbres/vegetales*
without meat *sin carne*
yam *el camote*

Drink

beer *la cerveza*
boiled *hervido*
bottled *en botella*
camomile tea *la manzanilla*
canned *en lata*
cocktail *el coctel*
coconut milk *la leche de coco*
coffee *el café*
coffee, small, strong *el cafecito*
coffee, white *el café con leche*
cold *frío*
condensed milk *la leche condensada*
cup *la taza*
drink *la bebida*
drunk *borracho*
firewater *el aguardiente*
fruit milkshake *el batido*
glass *el vaso*
glass of liquer *la copa de licor*
hot *caliente*

ice *el hielo*
juice *el jugo*
lemonade *la limonada*
milk *la leche*
mint *la menta*
orange juice *el jugo de naranja*
pineapple milkshake *el batido de piña con leche*
rum *el ron*
soft drink *el refresco*
soft fizzy drink *la gaseosa/cola*
sugar *el azúcar*
tea *el té*
to drink *beber/tomar*
water *el agua*
water, carbonated *el agua mineral con gas*
water, still mineral *el agua mineral sin gas*
wine, red *el vino tinto*
wine, white *el vino blanco*

Key verbs

To go *ir*
I go *voy*
you go (familiar) *vas*
he, she, it goes, you (formal) go *va*
we go *vamos*
they, you (plural) go *van*
To have (possess) *tener*
I have *tengo*
You (familiar) have tienes
He, she, it, you (formal) have tiene
We have tenemos
They, you (plural) have tienen

(Also used in 'I am hungry' *tengo hambre*)
There is/are *hay*
There isn't/aren't *no hay*
To be (in a permanent state) **ser**
soy; eres; es; somos; son
To be (positional or temporary state) **estar**
estoy; estás; está ; estamos; están.

This section has been assembled on the basis of glossaries
compiled by André de Mendonça and David Gilmour of
South American Experience, London, and the Latin
American Travel Advisor, No 9, March 1996

Food glossary

Food has always played an important role in Peruvian culture. The country's range of climates has also made it internationally famed for its cuisine.

Savoury dishes

Ají (hot pepper)
Ají is found in many varieties and is used to add 'spice' to everything from soup to fish to vegetable dishes. It is a staple in Peruvian kitchens from the coast to the most remote jungle villages. These peppers can be extremely spicy, so the inexperienced palate should proceed with caution!

Papa (potato)
The potato is as Peruvian as the Inca himself. There are more than 2,000 varieties of tuber although only a fraction are edible. *The International Potato Institute* is located on the outskirts of metropolitan Lima so those with a potato fetish might wish to visit. The *papa amarilla* (yellow potato) is by far the best-tasting of the lot.

Causa
A casserole served cold with a base of yellow potato and mixed with hot peppers, onion, avocado, with either chicken, crab or meat. A fantastic starter.

Estofado
A mild chicken stew, with lots of potatoes and other vegetables, served with rice.

Lomo saltado
Strips of sirloin sautéed with tomato, onion, *ají amarillo* (a spicy orange pepper) and french fried potatoes served with rice.

Papa Ocopa
A typical dish from the Arequipa region. A spicy peanut sauce served over cold potatoes with a slice of hard boiled egg.

Papa a la Huancaína
A dish which originated in the central department of Huancayo. This creamy cheese sauce served over cold potatoes is a common starter for set menus everywhere.

Papa rellena (stuffed potato)
First baked then fried, the potato is stuffed with meat, onions, olives, boiled egg and raisins. *Camote* (yams) can be substituted for potatoes.

Choclo (corn)
Another staple in the Peruvian diet. The large kernels are great with the fresh cheese produced all over the country.

Maíz morado (purple corn)
This type of corn is not edible for humans. It's boiled and the liquid is used to make *chicha*, a sweet and very traditional Peruvian refreshment.

Chicha de Jora
A strong fermented beverage mostly found in mountain communities. The people who make it use their saliva to aid in the fermenting process.

Granos (grains)
Kiwicha and *quinoa* are very high sources of protein and staples of the Inca diet. *Quinoa* is wonderful in soups and *kiwicha* is a common breakfast food for children throughout the country.

Arroz (rice)
Another major staple in Peruvian cooking.

Anticuchos (beef heart kebabs)
Beef heart barbecued and served with cold potato and a wonderful assortment of spicy sauces.

Cuy (guinea pig)
Prepared in a variety of ways from stewed to fried.

Cau cau
Tripe and potatoes.

Rocoto relleno (stuffed hot peppers)
Stuffed with meat and potatoes, then baked.

Pachamanca
Typical mountain cuisine, so popular it's now prepared everywhere. Beef, pork and chicken mixed with a variety of vegetables, and cooked together over heated stones in a hole in the ground.

Seco de cabrito
A favorite dish from the north coast. Roasted goat marinated with fermented *chicha*, served with beans and rice.

Ají de gallina
A rich mix of creamed, spicy chicken over rice and boiled potatoes.

Ceviche
The national dish of Peru. Raw fish or seafood marinated in a mixture of lime juice, red onions and hot peppers, usually served with a thick slice of boiled yam (*camote*) and corn. With a coastline of more than 1,800 km, the fruits of the sea are almost limitless. Sea bass, flounder, salmon, red snapper, sole and many varieties of shellfish are all in abundance. Keep in mind that *ceviche* is a dish served for lunch. Most *cevicherías* close around 1600.

Postres (desserts)

Arroz con leche
Rice pudding.

Manjar blanco
A caramel sweet made from boiled milk and sugar.

Picarones
Deep-fried donut batter bathed in a honey sauce.

Suspiro a la limeña
Manjar blanco with baked egg-white.

Turrón
This popular sweet, shortbread covered in molasses or honey, is sold everywhere during the October celebrations of *Señor de los Milagros* (Lord of Miracles) in Lima.

Fruta (fruit)

There's a great selection of fruit in Peru. Apart from common fruits such as mandarins, oranges, peaches and bananas, there are exotic tropical fruits to choose from.

Chirimoya
Custard apple. In Quechua means 'the sweet of the gods'.

Lúcuma
Eggfruit.

Maracuyá
Passionfruit, often served as a juice.

Tuna
Prickly pear.

Bebidas (drinks)

The national drinks are *Cristal, Cusqueña, Bremen* and *Pilsen*. There are also some dark beers.

Although not known as a great wine producing country, there are a couple of good quality wines to choose from. *Blanco en Blanco* is a surprisingly pleasant white wine from the Tacama winery which also makes a great red wine called *Reserva Especial*.

Pisco, a strong brandy made from white grapes, is produced in the departments of Ica, Moquegua and Tacna. *Pisco sour*, the national drink, is made with lime juice, egg white, sugar and a dash of cinnamon.

Index

Shorts' index

Advertisers' index

Map index

Complete title listing

Footprint publishes
travel guides to over 150
destinations worldwide. Each
guide is packed with practical,
concise and colourful
information for everybody from
first-time travellers to travel
aficionados. The list is growing
fast and current titles are noted
below.
Available from all good
bookshops and online

www.footprintbooks.com

(P) denotes pocket guide

Latin America and Caribbean
Argentina
Barbados (P)
Bolivia
Brazil
Caribbean Islands
Central America & Mexico
Chile
Colombia
Costa Rica
Cuba
Cusco & the Inca Trail
Dominican Republic
Ecuador & Galápagos
Guatemala
Havana (P)
Mexico
Nicaragua
Peru
Rio de Janeiro
South American Handbook
Venezuela

North America
Vancouver (P)
New York (P)
Western Canada

Africa
Cape Town (P)
East Africa
Libya
Marrakech & the High Atlas
Marrakech (P)
Morocco
Namibia
South Africa
Tunisia
Uganda

Middle East
Egypt
Israel
Jordan
Syria & Lebanon

Australasia
Australia
East Coast Australia
New Zealand
Sydney (P)
West Coast Australia

Asia
Bali
Bangkok & the Beaches
Cambodia
Goa
Hong Kong (P)
India
Indian Himalaya
Indonesia
Laos
Malaysia
Nepal
Pakistan
Rajasthan & Gujarat
Singapore
South India
Sri Lanka
Sumatra
Thailand
Tibet
Vietnam

Europe
Andalucía
Barcelona
Barcelona (P)
Berlin (P)
Bilbao (P)
Bologna (P)
Britain

Copenhagen (P)
Croatia
Dublin
Dublin (P)
Edinburgh
Edinburgh (P)
England
Glasgow
Glasgow (P)
Ireland
Lisbon (P)
London
London (P)
Madrid (P)
Naples (P)
Northern Spain
Paris (P)
Reykjavík (P)
Scotland
Scotland Highlands & Islands
Seville (P)
Spain
Tallinn (P)
Turin (P)
Turkey
Valencia (P)
Verona (P)

Also available
Traveller's Handbook (WEXAS)
Traveller's Healthbook (WEXAS)
Traveller's Internet Guide (WEXAS)

Footnotes Complete title listing

Map symbols

Administration

- □ Capital city
- ○ Other city/town
- International border
- Regional border

Roads and travel

- National highway
- Paved road
- Unpaved or ripio (gravel) road
- 4WD/track
- Footpath
- Railway with station
- ✈ Airport
- Bus station
- Ⓜ Metro station
- Ferry

Water features

- River
- Lake, ocean
- Seasonal marshland
- Beach, sand bank
- Waterfall

Cities and towns

- Sight
- Sleeping
- Eating
- Bars & clubs
- Building
- Main through route
- Main street
- Minor street
- Pedestrianized street
- Tunnel

→ One way street
⊨ Bridge
Steps
Park, garden, stadium
Ⓢ Bank
Hospital
Museum
Market
Police
Post office
Tourist office
Cathedral, church
Fortified wall
@ Internet
♪ Telephone
Petrol
Parking
A Detail map
A Related map

Topographical features

- Contours (approx), rock outcrop
- Mountain
- Volcano
- Mountain pass
- Escarpment
- Gorge
- Glacier
- Salt flat

Other symbols

- Archaeological site
- ♦ National park/wildlife reserve
- Viewing point
- ▲ Campsite
- Refuge
- Deciduous/coniferous trees

Credits

Footprint credits
Editor: Felicity Laughton
Map editor: Sarah Sorensen
Proofreader: Stephanie Lambe

Publisher: Patrick Dawson
Editorial: Alan Murphy, Sophie Blacksell, Sarah Thorowgood, Claire Boobbyer, Caroline Lascom, Davina Rungasamy, Laura Dixon
Cartography: Robert Lunn, Claire Benison, Kevin Feeney
Series development: Rachel Fielding
Design: Mytton Williams and Rosemary Dawson (brand)
Advertising: Debbie Wylde
Finance and administration: Sharon Hughes, Elizabeth Taylor

Photography credits
Front cover: Imagestate, llamas
Back cover: Imagestate, Sacsayhuaman Inca ruins
Inside colour section:
Alamy, Hilary Emberton, Robert Harding, Travel Ink, Jamie Marshall, South American Pictures.

Print
Manufactured in Italy by LegoPrint
Pulp from sustainable forests

Footprint feedback
We try as hard as we can to make each Footprint guide as up to date as possible but, of course, things always change. If you want to let us know about your experiences – good, bad or ugly – then don't delay, go to www.footprintbooks.com and send in your comments.

Publishing information
Footprint Cusco and the Inca Trail
2nd edition
© Footprint Handbooks Ltd
January 2004

ISBN 1 903471 80 X
CIP DATA: A catalogue record for this book is available from the British Library

® Footprint Handbooks and the Footprint mark are a registered trademark of Footprint Handbooks Ltd

Published by Footprint
6 Riverside Court
Lower Bristol Road
Bath BA2 3DZ, UK
T +44 (0)1225 469141
F +44 (0)1225 469461
discover@footprintbooks.com
www.footprintbooks.com

Distributed in the USA by
Publishers Group West

All rights reserved. No part of this publication may be reproduced, stored in a retrieval system, or transmitted, in any form or by any means, electronic, mechanical, photocopying, recording, or otherwise without the prior permission of Footprint Handbooks Ltd.

Neither the black and white nor colour maps are intended to have any political significance.

Every effort has been made to ensure that the facts in this guidebook are accurate. However, travellers should still obtain advice from consulates, airlines etc about travel and visa requirements before travelling. The authors and publishers cannot accept responsibility for any loss, injury or inconvenience however caused.

Acknowledgements

Writing a book about Cusco and the surrounding region has been an illuminating and inspiring experience, but all would have come to nothing without the help and advice of a multitude of valued friends and associates – without further ado Steve would like to thank: Marianne van Vlaardingen for her friendship and advice on the Manu Biosphere Reserve; David Ricaldi for his information concerning conservation projects in the Andes and Southern Peru; Boris Gómez for updates regarding changes to the status of protected areas in and around Manu National Park.

At **South American Explorers** the constant help and support of Branch Manager Ross Knutson was invaluable. Ross is a great friend and between games of *Risk* and episodes of *Celebrity Jeopardy* many good times were had. Fiona Cameron and Guillaume Gressino wrote the box about the Urubamba River Clean-up. Fiona was a great travelling companion on Steve's trip to the Pongo de Mainique and beyond.

Hugh Thomson wrote the Box on his discoveries in the Vilcabamba Range and he provided many insights into the pre-Columbian history of the region. Sean Nevis must be thanked for his invaluable advice on how to stay healthy in Cusco! Simon Leishman provided much information about hiking in the Cusco area's more isolated corners and he also updated the Cusco Internet section. Simon's advice on haircare at altitude will be treasured always!

Steve would also like to thank Carmen, of Casa de Carmen, for her warmth and friendship throughout his stay; Frank 'Big Moves' Donner for providing much inside information on kayaking on Cusco's rivers. Frank was also a mine of information on Cusco's infamous nightlife.

Alison Crowther of the **Inca Porter Project** gave valued advice concerning porters' rights and working conditions, and also considerable background information on the Inca Trail itself, as did her co-workers Lucy Brandram and Lucy Bertenshaw. Finally Kay Isbell deserves thanks and a big hug for her razor-sharp advice and editorial skills, specifically pertaining to the trek description from Huancacalle to Espíritu Pampa. Kay has been a mentor and great inspiration throughout Steve's life.

Our warmest thanks are also due to Mariella Bernasconi Cillóniz and Alberto Miori Sanz, who made significant contributions to the first edition and who, for this edition, sent new information on the alternative Cusco, the Museo de Arte Precolombino and tourism developments in Cusco generally.

Mention should also be made here of the other contributors to the first edition, Roger Perkins and Kate Hannay, Stephen Light, Barry Walker, John Forrest, Ricardo Espinosa and Wendy Weeks, whose efforts provided the firm foundation for the new edition. Specialist information was supplied by Paul Cripps (Mountain biking and Rafting, with new hands-on-paddle information from Steve Frankham), Mark Eckstein (Responsible tourism), Paul Heggarty (Language) and Charlie Easmon (Health).

We are also grateful to Víctor Melgar in Lima for updating a number of essential points and to all the travellers who have written to Footprint with advice, corrections and criticisms on the subjects of Peru and Cusco. In particular we'd like to thank Daan Mager and Dineke Veerman.

Last but not least, Steve and Ben would like to thank all at Footprint for their support: Felicity Laughton, Alan Murphy, Sarah Sorensen, Kevin Feeney, Claire Benison, Laura Dixon and Robert Lunn.

Experience the Best of Peru ...stay at Sonesta Hotels.

Sonesta Posadas del Inca

El Olivar - Lima • Miraflores - Lima • Cusco
Sacred Valley - Yucay • Lake Titicaca - Puno • Arequipa

Reservations: Phone: (511)222-4777 Fax: (511)422-4345
sales@sonestaperu.com   www.sonesta.com

Daily Departures

PERU EXPEDITIONS

More than 20 different expeditions & traditional tours in Peru, low cost flights, transfers, hotels. 10-year experience offering the best Peruvian quality.

Inca Trail to Machu Picchu, Amazon rainforest, Colca Canyon, Lake Titikaka, Taquile Island, Cuzco, Arequipa, Puno, Paracas & Ballestas Island, Nazca Lines.

- Mountain Bike
- Moto Adventures
- Trekking
- 4x4 Tours
- Overland Expeditions
- Private & Shared departures

Av. Arequipa 5241 - 504
Miraflores - Lima - Peru
South America
Fax   51 1 445-7874
Phone 51 1 447-2057

peruexpe@amauta.rcp.net.pe

www.peru-expeditions.com

Footnotes

Map 1 Urubamba & Vilcanota Valleys

To Chanquiri

Espíritu Pampa
Concevidayoc
Vilcabamba Vieja
Vista Alegre
Río Concevidayoc
Salinga Pass
Pampaconas
Punkuyoc
Yupanca
Lucma
Puqyura
Vitcos
Huancacalle
Yurac Rumi/ Chuquipalta
Vilcabamba La Nueva
Río Vilcabamba

To Icochote & Pongo de Mainique
Quillabamba
Choquechaca Bridge
Chaullay
Amaybamba
Umasbar
La Verónica (5,750m)
Santa Teresa
Aguas Calientes
Qorihuarach (km 88)
Machu Picchu
Wiñay Wayna
Sayajmarca
Runkuracay
Chille
Llactapa
Huayllabamba
Nev Salcantay (6,271m)

Choquetacarpo (5,512m)
Sacsarayoc/ Pumasillo (5,991m)
To Choquequirao
To Choquequirao

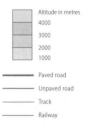

Altitude in metres
4000
3000
2000
1000

Paved road
Unpaved road
Track
Railway

N

0 km 5
0 miles 5

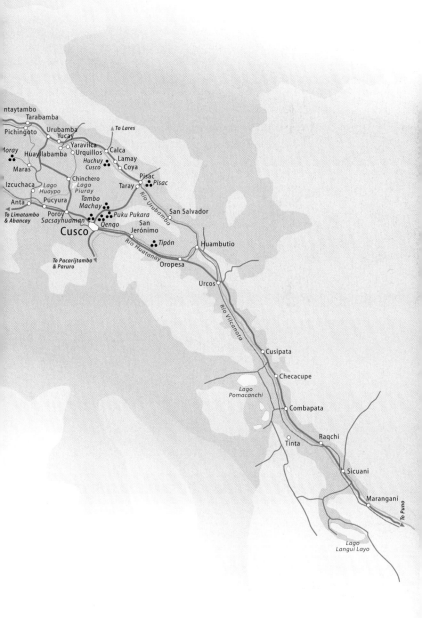

Map 2 Cusco region

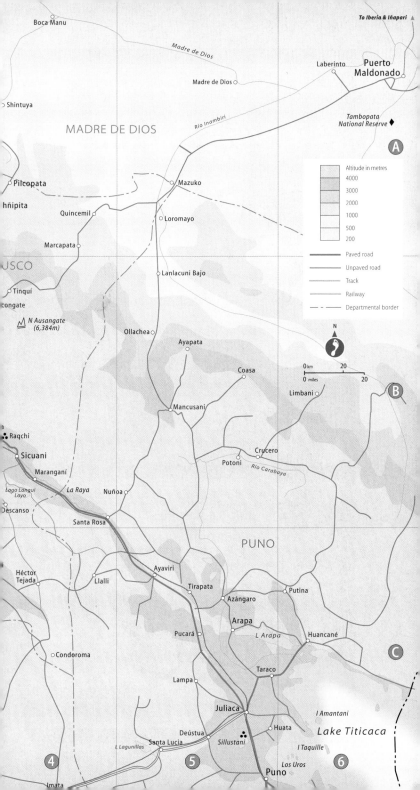

Boca Manu

To Iberia & Iñapari

Madre de Dios

Laberinto

Puerto Maldonado

Madre de Dios

Shintuya

MADRE DE DIOS

Río Inambiri

Tambopata National Reserve

A

Pilcopata

Mazuko

hñipita

Quincemil

Loromayo

Marcapata

Lanlacuni Bajo

USCO

Tinquí

congate

N Ausangate (6,384m)

Ollachea

Ayapata

Coasa

Limbani

B

Mancusani

Raqchi

Sicuani

Crucero

Maranganí

Potoni

Río Carabaya

Lago Langui Layo

La Raya

Nuñoa

Descanso

Santa Rosa

PUNO

Héctor Tejada

Ayaviri

Llalli

Tirapata

Putina

Azángaro

Arapa

L Arapa

Pucará

Huancané

C

Condoroma

Taraco

Lampa

Juliaca

I Amantani

Deústua

Huata

Lake Titicaca

L Lagunillas

Santa Lucia

Sillustani

I Taquille

4

5

Los Uros

6

Puno

Imata

Altitude in metres
4000
3000
2000
1000
500
200

Paved road
Unpaved road
Track
Railway
Departmental border

N

0 km   20
0 miles   20

318

Peru Rail

www.perurail.com
reservas@perurail.com

PeruRail - the service comprising some of the world's most scenic railways, and linking the tourist highlights of the Andes. It operates from historic Cusco to the famous ruins at Machu Picchu and to Puno's Lake Titicaca, connecting the most spectacular attractions of Peru. The trains are comfortable, the service is splendid and the views are unmatched. It is an unparalleled way to travel within Peru.

PERURAIL
Discovering the Andes

319

HOTEL
MONASTERIO

*The Leading
Small Hotels
of the World*

*We'll do whatever
it takes to make
you comfortable!*

**Cusco 3,300 metres above sea level.
Relief from High Altitude sickness...**

The Hotel Monasterio, with world
experts from the Scottish Pulmonary
Vascular Institute and Respiratory
Medicine, have counteracted the
problem of high altitude by using
oxygen concentrators to enrich the
atmosphere in the rooms, effectively
oxygenating the rooms down to an
atmospheric pressure low enough to
prevent altitude sickness. After sleeping
in an oxygen-enriched room, the
increased level of oxygen in the body
declines only gradually over a period
of 14 - 15 hours the following day.

ORIENT-EXPRESS HOTELS
PERU

www.orient-express.com   reservas@peruorientexpress.com.pe

For a different view of Europe, take a Footprint

"" Superstylish travel guides – perfect for short break addicts.
Harvey Nichols magazine

Discover so much more...
Listings driven, forward looking and up to date. Focuses on what's going on right now.
Contemporary, stylish, and innovative
approach, providing quality travel information.